YEAR-ROUND
OUTDOOR
BUILDING
PROJECTS

D1468339

YEAR-ROUND
OUTDOOR
BUILDING
PROJECTS

by Richard Demske
illustrated by Mary Kornblum

Service Communications, Ltd.

VAN NOSTRAND REINHOLD COMPANY
NEW YORK   CINCINNATI   TORONTO   LONDON   MELBOURNE

Copyright© 1977 by Service Communications, Ltd.

Library of Congress Catalog Number 77-73895

ISBN 0-442-22077-4

Printed in the U.S.A.

Published in 1977 by Service Communications, Ltd. and
Van Nostrand Reinhold Company
A division of Litton Educational Publishing, Inc.
450 West 33rd Street, New York, NY 10001, U.S.A.

Van Nostrand Reinhold Limited
1410 Birchmount Road, Scarborough, Ontario M1P 2E7, Canada

Van Nostrand Reinhold Australia Pty. Limited
17 Queen Street, Mitcham, Victoria 3132, Australia

Van Nostrand Reinhold Company Limited
Molly Millars Lane, Wokingham, Berkshire, England

First edition
16 15 14 13 12 11 10 9 8 7 6 5 4 3 2 1

Library of Congress Cataloging in Publication Data (CIP)
Demske, Richard, 1930—
    Year 'round outdoor building projects.

    Includes indexes.
    1. Garden structures — Amateurs' manuals. 2. Build-
ing — Amateurs' manuals. I. Title.
TH4961.D46   690   77-73895
ISBN 0-442-22077-4

Cover Credits

American Plywood Association, California Redwood Association, Sakrete, Filon Division of Vistron Corporation.

Credits

Alsynite Corporation of America; American Canvas Institute; American Plywood Association; AMF Wen-Mac Division; Brick Institute of America; Building Stone Institute; Buster Crabbe Pools; California Redwood Association; Canadian Office of Forest Industries; Cascade Industries; Chicago Combustion Company; Doughboy Recreational, Inc ; Filon Division of Vistron Corporation; General Electric Lamp Division; Georgia-Pacific; Glen-Gery Corporation; Hubbell, Inc.; Lighting Division; Louisiana-Pacific; Louisville Cement Company; Major Pool Equipment Company; Masonite Corporation; National Concrete Masonry Association; National Floor Products; National Pool Builders; National Swimming Pool Institute; Ozite Corporation; Portland Cement Association; Premier Peat Moss; Rain Jet Corporation; Red Cedar Shingle & Handsplit Shake Bureau; Sakrete, Incorporated; Sears, Roebuck & Company; Simpson Timber Company; Southern Forest Products Association; 3M Corporation; The Toro Company; Western Wood Products Association; Westinghouse Electric Corporation, Lighting Division.

Contents

PLANNING

In the last ten or fifteen years homeowners have come to realize more and more that the area outside the house—or at least a good portion of it—can be used for living and to increase quite markedly the quality of family life.

There are a variety of things one can install in this area—swimming pool, storage units, play devices for the kids, barbeque, a deck or patio, fences—the list goes on. In an ideal world—if you had the property and money—you could make a master plan, select the things you like in the book, lay out where they should be, and install them.

Most people will not be able to do that—the budget and property simply won't be there. But it is still important, no matter what your budget and property, to make a plan to at least maximize your outdoor living potential. Right now you may only be able to install a deck. But later, as money and time permit, you can add the other things you like: the fence, the play area for the kids, the pool.

The purpose of this section is to show you what's available and to give some hints on how best to effect the projects you plan. It is suggested that you read it thoroughly, digest it, then work with pencil and paper and figure out exactly what you can do now and what you will do in the future. If you're like most people, you'll find that just being able to do a few things now will be very exciting. And once you start using these things you'll be anxious to do all the other things you've planned. Indeed, you may wonder how you ever stayed indoors for so long.

Patios and Decks

Patio, terrace, porch, sun deck, your outdoor "floor" is normally the heart of any outdoor living area. Certain guidelines can be set down for its planning, for its construction, and for various little touches that will make it more useful.

Your property may allow one such area or it may allow a number—including, for example, a small, private fenced-in deck off the master bedroom as well as a large patio for family recreation and relaxation. Such an area should be spacious enough to ward off any cramped feeling—when you are outdoors this is the last impression you wish to create. Yet it may be made intimate—as the aforementioned enclosed sun area off the bedroom, for instance, or the shaping of the terrace or the use of plantings to provide conversation areas. The home itself and its immediate surroundings as well as your lot will be deciding factors in determining the size of the patio.

Perhaps the ideal place for the family patio is one that can be reached easily from the family room, living room, or kitchen. But these are not the only good places and your home's design may not invite an attached patio. You may prefer to locate the patio or deck in a far corner of the lot, or perhaps as a screened-in attachment to the garage. The important considerations are that you try to locate it where the surroundings invite pleasant relaxation, where the view (if any) is most advantageous, where traffic noises are as remote as possible, and where you will have some privacy as well as some sun and refreshing breezes.

As an extension of the home—although not necessarily a physical part of it—the patio should be planned so as to complement the home's architectural features. Shape and size should be considered in relation to the house and in relation to the shape and size of the lot. The setting should also be taken into account, and here the choice of materials is important. For example, patterns

Here's an example of good overall planning. The western pine deck is surrounded by a low wall for safety, and topped with a glass fence to retain the ocean view yet keep out strong winds. Louvered wall allows privacy, but lets the gentler breezes in from the side.

can be created with flagstone or a parqueted wood deck or modular concrete units to harmonize with the lines and textures of the natural surroundings.

Preliminary Planning

First think about how you intend to use your patio. Is it simply a place to put out a few chairs and catch the breeze on a hot summer night? Or do you intend to use it for outdoor dining, day or night entertaining, sunbathing, games, and other activities? How about the view—is it better on one side than on another? It is much better to look out upon a natural setting than your neighbor's garbage. Is there a lake or other beauty spot nearby which can be seen only from the second floor? In that case, perhaps an elevated deck is preferable. All of these factors should be pondered and discussed by the entire family before you put a shovel into the ground or a nail into the wood.

Location

A poorly located deck or patio may hardly be used at all; but one that is ideally placed may likely be the family gathering spot all during the warm weather. First of all, it must be convenient, and that usually means locating it close to the house. This is not always possible because of the design of your home and/or lot. A home on a small or unusually shaped lot may not have the physical room for an attached deck or patio. Even a home on a larger lot may not have room for an attached patio because of topography, zoning restrictions, or because the area is already utilized by a garden, driveway, pool, or other impediment.

Maybe the view from all sides of your house is not good, because of a gas station or noisy bar next door, but there may be a nice quiet area in the back of your lot. Or a remote part of your property may have a garden or some pleasant trees that make it just right for relaxation or private dining. In that case, it makes sense to locate your patio there.

The hostess will be able to enjoy outdoor dining more if it's close to the kitchen. Sliding sash at right on this house serves as a passthrough for food, dishes, and the like.

This raised deck provides a lovely lake view that would be missed from a ground-level terrace.

There may be other features which make it convenient to locate the patio away from the house. A swimming pool is a prime example. If your family spends a great deal of time around the pool, your outdoor living area should be located close by. Ideally the area between the house and the pool is the best choice.

Generally, however, a deck or terrace is most convenient when it doesn't mean taking a long walk from the house, particularly if you intend to do a lot of outdoor dining. Even a simple barbecue involves several trips with food, dishes, drinks, and the like. When the trips become long journeys some of the fun is lost. Then too, the deck or terrace seems more like a part of the home—truly an outdoor living room—when it is integrated with the rest of the house.

Orientation to the Sun

Depending on where you live, you will want to orient your outdoor living area to take advantage of, or to block out, the sun. Although it may be at the front or side of the house, nonsoutherly exposure is preferred where heat is oppressive. Even in northern climates, the noonday sun will be a problem for southern-facing terraces or decks. A roof or sun screen is advisable for patios at the south end of the home.

The deck or terrace need not be attached to the house. Here it is located at a far corner of the lot, away from street traffic noises.

Here's a small deck for water-lovers. The redwood overwater deck provides easy access to boating, swimming, and sunning.

If you have large trees on your lot, take advantage of them to shade your terrace.

Here the lounging deck is located away from the house to benefit from the shade of this gnarled but majestic tree.

Do you prefer the morning or afternoon sun? An eastward-facing patio or deck gets a lot of sun before noon, whereas the house blocks it in the afternoon. If afternoon sunbathing is your thing, face your outdoor area westward, where it will get plenty of post-meridian ultraviolet rays. If a shady area is your prime consideration, face your patio north or locate it under large trees.

Trees and Other Natural Elements

Trees should also figure in your plans. If you have none, of course, it's an academic question, but maybe you plan on planting them someday, and great trees do grow from saplings. You won't want to have to relocate the patio or pool when the trees mature. If your home is already surrounded by trees, they won't have much effect on where you locate the patio, because you'll be in shade most of the time anyway. But where there are trees on one side and not another, take this into account when planning.

The same holds true for prevailing breezes. The prevailing wind in most North American areas comes from the west. Check local weather statistics, and put your patio or deck where you can take advantage of cool breezes, if possible. In areas of high winds, plan to avoid or block them.

Traffic

Consider "people" traffic patterns when planning your outdoor living areas. For example, avoid placing a patio where bathers from your pool will have to pass back and forth across it into the house or dressing area; this will disrupt activities. And don't put the patio between the house and garage, in front of the main entrance, or in other heavily traveled areas, unless you haven't any other choice. Especially avoid areas where small children will be going back and forth with wet, sandy, or muddy boots and shoes.

The other type of traffic to be avoided is street traffic. If your house is on a corner near a busy intersection, place your deck or patio in an area away from the two streets if you can. The same holds true for a neighbor's busy driveway. Privacy is usually a prerequisite for outdoor comfort and pleasure.

There are some things you can do to block out heavy street traffic. Walls and fences can screen out much of it, although walls may interfere with sun and breeze. A good compromise is to build a louvered fence which lets in sun and air and still provides privacy. Hedges and bushes can also be effective—and usually look better than a barricade—but you have to either buy large, expensive shrubs or wait for them to grow. If privacy is the prime consideration, privet hedges are inexpensive and fast-growing, but they also require a lot of maintenance.

Size and Shape of Deck or Patio

As an extension of your home, the deck or patio should be planned to complement the house's architecture. Shape and size should be planned in relation to the house and lot. A rectangular patio is generally easier to plan and build, but a round or odd-shaped plan may fit better and be more esthetically pleasing.

Odd-shaped decks are difficult to engineer, especially if they are off the ground, but it can be done. If you build a second-story deck, take into consideration its overall effect on the architecture of the house. An oversized deck may detract from the looks of the house. Conversely, a deck can add desirable proportion and interest to a tall home with uninterrupted straight sides.

Basic Materials

Wood

There is a multitude of materials available for use in outdoor living projects.

When choosing wood, durability is the most important factor. Most woods are easy prey to the elements unless given some sort of protection. For those woods that do not have natural decay-resistance, a coat of wood preservative such as creosote oil or pentachlorophenol will help prolong life. Pressure-treated woods hold up very well, but these are relatively expensive.

Garden grades of redwood—lower in cost than architectural grades—have natural knots and sap streaks that give them a rustic look.

For outdoor use, the best woods are redwood and red cedar. Both are naturally resistant to rot and insects, but are higher in price than fir, pine, or spruce. Most redwood grades are higher priced than red cedar, but are generally considered better looking. Both woods mellow from their initial ruddy complexion to a silvery-gray appearance after several years' exposure to the elements. The cheaper grades, such as "garden grade" redwood, are just as good as more expensive grades for outdoor use, but open knots can cause structural weakness, especially dangerous in decks high off the ground. For posts or other supporting members which are in contact with the ground, use all-heart redwood or red cedar, incense cedar, or treated softwoods such as pine, fir, and similar species.

Redwood and red cedar are often used as divider strips and accent materials for patios, to provide visual relief to large areas or brick. Since they will be in contact with the ground and concrete or mortar, all-heart grades should be used.

Concrete

Concrete makes a carefree, low-maintenance patio or walkway surface. It is relatively easy to form and pour a concrete patio, and it can be used in just about any climate. Unless it is carefully blended in with the house and masked by shrubs and other plantings, however, plain concrete used in large doses tends to have a rather cold and unattractive appearance. Those who have tried to paint concrete know that the paint wears off all too soon and the surface takes on an ugly appearance. There are various coloring agents that give concrete a more pleasant look. Another alternative is to use rounded pebbles (exposed aggregate) at the surface to make it more attractive.

There are various other finishing methods for concrete as explained in the section on concrete building and installation techniques. Concrete can be alternated with brick or other materials to break up the monotonous look. Concrete also lends itself well to odd forms and shapes. For long life and durability, nothing beats concrete. Best of all, the material is relatively inexpensive.

Concrete Coverings

If you are building a concrete patio as an extension of a family room or other room within the house, you can emphasize the connection by using the same or complementary floor covering indoors and out. Such coverings can also be used to dress up a drab slab. Resilient flooring in sheet or roll form (normally 6 feet wide) is made of vinyl resins and colorfast pigments for both indoor and outdoor use. The material has a backing of fiberglass and asbestos, and is installed with epoxy adhesive. Epoxy is also used to fuse the seams so that dirt and moisture can not get under the flooring.

Indoor-outdoor carpeting is also available in a wide variety of colors and styles. It comes in 12-inch-square self-sticking tiles and in 6- and 12-foot-wide rolls. The carpeting is made of materials such as polypropylene fiber with an all-weather foam rubber backing and is installed with adhesive. The roll types have the advantage of fewer or no seams to collect dirt and moisture. You can even buy carpeting that simulates grass (the same as the artificial turf used in many modern sports stadiums)—this might appeal if you like to practice your putting on the patio.

Check the manufacturer's guarantee before buying resilient flooring or carpeting, and follow his instructions for installation. The sun can be more damaging to some types than the other elements, causing early fading and deterioration.

Another type of concrete covering is "seamless flooring." Before its application, the slab must be clean and all cracks patched. A special white base coat is rolled or brushed on the concrete, then colored vinyl chips are sprinkled on the surface, embedding themselves in the base coat in a random pattern. When the material has dried, excess loose chips are swept away, and one or more clear coatings (usually urethane or acrylic) are applied with brush or roller. A variation of this system uses colored sand in place of the vinyl chips.

Brick

Brick makes attractive terraces and walkways, and the brick itself is very long wearing. Brick can be laid either "dry" in a bed of sand or with mortar on a concrete slab (the latter method is preferred in frigid climates). Either way, there is a chance of brick heaving during alternating frost and warm spells. If it's laid in sand, you can reposition or replace the brick come springtime. The problem is not as common with brick laid in mortar, but when it does occur, it's more difficult to repair.

Brick is more expensive than concrete, but it makes a handsome terrace. It can be laid in a number of attractive patterns, but common brick is difficult to lay in modular patterns without mortar joints. If you plan to use any pattern other than "running bond" without mortar, modular "patio brick" which is exactly twice as long as it is wide, is recommended.

Patio Blocks

Patio blocks are made of precast concrete, and are usually laid like brick. They come in various sizes and shapes, but are generally larger than brick and less expensive per square foot. They are somewhat less durable then either

Precast concrete patio blocks come in a variety of shapes and sizes, and are easily laid in a bed of sand. The trellis is of knot-textured garden grade redwood.

brick or poured concrete, however, and are more likely to crack or break. Their big advantages are the wide variety of forms and colors, and the fact that they are easy to work with.

Visit local masonry and building supply yards to find out what is available in precast blocks, or cast them yourself using a nailed-together 2x4 form. Plan your patio so that you won't have to cut any of the blocks. It's a hard job, and the blocks will not look good unless used whole.

Flagstone

Flagstone is among the most handsome of outdoor materials, but a terrace of stone (the irregular-shaped type) is also one of the most difficult to lay out. Planning it is like working a jigsaw puzzle. Stone can be laid either in mortar or "dry" in sand, as with brick.

You can also buy stone cut into square or rectangular shapes. These are considerably easier to fit, but are more expensive than natural stone. Both irregular and cut stone are more costly than most other types of outdoor building materials. Flagstone comes in a surprising variety of colors. You can use all one color or a mixture, as you prefer.

Accents

Most large patios look better when different materials are combined to break up sizeable areas. Wood strips, as described above, are one method. Another is to intersperse beds of washed gravel with larger concrete or even wood areas. Gravel is not easy to walk on, however, so such areas are designed for looks rather than utility. Planters can be placed on the gravel beds, or they can just be left as is. You can also leave open areas of earth and plant trees or shrubs there for a natural look. Large trees require a lot of space, though. Other possibilities are built-in benches, garden pools, and beds of roses or other flowers.

Patio Roofs and Sun Screens

Whether you need a roof or sun screen depends on how you intend to use the patio. You will need a roof if you're an outdoor dining and cooking addict, because rain will almost certainly interrupt things otherwise. You will also need or want a roof or at least a sun screen if your patio is exposed to direct sunlight most of the day.

The advantages of having at least a portion of your outdoor living room covered are many. Properly planned, the patio roof can enhance the architecture of your house. A continuous roof line which includes your patio roof may make a disproportionately high dwelling appear lower, longer, and more balanced. It may tie in the patio area with a carport or storage area, which in turn can also serve as a patio wall to shut out an unsightly view or strong winds.

A patio roof can be built using standard roof construction techniques, with joists and/or rafters, plywood or lumber underlayment, and shingles. This type of construction may be especially appropriate if the patio roof follows the existing roof line, making the new roof appear to be an integral part of the original structure. Another possibility is to build the roof of fiberglass or translucent plastic, which lets in light but keeps out rain and the stronger rays of the sun.

When the patio is located away from the house, its roof may establish a harmonious relationship between the two structures through the use of similar roof lines or materials. You can also use a common trim color for both house and patio covering to visually tie them together.

Low stone retaining wall provides level planting area and interesting accent to this back yard.

A partial roof of spaced boards allows some sunlight to get through while filtering the rest and is technically a sun screen rather than a roof. This type of construction is preferred where harsh sun, rather than rain, is the primary problem. The boards are usually 1x2s, 1x3s, or 2x4s, either set on end or flat, whichever best suits your purposes.

Fences

Fences and wind screens serve a variety of purposes. They can be used simply to define property lines, in which case the construction can be open and primarily decorative. A split-rail fence is a good example of this. Where privacy is the prime consideration, a closed, high fence is best. If it is intended mainly to keep children or pets in bounds, the fence can be relatively open, but sturdy and not easily climbable. Chain link is a good example of this type.

A fence can also serve to define certain areas, such as separate play and sitting areas. These fences or "outdoor room dividers" are often of the screen type, allowing air to pass through and letting parents keep an eye on children at play while relaxing on the patio. Fences can also be built as screens against the wind and sun as well as for privacy.

Fences and wind screens can be of boards, pickets, panels, or masonry units in a virtually endless variety of shapes and patterns.

Retaining Walls

A retaining wall can be a functional part of your outdoor plan. Its primary purpose is to provide level space in a sloping lot, to prevent erosion or to create a raised bed for flowers or shrubbery. Careful planning is essential for a sloping lot in order to allow proper drainage and to fulfill the wall's essential function. Properly planned and executed, retaining walls can transform a dull landscape into an exciting and beautiful one. On the other hand, a poorly designed or built wall can be both ugly and dangerous. Those who have severe problems of this type are well advised to consult a landscape architect.

Retaining walls should be built as low as possible. Always prefer two small

Attractive redwood retaining wall holds back sloping hill, carves out a niche for secluded patio.

walls in a terraced design to one high one, and never build one higher than four feet. Common materials for retaining walls are building stone, brick, concrete block, and railroad ties.

Landscaping

Although all elements of your outdoor living plan are part of the landscape, the term is generally used to denote foundation plantings, trees, and other shrubbery. The type of flora used in landscaping varies depending on the area in which you live. All plantings should be adaptable to the soil and climate, with indigenous plants preferred. Compare the foundation plantings and trees of the Southwest, for example, with those of the Northeast, and you will find few similarities.

In colder regions, concentrate on winter-hardy plants. Milder areas can use varieties that will not flourish in northern climates. Soil acidity is another factor to be taken into consideration. Most broad-leaved evergreens such as rhododendron need an acid soil. Although soil conditions can be corrected by the use of proper additives, it is better to use these evergreens sparingly where the soil is alkaline. The opposite is true for plants that prefer "sweet" (alkaline) soils. Your nurseryman or state extension service can advise on conditions in your area.

There are many other factors to consider when choosing shrubs and trees. The size of your house and lot is important. A low house may appear dwarfed by high trees and large foundation plantings. A small lot is better served by smaller trees. You should always consider the mature size and shape of foundation plantings. That small shrub you place in front of a window, for example, may someday grow up to obscure your view and darken your living room, both indoor and out.

Outdoor Lighting and Plumbing

Often overlooked facets of the outdoor plan are electricity (primarily for lighting) and plumbing. A lighted patio is usable at night. Lighting can highlight your garden and make walkways safer. Outdoor receptacles allow you to plug in temporary lights for Christmas decorating or other purposes.

Plumbing may or may not be necessary depending on what else is in your plan. Outdoor bars, baths, and pools will need some type of plumbing, as will a garden waterfall. Swimming pools and sprinkling systems will need relatively complex plumbing systems. A gas barbecue may need a line from the main gas supply. When planning your outdoor living area, anticipate these needs. If, as most do, you're putting in a patio first, try to avoid laying it over the area where the electrical or plumbing lines will later be run. If this is impractical, install the lines before you put down the patio. You can then cap them until they're needed.

The Outdoor Kitchen

An essential element of outdoor living is the barbecue. If you will be using only a hibachi or a portable grill, the outdoor kitchen need not be a part of your early planning. But a more permanent, built-in barbecue unit may be desirable as an integral element of the patio.

All but the smallest barbecues require chimneys, and the chimney cannot be too close to the house. Chimneys need drafts, and when located close to an obstruction (such as a house) do not draw properly. The barbecue should be on an outside corner of the terrace, and away from high trees and shrubs which can block drafts or perhaps catch fire if branches are too close to the glowing embers.

This flagstone patio features a built-in storage closet for outdoor dining utensils.

You may be planning on using the traditional charcoal for your barbecue fuel. Fine. But if the barbecue is to be gas-fired, you'll need that gas line. You may prefer to use an LPG (Liquified Petroleum Gas) such as propane, but this requires a storage tank, which is unsightly if not effectively masked.

If your family really enjoys outdoor cooking, you may wish to plan a super barbecue unit that includes storage space for pots and pans, silverware, dishes, and other utensils. That way you won't have to go running back and forth to the house whenever you need a spatula to flip the hamburgers. It also gives you more flexibility in planning, since convenience to the house is less of a consideration. Your super barbecue could also include a built-in bar, which might save even more steps than the proximity of the pots and pans.

Storage and Other Structures

One way to avoid numerous trips back and forth to the house is to build a storage compartment into your barbecue area. Many types of storage facilities can be built to accommodate not only cooking utensils, but furniture and other outdoor living accouterments. Your basement or garage may be large enough to house all these items, but it's far more convenient to have a separate storage area near the patio.

Storage units can be built along the side of the house near the patio, or a separate (usually freestanding) storage structure can be placed immediately adjacent to the patio. If you plan carefully, the storage facility can serve more than one purpose, such as a privacy wall, a carport, or a potting shed, in additon to providing "a place for everything."

Outbuildings are not only for storage, however. A gazebo can be a lovely place to escape the warm summer sun. Cabanas and saunas are often part of the swimming pool scene. The serious gardener should consider a greenhouse as well as a potting shed. The kids will love a playhouse of their own. Finally, don't forget the family pet. An outdoor shelter will keep him safe and content too.

This redwood potting shed contains not only shelves and storage for the green-thumber, but also a wheel for making the pots. Note how it also serves as a privacy fence. Glass roof and gable provide light.

A swimming pool should be designed as an integral part of the landscape. Note how the dogleg shape of this model fits among the trees. Concrete pool-surround flows easily into the access steps.

Pool Planning

The ultimate outdoor project for most families is a swimming pool. Whether it's a small round above-ground wader or a concrete built-in, be sure to include pool possibilities when you do your outdoor planning. Even a small pool takes up a lot of space. Both kids and growups will want some room to stretch out in the sun around the pool, even if it's only a tiny wading type. A large pool requires facilities for filtering and heating equipment, walkways all around (preferably skidproof), and perhaps a bar, dressing rooms, and maybe a sauna.

There's more to pools than swimming. A concrete garden pool gives this back yard corner a little something extra to catch the eye.

Most people prefer to locate the pool adjacent to the patio. It should be reasonably close to the house unless you build a separate cabana. Make sure that you locate the pool as far away as possible from overhanging trees. Trees not only drop leaves and seeds into the pool, they shade sunbathers, too. The pool should also be close to the water supply, and to fuel and electricity if it's to be heated and lighted.

Other Considerations

There are some other factors to be considered when planning your outdoor living area. If your house is at the bottom of a hill on land with poor drainage, you should probably build a naturally drained patio of brick, patio block, or flagstone in sand. A ground-level deck should have the boards spaced so that water drains through. In any situation, concrete or other solid patios should be pitched away from the house, about ¼-inch for every foot.

If you live in a brick house, a brick patio may complement it best. The site should also be taken into consideration, with natural materials such as stone harmonizing well with an interesting natural topography. Where the home site slopes away steeply to the rear, a raised wood deck will take best advantage of the terrain. If your patio is located near a swimming pool, quick-drying and nonskid properties should be favored.

The Legalities

When you've got a general idea of what you want—and emphatically *before* you draw up final plans—check your local building codes and zoning ordinances to see what requirements, if any, apply to your project. One important thing to watch out for is the "setback." How far from your neighbor's house or your property line can you build? You may find that the ideal spot for your patio, pool, or gazebo infringes on the setback. The building department of your municipality will be able to supply a copy of the requirements of the local code.

Planning Checklist

1. Is you patio or deck in the best position with respect to the sun, wind, and privacy?
2. Will foot traffic disrupt activities on it?
3. Is the patio or deck conveniently located? Is it too far from the house?
4. When trees mature will they block out sunshine?
5. Will the materials used for the deck or patio (and other structures) harmonize or clash with house architecture? How about house and other structure architectural "lines" —do they clash?
6. Will foundation and other plantings blend well in their outdoor setting when they mature?
7. Will you have enough storage area near the patio?
8. Have you checked out your ideas with the local building code authorities?

CONCRETE

Slab Work

Carefree concrete makes a fine, durable surface, and there's no reason why the normally talented do-it-yourselfer who is willing to invest some time and perspiration cannot reap the satisfying reward of a considerable saving in the cost of his concrete slab work.

Concrete is a material with an unusual combination of desirable properties. For example, concrete sets or hardens in water, which is of great importance when building on the ground or in wet locations. It can be formed into practically any shape with a variety of finishes, textures, and colors. Since concrete is composed only of inorganic materials, it is impervious to decay and resists vermin, termites, and rodents. Concrete is made of materials that cannot burn. It is unaffected by the cold of the North or the heat of the South. Finally, concrete's basic ingredients are available almost everywhere at reasonable prices.

Concrete is a mixture of two components, paste and aggregates. The paste is composed of portland cement, water, and air. Aggregates are inert minerals such as sand, gravel, and crushed stone. The aggregates are divided into two sizes: fine and coarse. Fine aggregate is always sand, and coarse aggregate is usually gravel or crushed stone.

During mixing, the cement and water form the paste that surrounds every piece of aggregate. Within a few hours the concrete starts to harden due to hydration, a chemical reaction between the cement and the water. As hydration occurs, the paste binds the aggregates together into a strong, durable, solid mass.

The quality of concrete is directly related to the quality of the cement paste, which in turn is directly related to the amount of water mixed with the cement and the extent of curing. As the amount of water is reduced, the strength of the paste increases, making the concrete stronger and more durable.

Placing and finishing concrete is hard work. For the do-it-yourself project, the area to be paved is best broken down into a series of small jobs, or divided into sections with wood strips or preplanned construction joints. In this way, the amount of concrete placed in any one day can be predetermined.

Subgrade Preparation

The first step in any concrete work is preparation of the subgrade. Serious cracks, slab settlement, and structural failure can often be traced to a poorly compacted subgrade. The subgrade should be uniform, hard, free from foreign matter, and well drained.

Remove from the site all organic matter such as grass, sod, and roots, and grade the ground. Dig out soft or mucky spots; fill them with soil similar to the rest of the subgrade—or with granular material such as sand, gravel, crushed stone, or slag—and compact thoroughly. Loosen and tamp hard spots to provide the same uniform support as the rest of the subgrade. All fill materials should be uniform and free of vegetable matter, large lumps or stones, and frozen soil.

Granular fills of sand, gravel, crushed stone, or slag are recommended for

The subgrade for a concrete slab must be firm and well-tamped; otherwise uneven settlement and cracks may occur.

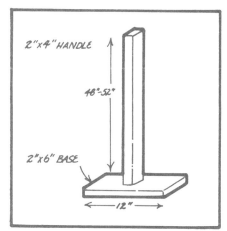

A simple tamper you can make yourself.

bringing the site to uniform bearing and final grade. Compact these fills in layers not more than 4 inches thick. It is best to extend the fill at least 1 foot beyond the slab edge to prevent undercutting during rains.

Cover poorly drained subgrades that are water-soaked most of the time with 4 to 6 inches of granular fill. The bottom of these granular fills must not be lower than the adjacent finished grade to prevent the collection of water under the slab.

Unless fill material is well compacted, it is advisable to leave the subgrade undisturbed. As support for concrete, undisturbed soil is superior to soil that has been dug out and poorly compacted. Subgrade compaction can be done with hand tampers, rollers, or vibratory compactors. For the small job, hand tampers may be used—you can even make your own by nailing a 2x6 base to a 2x4 handle. But for large-volume work, a mechanical roller or vibratory compactor is recommended. You can rent these.

A dry spot on the subgrade absorbs more water from the concrete slab than does an adjacent moist spot. This may result in dark and light spots in the concrete finish. The subgrade should be in a uniformly moist condition at the time of concreting. If necessary, dampen it by spraying with water. However, there should be no free water standing on the subgrade, nor should there be any muddy or soft spots when concrete is being placed.

Form Work

Forms are made of lumber or plywood, braced by stakes driven into the ground. All forms should be straight, free from warping, and of sufficient strength to resist concrete pressure without bulging. Stake and brace the

Stakes should be nailed to the form boards—not vice versa.

Wide-radius curvers can be forced by 1-inch lumber (the inside stakes will be removed after all outside stakes are in place).

Anchor permanent forms to the slab with 16d galvanized nails; concrete will be poured over them.

It's a good idea to mask the tops of permanent form boards to protect them from damage during the concrete placement.

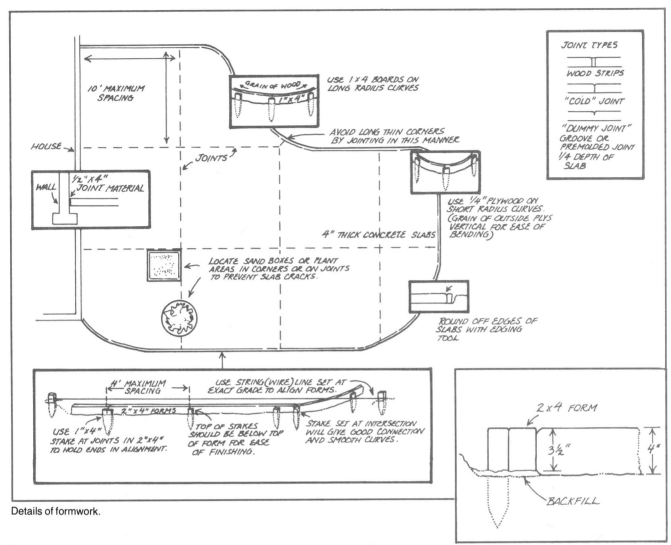

Details of formwork.

Since 2x4 forms are narrower than the slab, backfill to keep concrete from running out.

forms firmly to keep them in horizontal and vertical alignment. Setting forms to proper line and grade is normally accomplished by use of a string line.

For a 4-inch-thick slab—typical for most patios—1x4 or 2x4 lumber may be used. Since the actual dimension of 4-inch lumber is 3½ inches, the final grade should be slightly lower than the bottom of the form. A little back-filling outside the forms will prevent the concrete from running under them.

Wood stakes are cut from 1x2, 1x4, 2x2, or 2x4 lumber. They may be hand cut or purchased precut. Space stakes at 4-foot intervals for the 2-inch-thick form work. With 1-inch lumber, space the stakes more closely to prevent bulging. A maximum interval of 2 to 3 feet is recommended.

For ease in placing and finishing concrete, drive stakes slightly below the tops of the forms. All stakes must be driven straight and true if forms are to be plumb (perfectly vertical). For easy stripping after concrete is cured, use double-headed nails driven through the stakes into the forms—not vice versa.

Curves are formed with 1-inch lumber, plywood, hardboard, or sheet metal. Short-radius curves may be formed by bending ¼-inch plywood with the grain vertical. Tempered hardboard can be bent even more easily. To hold the forms at the proper curvature, set the stakes more closely together.

Wood side forms and divider strips may be left in place permanently for decorative purposes and to serve as control joints. Such forms are usually made of 1x4 or 2x4 redwood, cypress, or cedar that has been primed with a

Wood forms can be left in place permanently as a design element.

clear wood sealer. It is a good practice to mask the top surfaces with tape to protect them from abrasion and staining by concrete during pouring. Miter corner joints and join intersecting strips with neat butt joints. Anchor outside forms to the concrete with galvanized 16d nails driven at 16-inch intervals horizontally through the forms at midheight. Interior divider strips should have nail anchors similarly spaced but driven from alternate sides of the board. Drive all nail heads flush with the forms. Never drive nails through the top of permanent forms. All stakes that are to remain in place permanently must be driven or cut off 2 inches below the surface of the concrete.

Before pouring concrete, give all forms a final check for trueness to grade and proper slope for drainage—at least ¼-inch per foot away from the house or other structure. Check the subgrade with a wood template or string line to ensure correct slab thickness and a smooth subgrade. Finally, dampen forms with water or oil them for easier removal.

Concrete Requirements

If you are doing the job in easy stages—just a few 3- or 4-foot-square modules at a time—you can rent a small mixer and prepare your own concrete. But for any job other than a small patio or other inaccessible spot, you will find that ready-mix concrete, brought to the site by truck, is easiest and most satisfactory to use. Ready-mix is sold by the cubic yard, so determine the amount you will need, figuring the thickness of the slab at 4 inches. For an area 10 feet x 10 feet, for example, you will need to order 1⅓ cubic yards, allowing for waste and spillage; 10x15 will require about 2 yards; and 3 yards will do for about 250 square feet.

When you order concrete from a ready-mix supplier, you will have to specify certain things:
● Order the quantity of concrete in cubic yards, making allowances for uneven subgrade, spillage, and waste (about 5 percent).
● Specify at least six sacks of cement per cubic yard.
● Ask for not more than a 4-inch slump (a measure of the consistency of concrete). This will give a good, workable mix. Stiffer mixes are harder to finish by hand. Very wet, soupy mixes will not give a durable concrete.
● Specify a coarse aggregate (gravel) with a maximum size of between ¾ and 1½ inch. A maximum size of 1 inch is recommended.
● Ask for 6 percent ($\pm$ 1 percent) air entrainment to obtain good durability in concrete on all outside work.
● Specify where and when to deliver the concrete, and if possible place your concrete order at least one day ahead of time.

MIXING IT YOURSELF

If is not always possible to use ready-mix concrete on small jobs. In some cases, the amount of concrete you require may be less than most ready-mix producers will supply (usually, 1 cubic yard is the minimum order). And in some areas there is no ready-mix plant.

If you are faced with one of these circumstances, making your own concrete may be the only practical solution. This is hard work, but it has the advantage of low cost, and the amount of concrete mixed can be adjusted to suit your own work pace.

Quality concrete costs no more to make than poor concrete, but is far more economical in the long run because of its greater durability. The rules for making good concrete are simple:

● Use proper ingredients.
● Proportion the ingredients correctly.

● Measure the ingredients accurately.
● Mix the ingredients thoroughly.

Portland cement is not a brand, but a type. Most portland cement is gray in color. However, white portland cement is manufactured from special raw materials. It can be used instead of the normal gray, but it is more expensive.

You can buy portland cement in bags at your local building materials dealer. In the United States, a bag weighs 94 pounds and holds 1 cubic foot. Cement in bags should be stored in a dry location, preferably on raised wooden platforms.

Almost any natural water that is drinkable and has no pronounced taste or odor can be used to make concrete. Although some waters that are not suitable for drinking will make satisfactory concrete, to be on the safe side, use only water fit to drink.

Air is also an important ingredient for making good concrete. Air in the concrete improves its durability and virtually eliminates scaling due to freeze-thaw and de-icer salt action. Concrete containing such air bubbles is called air-entrained concrete.

Air entrainment is most important for concrete exposed to alternate cycles of freezing and thawing or use of de-icers. In cold climates, and even in mild climates that have several cycles of freezing and thawing each year, it should be used for all exterior concrete, including patios.

To create air-entrained concrete, chemicals specially made for this purpose, called air-entraining agents, are added to the mixing water. Building materials suppliers sometimes carry air-entraining agents. Ready-mix plants stock them for their own use and will probably sell you a small quantity. The amount to be added to the mix depends on the brand of air-entraining agent. This information can be obtained from the building materials supplier or ready-mix producer.

There is another method of obtaining air-entrained concrete. Many manufacturers market portland cements that contain an interground air-entraining agent. These cements are identified on the bag as "air-entraining" and are available from the same suppliers that sell regular portland cement.

Aggregates make up 60 to 80 percent of the volume of concrete. They act as a filler material to reduce the amount of cement required in concrete. Without aggregates, concrete would be very expensive. It would also shrink a great deal upon drying and this would cause excessive cracking. Aggregates restrain the shrinkage that occurs when concrete hardens.

Natural sand is the most commonly used fine aggregate; however, manufactured sand, made by crushing gravel or stone, is also available in some areas. Sand should have particles ranging in size from ¼-inch down to dust size. Mortar sand should not be used for making concrete since it contains only small particles.

Gravel and crushed stone are the most commonly used coarse aggregates. They should consist of particles that are sound, hard, and durable, not soft or flaky, with a minimum of long, sliverlike pieces. Particles should range in size from ¼-inch to a maximum of 1 inch for a 4-inch-thick slab.

Good fine and coarse concrete aggregates have a full range of sizes ranging from the smallest to the largest, but no excess amount of any one size. The big particles fill out the bulk of a concrete mix and the smaller ones fill in the spaces between the larger ones. Both fine and coarse aggregates for making concrete must be clean and free of excessive dirt, clay, silt, coal, or other organic matter such as leaves and roots. These foreign materials will prevent the cement from properly binding the aggregate particles together, resulting in porous concrete with low strength and durability.

HOW MUCH?

Before you get down to the job of measuring and mixing, you'll have to apply some good old basic math to determine how much cement, sand, and coarse aggregate you will neeed for your project. Start by figuring the cubic feet of concrete required, following this formula:

width (feet) × length (feet) × thickness (inches) = cubic feet

Ingredients Needed

Air-entrained concrete				Concrete without air			
Cement	Sand	Coarse aggregate	Water	Cement	Sand	Coarse aggregate	Water
Proportions by weight (pounds) per cubic foot of concrete							
24	39	70	9	24	45	70	10
Proportions by volume per cubic foot of concrete							
1	2¼	2¾	½	1	2½	2¾	½

For example, a 10-foot x 15-foot patio 4 inches thick would require $\frac{10 \times 15 \times 4}{12} =$ 50 cubic feet of concrete. Add about 10 percent for waste due to spillage, uneven subgrade, and other causes, and the total amount needed is 55 cubic feet.

The quantities of materials you will need can be calculated by multiplying the number of cubic feet of concrete (55 in this case) by the weights of materials needed for 1 cubic foot, as shown in the table. For example, assuming your project requires air-entrained concrete, the quantities for your 10 x 15-foot patio would be:

55 x 24 = 1320 pounds of air-entraining cement (approximately fourteen bags)

55 x 39 = 2145 pounds of sand

55 x 70 = 3850 pounds of coarse aggregate

Aggregates are sold by the ton or by the cubic yard (27 cubic feet). You can convert from weight to volume, or vice versa, by assuming a value of 90 pounds per cubic foot for sand and 100 pounds per cubic foot for coarse aggregate. Therefore, 2145 pounds of sand contains $\frac{2145}{90} = 23.8$ cubic feet, or $\frac{23.8}{27} = 0.88$ cubic yards. For the coarse aggregate on the 10 x 15-foot patio, 3850 pounds $\left(\frac{3850}{100}\right)$ contains 38.5 cubic feet, or $\left(\frac{38.5}{27}\right)$ 1.4 cubic yards. With a sharp pencil, you'll have your needs figured out in no time.

Placing Concrete

Advance planning and preparation will save time and prevent confusion on the job. Forms and subgrade must be ready; and the manpower, tools, and materials needed for placing and finishing the concrete must be on hand. For the average job, you will need a wheelbarrow, shovel, straightedge, bull float or darby, edger, groover, float, trowel, broom, water hose, and curing materials.

If concrete can be discharged from the truck onto the subgrade, one or two

Use a shovel to work concrete along the forms, eliminating voids and honeycomb.

helpers will generally be required. Additonal helpers will be needed if concrete must be wheelbarrowed from truck to subgrade.

Plan to get the heavy ready-mix truck as near as possible to the point of placement without driving it over existing sidewalks or driveways. If the site is especially difficult to reach, ask the ready-mix producer for suggestions before delivery of the concrete.

Place concrete uniformly to the full depth of the forms and as near as possible to final position. Start in a corner and do not drag or flow the concrete excessively. Overworking the mix in this manner causes an excess of water and fine material to be brought to the surface. This may cause scaling and dusting later on. Spade concrete along the forms to compact it firmly and eliminate voids and honeycomb.

Spreading and spading are best done with a short-handled, square-ended shovel. Spreading can also be done with special concrete rakes or come-alongs, which are hoelike tools. Ordinary rakes and hoes should not be used because they cause segregation (a separation of large pieces of gravel or stone from the mortar).

After concrete has been spread and compacted to fill the forms, strike-off and bull-floating or darbying should follow immediately. It is of utmost importance that these operations be performed before bleed water has an opportun-

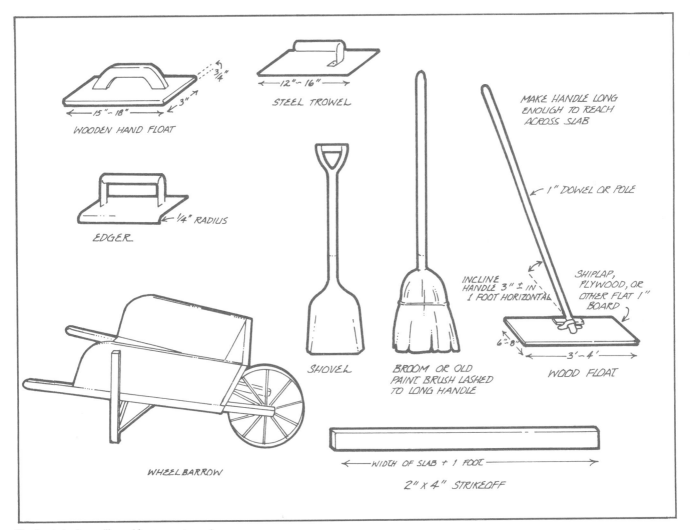

The basic tools you'll need for concrete work.

ity to collect on the surface. Concrete should not be spread over too large an area before strike-off, nor should a large area be struck off and allowed to remain before bull-floating or darbying. Any operation performed on the surface of a concrete slab while bleed water is present will cause serious dusting or scaling.

Strike-Off

Strike-off is the removing of concrete in excess of the amount required to fill the forms and bring the surface to grade. The tool used is a straightedge or strike-off. Straightedges may be of 2x4 lumber.

Move the straightedge back and forth with a sawlike motion. A small amount of concrete should be kept ahead of the straightedge to fill in low spots. As the straightedge is pulled forward, tilt it in the direction of travel to obtain a cutting edge. A second pass should be made, if needed, to remove any remaining bumps or low spots. During the second pass, tilt the straightedge in the opposite direction.

Move a straightedge back and forth across the newly poured concrete to strike off any excess.

When you are using permanent forms in your patio, you can do the job in small stages. Here, each square is poured individually, and struck off level with the form boards.

Bull-Floating and Darbying

Bull-floating or darbying follows strike-off immediately. The purpose of these operations is to level ridges and fill voids left by the straightedge and to embed all particles of coarse aggregate slightly below the surface. A bull float is used for areas too large to reach with a darby; otherwise a darby is used.

Bull floats are large, long-handled wood floats. The bull float should be pushed ahead with the front (toe) of the float raised so that it will not dig into the concrete surface. The tool should be pulled back with the float blade flat on the surface to cut off bumps and fill holes. If holes or depressions remain and no excess concrete is left on the slab, additional concrete should be added and the surface bull-floated again.

Darbies are hand-operated wood or metal tools, 3 to 8 feet long. The darby should be held flat against the surface of the concrete and worked from right to left, or vice versa, with a sawing motion, cutting off bumps and filling depressions. When the surface is level, the darby should be tilted slightly and again moved from right to left, or vice versa, to fill any small holes left by the sawing motion.

These operations should level, shape, and smooth the surface, and work up a slight amount of cement paste. Do not overwork the concrete; overworking will result in a less durable surface.

Bull-floating—note that the front edge of the toll is raised slightly so that it does not dig into the concrete.

The darby is held flat against the surface and worked in a sawing motion.

When the surface is level, the darby is tilted slightly and again worked over the surface. Darbies come in a variety of lengths.

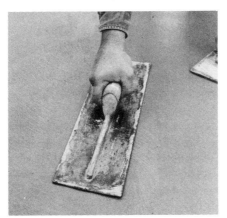

Magnesium hand floats are used on small areas. Wood floats can also be used.

Finishing

The finishing operations of edging, jointing, floating, and troweling must wait until all bleed water has left the surface and the concrete stiffens slightly. This waiting period, which is absolutely essential to obtain durable surfaces, varies with the wind, temperature, and relative humidity of the atmosphere and with the type and temperature of the concrete. On hot, dry, windy days, the waiting period is very short; on cool, humid days, it can be several hours. With air-entrained concrete, there may be little or no waiting. Begin finishing when the water sheen is gone and the concrete can sustain foot pressure with only about ¼-inch indentation. (A water sheen may not be visible on air-entrained concrete, so use the foot-pressure test.)

EDGING

Edging is the first operation. It produces a neat, rounded edge that prevents chipping or damage, especially when forms are removed. Edging also compacts and hardens the concrete surface next to the form where floats and trowels are less effective.

Edging tools are made of steel and bronze. Stainless steel edgers with a ½-inch radius are recommended for patios. The edger should be held flat on the concrete surface, with its front tilted up slightly while the tool is moved forward. When moving the tool backward over the edge, tilt the rear of the tool

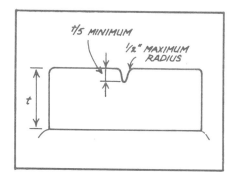

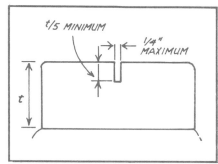

Types of control joints for concrete terraces.

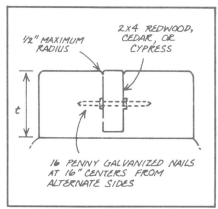

Use a pointed trowel to cut concrete away from the forms before edging.

Hold the edger flat on the surface, with the end tilted slightly upward so that it doesn't dig into the concrete.

slightly. Caution is necessary to prevent the edger from leaving too deep an impression, as these indentations may be difficult to remove in subsequent finishing operations.

JOINTING

Jointing is a most important finishing operation. Like other materials used in construction, concrete contracts and expands slightly under varying conditions of moisture and temperature. When newly placed, concrete attains its largest volume. When dry and cold, it contracts to its smallest volume. These changes in volume are normal in all concrete, but unless provisions are made to control them, cracks may result. Effective control is obtained with control joints and isolation joints.

Control joints, sometimes called contraction joints, are made with a hand tool, sawed or formed by using wood divider strips. The tooled or sawed joint should extend into the slab one-fourth to one-fifth of slab thickness. A cut of this depth provides a weakened section that induces cracking to occur beneath the joint where it is not visible.

Spacing of control joints in patios should not exceed 10 feet in either direction. If possible, the panels formed by control joints should be approximately square. Panels with excessive length-to-width ratio (more than 1½ to 1) are likely to crack. As a general rule, the smaller the panel, the less likelihood of random cracking. All control joints should be continuous, not staggered or offset.

Hand tools for jointing are called groovers or jointers. Like edgers, they are made of stainless steel and other metals and are available in various sizes and styles. The radius of a groover should be ¼ to ½-inch. The bit (cutting edge) should be deep enough to cut the slab a minimum of one-fifth, and preferably one-fourth, of the depth. Groovers with worn-out or shallow bits should not be used for making control joints, but may be used for decorative scoring of the surface.

It is good practice to mark the location of each joint with a string or chalk line on both side forms and on the concrete surface. A straight 1-inch board at least 6 inches wide should be used to guide the groover. The board should rest on the side forms and be perpendicular to the edges of the slab. The groover should be held against the side of the board as it is moved across the slab. To start the joint, push the groover into the concrete and move it forward while applying pressure to the back of the tool. After the joint is cut, the tool should be turned around and pulled back over the groove; this gives it a smooth finish. If

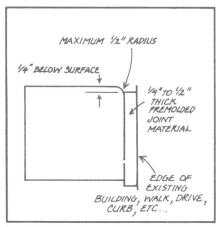

Details of an isolation joint.

More closely spaced control joints mean less likelihood of cracking.

the concrete has stiffened to the point where the groover will not penetrate easily to the proper depth, a hand ax can be used to push through the concrete. The groover should then be used to finish the joint.

Instead of being hand tooled, control joints can be cut with a concrete saw—an electric saw equipped with a masonry cutting blade. To function properly, a sawed joint must be cut as deep as a hand-tooled joint: one-fifth to one-fourth of the slab thickness. Sawing should be done as soon as the surface is firm enough not to be torn up or damaged by the blade. This is normally four to twelve hours after the concrete hardens.

The other type of joint required to control random cracks is the isolation joint, sometimes referred to as an expansion joint. It consists of a premolded strip of fiber material that extends the full depth of the slab or slightly below it. It need not exceed ½-inch in thickness, and in most instances ¼-inch is sufficient. Isolation joints are required at intersections of walks and drives and at points where patio slabs abut existing buildings or curves. They should be flush with the finished surface or, better still, about ¼-inch below. Joints that protrude above the surface are a safety hazard. For this reason, joint materials that extrude when compressed should not be used.

FLOATING

Following edging and jointing, the surface is floated to embed large aggregate just below the surface, to remove any imperfections left in the surface by

Edge marks made by the groover at control joints are removed during final floating.

Control joints can be cut with an electric saw fitted with an abrasive or diamond blade.

previous operations, and to compact the concrete and consolidate mortar at the surface in preparation for any further finishing operations.

Hand floats are made of metal, wood, plastic, and composition materials. Magnesium floats are light, strong, and slide easily over a concrete surface. They are recommended for most work, especially with air-entrained concrete. Wood floats drag more, hence require greater effort to use; but the wood produces a rougher texture, which may be preferred when good skid resistance is required and floating is used as the final finish.

Hold the hand float flat on the concrete surface and move with a slight sawing motion in a sweeping arc to fill in holes, cut off lumps, and smooth ridges. On large slabs, power floats can be rented to reduce finishing time.

Floating produces a relatively even (but not smooth) texture. Since this texture has good skid resistance, floating is often used as a final finish. In such cases, it may be necessary to float the surface a second time after some hardening has taken place to impart the desired final texture to the concrete.

Marks left by edgers and groovers are removed during floating. Therefore, if they are desired for decorative purposes, the edger can be rerun after final floating.

TROWELING

Immediately after floating, the surface can be troweled. This produces a smooth, hard, dense surface. Troweling should never be done on a surface that has not been floated; bull-floating or darbying is not sufficient.

On large slabs where you cannot reach the entire surface, you must work on knee boards. When hand finishing, you can float and immediately trowel an area before moving the knee boards. This operation should be delayed until the concrete has hardened enough so that water and fine material are not brought to the surface. Too long a delay, of course, will result in a surface that is too hard to finish. Premature finishing may cause scaling or dusting.

Hand trowels are made of high-quality steel in various sizes. Normally, at least two sizes are used. For the first troweling, one of the larger tools—18x4¾ inches, for example—is recommended. Shorter and narrower trowels are used for additional trowelings as the concrete sets and becomes harder. For the final troweling, a 12x3-inch trowel, known as a fanning trowel, is recommended. When one trowel is used for the entire operation, it should measure about 14x4 inches.

For the first troweling, hold the trowel blade flat on the surface. If it is tilted, ripples are made that are difficult to remove later without tearing the surface and causing pop-outs. Use the hand trowel in a sweeping arc motion, each pass overlapping one-half of the previous pass. In this manner, each troweling covers the surface twice. The first troweling may be sufficient to produce a surface free of defects, but additional trowelings will increase smoothness and hardness.

Allow some time after the first troweling to permit the concrete to become harder. When only a slight indentation is made by pressing your hand against the surface, the second troweling should be started; use a smaller trowel held with the blade tilted slightly. The final pass should make a ringing sound as the tilted blade moves over the hardening surface.

Curing Concrete

The hardening of concrete is brought about by chemical reactions between cement and water. This process, called *hydration,* continues only if water and a suitable temperature are available. When too much water is lost by evaporation from newly placed concrete, hydration stops. With near-freezing temperatures (32° F.), hydration slows almost to a standstill. Under these conditions,

The slab can be steel-troweled to a smooth, hard finish immediately after floating.

concrete ceases to gain strength and other desirable properties. The purpose of curing is to maintain conditions under which concrete hardens by keeping it moist and warm.

Supplying additional water through moist coverings is the most effective method of curing. Burlap, the most commonly used wet covering, should be free of any substance that may be harmful to concrete or cause discoloration. Place the burlap as soon as the concrete is hard enough to withstand surface damage and sprinkle it periodically to keep the concrete surface continually moist during the curing period.

Water curing with lawn sprinklers, nozzles, or soaking hoses is another method; it must be continuous so that there is no chance of partial drying during the curing period. Ponding is very effective for small patios that are reasonably level. Sand or earth dikes are used to confine water on the slab. A sufficient depth of water must be maintained to prevent dry spots.

Curing methods intended to seal the surface are not quite as effective as methods that supply water, but they are widely used for convenience. Moisture barriers such as plastic sheeting and waterproof paper are popular. They do not require periodic additions of water, but they must be laid flat, thoroughly sealed at joints, and anchored carefully along edges. Curing with these materials may cause patchy discoloration, especially if the concrete contains calcium chloride and has been finished by hard steel troweling. This discoloration is experienced when the plastic or paper becomes wrinkled. It is difficult and time-consuming on a large patio to smooth out the wrinkles that are apt to form.

Pigmented curing compounds provide the easiest and most convenient method of curing. These compounds are applied by spraying soon after the final finishing operation. The surface should be damp, but not wet with standing water. Complete coverage is essential. A second coat applied at right angles to the first is recommended.

Curing should be started as soon as it is possible to do so without damaging the surface. It should continue for a period of five days in warm weather (70° F. or higher) or seven days in cooler weather (50° to 70° F.). In very hot weather (above 90° F.) concrete work should never be attempted—for your own sake as well as for the concrete.

During the curing period, burlap may be used as a wet covering to prevent excessive evaporation.

A curing compound may be sprayed on the slab after finishing, but it is essential that the entire surface be covered.

Structural Considerations
Concrete Steps

Patio or other outdoor steps may not be needed for many homes, especially those built on a slab on level ground. Other homes, however, will require steps either from the ground up to the patio or from the patio to the house. In some cases, there will be steps leading from one ground level to another where the topography is uneven. Fortunately, steps of this type are relatively uncomplicated to build.

Often there is just one step to or from a patio. Such a single step can usually be formed and poured at the same time as the patio itself. The forms are placed a little higher or lower than the patio slab, depending on the circumstances. (Dimensions are as discussed below.)

Where more than one step is required, the procedures are somewhat more involved. The best material to use for forms is nominal 1x8 lumber (actual dimensions: ¾ inch x 7¼ inches). In most cases, the 7¼-inch dimension will be just right for riser height of the steps.

Steps should be a minimum of three feet wide. All risers should be exactly the same height—this is an important safety consideration. Another safety (as well as convenience) requirement is that treads be at least 11 inches wide; all

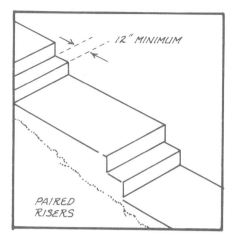

PAIRED RISERS

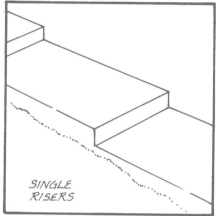

SINGLE RISERS

Steps for private walkways can be more casual. Ideal dimensions are given in chart.

should be of the same width. The rise for each step should not exceed 7½ inches (which makes the 1x8 form lumber ideal). Allow a ⅛-inch pitch on each tread for drainage. A landing is desirable to divide flights of stairs more than five feet high.

On a long slope, a stepped ramp is often used. Ramps should have a tread length that will provide two easy paces between the risers.

Basically, form-building for steps is simply an extension of the techniques used for patio forms. Just build them up, and make certain that they are securely staked to the ground all around. Steps with long treads will require nominal 1-inch-thick (actually 1½ inches) riser forms to keep from bending or bulging.

An efficient and economical way to keep steps from sinking is to dig two 6- to 8-inch-diameter post holes beneath the bottom tread, extending them below the frost line. The holes are then filled with concrete. The top step or platform is tied to the slab or house wall with two or more metal anchors.

Forms are placed, braced, and oiled (for easy removal). Well-tamped or granular fill is usually spread inside the forms to reduce the amount of concrete needed for the steps, but this should be at least 4 inches below the top edges of the forms.

The concrete mix for steps is the same as for patios. Pour the concrete inside the forms, spading it thoroughly around the edges. Tap the forms lightly to release entrapped air bubbles. Screed the concrete at tread level. Finish the treads with a float, then broom them for a nonskid step surface (these steps are explained in previous sections of this chapter). Use an edging tool to round the front edges of the treads. Moist-cure for at least five days. Remove the forms, then clean the steps with a wire brush. Fill in any holes or depressions with a mortar mix; chip off any projections and wire-brush smooth.

Precast concrete steps are available from many manufacturers. These steel-reinforced units are of many types; most have built-in lugs to hold railings and grill work. Because of their bulk and weight, precast steps are not normally a do-it-yourself installation, but most dealers have the special equipment needed to do this job quickly and easily.

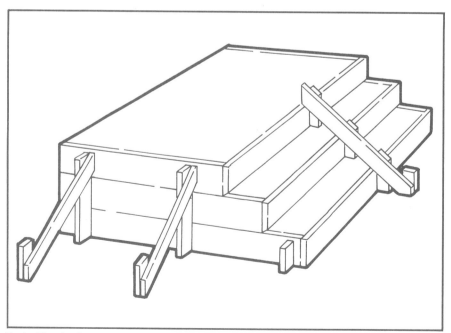

Typical forming for multi-level step construction.

Walks and Driveways

If walks or a driveway are part of your overall plan, it is a good idea to construct them at the same time as your patio. Although it may seem like an added burden at the time the savings in time and money are substantial in the long run.

Walks and driveways are basically concrete slabs, just as patios are. The mix, form work, and placing and finishing processes are the same. Dimensions, of course, will differ, and there may be more involvement with building codes and other local ordinances if your work involves municipal property. Sidewalks along the street and driveways are almost always subject to local regulations. Consult the municipal authorities about this during your planning stage.

The main walk leading to the front of your house should be 3 to 4 feet wide.

The private walk to the main entrance should be three to four feet wide. Shown is an exposed aggregate walkway with forms left in place.

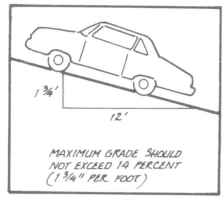

MAXIMUM GRADE SHOULD
NOT EXCEED 14 PERCENT
(1¾" PER FOOT)

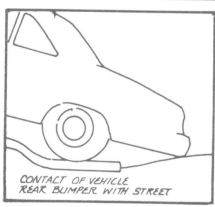

CONTACT OF VEHICLE
UNDERCARRIAGE WITH DRIVEWAY

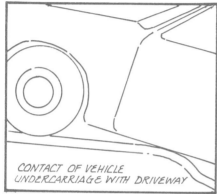

CONTACT OF VEHICLE
REAR BUMPER WITH STREET

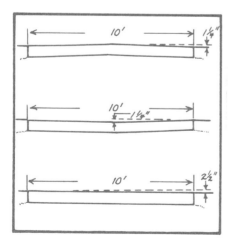

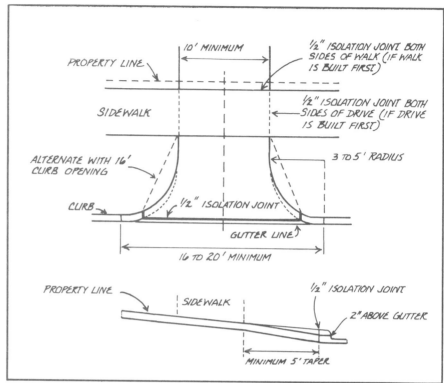

Points to remember when planning your driveway.

Other private walkways to the back door or elsewhere may be as narrow as 2 feet. Public walks along the street must be wide enough to allow two people to walk abreast, with enough room for a third to pass without crowding. This usually translates into 4 to 5 feet in an area with single-family housing. If you are located near a school, church, shopping center, or other area where pedestrian traffic is heavy, wider walks are advisable.

A 4-inch thickness is recommended for most walks, but in heavy traffic areas 5 or 6 inches may be required. The usual slope is ½-inch per foot toward the street to provide drainage. Again, check local authorities for possible variations.

Driveways for single car garages or carports are usually 10 to 14 feet wide, with a 14-foot minimum width for curving drives. The rule of thumb is that a driveway should be 3 feet wider than the widest vehicle it will serve. So if you plan on trading in your tiny CVCC for a mammoth Mark V, plan accordingly.

Long driveway approaches to two-car garages may be single-car width, but they must be widened near the garage to provide access to both stalls. Short driveways for two-car garages should be from 16 to 24 feet wide.

The thickness of a driveway is determined primarily by the weight of the vehicles that can be expected to use it. For passenger cars, 4 inches is sufficient. But if an occasional heavy truck (an oil delivery truck, for example) uses the driveway, a 5- or 6-inch thickness is recommended. It is far easier and more economical to pour an extra 2 inches of concrete initially than to be constantly patching and eventually digging up a slab that can't handle the load.

When a garage is considerably above or below street level and is located near the street, driveway grade may be critical. A grade of 14 percent (1¾ inch per foot) is the maximum recommended. The change in grade should be gradual to avoid scraping and damaging the car's bumpers and underside. The most critical point is when the rear wheels are in the gutter as a car approaches the driveway from the street.

This pleasant garden walk was formed with grassy intervals between slabs to add interest. Curved walkways are always more eye-appealing for this type of installation.

The driveway should have a slight slope so that it will drain quickly. A slope of ¼-inch per foot is generally recommended; its direction will depend on the particular building conditions, but usually it will be toward the street. A crown or cross-slope is sometimes used instead.

Walls

Poured concrete walls are not often used in outdoor living projects; when they are, their design is determined largely by the purpose they are intended to serve. Specific requirements for concrete retaining walls are discussed in a later chapter.

Concrete walls are sometimes used as foundations for wood decks and other outdoor structures. Building codes and ordinances are generally quite specific in their requirements for poured structural concrete, and you'd better be sure to check your local codes when planning a concrete wall. Building permits and inspections will probably be required. But what's good for the building code is good for you (usually), so don't knock it.

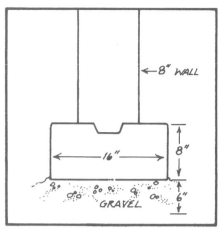

Typical footing proportions.

While the local code will be your ultimate guide, some general rules can be set for concrete wall construction. Footings will be required at the base to spread the load over as much area as is necessary for adequate support. Conventional wisdom has it that a footing should be as thick as the wall it supports and twice as wide—an 8-inch-thick wall would require an 8-inch-thick footing 16 inches wide. But poor soil conditions (sand or very porous earth, for example) may dictate larger footings to distribute the weight load. Your local building department may have requirements, or at least recommendations, about footing sizes. Check with them.

Excavation for wall footings should place them below the frost line, except in very moderate climates where this is not a factor. Again, check your local building code on this. Normally, a 6-inch bed or base of crushed rock is provided beneath. Form work is the same as for a walkway or patio. If the soil is sturdy and closely compacted, forms may not even be needed—the soil itself can serve as a form.

Generally, the mix for a footing will be about one part cement, two and one half parts sand, and four parts aggregate.

The poured concrete footing should be struck off level and floated—no other finishing steps are required. A keyway should be provided along the length of the footing to "tie in" the poured wall. Bevel the edges of the 2x4 the length of the footing to about 30 degrees. Coat edges and bottom with engine oil to facilitate later removal from the concrete. Pour the concrete to 1 inch from the surface, then place the 2x4 in the center of the footing, flush with the tops of the forms. Pour the remaining concrete and strike off. The keyway forms are removed as the concrete hardens.

For larger walls, steel reinforcing rods and tie rods may be required—again, your local building code should be your guide. The steel rods (usually $\frac{3}{8}$-inch for such purposes) are available at most building supply and masonry dealers. For a 16-inch-wide footing, three rods would normally be used, the outer ones approximately 2 inches from the edge of the footing and the third in the middle. About a third of the concrete should be poured, then the rods placed and covered with the remainder of the pour.

Where vertical tie rods are required—as on a retaining wall, for example—$\frac{1}{2}$-inch holes are drilled along the center line of the keyway form, usually at 24-inch intervals unless otherwise specified by the building code. Pour the concrete and place the keyway forms as above. Immediately after the final pour, carefully push the tie rods through the holes in the keyway forms. When the concrete is hard enough to support the vertical rods, remove the 2x4 forms.

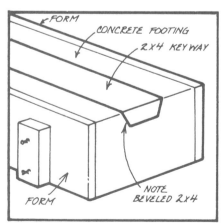

A beveled 2x4 is embedded in the concrete footing to form a keyway.

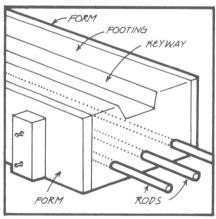

Reinforcing rods are inserted into the footing.

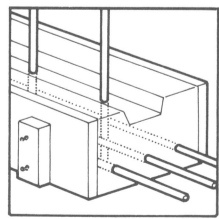

Insert vertical tie rods through keyway forms.

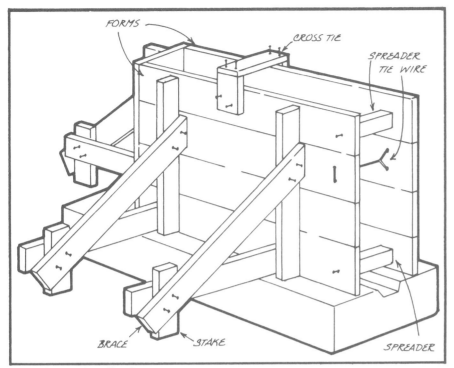

Typical form work and bracing.

Wall thickness will be determined by its intended function and, once again, the local code. The vertical loads of most outdoor structures on a concrete foundation wall are relatively small; a low wall serving such a purpose may be as little as 4 inches thick. A concrete retaining wall will probably be considerably thicker—perhaps 8 inches, and even more if it is over 6 feet in height.

Once the footing has thoroughly cured, you can begin the formwork. Forms for concrete walls must be strong, straight, and watertight. 1x6 or 1x8 tongue-and-groove boards or ⅝-inch plywood (plyscord is the usual choice—its smooth face should be on the inside of the form) are normally used by the do-it-yourselfer. (Professionals may use steel forms, but it would hardly pay to purchase these for just a single job. The boards or plywood of your forms can be put to some other use after they have served their form-work function). Forms must also be adequately supported and braced, strong enough to support the pressure of the concrete until it dries and hardens.

For very low walls, 1-inch lumber is adequate for bracing. Larger walls will require 2x3 or 2x4 braces. Use double-headed nails for building the forms; these are easily removed later on when you are knocking down the form work.

Assemble the braces in the form of a right triangle, with the angle at the top approximately 60 degrees. The vertical piece should be the same height as the form (and the wall to be poured) and must be perfectly plumb—your concrete wall will be no better than the forms into which it is poured. Anchor the outer ends of the braces to sharpened stakes driven well into the ground. The intervals between braces will depend on such factors as height and thickness of the wall and condition of the soil. Just make sure that you have enough—or too many—braces to keep the forms in place. Poured concrete is a heavyweight.

Spreaders of 2x2 or 2x3 lumber separate the forms until the concrete is poured. These should be placed every few feet horizontally and approximately every foot vertically. Tack them lightly through the outside of the forms—just enough to hold them in position.

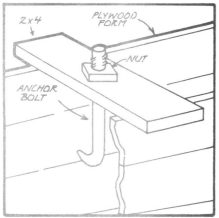

Suspend anchor bolts over cavity before pouring concrete.

Tie wires help hold the forms together (these are not needed for low walls). They are available in various types at building supply and masonry dealers. Some utilize nuts and threaded rod to allow proper adjustment—others are simply bent wire. Your local building code may have something to say on the subject; otherwise, your choice will be governed by what is most readily available. Tie spacing is the same as for spreaders (but, obviously, not in the same places). Finally, cross ties keep the tops of the forms from pulling apart when concrete is poured. Blocks of 2-inch lumber are nailed to the outsides of the forms midway between braces, and pieces of 1- or 2-inch lumber are nailed across these blocks. Coat the insides of the forms with engine oil to facilitate their removal after the concrete hardens.

If the concrete wall is to serve as the foundation for a deck or other structure, anchor bolts should be provided. These are bolts with a hook or plate on the bottom. They should be spaced at approximately 24-inch intervals. To hold the bolts in place during the pour, drill holes, $1/16$-inch larger than the diameter of the bolts, through lengths of 2x4 slightly longer than the width of the forms. Place the bolts through the holes, then thread nuts onto the bolts. Place the boards on the forms to suspend the bolts over the cavity.

When you are satisfied that your form work is straight, square, level, and plumb, it is time for the pour. The proportions of the mix will depend on local conditions; generally, one part cement, two and one half parts sand, and three and one half parts aggregate (by volume) is a good mix for walls. Begin placing the concrete at one end of the wall, pouring in even layers no more than 24 inches deep. Spade and tamp each layer before pouring the next, and remove the wood spreaders as you go along (tie wires are left in place). Work at a steady pace, and do not allow one layer to begin to harden before pouring the next. Be careful not to disturb the anchor bolts while pouring the concrete.

When the entire wall has been poured to the top of the forms, strike off the surface, then float it. After the concrete begins to harden, the boards holding the anchor bolts in place may be removed (if these were used). The rest of the form work must be left in place at least until the concrete is sufficiently strong to support its own weight. The forms also prevent premature drying of the concrete, much as damp burlap or other means do on a slab. Leaving the forms in place for five to seven days will help insure proper curing.

After the forms are removed, the tie wires are cut or broken off, depending on the type used. Holes left by the wires are filled with a cement-sand mixture troweled into place.

Temperature Considerations
Cold Weather Concreting

Although it isn't recommended for neophytes, concrete can be put down in temperatures below 50 degrees when necessary. Contractors often use calcium chloride and high early-strength concrete to speed up drying time and reduce the chance of freezing. The do-it-yourselfer can employ similar techniques, following the other precautions described below, when necessary, although it is a risky process and should be avoided if possible.

A single freezing and thawing cycle can damage even concrete that has been carefully laid. Several such cycles will so decrease the water tightness and surface resistance that the concrete will surely deteriorate within a few years.

The most helpful cold-weather installation technique is to heat the water so that the entire mix will be placed at the optimum temperature of 50 to 70 degrees. Since water is only one part of the mix, you must more or less play it by ear to estimate what effect the winter temperature will have on the concrete as a whole. If the outside temperature is only slightly below 50 degrees, the water need not be too hot. When it approaches 32 degrees, the water should be quite hot (but never over 140 degrees). When the air temperature goes below freezing, the sand and even the coarse aggregate may have to be heated.

It is also necessary to find some method of heating up the ground inside the forms if it is frozen. Use a blowtorch, burn some wood inside the forms, or use some other method to remove the chill. Add about a pound of calcium chloride per sack of cement to the water. Don't use antifreeze compounds, which will reduce the strength and wearing quality of the concrete.

Mute evidence of improper curing during weather extremes is this patio surface, scaled beyond repair.

The best way to get a warm concrete mix is to order it that way from a ready-mix supplier. Many dealers have trucks that will keep the mix heated until it is ready to pour. Needless to say, you must lay and finish such a mix quickly.

After placing, the concrete must be kept from freezing for at least four days. Ideally, the temperature at the concrete surface should be kept at 70 degrees for three days and at 50 degrees for five days.

Portable heaters should be used to maintain the required temperatures. If these are not available, lay tarpaper and a thick blanket of straw or other insulating material over the surface during the curing process. Wood or tarpaulins over the straw will provide additional protection. Moist and warm air should be circulated over the surface whenever possible. The insulating and heating materials can be removed after a week.

Hot Weather Concreting

Laying concrete in hot weather is another story. Although it too has its risks, the job can be done with the proper precautions. Good planning cannot always take a sudden heat wave into account. Whenever the temperature rises above 70 degrees, there is a greater chance of cracking due to too-rapid drying. Between 70 and 90 degrees, quick installation work and proper curing should keep problems under control. When the thermometer goes over 90, however, more drastic measures are in order.

Rapid evaporation can be prevented at least in part by beginning work in the late afternoon. Ice in the mixing water and cold water sprinkled on the aggregate will help on very hot days. The most crucial time, however, is during the finishing and curing processes. Windbreaks of canvas or polyethylene will keep hot, drying winds off the surface. Wet burlap should be placed on the surface between finishing steps, and as soon thereafter as possible. Ponding is also recommended for at least eight hours thereafter. The usual curing methods should be religiously followed for at least a week.

Special Finishes and Effects

Many decorative finishes can be built into concrete during construction. Color may be added to the concrete through the use of pigments or by exposing colorful aggregates. Textured finishes can be as varied as you wish, from a smooth polished appearance to the roughness of a gravel path. Geometric patterns can be scored or stamped into the concrete to resemble stone, brick, or tile paving. Other interesting patterns are obtained by using divider strips to form panels of various sizes and shapes—rectangular, square, or diamond. Special techniques are available to render concrete slip resistant and sparkling. The possibilities are almost unlimited.

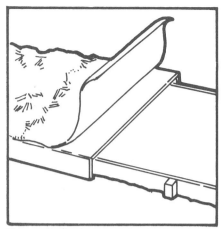

The most effective protective method in cold weather is to cover the concrete with wood, tarpaper and straw.

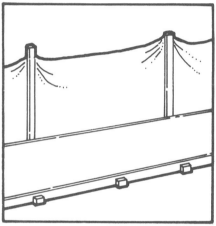

A plastic screen will protect the slab from hot sun and drying winds during very warm weather.

Colored Concrete

There are three methods of coloring concrete during construction: one-course, two-course, and dry-shake. The one- and two-course methods are similar. In both, the concrete mix is integrally colored by addition of a special mineral oxide pigment. The amount of pigment used should never exceed 10 percent by weight of cement.

Pigments in white portland cement will produce brighter colors or light pastel shades when used with light-colored sand. White cement should be used in preference to normal gray portland cement, except for black or dark gray colors. All materials in the mix must be carefully controlled by weight to maintain a uniform color from batch to batch. Mixing of color pigments and cement should always be done in the dry state. To prevent streaking, separate mixers and thoroughly cleaned finishing tools are required for colored concrete. When using the one-course method, uniform moistening of the subgrade is important for uniform color results. The best means to accomplish this is to soak the subgrade thoroughly the evening before placing concrete or to use a moisture barrier under the slab.

The only difference between the one- and two-course methods is that the latter uses a base course of conventional concrete. For a patio slab, this should be 3½ to 4 inches thick. The surface of the base is left rough to help provide good bond for the topping. After the base stiffens slightly and the surface water disappears, the top course of ½ to 1 inch of colored concrete is placed.

The dry-shake method consists of applying a factory-prepared dry color material over the concrete surface after preliminary floating, edging, and grooving. Two applications of the dry-shake are made, the first using about two-thirds of the total amount specified by the manufacturer. The surface is then floated, edged, and grooved again before the final application. Repeat the finishing operations to make sure the color is uniformly worked into the concrete. If a smooth, hard surface is desired, troweling follows floating in the usual manner.

Concrete Color Guide	
Color Desired	Materials to Use
White	White portland cement, white sand
Brown	Burnt umber or brown oxide of iron (yellow oxide if iron will modify color)
Buff	Yellow ocher, yellow oxide of iron
Gray	Normal portland cement
Green	Chromium oxide (yellow oxide of iron will shade)
Pink	Red oxide of iron (small amount)
Rose	Red oxide of iron
Cream	Yellow oxide of iron

Exposed Aggregate

Exposed-aggregate finishes offer unlimited color selection and a wide range of textures. These finishes are not only attractive, but they can be rugged, slip resistant, and highly immune to wear and weather.

Exposed-aggregate finish gives a rugged, natural look to the concrete terrace.

One of the most practical ways to obtain an exposed-aggregate finish is called *seeding*. The base concrete is placed, struck off, and bull-floated or darbied as usual, except that the surface level is about ½-inch lower than the forms. Aggregate is then spread uniformly over the entire surface by shovel or by hand, and embedded by tapping with a wood hand float, a straightedge, or a darby. Use a bull float or hand float for final embedding; the surface should be similar to that of a normal slab after floating.

When the slab can bear the weight of a person kneeling on a board, it's time for the exposure operation. Brush the slab lightly with a stiff-bristled broom to remove excess mortar. Next, fine-spray the slab with water while brushing. If aggregate is dislodged, delay the operation. Continue washing and brushing until flush water runs clear and there is no noticeable cement film left on the aggregate.

Another method is to expose the aggregate in conventionally placed concrete. With this method, the mix should contain a high proportion of coarse to fine aggregate. The coarse aggregate should be uniform in size, bright in color, closely packed, and properly distributed. The concrete slump must be low (1 to 3 inches) so that the coarse aggregate remains near the surface. In placing, striking off, bull-floating, or darbying, the usual procedures are followed. Care should be taken not to overdo floating, as this may depress the coarse aggregate too deeply. The aggregate is ready for exposing when the water sheen disappears, the surface can support your weight without indentation, and the aggregate is not overexposed or dislodged by washing and brushing. Expose by spraying and brushing as above.

In still another method of producing exposed-aggregate finishes, a thin topping course of concrete containing special aggregates is placed over a base slab of conventional concrete. This is the technique used for terrazzo construction. Terrazzo toppings for outdoor work are ½-inch thick and contain decorative aggregates such as marble, quartz, or granite chips. The colorful aggregates are exposed by brushing and washing with water. Brass or plastic divider strips set in a bed of mortar are used to eliminate random cracking. They also permit the use of different color terrazzo mixtures in a wide variety of patterns. This type is called rustic or washed terrazzo, and should be left to the professionals.

Textured Finishes

Decorative and functional textures can be produced on a concrete slab with little effort and expense by using floats, trowels, and brooms. More elaborate textures are possible with special techniques using a mortar dash coat or rock salt.

A swirl finish lends visual interest as well as surer footing. To produce this texture, the concrete is struck off and bull-floated or darbied. A hand float then is worked flat on the surface in a semicircular or fanlike motion, using pressure. Patterns are made by using a series of uniform arcs or twists. Coarse textures are produced by wood floats, and medium textures by aluminum, magnesium, or canvas resin floats. A fine-textured swirl is obtained with a steel trowel. Care must be taken to allow the concrete to set sufficiently so that these textures are not marred during curing.

Broomed finishes are attractive, nonslip textures made by pulling damp brooms across freshly floated or troweled surfaces. Coarse textures suitable for heavy traffic are obtained by using soft-bristle brooms on newly floated concrete. Medium to fine textures are obtained by using soft-bristle brooms on floated or steel-troweled surfaces. Best results are obtained with a broom that is specially made for texturing concrete. A broomed texture can be applied in many ways—straight lines, curved lines, wavy lines.

A travertine finish, sometimes called keystone, is created by applying a dash coat of mortar over freshly leveled concrete. The dash coat is mixed to the consistency of a thick paint and usually contains a yellow pigment. It is applied in a splotchy manner with a special dash brush so that ridges and depressions are formed. After the coating hardens slightly, the surface is flat-troweled to flatten the ridges and spread the mortar. The resulting finish is smooth on the high areas and coarse-grained in the depressed areas, resembling the appearance of travertine marble. Many interesting variations of this finish are possible, depending upon the amount of dash coat applied, the amount of color used, and the amount of troweling.

A similar texture can be produced by scattering rock salt over the surface after hand-floating or troweling. The salt is roled or pressed into the surface so that only the tops of the grains are exposed. After the concrete has hardened, the surface is washed and brushed, dislodging and dissolving the salt grains and leaving pits or holes in the surface. The salt distribution and grain size should be such that holes of about ¼-inch diameter are created.

Neither the rock salt nor the travertine finish is recommended for use in areas subject to freezing weather. Water trapped in the recesses of these finishes may freeze and spall the surface.

Geometric Patterns

A wide variety of geometric designs can be stamped, scored, or sawed into a concrete slab to enhance the beauty of the project. Random flagstone or ashlar patterns may be produced by embedding 1-inch-wide strips of 15-pound roofing felt in the concrete. After floating, the strips are laid on the surface in the desired pattern, patted flush, and floated over. At this time, a color dry-shake can be applied or the slab can be left to finish in its natural color. The strips are carefully removed before the slab is cured.

An alternate method of producing these patterns is to use an 18-inch-long piece of ½- or ¾-inch copper pipe bent into a flat S shape to score the surface. Scoring must be done while the concrete is still plastic, since coarse aggregate must be pushed aside. The best time is soon after darbying (or bull-floating). A second scoring to smooth the joints is done after hand-floating.

Stone, brick, tile, and other patterns can be cut into partially set concrete with special stamping tools. These operations are best done by the professional because the cost of the stamping equipment is prohibitive and is not the type of equipment which is readily rentable. The concrete may be colored integrally or by the dry-shake method and the joints filled with plain or colored mortar to create any number of striking effects.

Divider strips and borders of wood, metal, or masonry serve a number of

Concrete rounds made of exposed aggregate form an interesting pattern when combined with standard finishing.

One way to make exposed aggregate is to strike off the mix ½-inch below the forms, then seed it with aggregate. Note the aggregate at left of photo, ready for seeding.

After the aggregate is worked into the surface, the top is alternately washed and scrubbed with a stiff bristle—preferably nylon—broom.

purposes. Unusual patterns and designs can be created with rectangles, squares, and diamonds; concrete work can be segmented into small areas for better control of placing and finishing; combinations of various surface finishes are possible; and—very important—random cracks are greatly reduced or eliminated because divider strips act as control joints. Wood divider strips should be of rot-resistant lumber such as redwood, cedar, or cypress. Concrete masonry, brick, or stone divider strips and borders may be set in a sand bed with or without mortared joints. For more permanent work, masonry units should be set in a mortar bed with all joints mortared.

Nonslip and Sparkling Finishes

Surfaces that are frequently wet or that would be dangerous if slippery can be given special nonslip finishes. These can be made by hand tools such as floats, trowels, or brooms with dry-shake applications of abrasive grains. The latter method provides a long-lasting, nonslip surface.

The two most widely used abrasive grains are silicon carbide and aluminum oxide. Silicon carbide grains are sparkling black in color and are also used to make "sparkling concrete." The sparkle is especially effective under artificial light. Aluminum oxide may be gray, brown, or white, and is used where the sparkle of silicon carbide is not desired. Application of the abrasive grains essentially follows the same procedure as for a dry-shake color. The grains should be spread uniformly over the surface in a quantity of from ¼ to ½ pound per square foot and lightly troweled.

The "brickwork" here is actually concrete. The pattern is cut with special stamping tools. Because of the equipment and special skills involved, this job is best left to the professionals.

Combinations

In using concrete decoratively, striking effects can be obtained by combining colors, textures, and patterns. For example, alternate areas of exposed aggregate can be eye-catching when combined with plain, colored, or textured concrete. Ribbons and borders of concrete masonry or brick add a distinctive touch when combined with exposed aggregate. Also, light-colored strips of exposed aggregate may divide areas of dark-colored concrete or vice versa. Scored and stamped designs are enhanced when combined with integral or dry-shake color. These are just a few possibilities; with a little imagination, a concrete patio can be tailored to fit the mood and style of any architecture or landscape.

Concrete Coverings

If you are building a concrete patio as an extension of a family room or other room within the house, you can emphasize the connection by using the same complementary floor covering indoors and out. Such coverings can also be used to dress up a drab slab. Resilient flooring in sheet or roll form (normally 6 feet wide) is made of vinyl resins and color-fast pigments for both indoor and outdoor use. The material has a backing of fiberglass and asbestos, and is installed with epoxy adhesive. Epoxy is also used to fuse the seams so that dirt and moisture can't get under the flooring.

Indoor-outdoor carpeting is also available in a wide variety of colors and styles. It comes in 12-inch-square self-sticking tiles and in 6- and 12-foot-wide rolls. The carpeting is made of materials such as polypropylene fiber with an all-weather foam rubber backing and is installed with adhesive. The roll types have the advantage of fewer or no seams to collect dirt and moisture. You can even buy carpeting that simulates grass (the same as the artificial turf used in many modern sports stadiums). This might appeal if you like to practice your putting on the patio.

Check the manufacturer's guarantee before buying resilient flooring or carpeting, and follow his instructions for installation. The sun can be more damaging to some types than the other elements, causing early fading and deterioration.

Another type of concrete covering is "seamless flooring." Before its application, the slab must be clean and all cracks patched. A special white base coat is rolled or brushed on the concrete, then colored vinyl chips are sprinkled on the surface, embedding themselves in the base coat in a random pattern. When the material has dried, excess loose chips are swept away, and one or more clear coatings (usually urethane or acrylic) are applied with brush or roller. A variation of this system uses colored sand in place of the vinyl chips.

Carpeted conversation pit is a sunning spot outside a lower-level recreation room (left). If you are an avid golfer, you can have your own mini-course on the patio covered with carpeting that simulates grass; but never needs cutting (right).

Building & Installation Techniques:

PRE-CAST CONCRETE BLOCKS

Precast concrete patio blocks in a wide range of sizes, style, colors, and textures are readily available from local concrete masonry producers, building supply dealers, and nurserymen. It is also relatively simple to cast them yourself. The units are easy to handle and install for walkways, pool surrounds, patios, and the like.

Commercially made precast units are commonly available in square and rectangular shapes, measuring from 12 to 36 inches and thicknesses of 2, 2½, and 3 inches. The 2-inch thickness is suitable for patios. Other sizes and shapes are also manufactured. Round, triangular, diamond, and hexagonal shapes are among the most popular.

The slabs may be a natural gray or white cement color, or pigmented in tones of red, black, brown, green, or yellow. Slabs with exposed-aggregate finishes are available in some areas. Combinations of plain and colored or exposed-aggregate blocks add interest and pleasing contrast.

Precast concrete "rounds" are used as a stairway to this hillside home and its wood screened terrace.

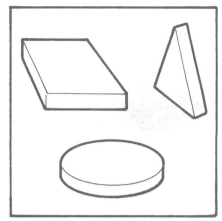

Patio blocks can be made in just about any shape that suits your fancy.

Precast concrete comes in a variety of shapes and sizes, like these diamond-shaped blocks, which are interspersed with ground cover.

Making Patio Blocks

You can make blocks in your garage or basement during the winter so that you can get an early spring start on your patio. Forms for square-, rectangular-, or diamond-shaped patio blocks can be made from 2x2 lumber. Cut the form pieces 7 inches longer than the size of the finished blocks. Cut ¾-inch deep, 1½-inch wide notches 2 inches in from each end of the form boards so that they fit together tightly, yet come apart easily for reuse. To speed up the job, make several forms.

A form for round blocks can be made of tempered hardboard secured inside a square lumber frame so that it holds its shape while the concrete is being poured.

Grease the inside surfaces of the form and set in on tarpaper. Since relatively small amounts of concrete are needed, a premix is ideal for the job; just add water according to the manufacturer's directions given on the bag. Pour the concrete into the form. For added strength, cut and straighten coat hanger wire and embed it in the concrete. Then fill the form to the top and level it with a strike board drawn across the form boards.

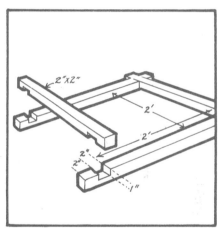

A simple form for making concrete patio blocks is constructed of 2x2s notched at the ends to fit together.

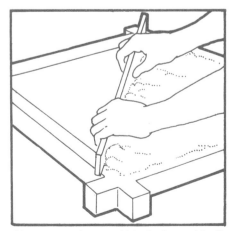

After concrete is poured into the form, strike it off flush with the top of the form boards.

Use an edging tool to round off the edges of the poured block.

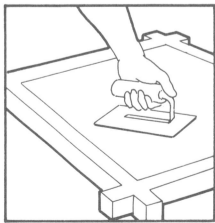

Trowel the surface to the desired finish.

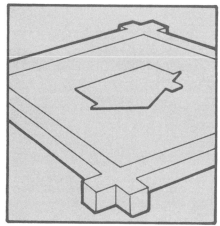

Cut out the design from heavy roofing paper and embed it in the surface of the concrete.

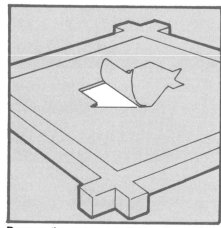

Remove the paper cutout after twenty-four hours; the impression will remain in the concrete.

Smooth the surface with a wood float, moving it over the surface in a half-arc motion while applying light pressure. Round off the edges of the block with an edging tool. Allow the concrete to set for an hour, then finish the surface with a steel trowel (or use a wood float if a rough finish is preferred). Hold the leading edge up slightly as the trowel is moved over the surface. Moist-cure the concrete for one week, following the recommendations given in the chapter on concrete. Forms can be removed and reused after a day or two.

You can customize your patio blocks with your initials or any design of your choosing, subject only to the limitations of your artistic capabilities. Cut the

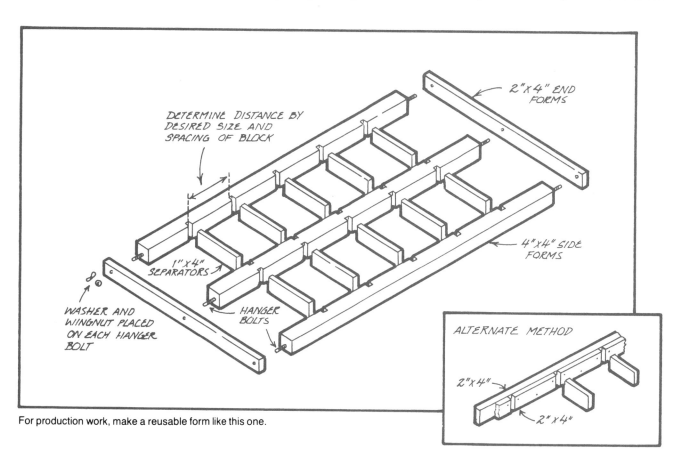

For production work, make a reusable form like this one.

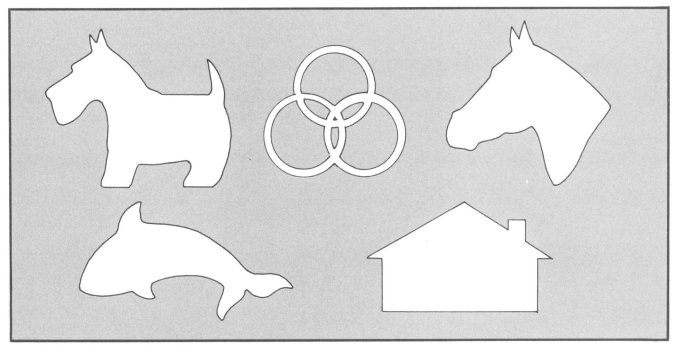

You can customize your patio blocks by incorporating any design of your choice. Here are just a few examples.

designs from heavy roofing paper. After troweling the poured concrete, when the water sheen disappears, place the cutout design on the block. Trowel over it to set it flush with the surface—be careful not to get too much concrete on top of the paper. After twenty-four hours, remove the cutout.

Concrete Masonry Block

Small concrete masonry patio blocks are available for projects such as patios and walkways. Paving blocks are similar but denser, for more rugged applications such as driveways. The most common units are brick shaped, but other shapes are also available. They are laid similarly to precast concrete blocks and standard brick (see Building Techniques: Brick).

When paving block is used in areas of heavy traffic, a 3- to 12-inch crushed stone or gravel subbase should be placed beneath the 2-inch sand leveling

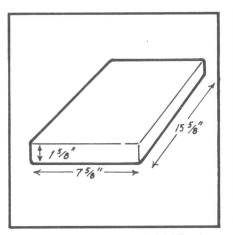
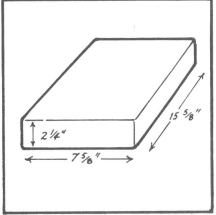
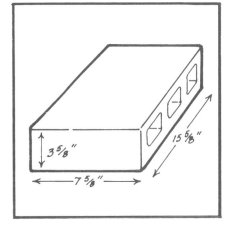

Patio block is light and comes in bricklike shapes.

Paving block is similar to patio block but has a greater density and can handle heavier loads. Many interlocking shapes are available for use in driveways or other high-traffic areas.

The key to a sturdy patio-block patio is locking the units together with sand brushed into the crevices.

bed. The thickness of the subbase will depend on the condition of the soil and the anticipated weight of traffic. The poorer the soil and the heavier the traffic, the deeper the subbase. Both the subbase and the leveling bed should be well compacted.

The masonry units are placed atop the sand bed in the desired pattern. By careful planning, cutting to fit can be avoided, but the units can be cut if necessary. Use a brick chisel and a heavy ball peen or mash hammer. Score

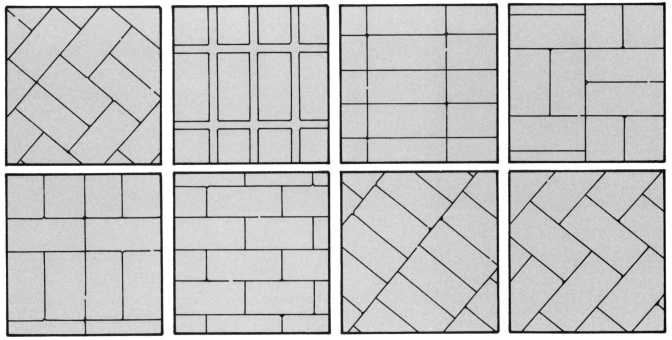

Some of the many patterns that can be used with standard patio block.

the block on all sides, then keep striking until it breaks off.

After all units are in place and leveled, sand is spread over the surface and swept into the cracks. The sand is watered down, and the process repeated until sand tightly fills all the joints.

Freeze-thaw cycles and heavy rainfalls may cause some blocks to rise ("heave") or sink. This is easily corrected by lifting out the offending block or blocks. Sprinkle in and compact some sand where the base is too low, or scrape some away and level it where it is too high. Then replace the block(s) and fill the joints as above. If a block doesn't quite line up properly, use a trowel or stick to shift its position.

Block Laying

Installation of precast blocks can begin in spring as soon as the frost is gone and ground conditions permit. In the fall, installation is possible until frozen ground prevents proper compaction of the subgrade material. The blocks are placed in a sand bedding.

Stake off the area, making sure it is large enough to accommodate the full-size blocks (cutting the concrete units is definitely not recommended). String a level line between the stakes. Excavate to a depth of about 4 inches, using the line as a guide.

Replace the excavated soil with slightly damp sand. Embed straightedged 2x3 boards in the sand about a foot from each side of the patio and level the boards to the proper height of the sand bed, allowing ¼-inch per foot for drainage. Place another straightedge across the two boards to make sure that they are even.

Compact the sand firmly by tamping. Check to make sure that the boards are level and even. Draw a strike board over the leveling boards, smoothing the sand. Fill in any low spots, then use the strike board again to level the sand. Remove the 2x3 leveling boards.

Embeded 2x3 leveling boards in the sand; place a third board across them to make sure they are level and even.

Fill the area with sand up to the leveling boards, then use a third board to make the bed perfectly level.

Starting in a corner, lay the precast blocks in the desired pattern. Square and rectangular units can be laid with joints butted tightly together. Use a level frequently. If a block needs leveling, force sand under the low part.

When all blocks are laid, sweep sand across the surface to fill the joints.

Casting in Place

Another way to use concrete in precast units is to remove the sod from the area to be concreted and cast the blocks in place. For a formal walkway with repetitive patterns, you can make a reusable form. Form boards should be beveled slightly and oiled before use; attaching screen door handles will further facilitate removal of the forms after the concrete has set. Cast one section, remove and clean the forms, reoil, and go on to the next section. An irregular-shaped form can be reversed to vary the pattern.

Another method achieves a flagstone effect. Dig away the earth in the desired shape and simply fill the excavated area with concrete, using the surrounding earth as a form. Patterns of paper or cardboard can be cut out and used as a guide for digging. Use a square-ended garden spade or a trowel to cut the sod, keeping the sides of the excavation square.

Tamp the sand bedding to compact it firmly.

Lay the precast concrete units on the sand bedding, filling in beneath with extra sand as necessary. Note the impressions left by the 2x3 leveling boards.

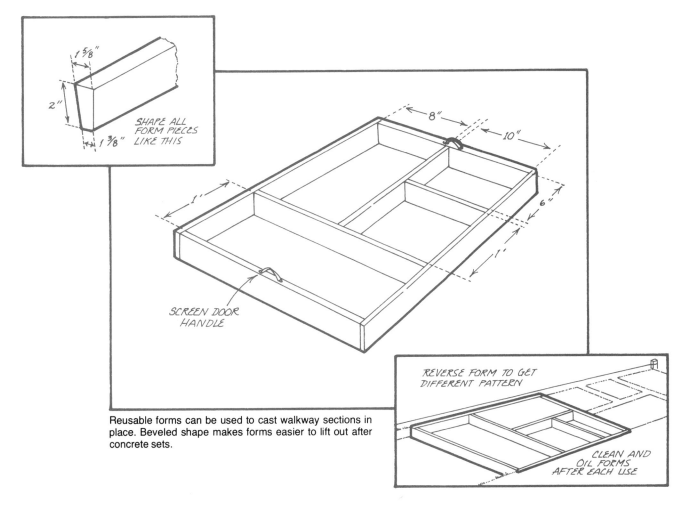

SHAPE ALL FORM PIECES LIKE THIS

1 5/8"

2"

1 3/8"

8"

10"

1"

6"

1"

SCREEN DOOR HANDLE

REVERSE FORM TO GET DIFFERENT PATTERN

CLEAN AND OIL FORMS AFTER EACH USE

Reusable forms can be used to cast walkway sections in place. Beveled shape makes forms easier to lift out after concrete sets.

A 2-inch thickness is normally sufficient for this type of concrete application. The bottom of the excavation should be as level as possible, but slight variations are not critical. It is more important to make sure that the earth is well tamped with no "soft" areas.

The surface of the pour should be leveled with a straightedge and wood-floated to leave a textured surface.

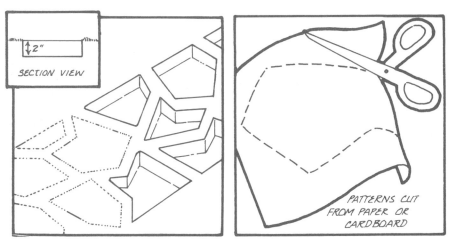

2"

SECTION VIEW

PATTERNS CUT FROM PAPER OR CARDBOARD

Irregular shapes, like the flagstone type shown here, can be cast in place by cutting out the earth in the desired shape. Patterns make it easier.

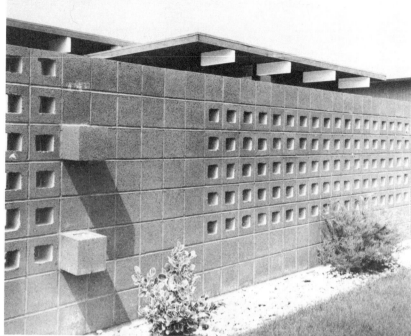

Concrete masonry units can be used in a variety of ways as walls, fences, and screens in the outdoor living area.

Concrete Block Walls

Concrete block is used to build upward as well as for paving flat surfaces. While commonly used for house foundation walls, it may also be used to build a foundation wall for a deck or other structure, or as a retaining wall. It is also frequently used in garden walls, fences, and wind screens, and in building outdoor barbecues, which are discussed later in this book.

There is a wide range of concrete blocks available, and your selection will depend on aesthetics as well as the use to which they will be put. Most common are the 8x8x16-inch units, cored with two or three holes. These are normally used when building a foundation wall, but they can also be laid sideways so that the holes are exposed, making a decorative garden wall. Screen and grille wall units, usually 12 inches square and 4 to 8 inches thick, are sold in an almost infinite variety of designs, and you are almost certain to find one that provides the perfect backdrop for your patio setting. Patterns of squares, rectangles, and strong diagonal lines can add a feeling of movement to ordinary garden walls, whether they are built for privacy or as wind screens. Lacy, intricate patterns of screen block walls add beauty and grandeur.

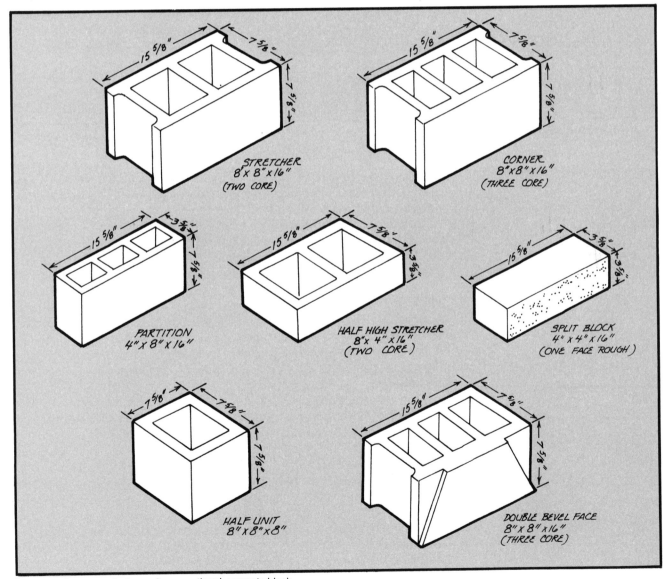

Common shapes and sizes of conventional concrete block.

Many striking patterns are available in screen block. Here is just a sampling; check your local building supply or masonry dealer to see what designs he carries.

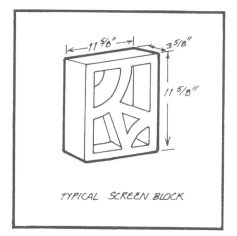

TYPICAL SCREEN BLOCK

Extruded mortar or offset block in the wall add a rugged appearance, if this is desired. Split block and textured block capture shadows and highlights, creating ever-changing patterns and designs.

Block sizes, as given above, are nominal. There may be some slight variation according to the individual manufacturer. But usually, the nominal dimensions are ⅜-inch greater than the actual dimensions, allowing for a ⅜-inch mortar joint. The common 8x8x16-inch block actually measures 7⅝x7⅝x15⅝ inches. A 6x12x12-inch screen block will measure 11⅝ inches square, but the 6-inch thickness may be full because it is unlikely that there will be a double thickness of block, thus there is no need to allow for a mortar joint. On the other hand, it might be less than 6 inches because such block is not intended for structural use. The lesson in all this is to measure the block that you purchase before you get too far into the actual planning and work on your concrete masonry wall.

When planning your masonry wall, try to avoid having to cut any blocks. This will save a lot of time and misery, and will certainly mean a much better looking result. The normal blocklaying pattern has each course of block offset so that the center of the block is above the joints of the course beneath. However, screen block is often laid on top of the block beneath to continue a pattern.

A concrete footing must be built to support the concrete block wall. It should be deep enough to be below the frost line so that it will not heave during winter weather. Footings are discussed at length in the previous chapter on techniques of building with concrete; the same techniques apply here. If there will be a force working sideways against the block wall (other than the gentle breezes of springtime), the footing should be keyed. For a high, solid wall, vertical tie rods may also be implanted in the footing. The cores of the block are placed over the rods and cement is poured into the cores, making the wall and the footing a monolithic structure.

The tools you will need for building with concrete block are a large pointed trowel, a level, a string line, a mason's hammer (especially if you must cut blocks to fit; it has a square head on one end and a chisel point on the other for chipping along a line to break a block) and a jointer. The latter tool should be at least 22 inches long and bent outward at both ends to prevent it from gouging mortar as you tool the joints. For forming V joints, you will need a ½-inch square bar, also bent up at the ends.

A good mortar mix is vital to insure a well-bonded masonry wall. It should be mixed with a shovel or hoe in a mortar box or, in smaller quantities, on a clean surface such as a piece of plywood. The ingredients for a normal mix are one part masonry cement or portland cement, one-half part lime, and 3-and-one-half parts of clean, dry sand. Water should be added in quantity to make a relatively stiff mortar—the block is heavy, and the mortar must be strong enough to support it while it is still wet. Evaporation occurs quickly, so mix only as much as you will use in a half hour or so, and remix frequently during that period, adding water as needed to keep it workable.

Before beginning your wall-building in earnest, make a "dry run" with the base course of block, laying them along the footing and allowing a ⅜-inch gap between each to allow for mortar. If things don't come out just right, make whatever allowances are necessary, such as reducing the mortar joints slightly. It is much easier to do this now than when an entire mortared course is in place and you suddenly discover that the last block is hanging over the edge of the footing. Think ahead!

When you have exact placement figured, remove the blocks and dampen—but don't flood—the footing. While professional masons normally build up the corners first and then fill in between (as outlined in a later section on bricklaying) it is generally easier for the do-it-yourselfer to take things a course at a time when laying block. Lay a bed of mortar approximately ½-inch thick for the first corner block to set in. If you are using core block, place mortar around the perimeter of the block area and where the core dividers are; for solid block, such as screen block, place mortar on the entire base. Set the first block in the mortar bed, tapping it into place with the trowel handle or hammer. Carefully level it both across its width and longitudinally, and measure its height from the footing. It should be the height of the block plus ⅜-inch (for a nominal 8-inch block, this will be exactly 8 inches).

The next block to be laid is at the other end of the wall. If the footing is

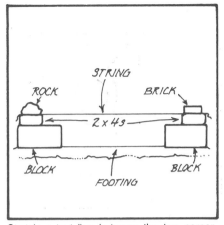

Stretch a taut line between the two corner blocks to serve as a guide for laying intermediate blocks.

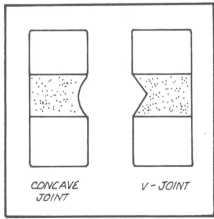

Two types of tooled joints.

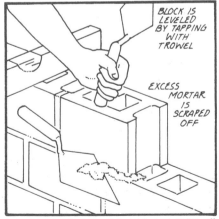

Level each block as it is laid, and strike off excess mortar.

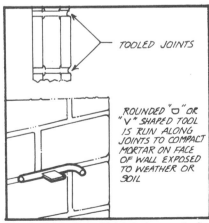

Use the jointer to tool joints before mortar begins to harden.

perfectly level (and it is, of course, after your painstaking labors in building it), it will be a simple matter to have this block in perfect alignment with its opposite number. Place 2x4 wood scraps at the outer ends of the two corner blocks and stretch a string line between the blocks, on top of the 2x4s and held taut by weights such as bricks or stones.

Fill in the course, working from one corner block to the other. Place a mortar bed (a block at a time) on the footing, then use the trowel to "butter" the in-place block and lay the next block in place, pushing it against the previously laid block, tapping it in and leveling, and checking the set against the taut string. The block should be exactly 1½ inches below the string. When the last block of the course is ready to be slotted into position, butter the sides of the two adjacent blocks, then fit in the "closing" block.

As you work along, frequently strike off excess mortar with the trowel. If you are building a large wall, tool the joints as you go, before the mortar has a chance to harden. Run the jointing tool (or square bar for V joints) evenly along the mortar, then clean away excess with the trowel.

Start the second course of block in the same way as the first. Where the wall turns a corner, the corner blocks should overlap, tying both sides together. Set each block gently into a mortar bed laid on the block below, taking care not to disturb the undercourse. Complete your wall in this way.

If your block wall is to support a deck, roof, or other structure, embed anchor bolts in the cores of the top course, spaced approximately 2 feet apart. To prevent the mortar that holds these bolts in place from falling all the way to the bottom of the wall, place small-mesh wire cloth between the second and third courses from the top. Or you can stuff wadded newspapers into the cores of the third last course—these will hold until the mortar has dried. Drill holes through 2x4s approximately as wide as the blocks and insert the hooked or plated anchor bolts, securing them with nuts. Lay the 2x4s across the top course of block, with the bolts suspended in the cores, and fill the cores with mortar. When the mortar hardens, remove the nuts and the 2x4 supports.

Allow the mortar to cure completely before building on top of the block wall. A minimum of a week is normally recommended in dry summer weather. Under damp conditions, allow ten days to two weeks.

Concrete block may be finished for decorative purposes with masonry paint, which comes in a variety of colors. It provides a durable and long-lasting surface. Dampen the wall with water before application, then put on the paint with a stiff-bristled brush. Allow to dry thoroughly, then apply a final coat.

When a roof, deck, or other structure is to be built on top of the block wall, anchor bolts are embedded in mortar in the top course. Wood plates are later bolted to the wall.

Apply cement paint to the wall, using a stiff-bristled brush.

Beautiful brick harmonizes with other natural materials, such as the redwood bench alongside this terrace.

Basket weave is a popular bricklaying pattern. Here the brick is set on a leveling bed of sand.

Building & Installation Techniques:

BRICK

Color, pattern, high abrasion resistance, and relative working ease make brick a highly desirable material for patios, walkways, steps, and walls. The brick patio or walkway may be laid over a concrete slab or set in a leveling bed on well-tamped, compacted earth in any number of pleasing designs. Brick stairways or walls generally require a concrete or masonry foundation.

A visit to your local brickyard or building materials dealer will introduce you to the wide range of sizes, textures, and colors available. Brick may be either solid or cored with rows of holes down the length of the brick. In most paving projects, the brick is laid flat, and solid must be used. But if the brick is to be placed on edge, the cored type will work just as well and may be cheaper. For walls the lighter cored brick can be used except for top courses, unless these are laid on edge.

Building-brick units usually measure 2¼ x 3¾ x 8 inches or 2¼ x 3⅝ x 7⅝ inches (dimensions may vary slightly according to manufacturer). Norman brick (2¾ x 3¾ x 12 inches) and Roman brick (1½ x 3¾ x 12 inches) are not normally used for paving but make handsome walls. Paving bricks, specially designed for mortarless walks and terraces, measure 4 x 8 inches, in thicknesses of 1½, 2, and 2¼ inches.

The color of most brick is in the range of the reds, buffs, and creams, varying with the type of clay used and the production process. By adding chemicals,

An edging is put down first to prevent the brick paving from shifting. Here an edger course of brick is laid on a masonry foundation.

brickmakers can produce an endless variety of colors and textures, allowing a wide choice for your patio and back-yard walkways.

A tribute to the material's durability is the popularity of "old brick." This is brick that has already seen one lifetime of service as part of a wall or some other structure and is ready for another go-round. Its patina of warmth and mellowness is hard to match, and good used brick often costs more than new brick.

In most areas of the country, SW grade (Severe Weather) is recommended for outdoor projects. The table will help you to estimate quantities of brick and mortar needed. Buy a little extra to allow for breakage and waste, especially if the brick must be cut (about 5 percent should do it). For a mortared project, premixed mortar is a practical choice. It is a little more expensive but saves time and trouble. Allow 15 to 25 percent extra for waste.

Estimating Brick and Mortar			
Brick size	Bricks per 100 square feet	Cubic feet of mortar per 100 bricks (includes ½-inch leveling bed) ⅜-inch joint	½-inch joint
2¼ x 3¾ x 8	400		1.84
2¼ x 3⅝ x 7⅝	450	1.49	
4 x 8 pavers	450	no mortar required	

Drainage

Drainage is an important factor in the construction of a brick paving area. When subjected to excessive moisture, brick terraces and walkways may be susceptible to efflorescence (a whitish crust on brick caused by mineral salts rising to the surface), stains, growth of fungi or molds, or disintegration caused by freezing and thawing.

When a concrete slab is to be poured as a base for the brick, slope it ⅛-to ¼-inch per foot away from buildings, retaining walls, or other places that will hold water on the surface. Or provide drainage gutters on the paving area and gutters around the perimeter to prevent adjacent areas from draining onto the project.

When brick is laid on a sand leveling bed, there may be adequate drainage through the joints into the ground beneath. Just make sure that there are no low areas where water can collect. In localities having relatively high water tables, or where the soil is heavy clay, lay the brick on a cushion of gravel to provide subsurface drainage and to prevent any large upward capillary flow of moisture. Omit the sand when using gravel, for it will sift down into the larger material and block drainage, cause uneven settling, and provide a capillary path for subsurface moisture. Most sandy or silty soils will provide adequate drainage without the gravel layer.

Edging

Brick pavings may spread or shift unless restrained. This is particularly true of mortarless construction. For this reason, an edging must be provided around the perimeter. This is placed before the brickwork. One type of edging consists of a soldier course (set on end) of brick emplaced in concrete, either

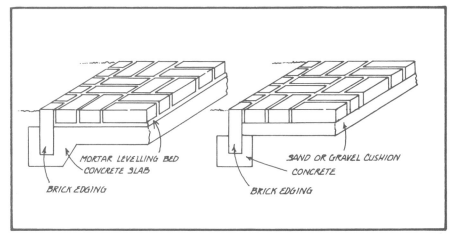

At top, brick laid in a mortar bed on a concrete slab, with an edging of brick in a soldier (upright) course. Below that, the brick rests on a bed of sand or gravel; the edging is set in concrete.

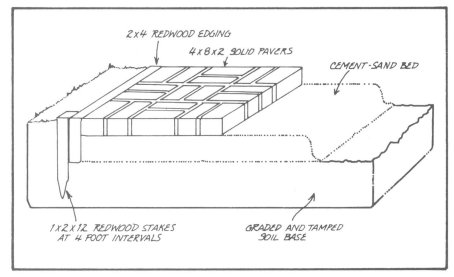

Here a lumber edging is used around a terrace of pavers on a sand-cement leveling bed.

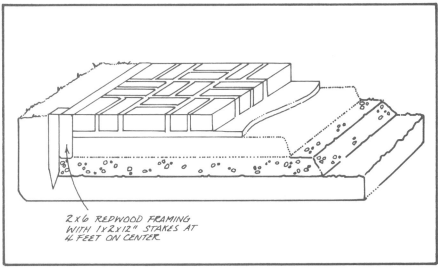

Lumber edging can also be used when the brick is laid on a concrete slab. Use redwood, or treat a less decay-resistant species with preservative.

as part of the concrete slab (if your project will be on a slab), or in a concrete footing around a mortarless terrace or walkway. Another type of edging has the brick laid on edge.

Edging might be constructed of redwood, or some other lumber that has

Brick is cut by scoring it with a broad chisel, then breaking it apart with a sharp blow.

been thoroughly treated with a preservative, held in place by stakes driven into the ground. This type of edging is more commonly used with mortarless construction, but it could also be used around a concrete slab, with the lumber placed just outside the concrete.

Cutting

You may be able to plan your project so that only full bricks will be needed. But for some designs, cutting will be inevitable. With a little practice, you will be able to master the art.

A broad-bladed chisel is used to cut brick. Tap the chisel with a hammer to score the brick along the line of the desired cut. Turn the brick over and score the other side in the same way. Then, pointing the chisel inward, strike a sharp blow with the hammer. The brick should break cleanly.

When a large number of bricks must be cut, you might want to buy a masonry blade for your power saw (or rent a saw, if you don't have one in your tool arsenal). You can also rent a manual cutting machine called a guillotine, the modus operandi of which should be obvious from its name.

Types of Brickwork

Brick-in-Sand

Outline the terrace or walkway with stakes and string. Suspend a line level from the center of the string between each stake, and mark each stake to establish a level grade line. Then mark the drainage slope (⅛-to ¼-inch per foot) on each stake. These marks will serve as guidelines for excavation and later for laying the brick.

Excavate the area to a depth of 3½ inches. Excavate a trench around the perimeter deep enough to accommodate the edging (10 inches for a soldier course of brick in concrete). Make frequent checks during the excavation, taking measurements against the marks on the stakes and occasionally stretching a line across the area between the stakes and measuring the depth. Don't be concerned with minor lumps or depressions. However, should you dig too deeply at any point, fill it in and tamp down firmly. Soft spots may cause future settling.

Install the edging around the perimeter of the project. The top of the edging should be flush with the top of the future patio or walkway, following the same drainage slope.

For a 100-square-foot terrace (10 feet x 10 feet) you will need approximately 1,250 pounds of loose sand. Set aside a few shovelfuls of sand for later use, then pour the rest into the center of the excavation.

For a more stable terrace or walkway, you can add cement to the sand in the leveling bed at the rate of four sacks (94 pounds each) per 100 square feet. Add the cement a sack at a time and mix in thoroughly. Since the sand will almost certainly be damp, the cement will begin to set almost immediately, so the mixture should be spread as soon as possible. Use a rake to spread it over the floor of the excavation to a level about 1¾ inches below the top of the edging (for 2-inch paving brick) or 1½ inches below the edging for standard 2¼-inch brick.

Screeding, or leveling, the bed is a most important operation. Use a straight-edged 2x4 long enough to fit across the area and rest on the edging. Notch each end of the 2x4 to a depth ⅛ inch less than the thickness of the brick (1⅞ inch or 2⅛ inch). Rest the notched ends on the edging, then draw the board

A large terrace or walkway can be done in sections. This is especially important where a sand-cement base is used, because the cement will begin to harden almost immediately after mixing. Use a rake to spread the mix in the excavation.

across the sand or sand-cement bed, leveling high spots and filling in low spots. Repeat until the bed is smooth and level.

Tamp the bed to make it firm and solid. (You can make a tamper by nailing a short length of 2x6 to a 2x4 handle.) Then repeat the screeding procedure and fill in any low spots. When the bed is finally prepared, stay off it.

Start laying brick at a corner, butting the units tightly together in the pattern of your choice. Tap each brick firmly in place with a hammer handle or a mallet of wood or plastic. Stand or kneel on previously placed brick as you progress, rather than on the bed. If you have prepared the bed properly, the brick should be level, but check each one and fill beneath it with sand, if necessary, to bring it up to level.

When the last brick has been placed, cover the surface of the terrace with a thin layer of sand. Work it around with a broom until the joints are filled, then sweep the surface clean. Spray with a fine stream of water to compact the sand, but be careful not to flood the joints and wash out the sand. Repeat the sanding and spraying procedures until all joints are packed flush with the surface.

One of the best things about this type of terrace is that it is ready to use as soon as it is finished—no waiting around for materials to dry or cure. You can just roll out a comfortable chaise, sink down into it with a cool refreshing drink, and instantly enjoy the fruits of your labors.

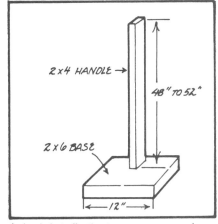

A simple but effective tamper you can make.

Brick on Concrete Slab

For a more permanent pavement, brick may be laid in mortar on a concrete slab. This might be your choice if you live in an area that suffers severe winter weather. The slab foundation will minimize ground swell and upheaval of the brick. Building brick, rather than pavers, should be used to allow for mortar joints.

Lay out the terrace or walkway with stakes and string, marking on the stakes the drainage slope, as with the mortarless terrace. Excavate the area to a depth of approximately 10½ inches. You could simply pour a "floating" slab, but, especially in colder climates, it is better to have a footing around the perimeter of the slab. This should be below the frost line. Your local building department can give you this information for your locality. The footing trench should be 10 to 12 inches wide.

Tamp the earth within the excavated area until it is firm and solid. If the earth

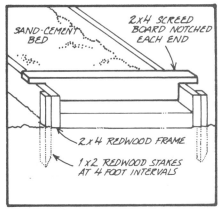

To level the sand or sand-cement bed, use a screed board made from a straightedged 2x4. Notch the ends to fit over the edging.

Spread sand in the base of the excavation, leveling it as much as possible before screeding.

Fill in low spots by adding sand as needed when laying the brick. Scrape away sand from high spots.

After completing a section, check to make sure that the surface is level (allowing for the desired drainage slope). Lift bricks where necessary to fill in low spots and take down high spots.

Spread sand over the surface.

Sweep the sand into the joints.

After wetting the surface to compact the sand in the joints, sweep more sand over the brick. Repeat the process until all joints are filled, "locking" the brick in place.

around the excavation is firm, it can serve as a form for the slab. In loose or sandy soil, forms will have to be built. Make them of lumber or plywood, built up to the top of the slab, following the drainage slope. Stakes driven into the ground outside the form boards hold them in place.

Spread gravel within the excavated area to a depth of approximately 4 inches, raking it as close as possible to the edge of the footing trench. Footing and trench are poured at the same time. For a large slab, ready-mix concrete, trucked to the site, will save you a lot of work. Or you can rent a mixer and mix your own, using one part cement, 2 parts sand, and four parts aggregate.

Pour the concrete into the footing trench and spread approximately 2 inches of concrete in the excavation. Place reinforcing mesh (6-inch x 6-inch, 10-gauge) across the concrete to within 6 inches of the edges (if you are using a soldier-course brick edging; otherwise, run the mesh to the edge of the slab). Pour the remaining concrete to the top of the form boards. Strike it off even with the boards, then embed the brick edging in the concrete, approximately 4 inches from the edge, with their tops 2¾ inches above the slab surface. Use string stretched between stakes at each end of the slab to align the bricks and keep them straight and even. After the concrete has begun to harden (about an hour after pouring), roughen the surface with a stiff-bristled broom to provide a bonding surface for the brick mortar.

To insure proper curing, wet down the concrete and cover it with burlap or straw to retard evaporation. Keep it damp for at least five days before beginning to lay brick.

When the slab is ready, try a "dry run" before actually laying brick. Set the brick on the slab without mortar, allowing a ⅜-or ½-inch space between units for mortar joints, depending on the size of brick you are using. This will show you whether any cutting will be necessary; perhaps by shifting the brick slightly you can avoid cutting altogether. If you must cut bricks, it's a good idea to do it beforehand, so that they are ready when you need them.

Brick should be slightly damp when laid. Otherwise, it will quickly absorb the moisture from the mortar, not allowing enough time for proper setting. But if the brick is *too* wet, it will dilute the mortar, causing the brick to sink or slip. The best bet is to spray the brick with a hose an hour or so before use.

If you are mixing your own mortar rather than using a premix, use one part cement, a half part hydrated lime, and four-and-a-half parts clean sand. Order the sand from your building supply dealer—the free kind you get at the beach is too coarse and dirty, and will result in weak mortar joints.

Thoroughly blend together the dry ingredients, turning them over and over with a shovel. Scoop out a hollow in the middle of the mixture and gradually add water, mixing it in with the shovel. The mortar should have the consistency of soft mud ("mud" is one of the names the professionals have for it) and slide easily from the mixing shovel. Make only as much as you can use in a half hour or so, and add a little water occasionally to keep it workable. If it becomes too stiff, discard it and make a new batch.

Slightly dampen the slab where the brick is to be laid. Take a slice of mortar on a bricklayer's trowel (10-inch is a good size) and place a ½-inch-thick bed of mortar in one corner of the slab, large enough for two bricks. (As your technique improves, you can work three or more bricks at a time, but it's better to start slowly.) Spread or "butter" the end and one edge of a brick with mortar and set it in place, making sure the corner is perfectly square. Butter a second brick and set it in place against the first, allowing the proper joint width. Clear away excess mortar with the trowel. Continue in this manner, following the design pattern of your choice. Joints can be flush with the surface, or you can tool them to a concave pattern by drawing a ¾-inch steel pipe along the joints before the mortar hardens. Use a piece of damp burlap to wipe excess mortar from the face of the brick as you go along.

Wet the finished terrace down with a light spray from a garden hose (a pressured spray will damage the mortar joints). This will loosen masonry crumbs and allow the masonry to cure properly. If the terrace still doesn't look clean, sprinkle sand on the mortar smears that remain and sweep them away gently with a broom, taking care not to dig into the mortar joints.

You can't use this brick area right away, as you would its laid-in-sand cousin. It takes about a week for the masonry to cure. If mortar smears still remain, clean them off with a solution of one part muriatic acid to nine parts water, mixed in a plastic bucket. Wear rubber gloves and protective clothing when working with this solution. If any spills on your skin, wash it off immediately with plenty of clear water. Wet the terrace first to keep the acid solution from soaking too far into the brick. Apply the solution with a fiber brush (metal will react with the acid and stain the brick), soaking thoroughly. Flush completely with a pressure spray from the garden hose.

The muriatic acid solution will also clean efflorescence from the brick if that should appear.

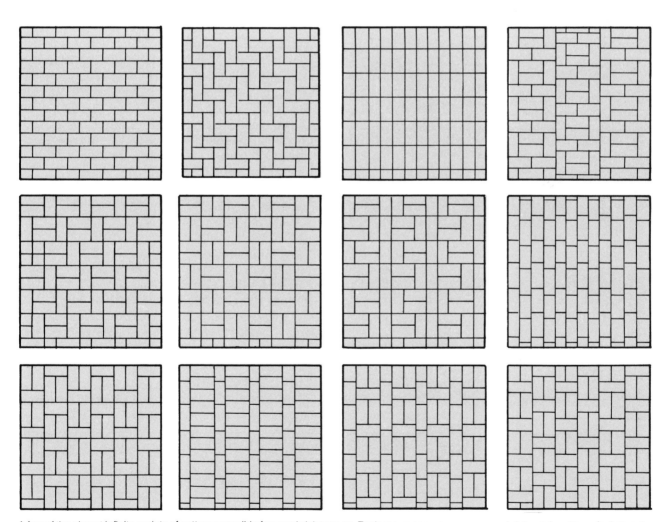

A few of the almost infinite variety of patterns possible for your brick terrace. For larger areas, you can even mix 'n' match patterns for interest.

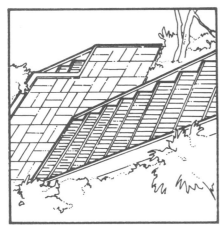

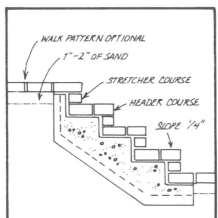

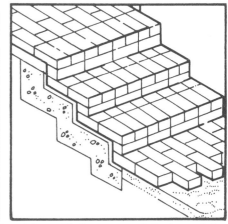

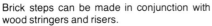

Brick steps can be made in conjunction with wood stringers and risers.

Here bricks are laid in mortar on a concrete foundation, with the terrace at the base of the steps set on a sand bed. Note that the steps slope forward.

Brick Steps

Brick steps are a practical solution to the problems of landscaping a slope, especially where they lead to or from a brick terrace. The relatively small sizes of brick permit flexibility of design, such as adjustments of tread and riser dimensions and construction of curves. Safety and comfort are important considerations, but steps should also be in scale with the outdoors, usually with greater tread area than is customary with interior steps. Various riser-tread relationships are possible, depending to a large extent on the topography and the area allotted for the stairs. Treads should never be less than 11 inches wide; narrower treads will present extra hazards when covered with ice or snow. Steps should pitch forward with a slope of about ¼-inch per foot. Ramplike stairways can be effective using only a 2-or 3-inch riser, but the tread must then be significantly wider—at least wide enough to allow two normal paces. Brick lends itself well to any tread and riser combination.

If space is restricted, the choice of riser and tread combinations will be limited. A change of stair directions with landings may be the solution. A good way to work out a step problem is to plot it on paper to scale. A final on-site check can be made using a wide board on which step positions are indicated.

Step width is mostly a matter of proportion—of choosing a width that best fits the surroundings. There are some minimum requirements. Four feet is considered the minimum for a one-person stairway, 5 feet for a two-person stairway. Auxiliary steps built for purely functional reasons can be as narrow as 2 feet.

Techniques for construction of brick steps are similar to those employed for paving. For steps of the brick-in-sand type, it is very important that the subsurface be well-compacted. The edging (in this case, the "stringers" of the stairs) can be of masonry or wood. Wood (again, redwood, cedar, or a pressure-treated lumber) makes the job relatively simple; the edging at the front of the steps can also be of wood, doubling as stair risers, nailed between the stringers (use 16d galvanized nails).

For brick steps that are mortared on top of a concrete foundation, edging is not really necessary (although it may be desirable for cosmetic reasons). Building forms for the concrete is as outlined in the concrete chapter, and the bricks are laid just as on a walkway or terrace.

Brick Walls

A garden wall or fence constructed of brick provides an interesting backdrop for shrubs and flowers. It may be designed for shelter against winds or for privacy in a secluded spot. Such a wall must be built to withstand considerable abuse from the weather. It should be on a stable foundation, and in areas of heavy wind reinforcement may be needed.

Always check your local building code when planning a structural brick project (anything more complex than a simple terrace or walkway, that is). These often contain quite specific regulations regarding brick work and, of course, must be followed to the letter. Simple decorative walls may not be covered by the code, but supporting walls and retaining walls usually are, especially if they are more than a few feet high.

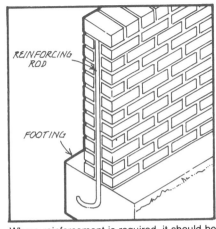

Where reinforcement is required, it should be anchored in the footing.

FOOTINGS

Footings must be provided for brick walls. The footing should be as thick as the wall is thick (8 inches for a wall that is as thick as the length of a single common brick, 12 inches for one as thick as the length of a Norman or Roman brick, 8 inches for a double wall of common brick laid side by side) and at least twice as wide (16 inches and 24 inches in the above examples). Where soil conditions are unstable, the footing should be even wider to insure an even spread of the wall's weight. Check the local code or county extension service for specific recommendations in your area.

The footing must be perfectly level, with its base below the frost line. All bricks that rest on the footing and all others below the ground level must be SW grade; ordinary brick is porous and may absorb surface and ground moisture, which in turn may freeze and break the brick. If the footing is considerably below the ground surface, concrete block may be laid up to the ground level, and the brick on that.

For details on building footings and concrete block walls, refer to earlier sections. Generally, a keyway need not be provided in the footing if brick is to be laid directly on it. Vertical reinforcing rods, as described in the concrete chapter, may be required by the building code, or perhaps by structural considerations for the project you are building. These should be provided when the footing is poured.

PATTERN BONDS

While structural strength is the first determinant in a bricklaying pattern, the varying arrangements that are possible introduce a design element as well. This is referred to as pattern bond; there are five basic ones commonly used.

Running bond.

Common or American bond.

Flemish bond.

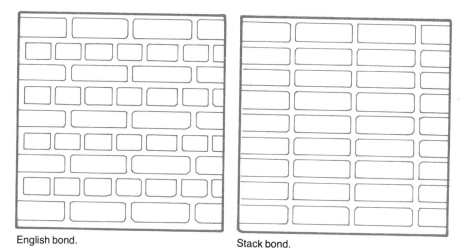

English bond.

Stack bond.

Running bond consists of all "stretchers,"—bricks laid with their length parallel to the face of the wall and with the joints of each course (or row) offset from the course beneath. While suitable for low garden walls, this type of pattern alone does not provide suitable structural strength for larger structures.

Common or American bond is a variation of running bond, with a double row of stretchers and a course of full-length "headers"—bricks laid lengthwise across the wall at regular intervals, usually every fifth, sixth, or seventh course. The headers provide structural bonding, as well as a visual break in the pattern lines of the wall.

Flemish bond is a variation with each course of brick made up of alternate stretchers and headers, with the headers in alternate courses centered over the stretchers. Flemish bond is sometimes varied by increasing the number of stretchers between headers in each course. Where three stretchers alternate with a header, it is called a "garden wall" bond—which may be just what you are looking for. A "double stretcher garden wall" bond has two stretchers between headers. Garden wall bond may also be laid with four or even five stretchers between headers.

English bond is composed of alternate courses of headers and stretchers. The headers are centered on the stretchers, and joints between stretchers in all courses line up vertically. "English cross" or "Dutch" bond is a variation with vertical joints between the stretchers in alternate courses centered on the stretchers in the courses above and below, rather than being vertically aligned.

Stack bond is purely a pattern bond. There is no overlapping or offsetting of bricks—all vertical joints are aligned. For all but the lowest of garden walls, a stack bond wall will require reinforcement, not only with vertical rods but also with steel rods placed in the horizontal mortar joints of adjacent courses.

HOW TO . . .

Estimating brick needs depends on the type of bond planned as well as the size of the wall to be built. As a general guideline, figure approximately seven common bricks per square foot of 4-inch wall without headers, or seven-and-a-half for a wall with headers. For ½-inch joints, figure from 8 to 8½ cubic feet of mortar per 100 square feet of wall.

Tools you'll need include a brick trowel, brick chisel, mason's hammer (don't use your claw hammer, which is for carpentry projects only), a shovel, a mason's level, cord (mason's line or any stout cord), a line level, a jointer, a folding rule, and a bucket and brush. A story pole—a board marked at intervals

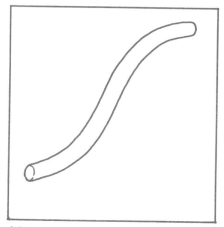

Jointer.

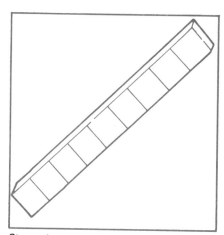

Story pole.

corresponding to the height of each course in a wall—is a big help, especially for higher projects. Plastic corner blocks to hold the line in place also simplify the job. You will also need a mortar box or, for a small job, a clean piece of plywood on which to mix mortar. You may also need a wheelbarrow if the mortar must be transported any distance to the building site; it is also a convenient container for the mortar that can be moved along the wall as you progress.

Do not attempt to lay brick in very cold weather. Mix the mortar as described previously for a mortared slab. Bricks should be wet when laid so that they do not absorb the moisture from the mortar.

The first step is to make a "dry run." Establish the exact locations of the bricks at each end of the wall. Stretch a line between stakes driven into the ground to mark the top outer edge of the first course of bricks. The line should be taut and level—check it with the line level. Set the corner bricks and the intermediate bricks on the footing, allowing for a ½-inch mortar joint between bricks. The corner construction will depend on the design of the wall. A straight, double-thickness wall can have columns of headers at the ends. A double wall that turns a corner may be made of two quarter bricks and two three-quarter bricks, with the rest of the first course made of headers. Determine the best corner arrangement for the type of wall you are building before proceeding.

If you must cut bricks to fit, as in the corners, use the chisel and hammer. Score the brick on all sides. Place it on edge on a bed of smooth, wet sand. Strike it with the chisel and hammer to break it off at the score mark.

When you are satisfied with the positioning of bricks in the first course, remove them from the footing. Dampen the footing slightly, then spread a bed of mortar in one corner, as wide as the wall and long enough to lay three or four bricks (as your bricklaying skills develop, you will be able to increase this to eight or ten bricks, or even more). The edges of the mortar bed should be about 1 inch thick, with the center somewhat less. Furrow it slightly with the trowel.

Lay the first corner brick in the bed and tap it into approximate position, making sure that it is squarely aligned. Spread ("butter") a layer of mortar about ¾-inch thick on the side or end of the brick next to the corner brick (depending on the construction of the corner) and lay it in place in the mortar bed. Place six or eight bricks out from the corner, adding mortar to the bed as necessary. Now make sure that all are properly aligned with the line and with

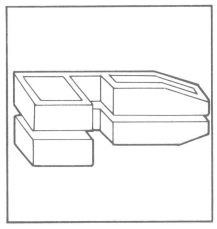

Corner block.

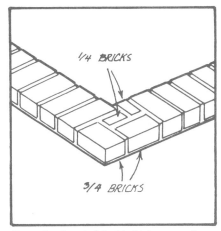

Corner treatment of double thickness wall.

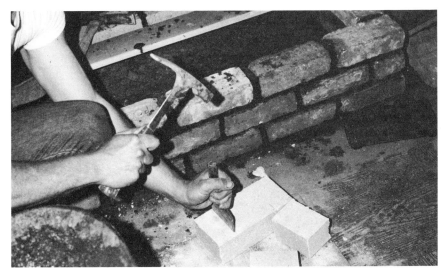

Score brick with a chisel to cut.

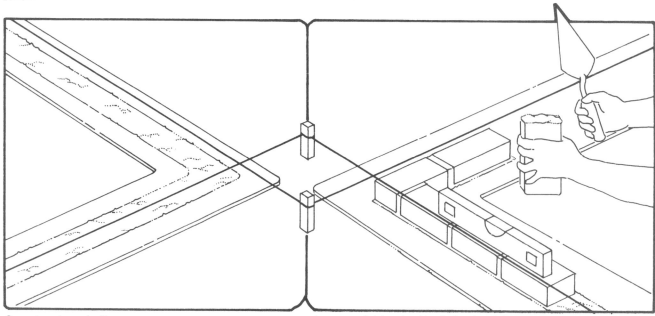

Spread mortar on footing.

Lay corner bricks, checking for level and alignment.

each other, horizontally level, and vertically plumb. Tap the brick about ½-inch into the mortar bed, using the handle of the trowel. Check that all mortar joints are approximately ½-inch wide. Use the point and edge of the trowel to remove excess mortar from the joints and face of the bricks. The excess can be spread on the next brick or it can be remixed with that in the wheelbarrow or mortar board.

Now repeat the process at the other end of the wall. When both corners are in place, lay the intermediate bricks of the first course, working from both ends toward the middle. Check frequently to make sure that mortar joints are the correct thickness, and that the bricks are properly aligned with the string and each other, level and plumb.

The last brick in a course is the "closure" brick. Spread a layer of mortar about ¾-inch thick on the sides or ends (depending on the bond) of the bricks on each side of the closure. Spread a similar layer on both sides or ends of the closure. Carefully set the closure brick in place, taking care not to knock the mortar out of the joints. Align the closure brick with the string and the other bricks, and make sure it is plumb and level.

With the first course laid, the corners or ends of the wall are built up several courses ahead of the stretcher, or intermediate, courses. Plastic corner blocks are hooked around the corner brick in each course to hold the guide line in position (you can also tie the string to nails pushed into mortar joints in the corners, but this is not quite as accurate and also requires some mortar patching later on). Make frequent checks to see that the bricks are aligned with the string and are perfectly plumb and level. As the wall grows higher, check also with the story pole to make sure that each course is at the proper height. Continue building up the corners, then filling in the stretchers, until the wall is completed.

Mortar joints must be finished after the mortar stiffens but before it hardens. On a very small project, you can probably do this after all bricks have been laid, but in most cases you should do it as you go along. Mortar may be troweled flush with the face of the wall. You can also use the trowel to make a "struck joint" (mortar flush at top and angled in toward the bottom) or "weathered joint" (the opposite of a struck joint). A round or square mason's jointer (see section

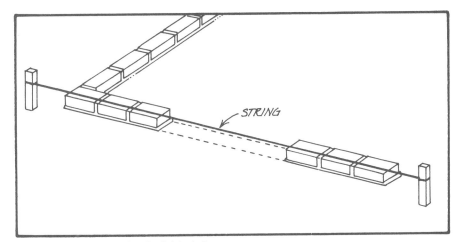

Repeat at opposite end, then lay bricks between.

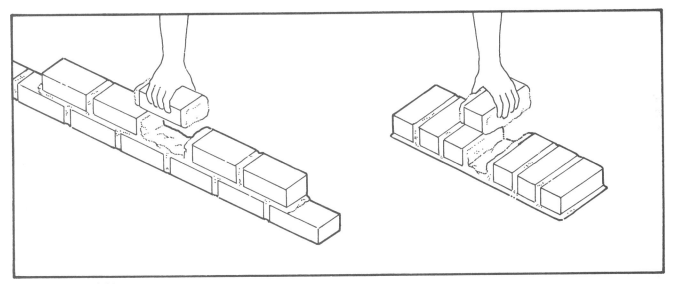

Laying the closure brick.

Build up corners several courses ahead of stretchers.

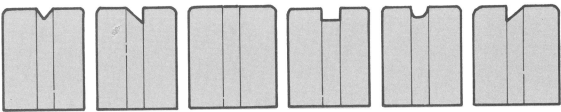

Joint treatments, top to bottom: flush, struck, weathered, concave, V, raked.

on laying concrete block) can be used to make concave or V joints. The square jointer will also make a "raked joint," from which the mortar has removed to a desired depth.

The best way to avoid cleanup after a bricklaying job is to be as neat as possible during the job. Keep the bricks clean of mortar droppings while you are working. If mortar does drop on the wall, scrape it away with the trowel or a putty knife, and wipe it off with a piece of damp burlap. After the mortar hardens, clean the wall with a commercial masonry cleaner. These usually contain muriatic acid, so follow label directions carefully and wear protective clothing and glasses. If some splashes on your skin, wash it off immediately with water.

Repair Work

Since brickwork is made up of small units, there are a lot of "little things" that might go wrong. Problems are most likely to appear along with the crocuses, after chilling winter frosts have vacated your patio for colder climes. Fortunately, repairs are relatively "little" too, and can usually be accomplished in plenty of time to greet the appearance of the first rosebuds and the advent of your outdoor living season.

A brick-in-sand project is more likely to heave and/or settle than is one on a well-constructed concrete slab, but it is also far more simple to put back into shape. Remove any bricks that have risen or sunk, using an old screwdriver, beer can opener, or other tool to dislodge the first one, then lifting out the surrounding ones.

Where settling has occurred, just lay in some extra sand and tamp it down firmly—in small areas, you can do this with a short length of 2x4. The application of some water helps to settle and compact the sand. When the bed is up to where it should be and level, relay the bricks the same way they were laid before, butting them as tightly together as possible. (If your edging has shifted, there may be spaces between the bricks; in that case, allow even gaps for as uniform an appearance as possible). When all bricks are in place, spread more sand over the top of the entire terrace (even where the bricks were not disturbed, the joints may have settled) and work it into the joints with a stiff-bristled broom. Use a garden hose to spray the terrace or walkway, then sweep in more sand. You may have to repeat the process a few times until the sand is worked between the bricks right up to the surface.

Heaving and settling of brick on a concrete slab should be relatively rare. If an area of the brick does present such problems, use a cold chisel or brick chisel with a ball peen or mash hammer to chip out the mortar so that you can remove the bricks. If you have trouble raising the brick, pry it up with a chisel or wrecking bar.

When settling is the problem, chip out the mortar that was underneath the brick down to the slab. Mix new mortar and lay in enough to bring the settled brick back up to surface level. Then "butter" the sides of the individual bricks and relay them as before. Allow sufficient setting time before standing on that area of the terrace to toast the rosebuds.

Heaved brick on a concrete slab poses a slightly more difficult repair problem. Remove the mortar and brick as above. Then chip off the concrete base to lower it to the surrounding level. If you suspect invading tree roots as the cause of the raised slab, you should remove all the concrete in the affected section—no mean feat. Concrete is meant to last, so expect to use some muscles you forgot you had when you swing that sledgehammer. You may be able to rent a jackhammer if the area is sizable, but this is not recommended for weaklings.

However you bare the earth, chop off the offending root as far back as possible. Don't worry about hurting the tree. Any tree big enough to lift a concrete-and-brick terrace can afford the loss of a root—it's like a slap on the fingers. Then pour new concrete, as detailed in an earlier chapter. After it has cured, relay brick as previously described.

When large areas of pavement are badly heaved or settled, it is likely that the concrete slab was poorly constructed originally (obviously, not by you). In that case, it is best to remove all the brick and either break up the slab and start all over or pour a 2-inch topping of new concrete over the old.

Most repair jobs to mortared brick are not that drastic, fortunately, but simply involve repairing or "tuck-pointing" crumbled mortar. You can spare yourself some future labor by repointing all loose or weak joints at the same time as those that are badly crumbled. Chisel out the damaged mortar to a depth of about one inch, even though the deterioration seems to be only on the surface. If new mortar is laid in too thinly, it will not hold.

Use a stiffer-than-normal mortar mix for tuck-pointing—one part masonry cement to two-and-a-half parts clean sand mixed with less than the usual amount of water so that the mortar clings to the trowel when it is turned upside down (it should slide off the trowel when held sideways). You may prefer to buy special repointing mortar, available at most building supply dealers.

Dampen the joints to be repaired, but do not soak them so that water is left standing. Use the trowel to force mortar into the joints, doing the short sides of the brick first, then the long ones. Allow the mortar to cure as above.

Repairs to brick walls are practically the same as for paving. Tuck-pointing is the most common. Chisel out the old mortar to at least ½-inch depth and clean the area with a brush. Dampen the joint and fill with new, tooling to match the existing joints. If extensive tuck-pointing is required, do it a section at a time—do not chisel out all the joints at once before refilling. Where mortar joints are very badly crumbled, you may have to remove a brick completely. In that case, chisel out the mortar behind the brick as well. Lay in new mortar, then butter the brick on all sides and replace, taking care not to drop mortar on surrounding bricks.

Where crumbling mortar is a major problem, the joints may be treated with a special waterproofing compound available at masonry supply dealers. The compound is brushed on, a very time-consuming process and one that should probably be considered only as a last resort.

In this variation, large, square stones are laid on a raised concrete slab; joints are left unfilled.

Dry-built patio of rectangular-cut stone is simply laid in a bed of sand.

Building & Installation Techniques:

STONE

Stone is man's oldest building material, and its durability and rugged natural beauty make it still a favorite. Granite, limestone, marble, sandstone, slate, and quartzite are commonly used for outdoor projects. These are available in a myriad of colors and textures. Most stone yards stock primarily what is native to the region or nearby regions, but they will probably order whatever you want—provided you are willing to pay the extra cost for transportation.

Flagstone is stone cut to various thicknesses specifically for use as paving. It is normally sold by the square foot and comes in either irregular, rectangular-cut, or square-cut forms. The smallest common cut size is 12x12 inches (actually about 11½ inches square); the largest common size is 24x36 inches. Smaller and larger sizes can be specially ordered—again, usually at extra cost.

Flagstone is also used for building walls, but here irregularly shaped field-stone may also be used. In many areas, you can find these right on your property, or (in rural areas) on the property of a farmer who will be happy to have you take them away for nothing. (If you are a really shrewd bargainer and he really wants a field cleared, he may even pay you—but farmers tend to be

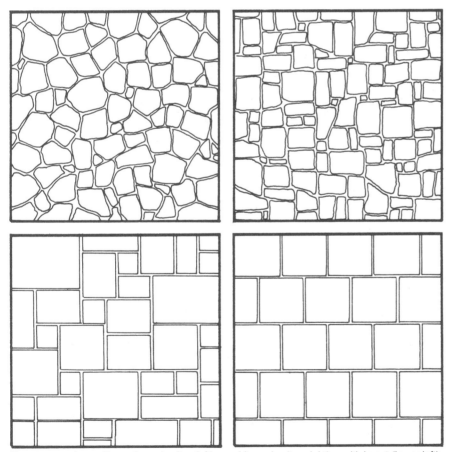

Flagstone paving patterns: irregular (top left), semi-irregular (top right), multiple cut (lower left), and staggered all one size.

shrewd bargainers too, so don't count on that.) Many building supply yards also stock fieldstone, or can order it for you.

Wherever you get it, just remember that stone is a heavy material. If you can have it delivered to your lot, do so. If you have to transport it yourself—whether from the building supply dealer's or the farmer's fields—take it easy on your car and yourself. That station wagon's springs have definite load limitations. So does your back. Don't overload either one.

There are two basic methods of building with stone—wet construction and dry construction. In wet construction, the stone is bonded together with a grout. In dry construction, it is simply laid out on a bed of sand (in the case of patios or walkways) or built up (for walls).

Dry Pavement Construction

Dry construction is usually preferred by the do-it-yourselfer because it is easier and requires no great technical know-how or special equipment. When choosing stone for a patio or walkway laid in sand, bear in mind that larger, thicker 1½-inch minimum pieces will stay level longer than smaller, thinner pieces. Also, when using irregularly shaped stones, select pieces that fit well together, keeping joint width to a minimum (not a problem if you choose cut stones for your project).

Determine the size of the patio and outline the area with stakes and string. Excavate to a depth of approximately 5 inches.

Edging is not essential to a flagstone patio, but it does make it easier to set the stone and retain the sand, especially where the pavement is raised above ground level. Edging can be of stone, approximately 1½x6 inches, set on edge. Or a wood edge of 2x6 lumber can be staked into the earth. In the latter case, a decay-resistant wood such as redwood or cedar, or another species that has been treated with preservative, should be used. Make sure that the edge is level.

Wet and tamp the earth in the excavated area. Fill with sand to approximately 1 inch from the top of the edging. Starting in a corner, begin laying flagstone on the sand base, tapping each piece with a rubber mallet or block of wood to set it firmly. If the stone sinks too far into the sand, pick it up and place more sand underneath. If it does not sink into the sand bed deeply enough to be level with the edging, pick it up and scrape away some of the sand underneath. By placing a straight board across the edging, you can determine that each stone is level and at the proper height.

When all the stones are laid, spread sand across the patio and sweep it into the joints. Wet down the patio with a hose to compact the sand. Then sweep more sand into the joints, making it almost level with the surface of the flagstones. Crushed stone or decorative gravel may be used in place of the sand, adding a custom touch to the patio.

Wet Pavement Construction

Wet construction is not only more difficult, but also more expensive, than the dry method. However, it gives you a permanent, maintenance-free patio. In wet construction, the flagstones are set in a 1-inch bed of grout on top of a 4-inch reinforced concrete slab with a perimeter footing to the frost line.

As in dry construction, first lay out the patio with string and stakes. Excavate the area to a depth of 8 inches. Around the perimeter, dig a trench the width of a shovel to the depth of the frost line in your locality. (Check with your local

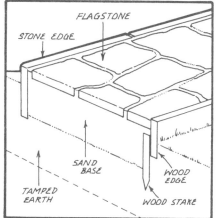

Dry construction method of laying flagstone.

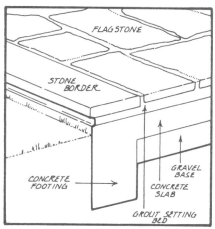

Wet construction method of setting flagstone. Thicker stone border piece is used because the patio is above grade level. For a patio at grade, no special border is needed.

After the stones have been set in the grout bed, joints are filled with mortar. The effect is generally more formal than dry construction.

building department for this information. In some warmer climates, a footing may not be necessary.)

After excavation is complete, set form boards around the perimeter, with the tops of the boards at the level of the finished slab. For proper drainage, the patio should be pitched ¼-inch per foot, away from the house if the patio is located adjacent to it. Set the form boards to this pitch.

Spread approximately 4 inches of gravel inside the excavation, raking it as close as possible to the edge of the footing trench. Footing and slab are poured at the same time. Use a mixture of one part cement, two parts sand, and four parts gravel. Fill the footing trench first, then spread approximately 2 inches of concrete in the excavation. Place reinforcing mesh on the concrete, then pour the remaining concrete to the top of the form boards. Strike off the concrete even with the boards. No trowelling or smoothing is necessary—a rough surface is desirable to provide a firm bond for the grout setting bed. Let the concrete slab harden for at least forty-eight hours before proceeding.

The grout bed consists of one part cement and three parts clean sand mixed with water to a consistency that could be balled and thrown (like a "good-packin' " snowball). Starting in a corner, spread only enough of the grout on the slab for one or two stones, to a thickness of 1 inch. Lay each stone in place and tamp it level by hammering it lightly with a rubber-faced mallet or block of wood. Stakes supporting strings stretched across the patio are a help in maintaining the proper pitch when setting the stones.

After a dozen or so stones have been laid, lift each one up one at a time and pour a cement "butter" over the grout bed, then drop the stone back into place. The "butter" consists of cement and water mixed to the consistency of thick pea soup and serves to adhere the dry stone to the quite dry grout—otherwise, the bond would be weak.

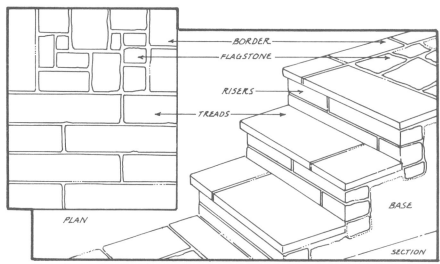

Stone step construction. A concrete or masonry foundation is required.

When setting stones into the grout, do not attempt to fill the spaces between them. Finish the entire patio first, and allow it to set at least overnight. Then make a mixture of one part cement and two parts sand mixed with water to a consistency a little wetter than the setting bed. Us a pointing tool to pack the mixture firmly into the joints. Be careful not to smear the cement on the face of the stone. If any spills accidentally, wash it off as soon as possible with a sponge and water before it has a chance to harden.

Steps

Flagstone steps could be laid on an earth base, but this is definitely not recommended since it would not be a very stable construction. It is far better to lay the flagstones on a base of concrete or masonry, constructed as described earlier in this book. (see concrete).

Select and have your dealer cut to size stone for the risers and treads, as well as border pieces and "cheeks" (side walls of steps) if these are to be built. Borders are desirable to give a finished appearance to the steps; these will be visible from both the top and edge, so select accordingly. Flagstone for the "field" (top platform) can be chosen to match the rest of the stone or to contrast with it, depending on the overall effect planned for the steps and walkway or patio. When measuring, allow for overhangs and keep in mind the thickness of the stone.

It is especially important that the bottom riser be set on a firm foundation. It cannot rest on a sidewalk or earth in front of the concrete or masonry base. The same applies to cheeks, if these are planned. It is necessary to dig along the front and sides of the step foundation to pour a concrete base.

If you are using stone risers as well as treads, the risers should be set first. Use a mortar mix of one part cement to three parts sand mixed with water to a workable consistency. The risers should be flush with, or just slightly above, the tops of the base steps.

To set the treads, spread the entire base surface with the cement mix. Place the stone tread in this bed, tapping it firmly into place with a rubber mallet and leveling it. If a stone tread is too high, lift it and scrape out some mortar from beneath; if too low, add more mortar. When you are satisfied that the stone is properly set, lift it up and pour the same "butter" as described previously over the bed and the back of the stone; then reset the stone.

Walls

A well-constructed stone wall is a thing of beauty—and endurance. In many more remote areas of the country, dry stone fences—built without mortar of the stones that were gathered when the land was cleared to allow the planting of crops—are all that survive to record the existence of farms long since abandoned and otherwise returned to their natural state. In some parts of the world where architecture and engineering were early sciences—Italy and China are two examples—it is not uncommon to find mortared stone walls that are five hundred years or even a millenium old, still sturdy and still a natural delight to the eye. Obviously, stone is here to stay.

Because of its weight and interfaced construction, a stone wall requires some different design considerations than other types of walls, such as those of brick or concrete block. As a general rule of thumb, a stone wall up to 3 feet high should be a minimum of 18 inches thick. For every foot of height above that, add another 8 inches of thickness; for a 6-foot wall, 7½ feet thick; a 9-foot wall, if you can spare the space and lift the stones that high, 5½ feet thick.

Because of this width-to-height ratio, a footing is not normally required for low stone walls—up to 3 or 4 feet, depending on the stability of the soil. It is usually sufficient to excavate about 6 to 8 inches and lay the first course of stone in this excavation after tamping the subsoil. For a higher wall of either wet or dry construction, a concrete footing should be poured below the frost line, as previously described. The stone can be laid directly on the footing, or a foundation wall of concrete or masonry units can be built up to near the grade and the stone laid on this.

Flat stones should always be laid in the flat position, both for appearance and strength. Fieldstone and "rubble" (rough-cut quarry stone) should have at least two (top and bottom) and preferably three (the face) flat sides. You will probably have to shape such stones with a hammer and chisel. Keep striking around the cut line until the stone breaks off, then clean the cut to the desired shape with the sharp end of a mason's hammer. Similar cuts will have to be made to fit irregular stones into the wall.

With the excavation dug and the footing and foundation in place, drive stakes in the four corners outlining the wall, extending a few inches higher than than the projected height of the wall. Figure the average height of the first course of stone (in some cases, the first course may be partly below ground level) and tie mason's cord between the end stakes, pulling it taut and using a line level to level it at this height.

Use the largest stones for the first course of the wall. Lay in a corner stone

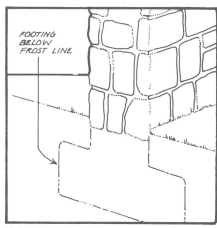

Higher stone walls require a footing below ground level and, in most instances, below the frost line.

Lay the first course of the stone wall roughly even with the guide line. Fill in between outer courses with backing stones.

Raise the guide line as you go along until the toppers are in place.

(if you have a stone the full width of the wall, use it here), working it in as level with the cord as possible. Lay a few more stones along the same side of the wall, fitting them as tightly together as possible, and sighting along the cord to see that they are as near level as possible. Go to the other side of the wall and lay in several stones from the corner, again keeping them aligned with the cord. Don't worry about the space between the outside courses at this time—these will be filled in later. Continue to lay the first course on both sides of the wall. If you have any particularly large stones that would extend up through the second course, place them strategically for strength and visual variety.

With the first course in place, fill the gap between the two sides with "backing" stones. These are smaller stones of any shape, and should fill the cavity as completely as possible without forcing the outer courses apart.

With the backing in place, it's time to separate the wets from the drys. If you are using the wet construction method, make a mortar of one part portland cement, one-quarter part hydrated lime, and three parts clean sand, with enough water to make a workable but not soupy mix. Use a trowel to place the mortar loosely into the crevices between the stones. Do not force the mortar into the joints. If any mortar gets on the face of the stone, wipe it off immediately with damp burlap. Because of the variations in width, mortar joints on stone work are not normally tooled.

After the first course has been mortared—or if you are using the dry construction method—raise the mason's cord on the stakes to the approximate level of the second course, pull it tight and level it. Starting at one end, proceed in the same manner as with the first course. Make sure that joints between stones do not fall over joints in the first course—these should be bridged for structural strength as well as for good appearance. If you have stones that are long enough, place an occasional "tie" across both sides of the wall. Check for plumb frequently, using a carpenter's or mason's level. While the generally rough surfaces of the stone will not form a perfectly vertical face, it should be made as close to it as possible.

Fill in the second course with backing and mortar if used, then proceed to build up the wall. "Toppers" are used to cap the wall. These should be stones as flat as are available, and with a large surface area. It is advisable to set this top course in a mortar bed, even on a dry wall. Once you've put the last topper in place, you have made your statement in stone for eternity—or at least for the next couple of hundred years. Congratulations.

Wood is a much-preferred patio material because of its natural beauty and versatility.

Building & Installation Techniques:
WOOD

Wood is the do-it-yourselfer's basic material, and with good reason. It is sturdy, versatile, easily worked, widely available in a variety of forms to suit many purposes, and relatively inexpensive (a few years back, we might even have said "cheap," but few things warrant that term today; still, wood is generally a bargain in comparison with other building materials). For outdoor projects, it is a natural—in a very literal sense. Wood belongs to the outdoors, and it blends well into almost any setting, adding its own beauty to its surroundings.

Most do-it-yourselfers have the required woodworking skills of swinging a hammer and wielding a saw. If not, these are easily acquired with practice. Beyond that, it takes some understanding of the properties of various woods, their capabilities and how to put it all together to make a fence, deck, storage shed, gazebo, doghouse, or whatever else is your project of the moment. It may take some careful calculations and meticulous measuring, but chances are very good that whatever your wood project is will turn out satisfactorily.

Lumber Species and Characteristics

Many lumber species will provide good service in outdoor applications. Some are more suited for these purposes than others. To select lumber wisely, you must first single out the key requirements of the job. Then it is relatively easy to check the properties of the different woods to see which ones meet these requirements. For example, beams or joists require wood species that are high in bending strength or stiffness; wide boards in railings should be species that warp little; posts and similar members that are exposed to long wet periods should be heartwood of species with high decay resistance. Follow the recommendations in the accompanying table to select wood for a specific use in your outdoor structure.

Ground-level decks, such as this one built of 2-inch-dimension western lumber, are as popular as those built on sloping sites. This type of design is particularly desirable for a free-standing unit, where direct access to the house is not feasible.

Pressure-treated southern pine is the choice for this deck. 2x4 deck boards are laid over beams set at 3-foot intervals, with joints staggered.

Wood Species Characteristics and Properties[1]

Kind of wood	Working and behavior characteristics							Strength properties			Freedom from pitch
	Hardness	Freedom from warping	Ease of working	Paint holding	Nail holding	Decay resistance of heartwood	Proportion of heartwood	Bending strength	Stiffness	Strength as a post	
Ash	A	B	C	C	A	C	C	A	A	A	A
Western red cedar	C	A	A	A	C	A	A	C	C	B	A
Cypress	B	B	B	A	B	A	B	B	B	B	A
Douglas fir, larch	B	B	B-C	C	A	B	A	A	A	A	B
Gum	B	C	B	C	A	B	B	B	A	B	A
Hemlock, white fir[2]	B-C	B	B	C	C	C	C	B	A	B	A
Soft pines[3]	C	A	A	A	C	C	B	C	C	C	B
Southern pine	B	B	B	C	A	B	C	A	A	A	C
Poplar	C	A	B	A	B	C	B	B	B	B	A
Redwood	B	A	B	A	B	A	A	B	B	A	A
Spruce	C	A-B	B	B	B	C	C	B	B	B	A

[1]A—among the woods relatively high in the particular respect listed; B—among woods intermediate in that respect; C—among woods relatively low in that respect. Letters do not refer to lumber grades.

[2]Includes west coast and eastern hemlocks
[3]Includes the western and northeastern pines.

—U.S. Department of Agriculture

Lumber Sizes

The nominal dimension of lumber is usually based on green sawn sizes. When the lumber has been dried and surfaced, the finish size (thickness and width) is somewhat less than the sawn size.

The following lumber sizes are those established by the American Lumber Standards Committee:

Nominal Size (inches)	Dry or Actual Size (inches)	Green (inches)
1	¾	$^{25}/_{32}$
$^5/_4$	$1^1/_{16}$	1⅛
2	1½	$1^9/_{16}$
3	2½	$2^9/_{16}$
4	3½	$3^9/_{16}$
6	5½	5⅝
8	7¼	7½
10	9¼	9½
12	11¼	11½

Thus, a nominal 2x4 would have a surfaced dry size of 1½ x 3½ inches; a 2x10 measures 1½ x 9¼ inches.

Moisture content of wood during fabrication and assembly of a wood frame structure is important. Ideally, the wood should have about the same moisture content it will reach in service. If green or only partially dried wood is used, wood members may frequently shrink, resulting in poorly fitting joints and loose fastenings after drying has occurred.

Although not as important for exterior use as for interior use, the moisture content of the lumber used and exposed to exterior conditions should be considered. The average moisture content of wood exposed to the weather varies with the season, but kiln-dried or air-dried lumber best fits the mid-range of moisture content that wood reaches in use.

Plywood

Plywood is adaptable for use in wood decks and is often recommended for solid deck coverings, fences or wind screens, sheathing and other applications. Plywood is made in two types—*exterior* and *interior*. Only the exterior type is recommended where any surface or edge is permanently exposed to the weather. Interior-type plywood, even when made with exterior glue and protected on the top surface, is not recommended for such exposures.

There are several appearance grades of exterior plywood (as there are of interior). These are designated A, B, C, and D, and are determined by the veneer grade on the back and face of the plywood panel. An A-C grade, for example, would have a smooth face veneer (A) and a back veneer (C) that would contain some splits and knots. This is often referred to as "good-one-side" and is perfectly acceptable for an application where only one side (the A side) will be exposed.

Appearance grades are identified in the American Plywood Association's APA grade-trademark stamp on each panel, along with a group number referring to the wood species. Plywood is manufactured from over seventy wood species of varying strengths which have been classified into five groups. Within each group, each species must meet a common criterion. Lower group numbers indicate greater stiffness and strength; Group 1 woods are the strongest. Where face and back veneers are not from the same group, the number is based on the weaker group, except for decorative panels ⅜-inch or less, which are identified by face species group.

Veneer Grades

A Smooth and paintable. Neatly made repairs permissible. Also used for natural finish in less demanding applications.

B Solid surface veneer. Circular repair plugs and tight knots permitted.

C Knotholes to 1″. Occasional knotholes ½″ larger permitted providing total width of all knots and knotholes within a specified section does not exceed certain limits. Limited splits permitted. Minimum veneer permitted in Exterior-type plywood.

C Improved C veneer with splits limited to ⅛″ in width and knotholes and Plgd borer holes limited to ¼″ by ½″.

D Permits knots and knotholes to 2½″ in width and ½″ larger under certain specified limits. Limited splits permitted.

TYPICAL BACK-STAMP

Grade of veneer on panel face
Grade of veneer on panel back

A-C

Species Group number — **GROUP 2**
Designates the type of plywood — **EXTERIOR**
Product Standard governing manufacture — **PS 1-74** 000

Mill number

TYPICAL EDGE-MARK

Grade of veneer on panel face
Grace of veneer on panel back
Designates the type of plywood Exterior or Interior
Product Standard governing manufacture

A-B · G-1 · EXT-APA · PS 1-74 000

Species Group number   Mill number

Plywood comes in a wide range of thicknesses. For most outdoor projects, ¼-, ⅜-, ½-, ⅝-, or ¾-inch will be used. Common panel size is 4x8 feet, although larger panels are available, usually on special order. Many lumber dealers also sell half panels (4x4 feet), and most will also cut the panels to your specified size, usually at a nominal fee. This can be a real time-saver, especially if your project requires a lot of cutting. Their large power saws make short work of the job.

Decay Resistance of Wood

Every material normally used in construction has its distinctive way of deterioration under adverse conditions. With wood it is decay. Wood will never decay if kept continuously dry (at less than 20-percent moisture content). Because open decks, fences, and other outdoor components are exposed to wetting and drying conditions, good drainage, flashings, and similar protective measures are more important than in a structure fully protected by a roof.

Plywood Grades for Exterior Uses

GRADE (EXTERIOR)	FACE	BACK	INNER PLIES	USES
A-A	A	A	C	Outdoor, where appearance of both sides is important.
A-B	A	B	C	Alternate for A-A where appearance of one side is less important. Face is finish grade.
A-C	A	C	C	Soffits, fences, base for coatings.
B-C	B	C	C	For utility uses such as farm buildings, some kinds of fences, etc., base for coatings.
303 ® Siding	C (or better)	C	C	Panels with variety of surface texture and grooving patterns. For siding, fences, paneling, screens, etc.
T 1-11®	C	C	C	Special ⅝″ panel with deep parallel grooves. Available unsanded, textured, or MDO surface.
C-C (Plugged)	C Plugged	C	C	Excellent base for tile and linoleum, backing for wall coverings, high-performance coatings.
C-C	C	C	C	Unsanded, for backing and rough construction exposed to weather.
B-B Plyform	B	B	C	Concrete forms. Re-use until wood literally wears out.
MDO	B	B or C	C	Medium Density Overlay. Ideal base for paint; for siding, built-ins, signs, displays.
HDO	A or B	A or B	C-Plugged or C	High Density Overlay. Hard surface; no paint needed. For concrete forms, cabinets, counter tops, tanks.

Classification of Species

Group 1	Group 2		Group 3	Group 4	Group 5
Apitong (a), (b)	Cedar, Port Orford	Maple, Black	Alder, Red	Aspen	Basswood
Beech,	Cypress	Mengkulang (a)	Birch, Paper	Bigtooth	Fir, Balsam
American	Douglas Fir 2 (c)	Meranti,Red (a),(b)	Cedar, Alaska	Quaking	Poplar, Balsam
Birch	Fir	Mersawa (a)	Fir, Subalpine	Cativo	
Sweet	California Red	Pine	Hemlock, Eastern	Cedar	
Yellow	Grand	Pond	Maple, Bigleaf	Incense	
Douglas Fir 1 (c)	Noble	Red	Pine	Western Red	
Kapur (a)	Pacific Silver	Virginia	Jack	Cottonwood	
Keruing (a), (b)	White	Western White	Lodgepole	Eastern	
Larch, Western	Hemlock, Western	Spruce	Ponderosa	Black (Western	
Maple, Sugar	Lauan	Red	Spruce	Poplar)	
Pine	Almon	Sitka	Redwood	Pine	
Caribbean	Bagtikan	Sweetgum	Spruce	Eastern White	
Ocote	Mayapis	Tamarack	Black	Sugar	
Pine, Southern	Red Lauan	Yellow-poplar	Engelmann		
Loblolly	Tangile		White		
Longleaf	White Lauan				
Shortleaf					
Slash					
Tanoak					

(a) Each of these names represents a trade group of woods consisting of a number of closely related species.

(b) Species from the genus Dipterocarpus are marketed collectively: Apitong if originating in the Philippines; Keruing if originating in Malaysia or Indonesia.

(c) Douglas fir from trees grown in the States of Washington, Oregon, California, Idaho, Montana, Wyoming, and the Canadian Provinces of Alberta and British Columbia shall be classed as Douglas fir No. 1. Douglas fir from trees grown in the states of Nevada, Utah, Colorado, Arizona and New Mexico shall be classed as Douglas fir No. 2.

(d) Red Meranti shall be limited to species having a specific gravity of 0.41 or more based on green volume and oven dry weight.

Courtesy American Plywood Association

To provide good performance of wood under exposed conditions, take one or more of the following measures:
● Use the heartwood of a decay-resistant species.
● Use design details which do not trap moisture and which allow easy drainage. (Quick drying is always desirable.)
● Use wood that has been given a good preservative treatment.

Preservative Treatments

The best treatment of wood to assure long life under severe conditions is a pressure preservative treatment. However, the wood parts of most outdoor structures are exposed only to moderate conditions except at joints and connections. There are two general methods of preservative-treating wood: pressure processes applied commercially and nonpressure processes which normally penetrate the ends and a thin layer of the outer surfaces and require frequent maintenance. The nonpressure processes are treatments with water-repellent wood preservatives.

Two general types of preservatives are recommended for severe exterior conditions: oils, such as creosote or pentachlorophenol in oil or liquefied gas carriers, and nonleachable salts, such as the chromated copper arsenates or ammoniacal copper arsenite applied as water solutions. If cleanliness or paintability is a factor (as on exposed parts of a deck), creosote or penta-chlorophenol in heavy oil should not be used. Nonleachable water-borne preservatives and pentachlorophenol in light or volatile petroleum solvents should be selected.

Where preservative treatment of wood not in contact with the ground is desirable because the more decay-resistant woods are not available, the use of a more easily applied, less expensive but less effective treatment may be considered. A pentachlorophenol solution with a water repellent is one of the better materials of this type. It is available at most lumber or paint dealers as a clear, water-repellent preservative. It should be applied by soaking, dipping, or flooding so that end grain, machine cuts, and existing checks in the wood are well penetrated. Dipping each end of all exterior framing material in a water-repellent preservative is recommended, and this should be done after all cutting and drilling is completed. Drilled holes can be treated by squirting preservative from an oil can with a long spout. Dry wood absorbs more of these materials than partially dry wood and, consequently, is better protected.

Design versatility is one of the reasons for the popularity of wood as a material for an outdoor living area. Note the interesting geometric patterns created by the deck boards, planter/rail, and house wall shingles.

General Rules for Outdoor Wood Use

● When a wide member is required, use edge-grain boards, since they shrink, swell, and cup less than flat-grain boards during moisture changes.

● Do not use wood in direct contact with soil unless members are pressure-treated.

●Provide clearance of wood members from plant growth and ground to minimize high moisture content. Bottoms of posts supported by piers should be 6 inches above the grade.

● Use forms of flat members which provide natural drainage (a sloped top of a cap rail, for example).

● Use rectangular sections with width and thickness as nearly equal as possible, for example, 3x4 instead of 2x6.

● Dip all ends and points of fabrication in a water-repellent preservative treatment prior to placement.

Exterior Finishes

Exterior finishes which might be considered for wood components exposed to the weather include natural finishes and penetrating stains and paints. In general, natural finishes containing a water repellent and a preservative are preferred over paint for exposed flat surfaces. The natural finishes penetrate the wood and are easily renewed, but paint forms a surface film that may rupture under repeated wetting and drying.

Natural finishes (lightly pigmented) are often used for exposed wood decks, railings, stairways, and other structures, not only because they can be easily renewed but because they enhance the natural color and grain of the wood. Such finishes can be obtained in many colors. Light tones are better for deck surfaces subject to traffic, since they show the least contrast in grain color as wear occurs, and appearance is maintained longer. One type of natural finish contains paraffin wax, zinc stearate, penta concentrate, linseed oil, mineral spirits, and tinting colors. Such finishes are manufactured by many leading producers of wood stains and are generally available from paint or lumber dealers.

Penetrating stains (heavily pigmented) for rough and weathered wood may be used on the large sawn members such as beams and posts. These are

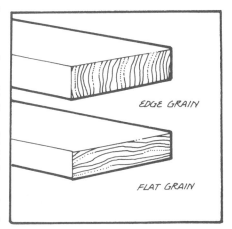

EDGE GRAIN

FLAT GRAIN

similar to the natural finishes but contain less oil and more pigment. They are also produced by many companies.

Paint is one of the most widely used finishes for wood. When applied properly over a paintable surface with an initial water-repellent preservative treatment, followed by prime and finish coats, paint is a highly desirable finish for outdoor structures or as an accent color when used with natural finishes. Exposed flat surfaces with end or side joints are difficult to protect with a paint coating unless there is no shrinking or swelling of the wood to rupture the paint film. A crack in the paint film allows water to get beneath the film where it is hard to remove by drying. Retention of such moisture can result in eventual decay.

Good painting practice includes an initial application of water-repellent preservative. After allowing two sunny days for drying of the preservative, a prime coat is applied. This can consist of a linseed oil-base paint with pigments that do not contain zinc oxide.

The finish coats can contain zinc oxide pigment and can be of the linseed oil, alkyd, or latex type. Two coats should be used for best results. A three-coat paint job with good-quality paint may last as long as ten years if the film is not ruptured by excessive shrinking or swelling of the wood.

Coverings and Coatings for Plywood

Tough, skid-resistant, elastomeric coatings are available for plywood deck wearing surfaces. These coatings include neoprene, neoprene/Hypalon, and silicone- or rubber-based materials. Plywood joints for these systems are usually sealed with a high-performance caulk such as silicone or Thiokol (silicone caulks require a primer). Joints may also be covered with a synthetic reinforcing tape, prior to application of the final surface coat, when an elastomeric coating system is used.

Silicone or Thiokol caulks are applied to ¼-inch gaps between panels over some type of filler or "backer" material, such as a foam rod. The caulk "bead" is normally about ¼-inch in diameter. An alternate method is to bevel the panel edges first, then fill the joint with the caulk before the finish coating is applied.

If outdoor carpeting is to be used on plywood exposed to the weather, it is advisable to use pressure preservative-treated plywood, with the underside well ventilated, for both low and elevated decks. Carpet may be readily applied to untreated plywood deck areas that are not subject to repeated wetting.

Canvas is sometimes used as a wearing surface on plywood. It should be installed with a waterproof adhesive under dry conditions. A canvas surface well fused to the plywood may be painted with regular deck paints.

Plywood used for exterior applications other than decks can be finished in a variety of ways. Plan ahead, because many of the finishing operations are best done before the panels are put in place.

Special care should be taken to seal the panel edges. If plywood is to be painted, give the edges a liberal application of a high-quality exterior house paint primer or similar sealer. Both the edges to be exposed as well as those that will be covered or blind should be sealed, with particular attention given to lower edges of siding panels exposed to severe wetting. Sealing is best done when the panels are in a stack, but edges cut later should also be sealed.

Where the plywood will not be painted, give the edges a liberal application of a good water-repellent preservative. This can be applied with a brush or roller when the panels are stacked. The preservative penetrates rapidly, so apply several coats.

For plywood to be painted, a prime coat should be applied as soon as possible after the panels are cut to size, or at least immediately after they are installed. High-grade exterior primer should be brushed on thoroughly, following manufacturer's directions. Don't thin primer beyond what is recommended; this is invitation to early paint failure.

Back-priming of plywood siding with the same primer that is used for the exposed surface is good practice, but too often neglected. It is especially important in unusually damp locations. A water repellent may be applied instead.

Many plywood manufacturers apply a prime coat in the mill. When factory-primed plywood is used, the manufacturer's instructions should be followed simplicity, particularly with regard to the type of finish paint to be used. The finish must be applied before the primer has had a chance to age or "weather."

While the prime coat should be brushed on to assure best coverage and adhesion, paint itself can be applied with a roller, making the job go much more quickly. Sprayer application is not recommended, since it is essential to work the finish into the wood surface.

Use only high-quality paints formulated for exterior wood service. Water-base acrylic paints are easy to apply and clean up, and excellent in performance. When properly applied over the recommended primer, they adhere exceptionally well to plywood—both smooth and textured surfaces. They will generally remain well bonded to the surface and will not curl or flake. They resist blistering and retain color well. They brush on easily, but care should be taken not to brush them out too thin. Two coats are better than one; three are better yet, but not a necessity. Oil-alkyd paints can be used on smooth plywood, but should not be applied to sanded or textured plywood surfaces.

Stains are a popular exterior finish, expecially for rough or textured plywood. They should be applied in one or two coats according to manufacturer's directions. As with paint, they are best applied with a brush, which helps work the stain into the wood surface. A long-nap roller can be used for textured panels. Stain can also be sprayed on, if applied liberally and then dry-brushed or wiped with a carpet section tacked to a block on a pole handle to help work the stain into the surface and give a uniform appearance.

Semitransparent or penetrating oil stains provide maximum grain show-through and display of surface texture. High-quality oil-base or latex-emulsion stains are recommended because they penetrate the surface and add color without forming a continuous film, and provide a breathing, durable surface. Where maximum wood color and grain show-through are desired and where color differences in the wood are not objectionable, a semitransparent stain may be used. One or two coats should be applied according to directions; two coats give greater color depth and longer life.

Opaque stains penetrate the surface to protect the wood but leave a thin coating of solid uniform color on the surface, obscuring grain pattern but not texture. These highly pigmented stains are recommended for covering color differences in or between panels, and usually require only a single coat for adequate coverage.

Clear finishes on exterior plywood are generally unsatisfactory and should be avoided.

Fasteners

The strength and utility of any wood structure or component are in great measure dependent upon the fastenings used to hold the parts together. The most common wood fasteners are nails and spikes, followed by screws, lag screws, bolts, and metal connectors and straps of various shapes. An important factor for outdoor use of fasteners is the finish selected. Metal fasteners should be rustproofed in some manner or made of rust-resistant metals. Galvanized and cadmium-plated finishes are the most common. Aluminum,

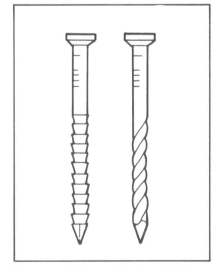

Two types of deformed shank nails that provide extra holding power: annular grooved (left) and spirally grooved.

General Rules for Fasteners

● Use nonstaining fasteners.

● Always fasten a thinner member to a thicker member (unless clinched nails are used).

● A nail should be long enough to penetrate the receiving member a distance twice the thickness of the thinner member but not less than 1½ inches (i.e., to fasten a ¾-inch board, the nail should penetrate the receiving member 1½ inches; use at least a 7d nail).

● A screw should be long enough to penetrate the receiving member at least the thickness of the thinner (outside) member but with not less than a 1-inch penetration (e.g., fastening a ¾-inch member to a 2x4 would require a 1¾-inch-long screw).

● To reduce splitting of boards when nailing:
   Blunt the nail point.
   Predrill (three-fourths of the nail diameter).
   Use smaller-diameter nails and a greater number of them.
   Use greater spacing between nails.
   Stagger nails in each row.
   Place nails no closer to the edge than one-half of the board thickness and no closer to the end than the board thickness.
   In wide boards (8 inches or more), do not place nails close to the edge.

● Use a minimum of two nails per board for 4- and 6-inch widths and three nails for 8- and 10-inch widths.

● Avoid end-grain nailing. When unavoidable, use screws or a side-grain wood cleat adjacent to the end-grain member.

● Lag screws
   Use a plain, flat washer under the head.
   Use a lead hole and turn in full distance; do not overturn.
   Do not countersink.

● Bolts
   Use flat washers under the nut and head of machine bolts and under the nut of carriage bolts. In softer woods, use a larger washer under carriage bolt heads.
   Holes should be exactly the size of the bolt diameter.

---

stainless steel, copper, brass, and other rustproof fasteners are also satisfactory. The most successful for such species as redwood are hot-dip galvanized, aluminum, or stainless steel fasteners. These prevent staining of the wood under exposed conditions. A rusted nail, washer, or bolt head is not only unsightly but difficult to remove and replace.

Smooth shank nails often lose their holding power when exposed to wetting and drying cycles. It's better to use a deformed shank nail or spike. The two general types most satisfactory are the annular grooved (ring shank) and the spirally grooved nail. The value of such a nail or spike is its capacity to retain withdrawal resistance even after repeated wetting and drying cycles.

Wood screws may be used if cost is not a factor in areas where nails are normally specified. Wood screws retain their withdrawal resistance to a great extent under adverse conditions. They are also superior to nails when end-grain fastening must be used. Because of their larger diameter, screw length need not be as great as that of a deformed shank nail.

The flathead screw is best for exposed surfaces because it does not extend beyond the surface. The use of a lead hole about three-fourths the diameter of the screw is good practice, especially in the denser woods, to prevent splitting. Screws should always be turned in their full length and not driven part way.

Lag screws are commonly used to fasten a relatively thick (such as 2x6) member to a thicker member (3-or-more-inch) where a through bolt cannot be used. Lead holes must be drilled, and the lag screw must be turned in its entire length. Use a large washer under the head. Lead holes for the threaded portion should be about two-thirds the diameter of the lag screw for the softer woods such as redwood or cedar, and three-fourths the diameter for the dense hardwoods and for such species as Douglas fir. The lead hole for the un-threaded shank of the lag screw should be the same diameter as that of the lag screw.

Bolts are among the most rigid fasteners. They may be used for small connections such as railings-to-posts and for large members when combined with timber connectors. The two types of bolts most commonly used in light-frame construction are the carriage bolt and the machine bolt. When obtainable, the step bolt is preferred over the carriage bolt because of its larger head diameter.

The carriage bolt is normally used without a washer under the head. A squared section at the bolt head resists turning as it is tightened. Washers should always be used under the head of the machine bolt and under the nut of both types. Bolt holes should be the exact diameter of the bolt. When a bolt-fastened member is loaded, such as a beam to a post, the bearing strength of the wood under the bolt is important, as well as the strength of the bolt. A larger-diameter bolt or several smaller-diameter bolts may be used when the softer woods are involved. Crushing of wood under the head of a carriage bolt or under the washer of any bolt should always be avoided. The use of larger washers and a washer under the carriage bolt is advisable when the less dense wood species are used.

Other methods are sometimes used for fastening wood members together or to other materials. These include metal anchors for connecting posts to concrete footings; angle iron and special connectors for fastening posts to beams; joist hangers and metal strapping for fastening joists to beams.

Design considerations will vary, but as a general rule 4x4 posts spaced 6 feet apart will adequately support 4x6 or 4x8 beams on 6-foot centers to a height of 12 feet. For 4x10 or 4x12 beams at the same spacing, a 9-foot height is the maximum for 4x4 posts; over that, use 4x6s. For 6-inch-wide beams, 6x6 posts should be used except for very low decks.

The tables show suggested spans for beams, joists, and deck boards. The figures are intended as general guidelines only, and are based on minimum-strength lumber species (see earlier section).

Suggested Beam Spans

Size	Width of Deck			
	6'	8'	10'	12'
	Maximum Span			
4x6	5'6"	5'0"	4'6"	4'0"
4x8	8'0"	7'0"	6'0"	5'0"
4x10	10'0"	8'6"	7'0"	6'6"
4x12	12'0"	10'6"	9'0"	8'0"
6x10	—	—	11'0"	9'6"
6x12	—	—	12'0"	11'0"

Suggested Joist Spans

Size	Maximum Span
16″ spacing	
2x6	8′0″
2x8	10′0″
2x10	13′0″
24″ spacing	
2x6	7′0″
2x8	8′0″
2x10	10′0″

Size	Maximum Span
1x4	16″
2x4, laid flat	36″
2x6, laid flat	42″
2x3, laid on edge	72″
2x4, laid on edge	120″

Wood Decks

One of the beauties of a wood patio or sun deck is its design flexibility. It can be tailored to the house, it can be tailored to the terrain, it blends in just about anywhere. It can easily be adapted to the activity or degree of formality desired. For all these reasons, it allows the do-it-yourself designer a fairly free hand. Adherence to some basic principles and building techniques will insure a sturdy and long-lasting structure for your family's enjoyment.

2-inch dimension lumber laid on edge (A) allows much greater deck board span than laid flat (B).

B

Wood decks may offer the only means of providing outdoor living areas for steep hillside homes. They are also popular for homes on level ground. Low-level wood decks may be chosen in preference to a paved patio because of wood's nonreflective and resilient qualities. More frequently, the deck is chosen because of its design versatility, its adaptability to varied use, and especially for the rich natural beauty of the wood, which adds charm, style, and livability to the home.

Most low- or high-level decks are attached to the house for access and partial support. Low-level decks can be simply supported on concrete piers or short, closely spaced posts, or sometimes even on the ground itself if it is level enough, thereby simplifying the main horizontal structure. However, drainage can be a problem on low or level ground and provision to insure water runoff should be made before the deck is built. Good drainage not only keeps the ground firm to adequately support the deck but avoids dampness that could encourage decay in posts or sills.

The substructure of hillside decks is designed to provide solid support with a minimum number of members, especially if exposed to view from below. This may require a heavier deck structure and more substantial railings than are needed for low-level decks, but the general rules to insure satisfactory performance are the same.

Design Recommendations

The allowable spans for decking, joists, and beams and the size of posts depend not only on the size, grade, and spacing of the members but also on the wood species. Species such as Douglas fir, southern pine, and western larch allow greater spans than some of the less dense pines, cedars, and redwood, for example. Normally, deck members are designed for about the same load as the floors in a dwelling.

The arrangement of the structural members can vary somewhat because of orientation of the deck, position of the house, slope of the lot, and other such factors. Basically, the beams are supported by the posts (anchored to footings) and in turn support the floor joists. The deck boards are then fastened to the joists. When beams are spaced more closely together, the joist can be eliminated if the deck boards are thick enough to span between the beams. Railings are located around the perimeter of the deck if required for safety (low-level decks are often constructed without edge railings). When the deck is fastened to the house in some manner, it is normally rigid enough to eliminate the need for post bracing. In high, free-standing decks, the use of post bracing is good practice.

Common sizes for wood posts used in supporting beams and floor framing for wood decks are 4x4, 4x6, and 6x6. The size of the post required is based on the span and spacing of the beams, the load, and the height and spacing of the posts.

Site Preparation

Site preparation for construction of a wood deck is often less costly than that for a concrete terrace. When the site is steep, it is difficult to grade and to treat the backslopes in preparing a base for a concrete slab. In grading the site for a wood deck, you need consider only proper drainage, disturbing the natural terrain as little as possible. Grading should be enough to insure water runoff—usually just a minor leveling of the ground.

Often the soil under an open deck with spaced boards will absorb most of a moderate rainfall. If the deck also serves as a roof for a garage, carport, or living area below, drainage should be treated as a part of the house roof drainage, whether by gutters, downspouts, or drip and drain pockets at the ground level. In such cases, some form of drainage may be required to carry water away from the site and prevent erosion. This can usually be accomplished with drain tile laid in a shallow drainage ditch. Tile should be spaced and joints covered with a strip of asphalt felt before the trench is filled. The tile can lead to a dry well or to a drainage field beyond the site. Perforated cement or plastic tile is also available for this use.

There may be a need for control of weed growth beneath the deck. Without some deterrent, such growth can lead to high moisture content of wood members and subsequent decay hazards where decks are near the grade. Common methods for such control consist of the application of a weed killer to the plants or the use of a membrane such as 4- or 6-mil polyethylene or 30-pound asphalt-saturated felt. Such coverings should be placed just before the deck boards are laid. Stones, bricks, or other permanent means of anchoring the membranes in place should be used around the perimeter and in any interior surface variations which may be present. A few holes should be punched in the covering so that not all the rain will run off and cause erosion.

Footings

Some type of footing is required to support the posts or poles which transfer the deck loads to the ground. In simplest form, the bottom of a treated pole and the friction of the earth around the pole provide this support. More commonly, some type of masonry, usually concrete, is used as a footing upon which the poles or posts rest.

Posts or poles must be embedded to a depth which provides sufficient bearing and rigidity for the structure. This may require a depth of 3 to 5 feet or more, depending on the exposed pole heights and applied loads. In areas where frost is a problem, such as the northern states, an embedment depth of 4 feet is commonly minimum. But a lesser depth may be adequate in warmer climates. Check your local building department for recommended depths in your area. Soil should be well tamped around the pile.

Concrete footings below the surface are normally used for treated posts or poles. One type consists of a prepoured footing upon which the wood members rest. Embedment depth should be only enough to provide lateral resistance—usually 2 to 3 feet. The exception is in cold climates where frost may penetrate to a depth of 4 feet or more. Minimum size for concrete footings in normal soils should be 12x12x8 inches. Where spacing of the poles is over 6 feet, 20x20x10 inches or larger sizes are preferred.

Another type of below-grade footing is the poured-in-place type. In such construction, the poles are prealigned, plumbed, and supported above the bottom of the excavated hole. Concrete is then poured below and around the butt at the end of the pole. A minimum thickness of 8 inches of concrete below the bottom of the pole is advisable. Soil may be added above the concrete when necessary for protection in cold weather. Such footings do not require tamped soil around the pole to provide lateral resistance.

Footings or footing extensions for posts which are entirely exposed above grain of the wood with wet concrete to prevent decay or damage to the bottom soil. When the size of the footing is greater than the post size (which is normal) a pedestal-type extension is often used. The bottom of the footing should be located below frost level, which may require a long pier-type pedestal. Bolts, angle irons, or other post anchorage should be placed when pouring.

Post-to-Footing Anchorage

The anchorage of supporting footings with top surfaces above grade is important as they should not only resist lateral movement but also uplift stresses which can occur during periods of high winds. These anchorages

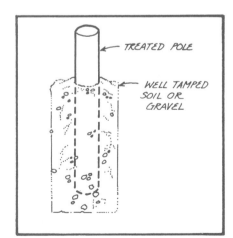

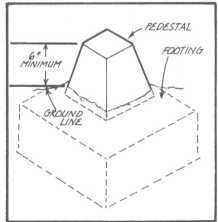

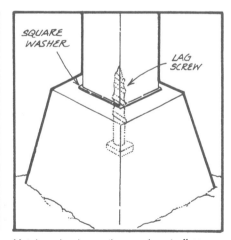

The simplest, and generally least satisfactory, method of supporting a wood deck is to embed a treated pole or post in well-tamped soil or gravel.

The top of an above-ground concrete pedestal foundation should be at least 6 inches above ground level.

Metal washer keeps the wood post off concrete pedestal, preventing decay.

Low-level parquet deck of Douglas fir is supported by posts resting on metal washers to keep the wood away from the concrete pedestals, preventing decay.

should be designed for good drainage and freedom from contact of the end gain of the wood with wet concrete to prevent decay or damage to the bottom of the wood post. It is also important that the post ends be given a dip treatment of water-repellent preservative. As recommended for nails, screws, bolts, and other fastenings, all metal anchors should be galvanized or treated in some manner to resist corrosion.

One system of anchoring small posts uses a galvanized lag screw turned into the bottom of the post with a large square washer (about 3x3x¼-inch thick for a 4x4 post) for a bearing area. The post is then anchored into a grouted predrilled hole or supported in place while concrete is poured. The washer prevents direct contact with the concrete and keeps moisture from wicking into the bottom of the post, and the lag screw head provides some uplift resistance.

An even better anchorage system utilizes a small steel pipe (galvanized or painted) with a pipe flange at each end. (A welded plate or angle iron can be substituted for the pipe flange. The plate or flange-to-post connection should be made with large screws or lag screws. The flange can be fastened to the post bottom and turned in place after the concrete is poured. When an angle iron is used, the entire assembly is poured in place.

Another type of anchor is the step-flange, which is positioned while the concrete is being poured. It should be located so that the bottom of the post is about 2 inches above the concrete.

Still another type of anchor for solid posts consists of a heavy metal strap shaped in the form of a U, with or without a bearing plate welded between. These anchors are placed as the concrete pier or slab is being poured. The post is then held in place with bolts.

Step-flange anchor is placed while concrete is being formed. The post is later bolted in position.

Beam-to-Post Connection

Beams are members to which the floor boards are directly fastened or which support a system of joists. They are fastened to the supporting posts. Beams may be single large members or consist of two smaller members fastened to each side of the posts. When a solid deck is to be constructed, the beams should be sloped at least 1 inch in, 8 to 10 feet away from the house.

Single beams when 4 inches or wider usually rest on the posts. When this system is used, the posts must be trimmed evenly so that the beam bears on all posts. Use a level and straightedge to establish this alignment.

One method of fastening a beam to a post is by the use of a 1x4 lumber or plywood (exterior grade) cleat located on two sides of the post. Cleats are nailed to the beam and post with 8d nails.

This redwood garden gazebo is built with posts and beams, following the same techniques as are used for building wood decks.

Another example of post-and-beam construction is this poolside cabana/guest house. Beams are anchored to posts by flanking trim boards.

Metal flange visible is connector between extended deck-support post and overhead beam is the same type as those used for floor beams.

Another good method of post-to-beam connection is the use of a metal angle at each side. A 3x3-inch or larger angle should be used so that lag screws can be turned in easily. A metal strap fastened to the beam and the post might also be used for single beams. A ⅛x3-inch or larger strap, preformed to insure a good fit, will provide an adequate connection. Use 10d nails for the smaller members and ¼-inch lag screws for the larger members.

For smaller posts and beams, a sheet-metal flange, which is formed to provide fastening surfaces to both beam and post, is a good connector. The flange is normally fastened with 8d nails. To prevent splitting, nails should not be located too close to the end of the post.

When a double post is used, such as two 2x6s, a single beam is usually placed between them. Fastening is with bolts or lag screws. Cleats over the ends of the posts provide end-grain protection.

Double or split beams are normally bolted to the top ends of the posts, one on each side. Notching the top of the post provides greater load capacity. A

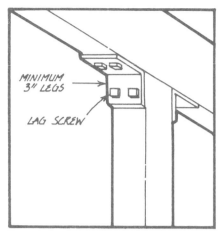

Beam-to-post fastening with metal angles.

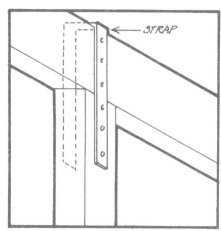

Beam-to-post fastening with a metal strap.

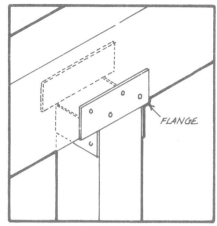

Sheet-metal flange fasteners can be used to connect smaller-dimension posts and beams.

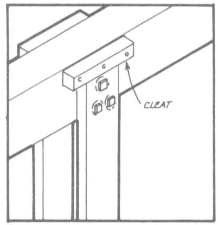

Cleats provide end-grain protection for double posts bolted to a beam.

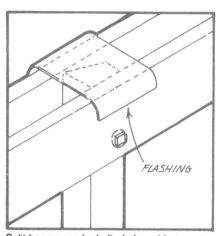

Split beams can be bolted alongside a post; asphalt felt or flashing protects the post end.

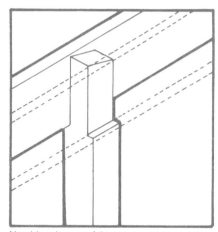

Notching the top of the post provides greater capacity for carrying split beams.

piece of asphalt felt or a metal flashing over the joint will provide protection for the post end.

Sometimes the post which supports the beam also serves as a railing post. Here, the beam is bolted to the post which extends above the deck to support the railing members.

Beam- and Joist-to-House Connection

When the deck is adjacent to the house, some method of connecting beams or joists to the house is required. This is done by use of metal hangers, wood ledgers, or angle irons. In some cases, you can utilize the top of the masonry foundation or basement wall. It is usually good practice to design the deck so that the top of the deck boards are just under the sill of the door leading to the deck. This will provide protection from rain as well as easy access to the deck.

Metal beam hangers may be fastened directly to a floor-framing member such as a joist header, or to a 2x8 or 2x10 which has been bolted or lag screwed to the house framing. Use 8d or longer nails or the short, large-diameter nails often furnished with commercial hangers. Hangers are available for all beams up to 6x14.

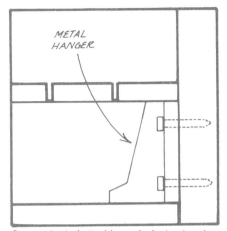

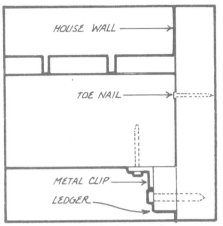

One method of attaching a deck structure to the house is with metal hangers tying beams or joists into a 2x8 or 2x10 lagged to the house.

A ledger fastened to the house wall can support the deck framing members; metal clips or angles strengthen the connection.

Beams can also be secured to the house proper by bearing on ledgers which have been anchored to the floor framing or to the masonry wall with expansion shields and lag screws. The beam should be fastened to the ledger or to the house with a framing anchor or a small metal angle.

When deck joists are perpendicular to the side or end of the house, they are connected in much the same manner as beams except that fasteners are smaller. A ledger can be lag-screwed to the house. Joists are toenailed to the ledger and the house or fastened with small metal clips. Another method of fastening joists is to lag a 2x8 or 2x10 to the house, then use metal joist hangers.

Bracing

On uneven sites or sloping lots, where posts may be several feet high, it may be necessary to use bracing between the posts for lateral strength. On a free-standing deck, bracing should be used on each side to provide racking resistance. When brace length is no greater than 8 feet, 2x4s can be used; 2x6 braces should be used when lengths are over 8 feet. Fastenings should normally consist of lag screws or bolts (with washers) to fasten 2-inch braces to the posts.

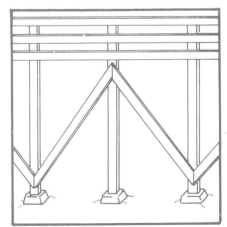

The "W" system of bracing.

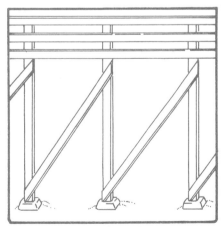

Another effective bracing system.

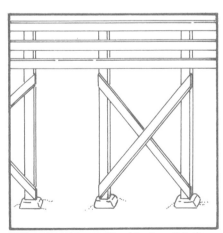

"X" bracing adds considerable strength to the structure.

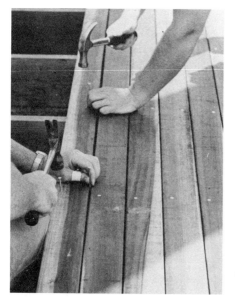

Deck boards should be spaced at least ⅛-inch apart to allow drainage. Good nailing practice calls for two nails at each joist.

One simple system of single bracing is the "W." Members are lag-screwed to the post and joined along the center line. Another single bracing method has members located from the base of one post to the top of the adjacent posts. Braces on the adjacent side of the deck should be placed in the opposite direction.

Another system of bracing used between posts is the "X" or cross brace. When spans and heights of posts are considerable, a cross brace can be used at each bay. However, bracing at alternate bays is normally sufficient. Bolting the braces together where they cross further stabilizes the bay.

For posts of a moderate height (5 to 7 feet) a plywood gusset or one made of short lengths of nominal 2-inch lumber can be used as a partial brace. A plywood gusset on each side of a post can also serve as a means of connection between a post and a beam. Use ¾-inch exterior-type plywood and fasten to the post and beam with two rows of 10d nails. The top edge of the gusset should be protected by an edge or header which extends over the plywood.

A partial brace of 2x4 lumber can be secured to the beam and posts with lag screws or bolts. Some member of the deck, such as a deck board or a parallel edge member, can overlap the upper ends to protect the end grain from moisture. When an overlap member is not available and the area is sufficient for two fasteners, a vertical cut can be used for the brace.

Joist-to-Beam Connections

When beams are spaced 2 to 4 feet apart and 2x4 Douglas fir or similar deck boards are used, there is no need to have support members for the deck boards. However, if the spans between beams are more than 4 feet, it is necessary to use joists between the beams or 2x3 or 2x4 on edge for decking.

Joists bearing directly on a beam may be toenailed with two 10d nails on each side. In high wind areas, supplementary metal strapping might be used in addition to the toenailing. Use 24- to 26-gauge galvanized strapping and nail with 1-inch galvanized roofing nails. When a header is used at the joist ends, nail the header into the end of each joist. Have the header overhang the beam by ½-inch to provide a drip edge.

Joists located between beams and flush with their tops may rest on 2x3 or 2x4 ledgers nailed to the beams; the joists are toenailed at each end. The joint can be improved by the use of small metal clips.

Another method utilizes a metal joist hanger. The hanger is first nailed to the end of the joist with 1- to 1¼-inch galvanized roofing nails and then to the beam. Several types of joist hangers are available.

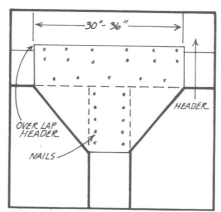

A plywood gusset strengthens the beam-post connection and also helps brace the structure.

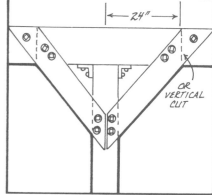

Lumber brace works on posts of moderate height, but provision should be made for protecting the end grain of brace pieces.

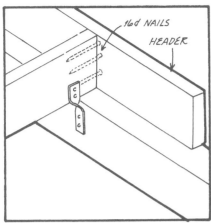

When a header joist is used, it should be nailed into the end of each joist.

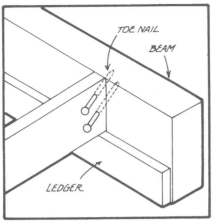

Joists between beams can be supported by ledgers nailed to the beams.

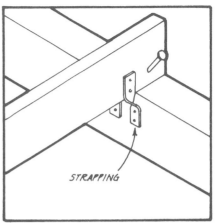

Joists may be toenailed to tops of beams; metal strapping strengthens the connection.

Fastening Deck Boards

Deck boards are fastened to floor joists or to beams through their face with nails or screws. Screws are more costly and time-consuming to use than nails but have greater resistance to loosening or withdrawal than nails. Both nails and screws should be set flush or just below the surface of the deck board.

Use two fasteners per joist for 2x3 and 2x4 decking laid flat. For 2x3s or 2x4s on edge, use one fastener per joist.

Space all deck boards (flat or vertical) ⅛- to ¼-inch apart (use 8d or 10d nails for ⅛-inch spacing). When deck boards are used on edge, spacers between runs will aid in maintaining uniform spacing. Spacers are recommended between supports when spans exceed 4 feet. An elastomeric adhesive on both faces of each spacer will prevent water retention in the joints.

Fastening Plywood

Plywood panels should generally be installed with a minimum $1/16$-inch space between edge and end joints. When caulking is used, a joint space of at least ¼-inch is usually required.

To avoid unnecessary moisture absorption by the plywood, seal all panel edges with an exterior primer or an aluminum paint formulated for wood. The panel edge sealant can be most conveniently applied prior to installation, while the plywood is still in stacks. Build some slope into the deck area to provide adequate drainage. A minimum slope of 1 inch in 8 to 10 feet should be provided when installing the joists or beams.

Provide ventilation for the underside of the deck area. For low-level decks, this can be done by leaving the space between the joists open at the ends and by excavating material away from the support joists and beams. For high-level decks over enclosed areas, holes can be drilled in the blocking between joists.

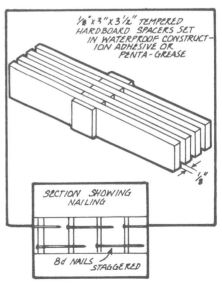

Spacers between deck boards laid on edge maintain uniformity, make nailing easier, and add strength to the structure.

Railing Posts

Low-level decks located just above grade normally require no railings. However, if the site is sloped, some type of protective railing or system of balusters might be needed, because of the height of the deck.

The key members of a railing are posts. They must be large enough and securely fastened to give strength to the railing. One method of providing posts for the railing is by the extension of the posts which support the beams.

Railing heights may vary between 30 and 40 inches, or higher when a bench

Post railings on this deck of garden-grade redwood are bolted sturdily to the end header of the framing.

Baluster-type railing provides protection around the edge of this deck.

or wind screen is involved. Posts should be spaced no more than 6 feet apart for a 2x4 horizontal top rail and 8 feet apart when a 2x6 or larger rail is used.

When supporting posts cannot be extended above the deck, a joist or beam may be available to which the posts can be secured. Such posts can be made from 2x6s for spans less than 4 feet, from 4x4s or 2x8s for 4- to 6-foot spans, and from 2x6s or 3x8s for 6- to 8-foot spans. Each post should be bolted to the edge beam with two ⅜-inch or larger bolts, determined by the size of the post. This system can also be used when the railing consists of a number of 2x2 or 2x3 baluster-type posts spaced 12 to 16 inches apart. The top fastener into the beam should be a ¼- or ⅜-inch bolt or lag screw. The bottom fastener can then be a 12d or larger nail. Predrill when necessary to prevent splitting. Wider spacings or larger-size posts require two bolts. A ⅛-inch to ¼-inch space should be allowed between the ends of floor boards and posts.

The ends of beams or joists along the edge of the deck can also be used to fasten the railing posts. Single or double (one on each side) posts are bolted to the ends of the joists or beams. Space the bolts as far apart as is practical.

Avoid mounting posts on a deck board. Not only will the railing be structurally weak, but the bottom of the posts will have end-grain contact with a flat

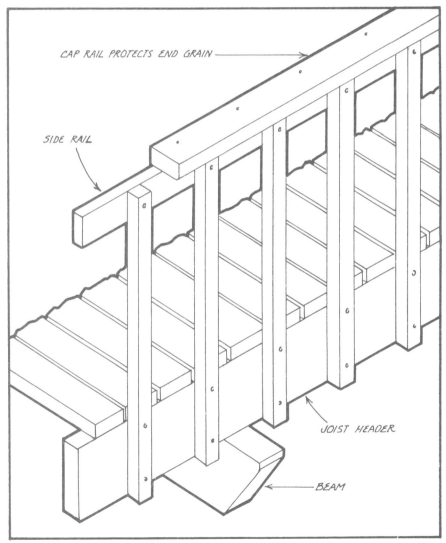

In this design, a side rail ties the balusters together at top, while a cap rail protects the end grain from excessive moisture absorption. Balusters are bolted to a header.

Railing is of 2x4 Douglas fir with 2x6 cap. Note absence of corner post.

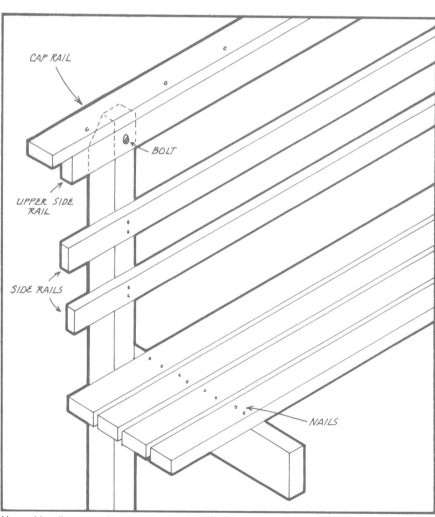

Here, side rails are used over supporting posts.

Side rails tie the railing posts together, while a redwood cap keeps out moisture.

surface. This could become a water trap and induce quick decay.

Often, a built-in bench is included around the perimeter of a deck, combining utility with protection. Railing posts are generally used to support the bench as well. In this case, the posts should be no more than 6 feet apart. Horizontal supports (usually 2x4s) are then bolted to the posts and a front vertical support (another 2x4); or a frame of 2x3s or 2x4s can be built to support the bench, and secured to posts or beams. The bench seat is made of the same lumber as the deck, set either flat or on edge, and fastened in the same manner as the deck boards.

Intermediate rails are nailed to the posts with a minimum of two nails into each post. A cap rail across the top of the posts protects the end grain.

Surrounding this deck of western wood, doubled main posts are supplemented by intermediate supports for the railing.

Stairway between upper and middle levels of this multilevel deck is supported by notched stringers of decay-resistant lumber.

Sometimes, a system of balusters may be preferred to a rail system. Posts are still needed to provide the main structural support. Balusters should be bolted to a beam or joist, using two bolts as widely spaced as possible. A rail is bolted across the top of the balusters to tie them all securely together. A cap rail is then nailed on to protect the end grain of balusters and posts.

Stairways

Often, a stairway must be built for access to a deck, or for use between decks at different levels. Exterior stairs are much the same as those within the house, except for the need to avoid moisture traps or exposed end grain of the wood.

The supporting members of a stairway are the stringers. These are usually 2x10s or 2x12s used in pairs not more than 3 feet apart. Stringers must be well secured to the deck framing. They are normally supported by a ledger or by the extension of a joist or beam. A 2x3 or 2x4 ledger can be nailed to the bottom of a framing member with 12d nails, then the stringers are notched to fit over the ledger. Toenailing or metal clips secure the stringers. If joists or beams are appropriately spaced, the stringers can be bolted to these structural members.

The lower ends of the stringers should be anchored to a solid base and isolated from any moisture source. If they are leading from one deck to another, normal wood-fastening methods are used. If the stairway leads to the

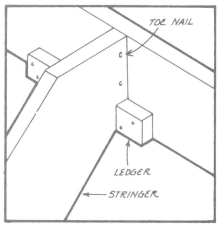
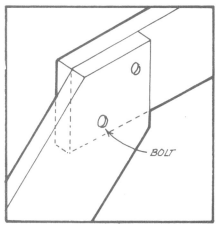
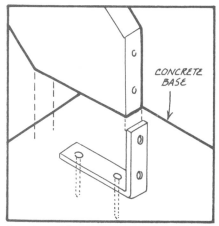

Two methods of attaching stair stringers to deck framing.

Securing a stringer to a concrete base. Metal angle should be thick enough to keep the wood from the concrete.

ground, a concrete footing should be provided, sloped for drainage, and each stringer anchored by metal angles thick enough to raise the wood off the concrete.

The relation of the tread (step) width to the rise (height) is important for both safety's sake and in determining the number of steps required. For ease of ascent, the rise of each step in inches multiplied by the width of the tread in inches should equal 72 to 75 inches. For example, if the rise is 8 inches (considered the maximum allowable), the tread would be 9 inches. Or if the rise is 7½ inches, the tread would be about 10 inches.

With this formula, you can determine the number and size of treads when the total height of the stair is known. Say that your deck is 6 feet 3 inches off the ground (75 inches). That works out neatly to a 7½-inch rise and 10 10-inch

Stairway leads from deck of garden-grade redwood to back yard. Treads are supported by cleats fastened to stringers.

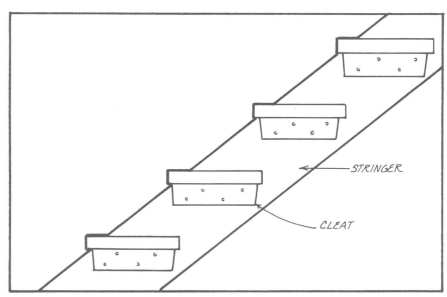

Tread-support cleats are fastened to the stringers with 8d nails.

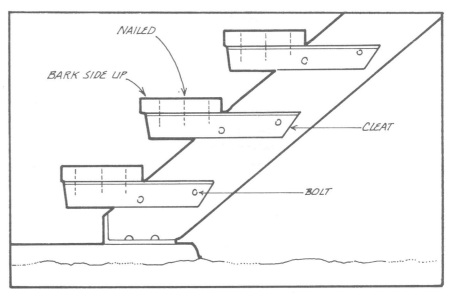

Ledgers bolted to the cleats are extended to support the treads in this design.

treads. The total run (the horizontal distance covered by the stairway) would thus be 100 inches (10 times the 10-inch treads).

Stair treads are often supported by dadoes, or notches, cut into the stringers. However, both these methods expose end grain and create water traps and should be avoided unless highly decay-resistant woods are used.

An alternate method of tread support is to nail 2x3 or 2x4 cleats to the stringers, then nail the treads to the cleats. An even better method in terms of avoiding water traps is to bolt 2x4 ledgers to the stringers and extend them to provide tread supports. The ledgers should be sloped back slightly so that the rain will drain off.

On high stairways with one or both sides unprotected, some type of railing is advisable. Railings for stairs are constructed much the same as deck railings—in fact, for the sake of appearance, they should be of the same design.

Other Structures

Fences and wind screens are frequently built of wood, but because of their unique design and purpose, a separate section is devoted to these later in this book.

Smaller projects such as a doghouse, storage shed, or garbage can garage may be built on the ground with no foundation, often of plywood, with or without corner bracing of lumber. Several such projects are shown in later pages.

Larger structures—a garden gazebo, a playhouse, a carport—may be built using the same post-and-beam techniques as for wood decks. Sheathing, lattice work, or whatever is applied to the sides of the posts to close in the structure, and a roof constructed as described in the section on patio shelters.

Another method of building enclosed structures is with platform framing—the same as is used for a frame house. The framing members are sole plates, top plates, studs (the vertical members), headers or lintels over openings, joists and rafters. The framing is assembled on the ground (or on a deck, if that is what you are enclosing), then lifted into place and secured. For most outdoor structures, the framing will be fastened to anchor bolts set into a concrete or masonry foundation, as described in an earlier section. If it is being built on a deck, it can be nailed in place through the deck boards to the joists or beams beneath.

For most buildings, 2x4s are used for plates and studs. (Very small structures can be built with 2x3 framing.) Cut sole and top plates the length of the wall you are building and lay them side by side on a flat surface. Use a framing square to lay out the positions of the studs. This handy tool has one side 16 inches long (the tongue), the other 24 inches long (the body). By happy coincidence, studs are normally spaced 16 inches center to center, or sometimes 24 inches center to center (check your local building code as to the allowability of the wider spacing). The tongue of the square also happens to be just 1½ inches wide—the thickness of a 2x4.

With a sharp pencil and the square, mark the location of the corner stud across both plates. Mark an "X" next to the line where the stud will be placed. Place the tongue or body of the square, depending on stud spacing, alongside one of the plates, with its end protruding ¾-inch beyond the ends of the plates. Mark a line across the plates, then an "X" to indicate stud location. Now move the square so that its end is aligned with the line and again mark ahead of the square. Continue marking like this until all stud locations are marked. Keep your pencil sharp! A slight error due to a dull pencil point will be compounded along the length of the wall and throw your calculations off, so that when it comes time to put on sheathing, nothing will fit and you'll be puzzling as to the cause while you try to set things right.

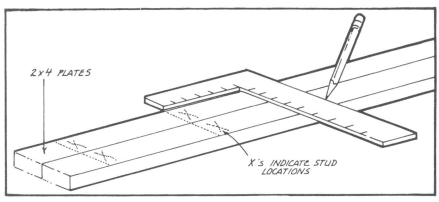

2x4 PLATES

X's INDICATE STUD LOCATIONS

Using the framing square to mark stud locations on sole and top plates.

Where door or window openings occur, the regular stud spacing may be interrupted, but it should be continued on the other side. Studs must be placed 5 inches outside the width of the projected door or window.

The final stud will be at the other corner, regardless of the spacing. Cut the studs 4½ inches less than the rough height of the wall (allow for ceiling- and floor-covering materials, if these are part of the project). Set the two plates on edge with the pencil marks facing inward, and place a corner stud between them. Nail through the plates into the stud, using two 16d nails. Place another stud between the plates, making sure it is aligned with and on the "X" side of the line, and nail. Continue until all studs are fastened.

At door and window openings, headers or lintels must be provided above the openings to support the weight of the structure overhead. These are made by nailing two pieces of lumber together with ½-inch spacers of plywood or lumber sandwiched between to make the header the full width of the wall. Most door and window openings require headers made of 2x6s. Wider openings will require 2x8s, 2x10s, or 2x12s. The headers are set on edge between the flanking studs and fastened with 16d nails driven through the studs. For door openings, short studs are nailed to the flanking studs between the sole plate and the header. Do not cut the sole plate in the door opening. For windows, a 2x4 sill is nailed across the bottom of the opening. Short studs are then nailed between the sill and the sole plate and the sill and the header. Finally, short studs are nailed at the regular intervals between the header and the top plate, and, in the case of a window, between the sole plate and the sill.

Additional framing will depend on what you are building. For example, if the interior of the structure is to be finished off, backing will have to be provided for wallboard or paneling at corners.

When all the walls are built, drill holes through the bottom plates for anchor bolts, if they are to be set on a concrete or masonry foundation. Lift the wall into position (four hands are definitely better than two at this stage, and six may be needed for long walls). Place washers over the anchor bolts and tighten down nuts—or nail through the plates into the beams or joists on a wood deck

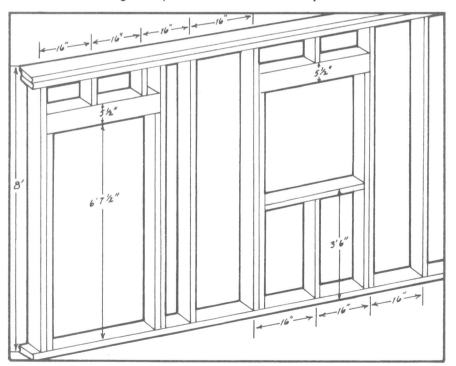

Door and window framing.

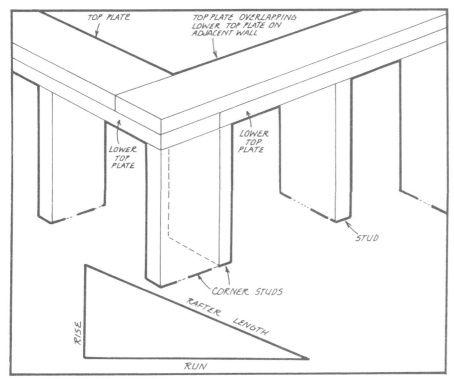

Top plates tie walls together at the corners. Run and rise are used to determine rafter length.

project. Level the wall and support it temporarily with wood braces staked to the ground. Set the adjacent wall in place, nailing through one corner post into the other. When all walls are in position, carefully check for plumb with the level. Cut top plates so that they overlap in the corners and nail to the lower top plate, effectively tying the structure together. Now you can cut the sole plates at door openings.

Joists and/or rafters are toenailed to the top of the wall framing. There is a wide variety of roof designs: flat, shed, gable, hip, to mention only the most common. Laying out roof framing (except for a flat roof) is basically an exercise in mathematics. As an example, consider a roof with a 4-12 pitch, which is fairly common for one-floor structures. This means that the rafters rise 4 inches for every 12 inches of run (the horizontal distance covered by the rafters). The rise and the run are two legs of a right triangle. The third and longest leg, the hypotenuse as you called it in sophomore geometry, is the length of the rafter. When you know the run and the rise, you can just apply the old $a^2 + b^2 = c^2$ formula to determine rafter length. For a roof with a 12-foot run and a 4-foot rise, rafter length would be just over 12 feet, 7¾ inches. We think.

But take heart, fellow math dropouts. There is a much easier way, called the roofing square. It looks like the framing square, but on both sides it is marked with a series of tables and scales that do the figuring for you. When you know the run and the rise of the roof (again, say 4-12), simply lay a straightedge across the square with one end intersecting the 4 mark and the other the 12 mark. Presto! The answer is there.

A ridge board is provided for nailing and stability where rafters meet at the peak of the roof. You will need help getting the end rafters in place against the ridge. Make sure that everything is plumb and square. Erect the rafters at both ends of the roof, then some intermediate rafters to hold the ridge straight. Then fill in with the remaining rafters.

With the framing in place, cover the walls and roof with plywood or lumber sheathing, or whatever else is planned for the structure.

Wholly or partially covering at least a portion of your outdoor living area will allow you many more hours of fresh-air fun.

Openwork covering has just a small roofed area to provide shelter from the midday sun.

Building & Installation Techniques:
PATIO ROOFS

Post-and-beam construction is most commonly used for patio covers. Here, post is anchored securely to its footing.

One method of securing beams to posts is with metal T-braces bolted to both members.

If your family is really committed to at-home outdoor living, you will almost surely want to have some sort of roof over at least part of your outdoor living area. In a region where frequent or even daily rainfall is as much a part of the warm-weather climate as is sunshine, the reason for a roof is obvious. But, no matter how much a sun-worshipper you may be, too much exposure to Old Sol will cut down on patio use too, unless your outdoor living room is built on the shady side of the street (or house).

Where sun, rather than rain, is the deterrent to all-day outdoor enjoyment, a simple openwork or lattice patio cover might provide enough shade to solve the problem. It can be designed to cast pleasing shadows on the deck or terrace, or climbing vines can be trained onto the roof members which, when grown, will provide cool leafy shelter beneath. On the other hand, where sometimes harsh breezes can be a discomfort, you may want to build not only a solid roof but one, two, or even three walls on your outdoor living room. Whatever your patio-covering needs may be, make sure that the structure is in harmony with the other materials of the deck or terrace, and with the house itself, whether attached to or remote from it.

The Basic Structure

Post-and-beam construction is favored for most types of patio covers. The basic structural techniques—setting the posts, fastening beams, bracing—are the same as those described in the earlier chapter on wood. Remember that open end grain, particularly of posts, must be kept from exposure as much as possible to guard against decay.

Small entry terrace is protected from the elements by a roof of translucent plastic.

Cantilevered redwood structure provides protection from the sun by overhead bamboo slats, from harsh breezes by canvas panels in the back.

Arched, airy enclosure of garden-grade redwood creates treeless shading for people and plants outside this home in the southern California desert.

Posts of 4x4 western wood support the roof framework of 2x6s and 2x4s; roof and walls are 1x2 slats, spaced to admit air but still providing shade.

Variation on a theme; here the slats are fastened to the bottoms of the redwood beams.

Rustic trellis-type roof extends beyond the edge of the patio over the pool.

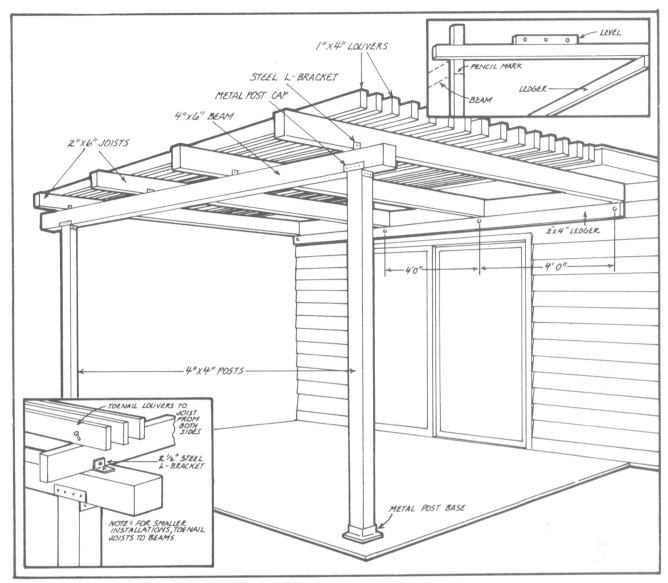

Typical construction details for a shade screen over a small terrace.

Openwork Covering

An openwork patio covering is usually (although not necessarily) flat. Lumber is simply nailed at intervals across the beams, or from a ledger attached to the house wall to the beam of the outer patio wall. Or joists can be fastened to the beams, and slats or louvers nailed across the joists. The size of lumber and spacing of the intervals will depend on the effect you wish to create and the span to be covered. For a relatively narrow deck or terrace roof, you might use 1x2s or 1x3s on edge, spaced the width of a single piece (¾-inch) apart. Short spacer blocks of the same size lumber placed between them at the beams will keep them perfectly aligned.

Over a larger span, 2-inch lumber should be used—2x3, 2x4, 2x6, or even 2x8—set on edge, usually with minimum spacing of 1½ inches (again, the width of the lumber). The spacing can be increased, according to your design, to as much as 24 or 30 inches, depending on the lumber dimensions. Use galvanized or aluminum nails or screws for all fastening.

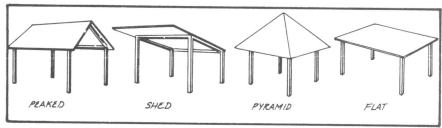

Possible shapes for patio roofs; peaked and shed are preferred for free-standing units.

Conventional

A conventional roof can also be built over post-and-beam framing, with some variations. While a flat roof can be built, a pitch of at least ¼-inch per foot is preferable. If the roof is built against the house, the slope will, of course, be away from the existing structure. If the patio roof is free-standing, the roof may either peak in the center or be pitched in only one direction, as a shed roof.

Unless the structure is quite narrow, rafters will have to be fastened between the beams or the beam and the ledger on the house. These can be spaced on 24-inch centers; their dimensions (2x4, 2x6, 2x8) will depend on the span to be covered. Generally speaking, 2x4 rafters of southern pine or Douglas fir can span up to 6 feet, 2x6s of the same species up to 9 feet, and 2x8s up to 12 feet.

Nail plywood or tongue-and-groove sheathing across the tops of the rafters. If, as is likely, you will be leaving the underside of the sheathing exposed, you may prefer the latter for appearance's sake. Boards which are $5/4$x4 are thick enough to take 1-inch roofing nails without the ends poking through, and can be stained or painted to make a handsome patio ceiling.

Conventional roof of western wood shelters this deck from sudden rainfalls.

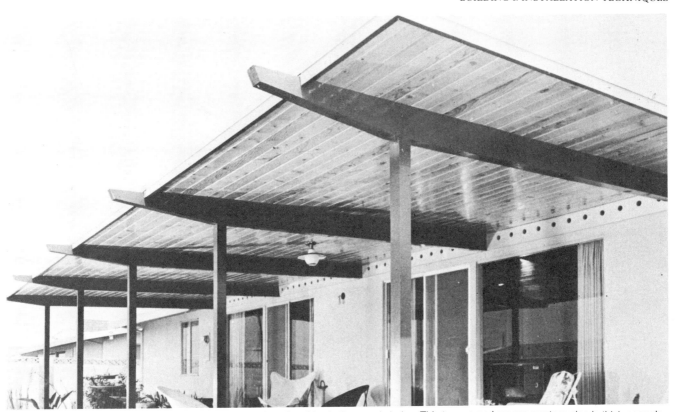

When the underside of a solid roof is to be exposed, lumber sheathing is the usual choice. This tongue-and-groove western pine is thick enough so that roofing nails do not penetrate and is a decorative asset as well.

Entry pergola of post-and-beam construction provides partial shelter and helps integrate house with its site; note rafters mingling with the treetops.

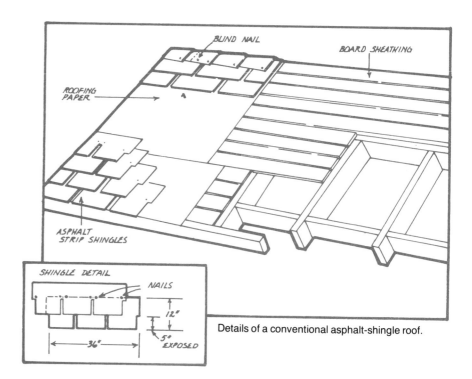

Details of a conventional asphalt-shingle roof.

Asphalt Shingles

Roofing on the patio covering should match that on the existing house roof as closely as possible. Asphalt shingles are the most likely choice. These come in a variety of shapes; the most common is the three-tab, square-butt strip shingle, measuring 12 x 36 inches. One bundle contains 27 strips, enough to cover approximately 33⅓ square feet.

Put an underlay of 15-pound asphalt-saturated felt over the roof sheathing. Lay the first piece (it comes in 36-inch-wide rolls) along the outer edge of the roof, stapling it in place. Lay the second piece overlapping the first by 4 inches, and continue in this fashion up the roof. If it is a peaked roof, cut an 18-inch-wide strip to fold over the top ridge.

Nail a starter course of shingles along the outer edge of the roof, overhanging the sheathing by about ½-inch. Shingles can be cut as necessary with a sharp knife. Nail a second course of shingles directly over the first, but with the slots offset half the width of a shingle tab. Follow manufacturer's recommended nailing procedures; normally, six nails are used for each strip, one at each end and two flanking each slot, all in a line about ¾-inch above the slots.

The second course of shingles is offset from the first—that is, the slots of the second course should fall in the middle of the tabs of the first course. Normal shingle exposure is 5 inches. Each upper course covers the nails in the one below, making a watertight surface. Keep the courses straight by aligning the shingle tabs with the slots in the course beneath.

For a peaked roof, ridge shingles are nailed over the top course on each side. If the new roof is butted against the house wall, install plastic or metal flashing under the siding and over the top course of shingles to make a watertight joint.

Wood Shingles

Wood roof shingles are often used for outdoor living structures because of their rustic appearance, although they are more expensive than the asphalt variety. They are generally available in lengths from 16 to 24 inches; 16-inch are normally laid with 5-inch exposure, 24-inch with 7½-inch exposure, in-between sizes are laid accordingly. The shingles are often dipped in stain before they are laid, both for appearance and as a decay-resistant measure.

As with their asphalt counterparts, the first course of wood shingles is doubled. Joints should be staggered so that each joint is at least 2 inches from the joint in the course above. Shingles should be spaced from ⅛- to ¼-inch apart to allow for expansion in wet weather. They should project from ½- to ¾-inch beyond the eaves at all sides. Each shingle should be fastened with at least two nails driven about ⅝-inch from the edges and about 2 inches above the butt line of the next course.

With the first course in place, snap a chalk line across the shingles as a guide for the next course. Proceed up the roof in this manner. Wood shingles are best cut for fitting with a roofer's hatchet. Simply split the shingle and trim as necessary with the cutting edge; then turn the hatchet around and use the hammer head to nail the shingle in place.

The ridge of a wood shingle roof is usually capped with metal bent to conform to the roof contour. 1x6 lumber can also be used, with caulking applied at the joint to seal it against the weather.

Shelter for this small deck is built of Douglas fir with conventionally framed roof.

Translucent

You can keep out the rain but let the sun shine in by building a roof of translucent, fiberglass-reinforced plastic (known as FRP). When it was first introduced twenty-five or so years ago, this material quickly acquired a bad reputation for uneven coloring and fading, but it has come a long way since then. It is lighter than plywood, yet stronger than steel. It can be sawed, drilled, and nailed like wood. It comes in a rainbow of colors and even in multicolored, striped patterns. If built-in color, light transmission, and ease of handling and construction are important to you, you should definitely consider FRP for your patio roof. On the other hand, if you are seeking to preserve a colonial or rustic appearance around your house, you will be better off with a conventional roof. FRP is definitely a modern-looking material.

Stick to regular roofing, too, if you're planning a patio roof in a "mountain fire district." Building codes usually require "noncombustible" materials in such areas. The same holds true if you're planning to fully enclose a patio or porch. Code officials consider an enclosed area to be an addition to the dwelling area, making the roof subject to the same regulations that apply to the house roof.

FRP panels will burn at about the same rate as wood of similar thickness. It takes a direct flame to ignite the panels (a lighted cigarette or a small ember won't do it) but, once lit, they will burn fairly rapidly. Just as with wood, you wouldn't (or shouldn't) start a roaring fire in a barbecue if the flames could come near the patio roof. And, if you're planning to cut a hole in an FRP-panel roof to permit passage of a metal chimney stack, you should use insulation between the metal and the panels. The stack should, of course, be equipped with a good spark arrester.

Some other factors enter into the FRP-panel decision: because it's rotproof and virtually verminproof, it can be installed in the earth, or be in constant contact with it, and no preservatives are needed. An FRP wind screen, for example, can be both simpler to erect and a "good neighbor" gesture as well; it

Fiberglass-reinforced plastic panels for patio roof construction come in ribbed or corrugated configurations.

FRP panels come in a wide variety of colors and patterns, such as the striped design over this terrace.

won't cut off light from plantings on either side, and it will offer privacy to both sides of the plot line.

There is one other aspect to consider, with both advantages and drawbacks: In overhead applications, the same light-admitting feature that is FRP's greatest attraction also produces a need to keep the panels cleaner than you would completely opaque materials. Accumlations of dirt, dead leaves, and other debris will show up as unsightly shadows below, and, even more important, can hasten the day when the panels will need refinishing with a clear acrylic liquid. On the other hand, keeping the panels relatively clean is simply a matter of rinsing them with a garden hose a few times a year.

FRP panels come in a variety of shapes, weights, and colors. There are flat sheets, corrugated panels, and rib-shaped panels. Flat sheets of equal weight are as strong as the other two and much more flexible, but more difficult to make watertight. They are more suited, therefore, to vertical uses (fences, partitions, dividers), where they do not need to span more than 18 to 24 inches in width or height. The choice between the curved or wavy corrugated shape and the crisper, angular ribbed shape is mainly one of aesthetics and often what's available at your dealer. (Check manufacturer's catalogs as well as dealers' stock—the varieties that are offered are almost endless, and can be ordered if they are not on hand.)

Weight is expressed in ounces per square foot of panel. For residential construction, this is usually 4 or 5 ounces per square foot, although dealers in heavy snow areas also usually stock 6-ounce panels, and sometimes 8-ounce. "Economy grade" panels may be called "4-ounce weight" but chances are they'll be as much as 20 to 25 percent lighter. These are not recommended for load-bearing applications. Which weight is best for your roof depends on how much support structure you're planning to build. On a typical patio roof, a 5-ounce panel (corrugated or ribbed) needs purlins spaced 3 feet on center. A 6-ounce panel will cost about 20 percent more, but its purlin requirements are 4 feet on center for the same load-bearing capacity. In terms of cost, then, it's about an even trade-off. The 5-ounce panel has a slight edge in that it offers the widest choice of shapes, colors, and patterns.

Colors and patterns are far more varied than the boring choice of white, green, or yellow you'll find in most retail stocks, and therefore, on most patio roofs. The more enlightened retailers will also offer some of the striped patterns that have become popular in recent years. These are usually based on a white background, with bold passes of earth tones or brighter "sun-and-sky" colors for contrast. All blend well with the outdoors, and the choices include color patterns that can match or set off almost any home exterior. They are also made with much deeper background colors to reduce the transmission of solar energy; the striping here is merely accent bars of black.

Besides personal choice, the matter of color is directly related to comfort or discomfort under a patio or porch roof made with FRP panels. The color of the panel will change the color of light coming through, and the density of pigment will determine the transmission of total solar energy converted to heat energy. So while dark green might strike you as a cool-looking color, a panel in that shade can be made with relatively little pigment, meaning that a great deal of solar energy will pass through. And dark green light may not be too complimentary to skin tones or to the appearance of a steak.

This is probably the reason why white is by far the most popular FRP panel color among do-it-yourselfers. It transmits a considerable amount of light—without changing the color of the light—and the density of pigment required for a good-looking white panel virtually assures a comfortable level of transmitted solar energy.

Sizes for residential construction are pretty much standardized. Both the corrugated and ribbed shapes, solid or striped, are most generally available in 26-inch width, in lengths of 8, 10, and 12 feet. The standard width allows placement on rafters spaced on 24-inch centers with a 2-inch overlap. Longer lengths can be special-ordered—up to about 39 feet—but delivery times may be long.

Be cautious about extreme bargains in FRP panels. Reputable brands conform to fairly tight standards published by the National Bureau of Standards, but compliance is voluntary rather than mandatory. A very low price may indicate that the batch of panels being offered has nothing more wrong than visual blemishes that will not affect structural strength. On the other hand, they may have been manufactured with little or no regard for durability. A homeowner can't perform the elaborate tests required to determine panel quality, but there are a few hallmarks that provide a fair degree of assurance: Does each panel carry a label, giving at least the manufacturer's name and address? Does the label state the weight per square foot? Does it note conformance with the government's Product Standard? Does the dealer have instruction brochures from the same manufacturer? The more "yes" answers you find, the more you can be sure that you're buying an investment, rather than a headache.

Building with FRP panels is relatively simple. The wood understructure is generally of post-and-beam construction, quite similar to that described for wood decks in an earlier chapter. It must be planned to accommodate available sizes and the load-bearing capacity of the particular panel you'll be using. Rafters should be spaced 24 inches o.c. for 26-inch-wide corrugated or ribbed panels. While the panels derive their rigidity from the supporting members that run across the corrugations or ribs (purlins or girts), the rafter spacing provides overall structural integrity, while also serving to obscure the panel lap joint. As noted previously, spacing of cross supports depends on the panel weight per square foot. But there's another factor too: the depth of the panel's shape. In

Rafters are fitted on beams to support the FRP panels.

the case of panels sold for residential use, recommended spacings for roof purlins are: for economy grades—24 to 28 inches; for true 4-ounce weights—30 inches; for 5-ounce—36 inches; for 6- and 8-ounce weights—48 inches. In vertical installations, girt spacing may be increased about 20 to 25 percent.

Filler strips, sometimes called "wiggle molding" after their corrugated shape (they're also available to fit the ribbed panels), are installed to provide a solid fastening surface, needed because nails are driven into the crowns of the corrugations or ribs. Without the filler strips, you could overdrive the fasteners, distorting the panels, or else not fasten snugly enough, allowing the panels to rattle. Because the filler strips have a slight thickness, they raise the panels that much above the framework. You'll need filler strips atop all rafters, headers, and purlins. (On purlins and headers, use the corrugated or ribbed strips that match the FRP-panel shape.) Use a panel to make sure the strips (available in 6- or 8-foot lengths) are properly aligned before tacking them down with finishing nails. "Vertical" filler strips—half-round molding for corrugated panels, square for the ribbed shape—go atop the rafters. These can be cut to fit between the horizontal rows of the shaped moldings. They're also sold in 6- or 8-foot lengths.

No special tools are required for working with the FRP panels. Any ordinary saw—hand, saber, circular—will cut the panels, although a fine-tooth blade or an abrasive disc on a power saw work best. Fastening the panels is best done with aluminum screw-type nails, and manufacturers recommend predrilling with a $5/16$-inch bit. This helps avoid tiny cracks around the nail holes that could lead to leakage.

The aluminum twist-shank nails will not corrode or leave stains on the panels and they're equipped with neoprene washers under the heads to fill in the nail holes. To avoid water leaks, always fasten in the crowns of corrugations or ribs: valley-fastening produces nail holes in the channels that carry runoff and also invites cracking from misdirected hammer blows.

During construction use 1x12 boards or a piece of plywood when standing or kneeling on the patio roof. An FRP panel, when supported as recommended, will carry about 100 pounds per square foot. But a 180-pound man, standing with his feet together, will exert almost double that load. Using a board spreads the load.

A good-quality FRP panel will be uniform in both thickness and shape, allowing for a fairly tight overlap between adjoining panels. But water can creep into the tightest lap through capillary action, so you'll need to seal or caulk the joints between panels. The sealant should be nondrying and should remain flexible; otherwise, the normal expansion and contraction of the panels would break the seal. It should be clear, too, since a dark sealant would show up between the translucent panels. The butyrate-type sealants sold by FRP panel firms meet these requirements, as do the more expensive silicone sealants. Both are available in standard-size caulking cartridges.

After several years (just how many depends on their original quality, climatic conditions, sun orientation, and how clean you've kept them), FRP panels will begin to lose their characteristic glossiness. That's a sign that panels need refinishing right away. At this point, all you'll need to do is hose down the panels thoroughly, let them dry, then apply a coat of panel refinisher by either spraying or brushing. The refinisher is a clear acrylic liquid, generally available from dealers who sell the panels. It will last for about one to three years, depending on climate.

If you don't catch the problem when the panel gloss starts to go, you'll soon find the surface starting to get fuzzy as the reinforcing glass fibers near the surface become exposed. As more of the fibers appear, they'll trap dirt and

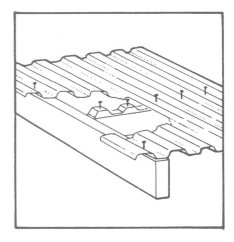

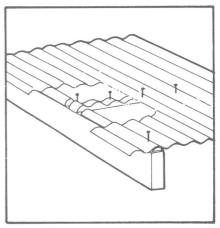

Filler strips for the ridged (top) and corrugated (bottom) FRP panels.

Holes for nails are predrilled in the panels to avoid cracking.

The lightweight panels are easily lifted into place on the roof.

Threaded aluminum nails with neoprene washers are used to fasten the panels.

As a safety precaution, use a board or a piece of plywood to spread your weight when working on the roof.

fungus, which simply cannot be hosed off. This doesn't mean your panels are ruined—just that it will be a bit more work to restore them to an almost-new appearance. You'll first have to scrape off the exposed fibers and matted dirt. The best way to do this is with 0-grade steel wool. (Use a 1x12 board or

Traditional canvas awning is still a popular choice as a covering for a deck or terrace.

This canvas roof is held by long dowels placed over and under redwood beams.

plywood to support your weight on the roof.) You can fashion a "brush" out of one of the filler strips left over from the construction job. Simply staple pads of steel wool to the corrugations or ribs and rub down the panels—you'll cover a lot more area with the same amount of effort. After the dirt and exposed fibers are removed, you'll find you have just about restored the original color, since the discoloration was only skin deep—just as a suntan only affects the topmost layer of your skin. A coat or two of resurfacing liquid will seal the panel surface, completing the restoration job.

Canvas

The traditional canvas awning with some very contemporary variations is still widely used as a patio cover. One big advantage is that a canvas awning can be designed to be drawn up out of the way when sunshine is the order of the day, then put into position to provide shelter when needed. Often, though, a canvas roof is permanently fixed over part or all of a deck or terrace.

The framework for a canvas cover can be of wood, just as for other patio roofs. It can also be of pipe (usually ¾- or 1-inch galvanized) which can be fabricated at your local plumbing shop. The pipe can be set into a concrete footing (just as with a wood post) or attached to a foundation with heavy-duty flanges into which the pipe is threaded.

Another way to support a canvas roof is by a network of cables or ropes suspended between the house and another structure (such as a garage) or simply a number of posts. In fact, there are many ways you can use this colorful material—put your imagination to work!

You can hem and sew canvas yourself, but it is quite a chore. You are probably better off having it sewn to your specifications at an awning shop, sailmaker's loft, upholsterer's, or even the local cobbler's (he should have the necessary needles and machinery). For fastening the canvas with ropes, first insert grommets in the material. You can purchase a grommet kit at any hardware store, and it includes the specialized tools needed as well as the grommets.

Scalloped canvas "ceiling" of this outdoor living room is supported by cables strung tautly between the house and the garage (not visible at right). Cables are attached to screw eyes at each end.

Large umbrella laced to a circular frame of thin-wall tubing is supported from above by a beam extending out from the house.

Building & Installation Techniques:

OUTDOOR LIGHTING

Warm glow is cast over this patio by pink flood bulbs in shielded bullet-type fixtures located on house roof and directed downward. Accents of white spot the young trees and create lacy shadow patterns across the walls.

Light from inside the strawberry pottery jar reflects a "face" in the water of this small corner pool. Lily pad lights are silhouetted against the calm surface of the pool. Realistic rock form at right conceals a bulb that accents the wall mosaic and shrubbery behind it.

Dining under the stars can be a delight—if the starlight is supplemented so that you can see enough to carve your steak without carving your hand.

It is difficult to imagine modern living without benefit of electricity—no television, no toaster, no instant hot water for coffee or almost instant ice cubes for cooling drinks on the patio, no air conditioners or electric blankets to keep us year-round comfy, no dishwashers or automatic clothes washers or refrigerators or stereo sets or blenders or you name it. And, of course, inferior and inconsistent nighttime lighting. Since your concept of outdoor living is as an extension of total home life, it is obvious that electricity will have its place in your plans.

Ourdoor lighting is a prime consideration, and should be designed as an integral part of the overall outdoor "floor plan." Strategically placed electrical outlets are also a convenience and are much safer than running lengthy extension cords from the house to various points in the yard where power might be required. You'll want a place to plug in the TV, radio, and portable record player, the electric lawn mower (several outlets are better in a large yard), and various gadgets in the outdoor kitchen, such as the rotisserie. If you are really big on back-yard living, you will probably want such amenities as a small refrigerator close at hand, along with provisions for plugging in a blender to help you concoct those delicious fruit drinks (have you ever tried a banana daiquiri, or an avocado daiquiri?). And if you have a swimming pool, you will need to provide electricity for pumps and filters.

Guidelines

Much of your outdoor living, and especially your entertaining, will probably take place in the hours after dark. For this reason, to make the most effective use of your outdoor living area, it is important to provide proper outdoor lighting. Good lighting will not only extend the hours of usefulness of the patio, it can also add striking beauty to your exterior decorating scheme. And it is

Cool blue lighting bathes a rock retaining wall in this yard, with warmer tints highlighting the stockade fence.

essential for nighttime safety, along garden paths and at poolside, and to discourage trespassers as well.

In many ways, you can apply the same standards for lighting your outdoor living room as you would for other rooms of the home. For example, soft indirect lighting is fine for conversation areas, but more powerful and direct light is needed for reading. But there are many other factors to consider, for generally there will be none of the reflections of light from the ceiling and walls that help to create an indoor room's level of illumination.

Do not make the mistake of planning your outdoor lighting as though you were trying to imitate the sunlight—it can't be done and you wouldn't want to do it if you could, for night lighting can give a whole new atmosphere to the outdoors. For general illumination of an area, the basic lighting should be floodlighting, provided by carefully aimed lights on the roof or under the

If a pool plays a part in your outdoor living, lighting—both above and below water—is just about essential.

Up-lighted trees are reflected in the lighted swimming pool, creating fantasy patterns on the surface.

eaves of the house, in trees or on tall posts. These should be high enough and so placed and shielded that they are not blinding or glaring to any of the general-use areas.

Be considerate of the neighbors, too, when placing the floodlights, so that glare is not directed into the next-door living room or bedroom.

Where illumination is provided for game areas, make sure it is adequate. Lighting fixtures should be so placed and spaced that they provide sufficient light to see the object in play—a ball, a shuttlecock, or whatever—while creating a minimum of shadows and protecting the players' eyes from glare. Generally, highly placed floodlights are best for game courts. Light coming from several directions reduces shadows and provides more uniform illumination.

Floodlighting alone creates a flat and monotonous effect. This can be

Charming garden setting by day takes on a uniquely different appearance at night as spots and floods create highlights and shadows.

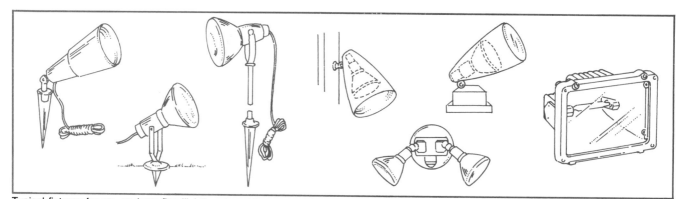

Typical fixtures for up- or down-floodlighting. 1 and 2 are portable types with cord, plug, and ground spike. 3 uses a tungsten halogen filament-type bulb. 4 has a ballast enclosed in the base to operate a 100-watt vapor PAR bulb. 5 and 6 are one- and two-socket fixtures for mounting on house or pole. 7 is an adjustable-pole fixture well suited for lighting game and barbecue areas.

overcome by accenting feature areas in the floodlighted area with spotlights, pointing up the outdoor fireplace, perhaps, or a planter box. The use of lighting for decorative purposes can, when properly handled, produce the most striking and gratifying results.

For a subtle effect in the garden, use a number of small lights rather than a few large ones. The beauty of garden lighting is the emphasis it gives to the contrast of highlights and shadows. The garden takes on a completely different aspect that it has in the daytime—not necessarily more delightful (although in certain cases, it may well be, simply because the darkness obscures distracting backgrounds and the lighting focuses attention where it should be), but certainly not less so.

You might arrange the lighting to accent those areas where the plants and flowers are at their seasonal loveliest. Then, as their beauty wanes, shift the accent to another area. Pools lend themselves well to lighting. Special underwater lights are available for dramatic effects. Remember, though, that water will reflect light, and take this into consideration when planning lighting for surrounding areas. A tree may be the star attraction in your nocturne. Light from a spotlight set a distance away, or from a reflector at the base of the trunk directing its light upward, or from a light concealed among the branches will create enchanting interplay among limbs and leaves.

Very dramatic effects can sometimes be had with colored lighting, but be extremely judicious in its use, for it is also capable of results that are bizarre, garish, and grotesque. Generally speaking, light of the same hue as the object lighted tends to heighten the color. Certain colors tend to deaden grass and foliage. Some colors may be mixed, but the wrong combination or a mixture of too many may give unexpected and usually undesirable results. If you wish to use color, it's best to experiment before making a permanent installation.

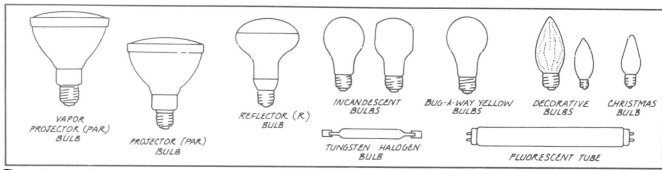

The most commonly used bulbs for 115-120-volt outdoor lighting.

To keep the family athletes in shape, it's important to provide good lighting for game-playing areas.

Down-lighting under the house eaves illuminates this terrace and also lights the way from the yard to the rear entrance. Side-lighting of the stairs is a safety feature.

Dramatic effects can be achieved by spotlighting large trees.

The placing of unobtrusive lighting fixtures alongside walks and paths, and especially at steps and other potential hazard spots, need in no way distract from the magical spell of night as you contemplate the starry wonders, but it will help you to stroll along without accident. There is a wide variety of fixtures available at electrical supply stores that will blend in almost unnoticed with any surrounding.

Unfortunately, the hospitable invitation of a lighted patio is usually also communicated to night-flying insects, who are attracted by bright light sources. Keeping floodlamps far enough away from places where people

Post fixture designed to be set in a concrete base.

This type of perimeter fixture can be bolted to a masonry or other base.

Stem-type garden fixture comes with junction box at base.

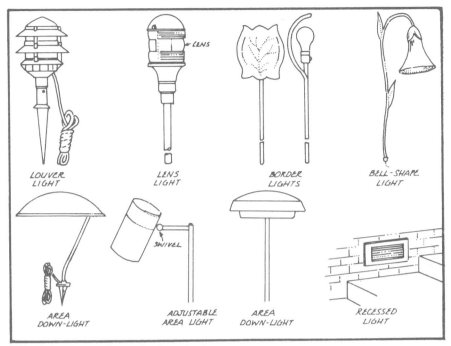

Fixtures for steps, paths, and patio perimeters.

normally congregate will keep these pests at a distance at least. Yellow lamps are almost invisible to insects while providing adequate light for human eyes, and these are often used for outdoor living areas. And, of course, there are numerous insect repellents available that can be placed about the patio to discourage the bugs.

Electric insect traps further minimize the threat of these night-flying nuisances. Equipped with special bulbs that are rich in insect-attracting blue light but practically invisible to humans, these traps are placed away from the main outdoor living areas to attract and kill most night-flying bugs.

Perimeter fixtures define the border of this brick terrace.

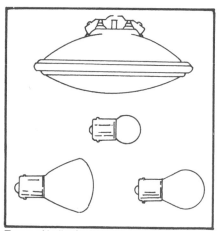

Types of bulbs for low-voltage systems.

Low-Voltage Landscape Lighting

The range of voltage commonly used in household circuits is 115-120. There is also a system known as low-voltage, which operates on 12 volts—the same voltage used to safely operate an electric train.

The heart of a 12-volt outdoor lighting system is the voltage-reducing transformer, which reduces the 115-120-volt supply to 12 volts. Weatherproof transformers are made for outdoor use and are easy to connect to an existing outlet. Fixtures of various designs may be easily attached to the 12-volt cable which extends from the transformer and then moved in perfect safety from one location on the resealing cable to another. The methods of connecting fixtures to this type of self-sealing cable differ with manufactuers. Some low-voltage systems come equipped with timers for turning lights on and off.

Fixtures for a 12-volt system, as with a 120-volt system, are available as portable types which spear into the ground and attach to a cable placed on the ground, and those supplied with a conduit mount for attachment to a terminal box and underground cable. There are 12-volt fixtures designed for up-lighting small plants and trees; down-lighting steps, paths, and foliage, dramatizing a reflecting pool or fountain, highlighting a statue or flower bed, accenting a wall, fence, or patio; and creating dramatic shadow patterns—not any one fixture, of course. It may take several fixtures, for they are designed to produce different lighting effects. Remember, the prime objective is to see what is lighted, not the source of light.

The size, shape, and bases of 12-volt bulbs differ from the usual 120-volt household bulbs which have screw-type bases. They differ also in that 12-volt bulbs are known by a number rather than by wattage. Some 12-volt bulbs are of the type used in automobiles and are available at most service stations.

Low-voltage outdoor lighting systems and equipment offer features not always found in standard 115-120-volt designs. These include low-voltage as a safety factor, ease of relocating fixtures on a resealing cable, small-scale

This low-voltage system includes a timer. Cord is run to desired locations in yard and colored lights with ground stakes are attached. Lights may be moved without disturbing the cord.

Plenty of light is used in a tasteful way in this back yard. Border fixtures around the terrace are complemented by lights highlighting the trees. Japanese lanterns signal a festive occasion.

fixtures that are useful in restricted spaces, and ease of do-it-yourself installation. For the myriad effects desired in the design of outdoor lighting, there needs to be a compatible partnership of both 120-volt and 12-volt lighting systems and fixtures.

Large, tall trees, expansive shrubbery, and other special attractions will require the power and punch delivered by standard 120-volt fixtures and light sources. Therefore, in planning your outdoor lighting, wed the two systems to combine the advantages of each.

Wiring

Proper wiring is essential for the complete enjoyment and safety of outdoor living after dark. A garden with underground wiring to switch-controlled permanent fixture locations and convenience outlets is a safe and convenient system. It allows for lighting and the use of electrical appliances and garden power tools too. But temporary wiring also has its place. It allows for some experiments you'll want to try before making final decisions.

For temporary wiring, use outdoor-type rubber extension cords of at least No. 16 wire. These come in lengths of 25, 50, and 100 feet with sockets and plugs molded in weatherproof rubber. Connect into the nearest outlet in or on

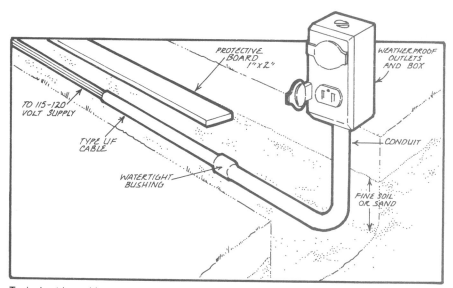

Typical outdoor wiring to a convenience outlet.

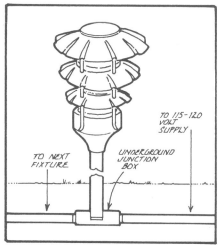

Fixtures can be permanently installed to underground junction boxes.

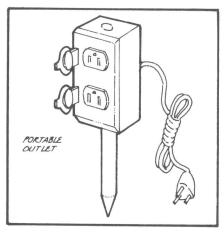

A portable outlet like this plugs in anywhere; the stake is driven into the ground.

the house or garage. Then you will need at least one outdoor-type portable double-convenience outlet fixture. Extension cords and outlet fixtures are available in two-conductor and three-conductor grounded types; three-conductor grounded wiring devices are recommended because of the likelihood of dampness conditions in outdoor usage. Some outdoor fixtures have a built-in outlet into which another fixture can be plugged. Be sure you don't exceed 1600 watts on a 15-ampere circuit, or 2000 watts on a 20-ampere circuit.

Permanent Wiring

Permanent wiring for lighting and other purposes should be your goal for the outdoor living area. Electrical work remains somewhat of a mystery to many homeowners (just as electricity itself does to even the most learned scientists); others will blithely forge ahead, making haphazard installations and connections that are almost certain to end in disaster. We would recommend that, unless you have had considerable experience in this sort of work, you seek the services of an electrical contractor. Many communities require that all electrical work be performed by a licensed electrician. If you want to do it yourself, consult a good book on the subject, take your time, and above all, never work on "live" wires or circuits. (We regret that space limitations prevent us from giving complete wiring installation instructions, but it is a major subject in itself.) In any event, consult your local electrical codes before starting any such project.

The principles and general techniques for outdoor wiring are the same as for interior electrical wiring, but wire and fixtures must be specifically made for outdoor use. Outdoor receptacles should have special gasket-fitted covers and other safeguards against the elements. Most codes require that above-ground cable be enclosed in metal conduit. Underground cable, run in trenches should be UF (underground fused) which is plastic-sheathed and can, unless a code forbids it, be buried without conduit. The trench should be below the frost line and, in any case, located where it is not likely to be damaged by future digging. The cable should be laid in and covered with sand or fine gravel to provide drainage. You can protect cable by laying boards over it before backfilling. This is satisfactory during a construction period, but remember that the boards will eventually rot away.

Cable is usually run through a hole drilled in the house wall to connect to the fuse or circuit-breaker box. Patch around the cable after installation to prevent leakage.

At the other end, the cable is connected to weatherproof outlet boxes or to underground junction boxes to which fixtures can be permanently installed. Convenience outlets can be located on the house walls, fence posts, trees, or individual posts or stakes wherever needed. All outlets should be above the "snow line" for your area, although recent winters make this a practical impossiblility in many regions. Who wants to climb a 15-foot ladder to plug in the TV? In any event, place them at least 18 inches above the ground except in no-snow areas where they can be lower. Also locate electrical equipment so that it cannot cause falls or be damaged by mowing.

Outdoor electrical circuits should be separate from those inside the house and controlled by a switch. Make a map of the wiring layout for ready reference in the event repairs are needed, or if additional fixtures are installed at a future date.

The National Electrical Code recommends and many local codes require that a Ground Fault Circuit Interrupter (GFCI) be included in any outdoor circuit. This is a device that protects against overloads and short circuits in the line, and, even more important, current leakage, which could be a serious hazard in an outdoor installation. There are several different types of GFCIs for both indoor and outdoor locations, and specific wiring instructions are included with whatever type you buy. Most local codes require a GFCI whenever electricity is used in conjunction with a swimming pool—and if they don't, you should have it anyway. In fact, you should have a GFCI for any outdoor electrical wiring circuit.

For purposes of beauty and security, you may want to install an electric eye or timer to control selected lighting units so that your grounds will be lighted at dusk whether you are at home or not. You will find a variety of such devices at any electrical supply outlet.

For Safety's Sake

● Work only when the ground is dry.
● Have a switch to control the outdoor circuits and turn off all current while you're working.
● Use only outdoor-type equipment with waterproof cords, plugs, sockets, and connections.
● Tape temporary connections with electrical tape. Elevate them to keep connections out of puddles.
● Some holders for bulbs come equipped with gaskets—round rubber rings. Use them. They create a seal around the neck of the bulb to keep moisture out of the socket.
● For lily pad fixtures and bulbs placed in water, us a cord with molded rubber sockets. Such sockets tightly grip the neck of the bulb, thus preventing water from seeping into the socket.
● Water and 120 volts of electricity don't mix. But it is safe if you use fixtures and bulbs specially designed for such usage. Make all connections and put the bulbs in the water first, then turn on the current.

This low privacy fence was planned along with the rest of the outdoor living area. Note how it seems to blend into the landscape. Interesting touch is the open space on both sides of the gate. It's to let the cat in and out when the gate is closed.

The bamboo fence shields the rustic brick garden area from the more utilitarian outdoor section behind. Bamboo posts are set between 4x4s to blend with Oriental-type garden.

Building & Installation Techniques:

FENCES & WINDSCREENS

A fence can be many things. It can be a privacy screen, shielding you from the prying eyes of neighbors and passersby. It can be a definition of your property line, a reminder that you (with a little help from the bank) are the owner of all that ½-acre you survey. It can block out eyesores such as your next-door neighbor's garbage cans, or irritants like his swimming pool, the delights of which he adamantly refuses to share (the solution here might be to build your own pool, rather than a fence—read about it in a later chapter). It can keep in young children and pets. It can also keep them out, if they are somebody else's. It can be a deterrent to the neighborhood vandals who use your lawn as a shortcut from wherever they are coming to wherever they are going. It can divide your outdoor living space into various functional areas, much like the partitions inside your house. It can protect you from, or at least cut down, lusty breezes and excessive sunshine. It can be purely cosmetic, either serving as a background for shrubs and plants or standing on its own as a decorative element in your overall outdoor plan.

Fences are not for everyone. Some homeowners, particularly in suburban and semi-rural areas, prefer an unfenced landscape that gives the neighborhood an air of freedom and openness. They like to look out onto a continuous row of sweeping lawns and shrubbery. But where there are neighbors, there is always the possibility that one or more of the above reasons will make a fence desirable, even if you don't especially like the idea. And if you should decide to build that pool, a fence will likely be mandated by local ordinance.

The primary purpose of this fence is as a foil for the prize shrubbery. The greens of the shrubbery and the multicolored crushed rock contrast nicely with the warm red cedar 1x1 strips spaced within a 2x6 cedar frame.

Latticework screen separates "Roman" courtyard from other areas, also serving as a classical backdrop. Ponderosa pine 1x2 strips are nailed to 2x2 uprights, 2x4 dividers, and 2x8 posts. Posts also support canopy behind.

Here's an unusual divider that separates a living area from the wooded property behind. The painted tempered hardboard is set into redwood frames, with redwood shelves for displaying the homeowner's Bonsai plants. Bamboo canopy lends Oriental touch and allows the play of light and shadow on the plants and fence.

Planning Your Fence

It is important to contemplate the effect on the neighborhood, as well as on your own property, of building a fence. Perhaps one that surrounds only a small area rather than framing the entire lot would answer your purpose while still retaining the open-greenery effect. Or perhaps your fence style can match that of your neighbor's, giving a pleasing continuity rather than a broken-up appearance.

First decide what it is that you are fencing in and/or out. As part of your overall plan for the outdoor living space, determine which areas might be enhanced by a fence. Try to visualize the effect of various fence styles, either by looking at the various fences shown in these pages or by sketching a design of your own. If you really want to do it right, get out your Polaroid and shoot a few views of the lot from various angles. Then draw the fence in scale on a tissue overlay and place it over the photo.

If you are fencing off a play area for the children, make sure that it is clearly defined. When children are small, you will want the play area at least partially visible both from the patio and from the house—preferably the kitchen—for easy visibility. If there are animals too, some provision should be made to keep them away from the children's area. A solid fence between the two will do the trick, but don't build it in the parents' line of sight.

If you are fencing off a utility area, leave easy access for taking out garbage from the house, and for taking garbage cans to the curbside collection point.

Where the principal purpose of the fenced-in area is private sunbathing, consider locating it off the bedroom or even the master bath (although this latter would likely require some alterations to the house wall), rather than the family room or kitchen. A solid, high fence is best here, perhaps a louvered type that will keep out peeping eyes while admitting cool breezes.

Where a boundary-line fence is in order, contact your local planning board or zoning board to find out about setbacks from the property line, maximum height, and other regulations governing fences. The same applies to fences around pools. Statutes in this regard are often quite specific, dictating where,

A little originality will turn an otherwise ordinary fence into an interesting and inviting work of art. Shown are a few examples.

This ruggedly handsome fence conceals the service area. Two garbage cans are hidden inside the lidded box, and two more are underground. Western cedar is used throughout, with 1x4 tongue-and-groove boards for fencing, capped by 1x2 slats and a 2x4 rail. Box lid is composed of 1x2 slats in a 2x2 frame.

A wind screen can be built as shown, with the open design cutting down on strong winds, but letting gentler breezes through.

Here's an example of judicious use of stockade fencing. Water view is kept for enjoyment on the patio-brick terrace, while close next-door neighbor's view is blocked off. (Homeowner violated unwritten law, however, by facing the "good" side toward him.)

what type, and what size the fence must be. In fact, it is wise to check local ordinances when you are building just about any type of fence to make sure that you don't unwittingly violate any of them. For example, "good-one-sides" often must be built with the side facing your neighbor (common courtesy suggests this even where the law doesn't). And make sure you carefully study your own survey to locate your property lines.

Fence Styles

Don't be one of those who automatically puts up stockade fencing from the building supply yard without considering the alternatives. The relatively inexpensive stockade is fine as a barrier between your lot and a busy highway or some other irritant, but this type of fencing is not calculated to make friends with your next-door neighbors. It is not the most attractive type of fence, and should never be used to define various outdoor living areas except, perhaps, to wall off the garbage cans or other eyesores.

Again, consider your neighbors' fences. If the other back yards are separated by split-rail fences, a continuation of that or the use of a similarly open style may be more pleasing. Of course, this will not help much when keeping in small children and pets is the objective. But you can staple relatively unobtrusive chicken wire to it until the children grow a bit or the dog is better trained. The wire is then easily removed.

With small children, safety and security are all-important. This chain-link keeps the kids in bounds and away from marauding dogs or other intruders.

If it's privacy you're after, there's nothing like a solid wooden fence. You don't have to make it ugly, though, as this board-on-board western pine design illustrates.

This basketweave fence keeps prying eyes out, but allows some airflow between the strips. The 1x6 western pine slats are woven between 1x1 supports. The whole fence is coated with an exterior stain.

The purpose of the fence will, of course, be a major factor in selecting a style. A privacy fence, obviously, cannot be an open type, or a chain-link (which most do-it-yourselfers firmly believe should be reserved for use around prison perimeters and top-security military installations and banned from suburbia). There are metal, plastic, or wooden strips that can be threaded between the links to provide some privacy for this type of fencing, but it is certainly more attractive to build a "solid" fence in the first place.

A solid fence doesn't necessarily have to be solid, or airtight. Boards can be staggered, set at angles, woven, or otherwise arranged to insure privacy—at least from certain points of view—and still allow the passage of fresh air and gentle breezes. The same arrangements can allow you to bask in the sunlight at certain hours without basking in the stares of nosy neighbors and peering passersby.

The young lady can sun herself without concern about the prying eyes of neighbors, even though there are slight gaps between the boards and the height of the fence is minimal. Since the house next door is lower, the small fence cuts off the line of sight.

Pools must be fenced in—by common sense if not by law. These corrugated fiberglass panels create privacy while allowing the sunlight through.

Rough-sawn board-on-board red cedar makes an effective barrier for dogs and other nuisances, but is also very attractive. The 1x8 boards are nailed on alternate sides of 2x4 stringers. This fence also allows free flow of breezes.

Another example of board-on-board design, but this time the southern pine boards are nailed so that they overlap one another.

Generally, a privacy fence should be as high as the law allows. But if your private area is on higher ground than the surrounding houses, a low fence might do the job. Line of sight is the important consideration.

A fence intended for shelter from wind and/or sun should be thoughtfully designed. Adjustable louvers, either horizontal or vertical, can be used to admit the gentle rays of the sun but shut it out when it becomes desert-intense. The same design can serve as a wind screen. If strong prevailing winds come from, say, the north, block them with either an airtight fence or one built of staggered, overlapping boards that breaks up gusty winds into gentle breezes. Louvers can also be used if the winds are only an intermittent problem. If you want to keep out southerly winds but admit the light and warmth of the sun, a translucent fence of plastic or fiberglass may be your choice. These can be employed as solid panels or louvers (techniques of working with these materi-

Plastic panels form a wind-barrier fence for this hilltop home.

For the ultimate in shelter from the winds, try these movable windbreaks, which can be adjusted for wind direction. Each red cedar screen has metal rods attached to bottom corners which fit into pipes set along the patio edge.

This redwood and opaque plastic fence gives plenty of privacy. Open sections at top and bottom let some air through.

When the terrain is hilly, a stepped fence such as the resawn cedar one shown is in order.

als are discussed in the earlier section on patio roofs). Clear plastic or fiberglass can be used to shield your deck or patio from strong ocean or mountain winds while retaining the view.

The contour of your land is yet another consideration in selecting a fence style. Designs that require long, straight runs—paneled or picket types, for example—are not suited to hilly ground. A rambling or stepped-down fence is a better choice. And don't overlook the appearance of the fence on the look of your property from the outside. Even if you are a recluse and could not care less what the neighbors think, there may come a time when you will want to sell the house. You won't want to have to tear down the fence just to make it saleable. That can be as much work as putting it up. Unless you have a passion for privacy, it is generally unwise to cut off the view of the house from the street.

This stepped-down open fence not only provides a backdrop for the shrubbery, but also acts as a trellis for it. The combination makes a solid privacy fence without looking like it. The western pine lumber was painted for longevity.

Be imaginative when choosing a fence style. The reason this fence blends in so well is that it's made of the same type of beveled siding as that on the house.

It is also unwise to cut off the view of the street from the driveway. And remember such practical aspects as getting in and out of the family car. Don't build a fence so close to the parking area that you have to go on a crash diet to fit through car doors that can be opened only a sliver.

While the term "fence" ordinarily connotes a wood structure, or sometimes metal or plastic, you may find that a masonry "fence" better suits your needs. A masonry fence is actually a wall, usually of brick, stone, or decorative concrete units. Techniques for building such walls are detailed in the appropriate sections for each material earlier in this book.

Fence Posts

Most wooden fence designs depend upon posts for stability. (An exception is the zigzag fence, where posts are used only to anchor it to the ground, or not used at all.) Posts will vary in dimension; 2x4s, 3x3s, 4x4s, and 3- to 6-inch logs are among the more commonly used dimensions. As a general rule, posts should have about one-third of their length below the ground; a 4-foot-high fence would require 6-foot posts.

Determine the spacing of the fence posts. Prebuilt fencing usually comes in 6- or 8-foot lengths, but check the type you are buying. If you are building your own fence, you have more leeway, so plan ahead. If, for example, the fence is to be 49 feet long, space the posts on 7-foot centers. If you use the more common 8-foot centers, you will wind up with six 8-foot sections and an awkward 1-foot section at the end. Remember to take into account the width of gates before setting the posts—you don't want to fence yourself in permanently.

After property boundaries and setbacks have been accurately established, mark off the fenceline with a line strung between stakes at each end. Using a 50- or 100-foot tape, measure along the string and mark locations of posts by driving stakes into the ground. Post holes can be dug with a square-end garden spade, but this is tedious work, especially where the ground is hard or rocky, and it gets more tedious the deeper you must dig. A much better tool for the job is a post-hole digger, which can usually be rented. Auger types are best for rockfree soils. Clam-shell diggers are preferred for rocky soils. If there are very many holes, a power-driven auger can make the going easier.

A clam-shell post-hole digger is best for rocky soils.

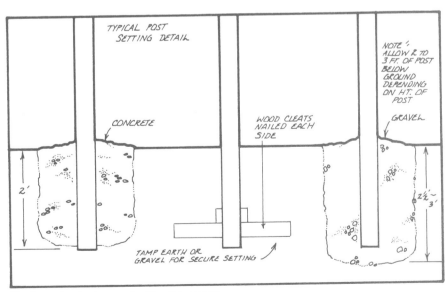

TYPICAL POST SETTING DETAIL

NOTE: ALLOW 2 TO 3 FT. OF POST BELOW GROUND DEPENDING ON HT. OF POST

CONCRETE

WOOD CLEATS NAILED EACH SIDE

GRAVEL

2'

2½'~3'

TAMP EARTH OR GRAVEL FOR SECURE SETTING

The three standard ways of setting fence posts.

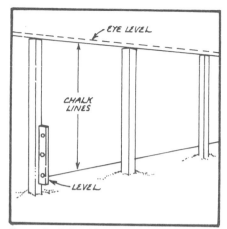

For perfectly level fencing, run a line between the corners and set all posts to the same height.

Dig the holes 4 inches deeper than the required burial depth of the post. Dump that much gravel into the holes to insure proper drainage away from the post bottoms.

Hole diameters will vary according to the size post you are using and how it will be set. Generally, if the posts are to be set into tamped earth, the diameter of the hole should be twice that of the post. If concrete is to be poured around the post, the hole should be two and one half to three times that of the post.

Treat the posts with preservative as described in the section on working with wood. Make sure that the bottom grain is thoroughly impregnated with the preservative.

If you are setting a post in tamped soil nail 1x2 cleats, as long as the diameter of the hole, near the bottom of the post in both directions. Set the two end posts first, then run a taut line between the tops and check with a line level to make sure that they are perfectly aligned. Use a carpenter's level to plumb each post, and brace it temporarily with boards nailed to stakes driven into the ground. Backfill with earth and tamp down firmly around the post. Recheck for plumb, and adjust as necessary before removing the bracing. Mound the earth slightly around the posts to direct drain water away.

Gravel may be used around the posts in place of soil. The technique is the same; just make sure the gravel is tamped down firmly.

The most sturdy anchorage for fence posts is concrete, but this can also accelerate rot at the post bottoms—make sure that the posts are in contact with the gravel in the holes (to allow good drainage) and not resting on concrete where puddles of water might collect. Posts are set and leveled as above. Techniques of working with concrete were detailed earlier. Build the concrete up around the post slightly above ground level, and slope it away so that water will flow away from the wood.

With end posts in place, set intermediate posts, using the string line as a guide for straightness and height.

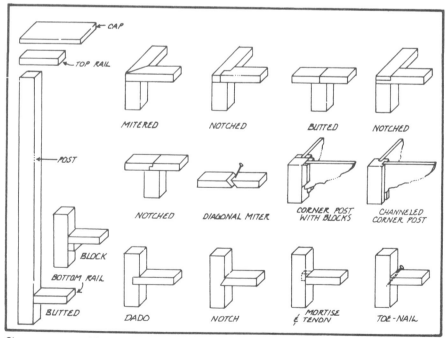

Shown are some of the many ways of attaching fence rails to posts. It is easiest to butt the top rails and nail to tops of posts, mitering at corners. Bottom rails can be toenailed, but should be braced with blocks when strength is required. The dado or mortise-and-tenon joints are the best, but are more difficult and should be made with power tools.

Louvered fences insure privacy from the desired angle, yet admit sunlight and breezes. Louvers are nailed to spacers.

Building the Fence

Plans for a variety of fences are included elsewhere in this book. In general, rails or stringers at top and bottom are 2x4s. Boards are generally 1x8s or 1x10s. Pickets are most commonly 1x3s or 1x4s. Nails are the usual fasteners, and should be galvanized or aluminum. 12d or 16d nails are used for fastening rails; 8d for boards. Louvers are fastened to cleats or spacer blocks.

Finishes for fences are the same as those for other outdoor lumber, as detailed in the section on working with wood.

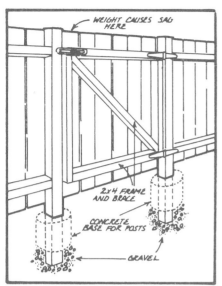

Typical gate construction.

Contrast is provided for this gate by painting it a different color and setting it at a lower height. Continuity is maintained, however, by using a matching design.

Gates

Because one end of a gate hangs free, gate construction should be even sturdier than a normal section of fencing. Gate posts also take a lot of abuse, and should be set a foot or so deeper than other posts. It is also advisable to set gate posts in concrete even if the others are set in tamped soil, and to use heavier lumber (4x6s instead of 4x4s, for example) if design permits.

Gates should be wide enough to accommodate two people walking abreast—at least 3 feet. For an opening much wider than that, it is better to use two gates latching in the center. Diagonal 2x4s from the top of the free end to

Fancy gate for use with a picket fence.

The attractive gate for this fence is different, but matches the fence because the same type of wood (pine) is used. It is stained the same color.

Gate can be blended into fence so that it's difficult to see. Can you find it in this picture? Note the latch in the pane, above the concrete walk.

the bottom of the post end provide extra strength; additional bracing may be required for larger or heavier gates.

Use long, heavy-duty hinges and screws to attach the gate to the post. Hinges should extend onto the top and bottom rails where possible. Allow ½-inch clearance at the free end. And, obvious as it may seem, make sure that there are no obstructions in the way of the gate's swing and that it does not swing uphill.

The design of the gate usually matches that of the fence, but sometimes a different, complementary style is chosen for visual impact. For "vestibule" effect, the gate may be recessed a few feet behind the adjacent fence.

Here's a truly elegant entryway. The fence is capped by brick columns, with a wrought-iron gate between. Note the iron stud, which can be raised to help prevent sag in the middle. When gate is latched, both sections are given support.

Plantings serve as "room dividers" in this pool-surround patio.

Building & Installation Techniques:

LANDSCAPING

Exterior decorating—landscaping the outdoor living area—is just as important for creating a pleasant setting for leisure-time activities as is indoor decorating. Entertaining friends on a patio in the middle of a dusty, barren desert of a back yard has about as much panache as holding the party in a grimy, cluttered garage, no matter how charming a host you are and how succulent the barbecued steaks may be. A well-maintained lawn and some carefully located shrubs and trees can make all the difference. Plantings can provide privacy or serve as "room dividers" between various activity areas. They can also serve other fencelike functions, as wind screens or sun shades.

Natural Factors

Nature is a somewhat limiting factor in your landscape planning. Your idea of patio pleasure may be sipping mint juleps under the spreading boughs of a magnolia tree, but if you live in Minnesota you'd better plant maple instead—that magnolia just won't make it.

You can't change the weather, but you can make allowances for it. Consider local temperature ranges, average rainfall, and distribution of rainfall throughout the year, and select trees and shrubs that are best suited to these climatic factors. The U.S. Department of Agriculture, state or county agricultural agent, or a knowledgeable nurseryman can advise on this. If you live in a region that suffers through prolonged dry spells, you may want to install a sprinkling system as described elsewhere in this book to help Mother Nature nurture trees and shrubs as well as your lawn. If strong prevailing winds are a problem, protect vulnerable plants and trees (at least during their youth) with wind screens.

The topography of your lot will figure into your landscape planning and the selection of plants. A flat plain can be given visual interest by grouping plantings in corners or defining a certain activity area. A steeply sloping bank where lawn mowing is difficult can be planted with trees, or groundcovers, or terraced and planted with shrubs or flowers. Of course, you could simply hack away the hillside, but this is a difficult and expensive solution that could cause more problems than it solves.

Landscaping liabilities can often be turned into decorative assets. A low, marshy spot in the yard can be lined with polyethylene sheeting to become a pool where water plants can be grown. An ugly outcropping of rocks can be transformed into a beautiful rock garden, or a small pool can be excavated alongside it with water recirculating over the rock to create a lovely "waterfall." Use your imagination.

The soil in your yard is another factor to be taken into account when planning your landscaping. It should be tested to determine its pH factor —whether it is acid or alkaline. Your county agricultural agent or a local nurseryman can perform such a test on a soil sample. Knowing the pH will give you an indication of what minerals will have to be added to the soil for the types of plants you want to grow.

Clay, hardpan, or very sandy soil that refuses to support plant life may have to be replaced, at least in selected areas where you want to plant. For lawns, an entire layer of topsoil may be required to provide a root zone that will allow moisture to soak in rather than run off or just stand on top.

Juniper ground cover on the sloping area of this yard makes the mowing easy and helps prevent erosion.

An example of a liability converted to an asset. The low, marshy area in the center of this yard was made into a garden pool with water plants and submerged lighting.

COLOR

Color is a key element in exterior decorating—again, just as indoors. Green is restful, and is provided in abundance by Nature. There are many shades of green, and you should be aware of the subtle differences between leaves of different types of deciduous trees, broad-leaved evergreens, and needle-leaved evergreens. Some landscapers work with green only and achieve satisfactory results with this monochromatic color scheme.

Most outdoor-living enthusiasts like more color, however—especially when the patio or deck beckons after a drab winter. What could be more inviting than the yellow, white, and violet crocuses popping up under the last vestiges of snow, even if you have to wear a sweater while admiring them? Daffodils and early tulips in a wide variety of colors add brilliant color to spring. Flowering ornamental trees supply reds, pinks, and whites. Roses come in oranges, corals, and even lavenders and near-purples as well as rich reds.

Colorful blooms are welcome in other seasons as well. Mimosa, larkspur, zinnia, asters, and pentunias flower in mid-summer. The flowering dogwood has bright red berries in the fall, in addition to its spring blossoms. Goldenrain, crape myrtle, and Chinese dogwood also extend the flowering season.

Very colorful plants should be used with restraint, however. A color scheme can be overdone outdoors as well as in, and violent clashes of brilliant colors hardly create a restful setting for the outdoor living room. Evergreens may be combined with flowering plants, especially alongside the deck or patio.

Both restraint and repetition are valuable guidelines in landscaping. Exer-

Color and texture are used to excellent advantage in this relatively small outdoor living area. The soft yellow marigolds on their long stems contrast nicely with the fluffy pink petunias and their crinkly leaves. The pitted surface of the patio blocks in several colors goes well with the verdant lawn. White fence provides an ideal backdrop.

Bright colors issue an invitation to outdoor living after a long, drab winter.

Avoid a cluttered look caused by planting too much of too many different varieties in one spot.

Good landscaping exercises both restraint and repetition. In this redwood courtyard, low, spreading juniper is planted on one side, broad-leaved evergreens on the other.

159

cise restraint in selecting types of plantings, and in the numbers of plants. For one thing, they need room to grow. For another, too many different kinds of planting materials will give the yard a cluttered appearance. It is also good to repeat the same plant texture and the same color, or various tones of the same color, in different parts of the yard. This helps to unify the landscaped area. But don't carry these themes too far. Avoid having all plants a uniform size, texture, and color. It's a matter of good taste and common sense, so exercise these.

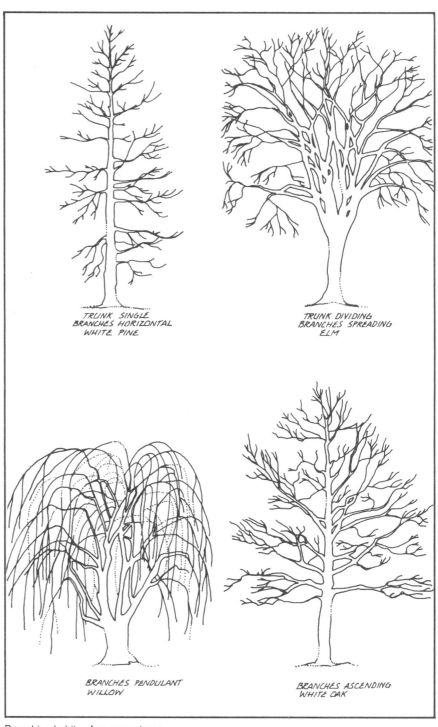

Branching habits of common trees.

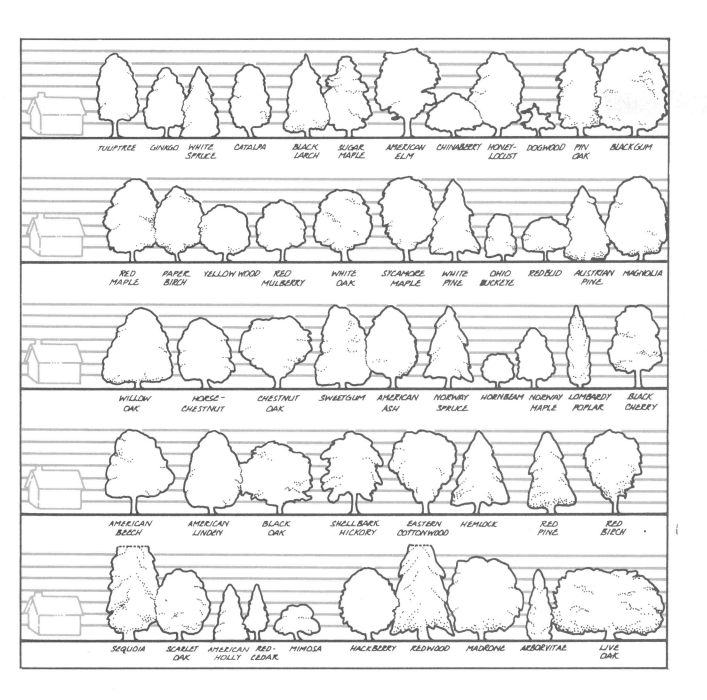

TULIPTREE · GINKGO · WHITE SPRUCE · CATALPA · BLACK LARCH · SUGAR MAPLE · AMERICAN ELM · CHINABERRY · HONEY-LOCUST · DOGWOOD · PIN OAK · BLACK GUM

RED MAPLE · PAPER BIRCH · YELLOW WOOD · RED MULBERRY · WHITE OAK · SYCAMORE MAPLE · WHITE PINE · OHIO BUCKEYE · REDBUD · AUSTRIAN PINE · MAGNOLIA

WILLOW OAK · HORSE-CHESTNUT · CHESTNUT OAK · SWEETGUM · AMERICAN ASH · NORWAY SPRUCE · HORNBEAM · NORWAY MAPLE · LOMBARDY POPLAR · BLACK CHERRY

AMERICAN BEECH · AMERICAN LINDEN · BLACK OAK · SHELLBARK HICKORY · EASTERN COTTONWOOD · HEMLOCK · RED PINE · RED BIRCH

SEQUOIA · SCARLET OAK · AMERICAN HOLLY · RED-CEDAR · MIMOSA · HACKBERRY · REDWOOD · MADRONE · ARBORVITAE · LIVE OAK

Trees

If you have mature trees on your property, you probably won't consider cutting them down unless they are diseased or blocking an outstanding view or are smack in the middle of the ideal location for the swimming pool. But most homeowners—especially those in newer homes—are not so fortunate. Bulldozing builders are notorious for knocking down all the trees on a piece of property to provide easier access for trucks and grading. Then it is necessary to start from scratch—or from sapling. Mature trees are very expensive and very difficult to transplant successfully.

 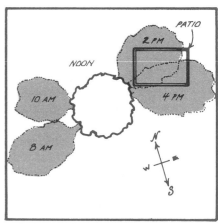

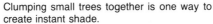

Clumping small trees together is one way to create instant shade.

A shade tree planted west and a little south of the target area provides the most shade during the hottest hours of the day in most areas of the U.S.

If you want to provide shade for the deck or patio, one large tree might do the job, but a cluster of smaller trees might accomplish the purpose sooner. Usually, shade trees should be planted west and a little south of the target area. Trees are often employed to give the landscape a third dimension. In this case, a canopy effect is desirable, and the location depends on the overall plan of the outdoor living area. Trees may also be planted to mark the boundary of the lot, or to screen an objectionable view. In no case, however, should trees be planted so closely together that their branches will intermingle when they are fully grown.

Ornamental trees are used just as the name implies. Flowering crab, Kwansan cherry, and similar species should be situated for maximum visual impact. Don't hide them in the far corners of the yard or behind other trees. Like flowers or flowering plants, don't use a hodgepodge of different varieties—plant them singly, or in small groups of the same species.

There are two main classifications of shade trees: evergreen and deciduous. The latter drop their leaves in the fall; evergreens keep theirs through the winter. Deciduous trees generally grow faster than evergreens, but the growth rate varies among all species and varieties and is also affected by soil fertility, rainfall, and temperature.

Cold-hardiness is the primary requirement in selecting tree species for planting. Trees native to an area can be presumed to be hardy, but some introduced species may also withstand winter cold. If you live in a very hot, dry region, some species will survive with good watering practices. Bear in mind, though, that water is becoming a precious commodity in many such regions, and a drought-resistant species may be preferable; in any event, it will require far less care.

Roots of elms, willows, poplars, and maples can clog sewers in their search for water, and therefore those trees should not be planted near drainage pipes. The roots of some trees grow near the surface of the ground, so such trees should not be planted too near a walkway or patio, since they can break up the pavement from below. Also, tree roots near the surface interfere with lawn mowing and may rob grass of water. And don't plant trees beneath power lines, for obvious reasons.

Regional map, indicating which areas will best sustain certain tree species.

Region 1

Evergreens, broadleaf
  Holly, American
  Magnolia, Southern
Evergreens, needle leaf and
    scale leaf
  Arborvitae, Eastern
  Arborvitae, Japanese
  Cedar, Deodar
  Cedar, Eastern Red
  Cedar of Lebanaon
  Cryptomeria
  Fir, White
  Hemlock, Canadian
  Juniper (*See* Cedar,
    Eastern Red)
  Lawson False Cypress
  Pine, Eastern White
  Pine, Red
  Spruce, Colorado Blue
  Spruce, White
Deciduous
  Ash, Green
  Ash, White
  Aspen, Quaking
  Baldcypress

Beech, American
Beech, European
Birch, Cutleaf European
Birch, Paper
Birch, White
Buckeye
Buckeye, Red (*See* Horse-
  chestnut, Red)
Catalpa, Northern
Catalpa, Southern
Cork Tree, Amur
Cucumber Tree
Elm, American
Elm, English
Elm, European Field
Elm, Scotch
Ginkgo
Goldenrain Tree
Hackberry, Eastern
Hickory, Bitternut
Hickory, Mockernut
Hickory, Pignut
Hickory, Shagbark
Honeylocust, Thornless
Hornbeam, American

Hornbeam, European
Hornbeam, Hop
Horsechestnut
Horsechestnut, Red
Horsechestnut, Ruby (*See*
  Horsechestnut, Red)
Japanese Pagoda Tree
Kalopanax
Katsura
Kentucky Coffeetree
Larch, European
Linden, American
Linden, Littleleaf
Linden, Silver
Locust, Black
London Plane
Magnolia, Cucumber (*See*
  Cucumber Tree)
Magnolia, Sweetbay
Maple, Norway
Maple, Red
Maple, Sugar
Maple, Sycamore
Mimosa
Oak, Black

Oak, Bur
Oak, Chestnut
Oak, Northern Red
Oak, Pin
Oak, Scarlet
Oak, Shingle
Oak, Turkey
Oak, White
Oak, Willow
Oak, Yellow
Pear, Bradford
Pignut (*See* Hickory,
  Pignut)
Sassafras
Silverbell
Sourgum
Sweetgum
Sycamore
Tamarack
Tulip Poplar
Willow, Weeping
Yellowwood
Zelkova

Region 2

Evergreens, broadleaf
  Camphor Tree
  Holly, American
  Holly, Chinese
  Holly, English
  Laurelcherry
  Magnolia, Southern

Oak, Laurel
Oak, Live
Wax Myrtle
Evergreens, needle leaf and
    scale leaf
  Arborvitae, Eastern
  Arborvitae, Oriental

Cedar, Atlas
Cedar, Deodar
Cedar, Eastern Red
Cedar, Incense
Cedar of Lebanon
Cryptomeria
Hemlock, Carolina

Pine, Eastern White
Pine, Loblolly
Pine, Longleaf
Pine, Shortleaf
Pine, Slash
Spruce, Colorado Blue
Spruce, Red

163

Region 2

Deciduous
Ash, White
Baldcypress
Beech, American
Beech, European
Birch, Cutleaf European
Buckeye
Catalpa, Northern
Catalpa, Southern
Cherry, Black
Chinaberry
Chinese Tallow Tree
Crape Myrtle
Cucumber Tree
Elm, American
Elm, Cedar
Elm, English
Elm, Winged
Ginkgo
Goldenrain Tree
Hackberry, Eastern
Hickory, Bitternut
Hickory, Mockernut
Hickory, Pignut
Hickory, Shagbark
Honeylocust, Thornless
Hornbeam, American
Hornbeam, Hop
Japanese Pagoda Tree
Katsura
Kentucky Coffeetree
Linden, American
Linden, Littleleaf
London Plane
Magnolia, Cucumber (*See* Cucumber Tree)
Magnolia, Sweetbay
Maple, Norway
Maple, Red
Maple, Silver
Maple, Sycamore
Mimosa
Mulberry, Paper
Oak, Black
Oak, Bur
Oak, Chestnut
Oak, Pin
Oak, Post
Oak, Scarlet
Oak, Southern Red
Oak, Water
Oak, White
Oak, Willow
Pear, Bradford
Pecan
Persimmon
Pignut (*See* Hickory, Pignut)
Redbud, Eastern
Sassafras
Silverbell
Sourgum
Sourwood
Sweetgum
Sycamore
Tulip Poplar
Umbrella Tree (*See* Chinaberry)
Yellowwood
Palms
Palmetto, Cabbage

Region 3

Evergreens, broadleaf
African Tuliptree
Bell Flambeau (*See* African Tuliptree)
Brazilian Pepper
Cajeput
Cocoplum
Fig, Fiddle Leaf
Fig, India Laurel
Fig, Lofty
Geiger Tree
Holly, American
Holly, Chinese
Indian Rubber Tree
Jacaranda
Laurelcherry
Magnolia, Southern
Mahogany, Swamp (*See* Mahogany, West Indies)
Mahogany, West Indies
Oak, Laurel
Oak, Live
Oxhorn Bucida
Pigeon Plum
Silk Oak
Silver Trumpet
Wax Myrtle
Evergreens, needle leaf and scale leaf
Pine, Longleaf
Pine, Slash
Pine, Spruce
Deciduous
Baldcypress
Bo Tree
Crape Myrtle
Cucumber Tree
Fig, Benjamin
Goldenrain Tree
Linden, American
Magnolia, Cucumber (*See* Cucumber Tree)
Maple, Red
Mimosa
Mimosa, Lebbek
Oak, Water
Orchid Tree
Pecan
Redbud, Eastern
Royal Poinciana
Sweetgum
Palms
Palm, Coconut
Palm, Cuban Royal
Palm, Fishtail
Palm, Florida Royal
Palm, Manilla
Palm, Mexican Fan (*See* Palm, Washington)
Palm, Washington
Palmetto, Cabbage
Leafless
Beefwood (*See* Casuarina)
Beefwood, Horsetail (*See* Casuarina)
Casuarina
Cunningham Beefwood
Scaly Bark Beefwood

Region 4

Evergreens, broadleaf
None
Evergreens, needle leaf and scale leaf
Arborvitae, Eastern
Arborvitae, Oriental
Cedar, Eastern Red
Cedar, Incense
Douglas Fir
Hemlock, Canadian
Juniper (*See* Cedar, Eastern Red)
Juniper, Rocky Mountain
Pine, Austrian
Pine, Ponderosa
Pine, Scotch
Spruce, Colorado Blue
Spruce, White
Deciduous
Ash, Black
Ash, Green
Ash, White
Birch, Cutleaf European
Birch, Paper
Birch, White
Catalpa, Northern
Cherry, Black
Cottonwood, Plains
Elm, American
Elm, Siberian
Hackberry, Eastern
Hackberry, Western
Honeylocust, Thornless
Katsura
Larch, Siberian
Linden, American
Linden, Littleleaf
Maple, Silver
Oak, Bur
Oak, Northern Red
Oak, Pin
Oak, Scarlet
Poplar, Plains (*See* Cottonwood, Plains)
Sugarberry (*See* Hackberry, Western)
Zelkova

Region 5

Evergreens, broadleaf
Oak, Live
Evergreens, needle leaf and scale leaf
Arborvitae, Oriental
Cedar, Atlas
Cedar, Eastern Red
Cryptomeria
Cypress, Arizona
Juniper (*See* Cedar, Eastern Red)
Juniper, Rocky Mountain
Pine, Austrian
Pine, Loblolly
Pine, Ponderosa
Spruce, Colorado Blue
Deciduous
Ash, Green
Baldcypress
Beech, European
Buckeye
Catalpa, Northern
Catalpa, Southern
Chinaberry
Desert Willow
Elm, American
Elm, Chinese
Elm, English
Elm, European Field
Elm, Siberian
Goldenrain Tree
Hackberry, Eastern
Hackberry, Western
Honeylocust, Thornless
Huisache
Japanese Pagoda Tree
Katsura
Kentucky Coffeetree
Maple, Silver
Maple, Sycamore
Mesquite
Mulberry, Paper
Mulberry, Russian
Oak, Bur
Oak, Chestnut
Oak, Pin
Oak, Post
Oak, Shumard (*See* Oak, Texas)
Oak, Scarlet
Oak, Spanish
Oak, Texas
Oak, Yellow
Pecan
Pistache, Chinese
Redbud, Eastern
Retama
Sassafras
Soapberry, Western
Sugarberry (*See* Hackberry, Western)
Sycamore
Umbrella Tree (*See* Chinaberry)
Zelkova
Palms
Palm, Mexican Fan (*See* Palm, Washington)
Palm, Washington

Region 6

Evergreens, broadleaf
  Olive, Common
  Olive, Russian
Evergreens, needle leaf and scale leaf
  Arborvitae, Giant
  Arborvitae, Oriental
  Cedar, Atlas
  Cedar, Eastern Red
  Cedar, Incense
  Douglas Fir
  Fir, White
  Juniper, (*See* Cedar, Eastern Red)
  Juniper, Rocky Mountain

Pine, Austrian
Pine, Ponderosa
Spruce, Colorado Blue
Deciduous
  Ash, Arizona (*See* Ash, Modesto)
  Ash, European
  Ash, Green
  Ash, Modesto
  Beech, European
  Buckeye
  Buckeye, Red (*See* Horsechestnut, Red)
  Catalpa, Northern
  Cottonwood, Plains

Elm, American
Elm, Chinese
Elm, European Field
Elm, Siberian
Ginkgo
Goldenrain Tree
Hackberry, Eastern
Honeylocust, Thornless
Horsechestnut
Horsechestnut, Red
Horsechestnut, Ruby (*See* Horsechestnut, Red)
Japanese Pagoda Tree
Katsura
Kentucky Coffeetree

Linden, American
Linden, Littleleaf
London Plane
Maple, Bigleaf
Maple, Norway
Maple, Sugar
Mulberry, Russian
Oak, Bur
Oak, Northern Red
Oak, Pin
Oak, White
Poplar, Plains (*See* Cottonwood, Plains)
Sweetgum
Zelkova

Region 7

Evergreens, broadleaf
  Carob
  Eucalyptus
  Gum, (*See* Eucalyptus)
  Olive, Common
  Olive, Russian
  Palo Verde, Blue
Evergreens, needle leaf and scale leaf
  Cedar, Atlas
  Cedar, Deodar
  Cedar, Eastern Red
  Cypress, Arizona
  Cypress, Italian
  Douglas Fir
  Fir, Silver
  Juniper (*See* Cedar,

Eastern Red)
Juniper, Rocky Mountain
Pine, Aleppo
Pine, Austrian
Pine, Canary Island
Deciduous
  Acadia, Baileys
  Ailanthus
  Ash, Arizona (*See* Ash, Modesto)
  Ash, Green
  Ash, Modesto
  Baileys Wattle (*See* Acacia, Baileys)
  Chinaberry
  Cottonwood, Fremont
  Cottonwood, Plains

Desert Willow
Elm, Chinese
Elm, Siberian
Ginkgo
Goldenrain Tree
Hackberry, Eastern
Hackberry, Western
Honeylocust, Thornless
Huisache
Linden, Littleleaf
Locust, Black
London Plane
Maple, Silver
Mesquite
Mulberry, Russian
Oak, Pin
Oak, Southern Red

Pecan
Pistache, Chinese
Poplar, Bolleana
Poplar, Carolina
Poplar, Plains (*See* Cottonwood, Plains)
Sugarberry (*See* Hackberry, Western)
Sweetgum
Tree of Heaven (*See* Ailanthus)
Umbrella Tree (*See* Chinaberry)
Wattle, Sydney
Palms
  Palm, Canary Date

Region 8

Evergreens, broadleaf
  Cajeput
  Camphor Tree
  Carob
  Cherry, Australian Brush
  Coral Tree
  Eucalyptus
  Fig, India Laurel
  Fig, Moreton Bay
  Gum (*See* Eucalyptus)
  Jacaranda
  Laurel, California
  Laurelcherry
  Laurel, Grecian
  Magnolia, Southern
  Oak, Canyon Live
  Oak, Coast Live
  Oak, Holly
  Oak, Live
  Palo Verde, Blue

Tanoak
Evergreens, needle leaf and scale leaf
  Arborvitae, Oriental
  Cedar, Atlas
  Cedar, Deodar
  Cedar, Incense
  Cedar of Lebanon
  Cryptomeria
  Cypress, Arizona
  Lawson False Cypress
  Norfolk Island Pine
  Pine, Aleppo
  Pine, Canary Island
  Spruce, Colorado Blue
Deciduous
  Ash, Arizona (*See* Ash, Modesto)
  Ash, Modesto
  Chinaberry

Chinese Lantern Tree
Cottonwood, Fremont
Desert Willow
Elm, American
Elm, Chinese
Elm, Siberian
Ginkgo
Goldenrain Tree
Hackberry, Eastern
Honeylocust, Thornless
Japanese Pagoda Tree
Locust, Black
London Plane
Maple, Bigleaf
Maple, Norway
Maple, Red
Mimosa
Mulberry, Russian
Oak, Bur
Oak, English

Oak, Northern Red
Oak, Pin
Oak, Scarlet
Oak, Valley
Orchid Tree
Pistache, Chinese
Sweetgum
Tulip Poplar
Umbrella Tree (*See* Chinaberry)
Palms
  Palm, Canary Date
  Palm, Mexican Fan (*See* Palm, Washington)
  Palm, Washington
Leafless
  Beefwood (*See* Casuarina)
  Beefwood, Horsetail (*See* Casuarina)
  Casuarina

Region 9

Evergreens, broadleaf
  Holly, English
  Madrone
  Magnolia, Southern
  Tanoak
Evergreens, needle leaf and scale leaf
  Arborvitae, Giant
  Arborvitae, Oriental
  Cedar, Atlas
  Cedar, Deodar
  Cedar, Incense
  Cryptomeria
  Lawson False Cypress
  Pine, Austrian

Pine, Ponderosa
Spruce, Colorado Blue
Deciduous
  Ash, European
  Ash, Green
  Ash, White
  Beech, European
  Birch, White
  Buckeye, Red (*See* Horsechestnut, Red)
  Cork Tree, Amur
  Dogwood, Pacific
  Elm, American
  Elm, Chinese
  Elm, English

Elm, Scotch
Elm, Siberian
Ginkgo
Golden Chain Tree
Goldenrain Tree
Honeylocust, Thornless
Hornbeam, American
Horsechestnut
Horsechestnut, Red
Horsechestnut, Ruby (*See* Horsechestnut, Red)
Japanese Pagoda Tree
Kentucky Coffeetree
Linden, American
Linden, Littleleaf

London Plane
Maple, Bigleaf
Maple, Norway
Maple, Red
Maple, Sugar
Mimosa
Oak, Northern Red
Oak, Oregon White
Oak, Pin
Oak, Scarlet
Oak, White
Silverbell
Sourwood
Sweetgum
Tulip Poplar
Yellowwood

Planting Methods

Trees may be purchased with the soil held around their roots by burlap and wire or plastic ("balled-and-burlaped"), or in a container, usually metal or plastic ("container-grown"), or with no soil around the roots ("bare-rooted"). Survival chances are good for balled-and-burlaped and container-grown transplants, somewhat less for bare-rooted trees.

In general, decidous trees are planted in autumn after their leaves change color and before the ground freezes, or they are planted in early spring after the ground has thawed but before budding. Spring is the best time to plant in areas where the ground freezes deeply, where strong winds prevail, or where soil moisture is deficient.

In cold regions, needle-leaved evergreens usually are planted in early fall or in spring after the ground has thawed. Those that are balled-and-burlaped or container-grown can be planted in cold regions anytime the ground is workable if they are mulched and watered after planting.

In warmer regions, needle-leaved evergreens may be planted anytime if they are watered regularly. Small varieties may be planted bare-rooted, but larger ones will have a better chance if they are balled-and-burlaped or container-grown.

Spring is the best season to plant such broad-leaved evergreens as rhododendron, magnolia, and holly, but they may also be planted in autumn if there is time for their roots to grow before the ground freezes. The best time to plant palms is during warm, wet months, but they may be planted anytime if they are adequately watered after planting.

Dig the planting hole for a bare-rooted tree wide enough so the roots can be spread in their natural position—they should never be doubled back. The planting hole for a balled-and-burlaped or container-grown tree should be about two feet wider than the diameter of the root ball or container so that soil can be placed around the planting. The hole should be deep enough so that the tree can be planted as deep as it was originally. Planting holes must be well drained. Most species will not grow well if they are planted where water stands for even a short period. A layer of gravel or crushed stone in the bottom of the hole will allow for drainage. In very wet or marshy areas, lines of 3- or 4-inch drainage tiles should be laid away from the hole to carry off excess water. The tiles should extend to a ground level lower than the bottom of the hole, to a dry well filled with gravel, or to a storm sewer.

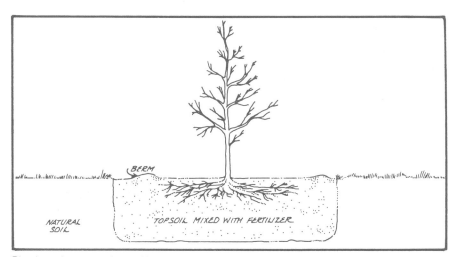

Planting a bare-rooted tree. Note the berm, which forms a basin around the tree to hold water inside the root area.

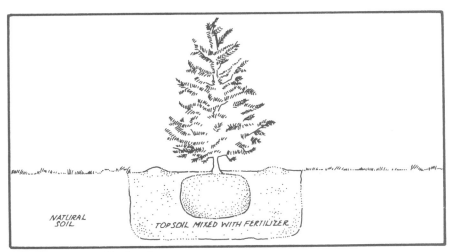

Planting a balled-and-burlaped tree.

A soil pH of 7.0 is neutral; below that is acid and above, alkaline. Adding lime decreases acidity, while adding sulphur or aluminum sulfate increases acidity. A pH of 6.0 to 7.0 is suitable for most shade trees. Generally, most needle-leaved evergreens grow best in acid soil, but junipers will grow in nearly neutral soil. Again, check with agricultural agents in your locality or a knowledgeable nurseryman.

Bare-rooted trees should be held in place while their roots are adjusted to their natural positions in the hole and covered with soil. If fertile loam was removed from the hole, it may be used to cover the roots. Otherwise, it should be mixed with fertilizer—well-decayed leaf mold, bone meal, or similar organic material may be used. For trees 6 to 10 feet tall (as most transplants are), mix about a half pound of fertilizer with every four bushels of filling soil.

Heavy clay soil can be made more permeable by mixing it with as much sand as necessary to obtain good percolation of water. Sandy soil can be made less permeable by mixing it with clay, loam, and organic materials such as peat moss. Do not use fresh manure or fresh green plant material in the planting hole—these materials release compounds as they decay that are toxic to tree roots.

Work the soil among the roots and pack it with a blunt tool. Gently shake the tree to settle the soil around the roots and eliminate air pockets. Continue to pack the soil until the roots are covered, then tamp the soil to settle it firmly. Water the soil to settle it, but do not tamp wet soil. When the water has soaked in, add more soil to form a low basin around the base of the trunk to hold water over the root area.

Balled-and-burlaped trees should be set in the planting hole with the covering around the root ball. If the hole has been dug too deep, add soil under the ball. Loosen the covering and drop it from the side of the ball. Burlap or other material need not be entirely removed from beneath the ball. Pack filling soil around the ball and settle it the same as for bare-rooted planting.

For container-grown trees, cut away the sides of the container with metal shears and carefully remove the root ball. Plant it the same way as a balled-and-burlaped tree.

Newly planted trees usually need support to hold them in position, or they may lean permanently away from prevailing winds. One to three stakes are usually adequate for smaller trees. They should be strong enough to hold the trunk rigidly in place. Set them 6 to 12 inches from the trunk, and fasten the trunk to the stakes with canvas tapes or loops of wire passed through sections of rubber or plastic hose or similar soft material. Never allow bare wire to

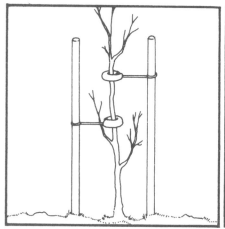 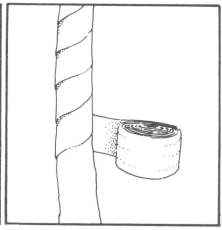

Newly planted trees should be supported by wires attached to stakes. Pass wire loops through pieces of hose to protect the bark.

Wrap the trunk with strips of burlap to prevent its drying out or being invaded by insects. Specially treated paper is also available for this purpose.

scrape the bark. Larger trees should be held securely by guy wires fastened to stakes in the ground and about two-thirds up the trunk of the tree. Remove stakes and wires after tree roots are firmly established, usually after about a year.

Fall-planted trees should be mulched after planting. Trees planted in the spring should be mulched after the soil has warmed. Leave the mulch around the trees until it decays. Broad-leaved evergreens should be mulched continuously. Protect the trunk of a newly planted deciduous tree from pests and from drying out by wrapping it spirally with strips of burlap.

Water trees regularly during the first and second growing seasons. A thorough weekly watering is better than light daily watering. Deep-rooted trees may require watering through holes punched or drilled in the ground. Watering "needles" are available at nursery supply centers to get the water down to where it is needed.

Foundation Planting

One other essential element of all successful landscaping is good foundation planting. Most homes have exposed foundations of concrete or masonry block. The patio may also be of concrete. Concrete is an excellent long-wearing building material, but by itself is not particularly attractive. In fact, it can be an eyesore, disturbing the esthetic contemplations of the person relaxing on the deck or patio. The intelligent use of shrubbery and other plantings offsets the stark look of plain concrete and helps blend the home into its natural surroundings.

Most do-it-yourself landscapers buy small plants because they are less expensive than large ones of the same variety. These small plants should be spaced to allow for several years' growth. The sparse appearance of this kind of planting may be disappointing at first, but planting ground cover between the shrubs will help overcome this temporary disadvantage. To achieve an almost immediate finished effect, mature plants can be purchased. But the higher cost may rule this out.

One school of thought teaches "plant thick and thin quick." This means using several small plants in an area that will be occupied by only one plant in a few years. The immediate effect is fairly good, but the procedure is impractical. Some of the plants will have to be removed and probably discarded, and the overall cost may be as much as or more than that would have been spent on a single mature plant. Also, close planting causes the individual plants to become more crowded and misshaped as they grow, losing their characteristic shapes.

Most of the plants around a patio or terrace should be low-growing varieties. Proportionately larger growing shrubs should be used near decks that are higher above the ground. Near very high decks, a tree or tree-form shrub may be preferred, not only for shade and some privacy, but also as an interesting variation.

Low-growing plants alongside steps give a feeling of easy access to the patio or garden. The same is true of plantings flanking a gateway.

Low plantings alongside a stairway suggest an inviting entry.

Simple box trellis on the screen leading to the walkway supports vines.

Vines

Vines are often used to ornament garden walls, retaining walls, and fences. They should be selected with regard to the type of construction and the space they are to occupy.

Twining vines can be used on wood structures, and on stone or brick walls if support is provided. Clinging vines are more frequently used on stone and brick walls, however. Vines such as bittersweet and Boston ivy cover large wall spaces; akebia and clematis, which are not so lush in growth, are better suited to smaller areas. Thorny vines such as climbing roses should not be used near gateways or alongside walkways.

Most clinging vines require artificial support only until they attach themselves to a wall, although heavy clinging vines such as big-leaved winter creeper and trumpet creeper may need permanent support. A thin lattice or other strip laid across the stem and nailed to the wall is usually enough to hold them. Twining vines must have a trellis or other support. Trellis designs should be kept simple. For smaller areas, a rectangular support is all that is needed.

Vines climbing the posts of this walkway shelter will soon cross over the joists and rafters, providing shade and a lacy shadow pattern below.

Self-contained prefabricated outdoor fountains such as this fiberglass-bowl unit actually require no plumbing. They are filled with water that is recirculated through a submersible pump.

Building & Installation Techniques:

PLUMBING

Mention plumbing and most people think of bathtubs, dishwashers, toilets, and the like. But you may very well want some plumbing installations in your outdoor living area as well. A sink is certainly handy in the outdoor kitchen, and a wet bar is always a step saver when entertaining out-of-doors. Somewhat more extensive plumbing is required if you want to install an automatic sprinkler system to keep your outdoor living room's "carpet" nice and green with minimal effort. Or you might want a drinking fountain to cool the parched throats of back-yard athletes. Perhaps the plumbing will serve a purely esthetic purpose—a fountain or waterfall that is part of the exterior decorating scheme. And, of course, if a swimming pool is in your plans, the plumbing assumes a major role.

If your outdoor living area is so arranged that plumbing fixtures such as a sink or drinking fountain are to be placed along the house wall, the installation is relatively simple. Supply and drainage pipes are run through holes drilled through the wall to connect the new fixture to the existing plumbing lines. Shut

171

Swimming pools require more elaborate plumbing installations. Sliding windows on this deck open to the kitchen sink, allowing it to serve double duty indoors and out.

off the water at a valve between the main and the point where the connection is to be made, and open faucets ahead of the connection to drain as much water as possible out of the line. Then cut through the existing line with a fine-tooth hacksaw or tubing cutter or, in the case of certain types of plastic pipe, a sharp knife.

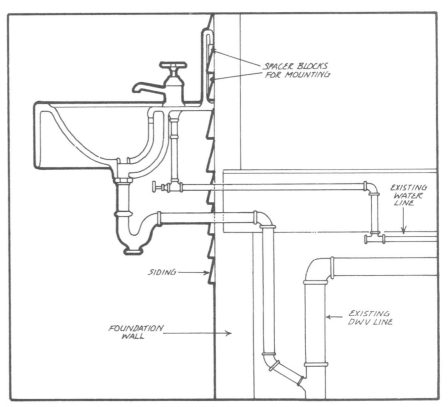

Typical installation of sink on the outside wall of a house.

This redwood A-frame shelter is the focal point of the back-yard garden, and is complemented by the urn-bearing statue to the right. Water is recirculated through the statue.

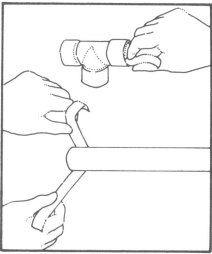

Clean the end of copper tubing and the inside of matching fitting with emery cloth.

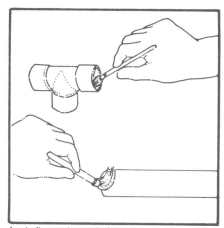

Apply flux to the end of the pipe and inside the fitting.

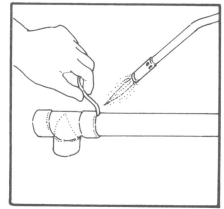

Apply heat with a propane torch; hold solder to joint.

If the existing plumbing lines are of copper, cut out enough of the line to fit a tee into it. With steel wool or fine emery cloth, clean the two pipe ends and the insides of the tee outlets. If you have dented the pipe by cutting it, ream or tap it until it is perfectly round.

Coat the pipe and the inside of the fitting with noncorrosive flux or soldering paste. Place the tee on the two pipes and rotate it back and forth a few times to spread the flux evenly. Wipe away excess flux.

If the connection is being made near a joist or other structural member, slip asbestos sheeting between the pipe and the flammable framing. Apply the heat from a propane torch to the fitting at the joint, heating it evenly. When flux begins to bubble out, back off the torch and apply the end of a strip of solder to the edge of the fitting. Capillary action will draw the solder into the joint, there should be a line of solder visible all around the joint. Wipe away excess and allow solder to harden, which should take less than a minute.

Saddle-type fittings make the job even easier. These are clamped over the existing pipe, then a hole is drilled inside the fitting through the pipe and the new pipe is attached to the fitting. The disadvantage of these is that they restrict the flow of water somewhat and are not suitable if the new line is to be the same size as the existing one.

Tapping into a plastic supply line is similar to the procedure for copper, except that a solvent, appropriate to the type of plastic pipe used (see below), is used instead of solder for the connections. If your house has galvanized steel piping, you can cut into it, thread the ends, and join the connecting tee to one of the pipes and a union fitting to the other to make the "tap." However, if your house has galvanized piping, chances are it is getting on in years, and it may be time to replace the whole system with copper or (where permitted) plastic pipe.

Drainage of water from such fixtures is connected similarly to the interior DWV (drain-waste-vent) system. Beneath the fixture, a water-filled P, J, or S trap is usually located to prevent backup of sewer gases. From the trap, the waste water is led to a drain pipe, usually in the basement or crawl space, or to a vertical drain pipe in a slab-foundation house. It is tied in with a tee or other

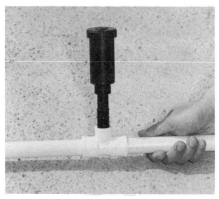

Plastic pipe makes outdoor plumbing jobs easy for the do-it-yourselfer.

The plastic pipe is easily cut with a saw or a sharp knife.

fitting, depending on the angle and on the comparative sizes of the fixture drain and the existing drain pipe. The fixture drain is usually copper or plastic pipe, and sometimes galvanized steel. The existing drain may be copper, cast iron, or plastic.

Underground Piping

For a plumbing installation remote from the house (perhaps a wet bar on a separate deck, or a spigot in a far corner of the lot), underground piping will be required. Today, the almost universal material choice for such purposes is plastic pipe. Over the past several years, most local plumbing codes have caught up with the twentieth century—in this regard, at least—and allow the use of plastic pipe. But many still do not allow its use for carrying water for drinking, and some still ban its use for any supply lines. So, as ever, make sure you check the local codes before installing this material.

Plastic pipe is ideal for underground use because it will not rust, rot, or corrode. It is easy to work with. Cutting is done with a saw or a sharp knife, and

Water trickles over a large shell into the birdbath at the right of this deck. Plastic piping is concealed in the planter behind.

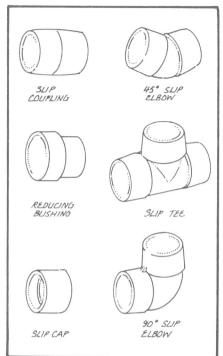

SLIP
COUPLING

45° SLIP
ELBOW

REDUCING
BUSHING

SLIP TEE

SLIP CAP

90° SLIP
ELBOW

Some common fittings for plastic pipe.

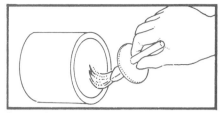

Apply solvent to the inside of the plastic fitting.

Apply solvent to the outside of the plastic pipe.

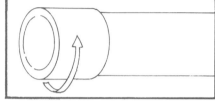

Place fitting on pipe and turn slightly to spread solvent evenly.

connections are secured with a solvent cement or, with some types, clip-on fittings.

There are several different types of plastic pipe, but three are commonly used by do-it-yourselfers. While all three are suitable for underground applications, only one can be used for hot water lines, as you may need for a sink. Chlorinated polyvinyl chloride (CPVC) pipe may be used for either cold or hot water lines. Polyvinyl chloride (PVC) pipe is a close cousin, but is not suited to hot water use because heat will soften the plastic. Polyethylene (PE) plastic pipe is more flexible than the others, making it especially useful for underground runs where hot water is not a factor. Whatever type you use, it must bear the seal of the National Sanitation Foundation if the water will be for drinking purposes.

Some types of plastic pipe are flexible, enabling you to negotiate curves and bends without fittings. But no matter where you want your plumbing line to go, there are fittings available to get it there: elbows, tees, couplings, reducers, adapters—you name it and chances are your hardware store has it.

The most common method of connecting plastic pipe and fittings is with a solvent cement, specially formulated for the type of plastic involved. First use a fine emery cloth to clean the pipe end and the inside of the fitting. Brush the solvent generously inside the fitting and on the outside of the pipe. Press the fitting onto the pipe and give it a quarter turn to spread the solvent evenly. Hold the pieces together for about fifteen seconds, until the curing process begins, then clean off excess solvent with a rag. Allow the solvent to set for at least twelve hours before trying the line under pressure.

Water supply lines should be buried at least 3 feet below the grade—at least below the frost line for your area. They are best insulated in a layer of sand. It is a good idea to make a "map" of the outdoor plumbing system, noting the locations of the various lines. If trouble should develop at some future time, it will simplify the repair tasks.

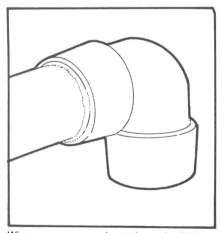

Wipe away excess solvent; there should be a continuous bead around the joint.

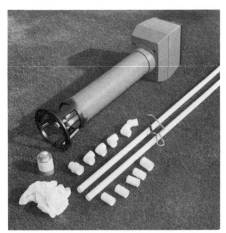

Sprinkler systems are easier to install because fittings and pipe are plastic—easier to cut and join with clamps or solvent cementing.

Underground Sprinkling Systems

Most people want their lawns to be healthy because it means the lawns will look good. But a healthy lawn also will control dust, prevent soil runoff (and mud being tracked into the house), and provide a nice play surface for the kids.

One of the most important needs of a healthy lawn, of course, is regular watering. A simple, sure way of doing it is with an automatic, underground sprinkler system. You don't have to remember to do the job in the first place and you don't have to lug out the hose on those hot days when you'd rather be sipping lemonade on a shaded patio. One other plus: The lawn will get the correct amount of water—not too much, not too little.

There are a variety of sprinkling systems one can install, but one of the easiest is one with mostly plastic components. Following are highlights of its installation, so you can decide if you want to do the job.

The only really tricky part is laying out the system according to your property; here it's best to consult with your dealer. If he has a plan of your property he can likely tell you exactly where to place the sprinkler heads. The plan should include flower beds, obstructions, trees—anything that could affect the installation. And you should keep a copy of the plan for the future so you won't accidentally run lawn machinery over the sprinkler heads.

The system uses a PVC pipe. It is laid out in the position it will occupy on the lawn, then laid in narrow trenches. To do this, a flat spade is used to turn back the sod to a depth of 4″. The pipe is placed in the trenches, tamped in place with a board, and sod replaced and tamped down.

At certain points—those most advantageous for your particular property—sprinkler heads are installed and other pipe connections made with Tee, Ell, and other fittings. It is here that plastic pipe shines. The pipe may be cut with a hacksaw or sharp knife as described; and parts held together with stainless steel clamps, or screwed together or glued together.

Laying out sprinkler heads and pipe. This is really something where the dealer should be consulted.

Digging trenches can be made infinitely easier by using powered device, such as shown here.

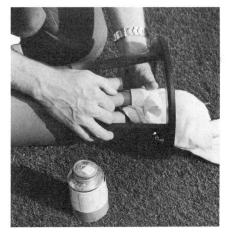

Fitting beging installed on control mechanism. Solvent is dabbed on with small applicator.

Control mechanism. Each of the pipes will carry water to other pipes which go to various lawn areas.

Ultimately, the pipe is connected by means of flexible tubing, to a control box to a galvanized valve assembly screwed to an outside faucet. Regulator valves are adjusted with a screwdriver to control water flow.

The control box itself is simple. It has a simple wiring system—a common neutral and a hot wire from each head in each sprinkling zone to its respective valve and then to the box. The box is plugged into ordinary house current.

The control box can monitor—in this particular system—up to four sprinkling zones or stations. These may be four wave sprinklers—these oscillate back and forth or the popup type with each station set for from three to sixty minutes of watering. You can slso rig things so the system goes on every day, or every other day—great flexibility, indeed, for watering schedules.

Other Installations

More elaborate water effects can be created in the outdoor living area. Waterfalls can be created over built-up rocks, or formal fountains can add beauty to the garden. (Fantastic nighttime effects can be achieved by combining the water effects with special lighting, as outlined in a previous chapter.) Such installations normally involve only minimal plumbing. Water is recirculated through the fountain or falls by means of a submersible pump. In the case of a waterfall, the water may be carried from the pump through plastic pipe or even garden hose to the top of the rock or hillside, where it cascades down to repeat the cycle. Submersible pumps are available at many nursery centers and most building supply stores.

Who needs the bay (background) when you can have a pool right in your own backyard? This vinyl-lined model is surrounded by a wood deck.

Building & Installation Techniques:
SWIMMING POOLS

The idea of a cooling dip on a hot day followed by a stint of poolside sunbathing accompanied by frosty drinks represents the ultimate to many outdoor-living enthusiasts, and it is indeed a pleasant concept. It can be a pleasant reality as well, for swimming pools have come well within the financial reach of many of today's homeowners. Persistent water shortages and the ever-mounting costs of fuel (as used in recirculating and filtering equipment and to heat a pool) may make some people postpone their pool plans, but the dream endures.

The Bad Side . . .

If there is a pool in your future, you should be aware that it is not all a waterbed of roses. To begin with, the community in which you live may be very demanding about what you must provide (and pay for) in addition to that hole in (or above) the ground. Building codes in most urban and suburban localities require that a pool (except for very small waders) be fenced in. But some go further, and insist that a screen of plantings, usually evergreens, conceal the fence. Detailed plans may have to be submitted not only for the pool, but also for fencing and landscaping. Types of lighting that are permitted may be narrowly restricted. And to add insult to economic injury, some communities require the owner to sign an agreement that the pool will be used only by himself and a limited number of guests. Make sure to check the building code in your community before you start digging that hole.

Some realtors warn that a pool may lower the resale value of a home rather than raise it. In a neighborhood of young homeowners with small children, a full-sized pool may be a sales liability. Prospective buyers might be more concerned with year-round safety than summertime fun, and will see the pool as a potential disaster area.

A pool may mean an increase in your real estate taxes. It will almost certainly mean an increase in food and liquor bills, along with other problems associated with the newfound popularity your family will acquire once the pool is open for swimming.

. . . And the Good

But there are compensations. Foremost is the incomparable pickup of a cool dip after a hard day's work—and right in your own back yard! The weary bones and the weary brain relax into instant euphoria as soon as hot flesh hits cold water. Sheer delight!

After the swim, as you lounge at poolside sipping a gin and tonic, you might ponder some other advantages of pool ownership. No more need you fight crowded traffic to get to a crowded beach where you can fight pollution and seaweed for a brief period of cooling off before you have to sweat your way through traffic to get home again, as miserable as before you left. Then there are the exercise benefits. Diets may be "in," but they are seldom fun. Jogging may impress the neighbors, at least those who are up at dawn (mostly other joggers), but it too can hardly be called fun. A swimming pool, though, is quite a different matter. Sure, swimming improves arm and leg muscles, firms up the torso, and trims off excess fat throughout the body, but you don't think of it as exercise. Swimming is fun!

And if there are small children in your family, what better place to teach them to swim than in your own back yard? As they grow, you can supervise their water activities and help them to improve their aquatic techniques. And when as teenagers they want to go to the beach on their own ("where the action is"), you will be secure in the knowledge that they can take care of themselves—in the water, at least.

Lighting extends the hours of pool usage, but this one should be surrounded by a fence for safety's sake.

Most pools are situated adjacent to house and patio. With a small lot, you don't have much choice. Finished job is a clever and eye-pleasing utilization of little space.

On a larger piece of property, you have more options as to where to place your pool. This one is the far corner of the yard where there is plenty of sun.

Pool Location

If you live on a small lot with very irregular terrain and, perhaps, areas of hard rock, your choice of pool locations might be limited or (at least in the case of an in-ground pool) nonexistent. Otherwise, you should give some careful consideration to the question of where.

It is convenient to have the pool next to the house, or next to a patio adjacent to the house. This facilitates the serving of poolside snacks and drinks and shortens the trip to dressing rooms and bathrooms. (Often a bathroom is located right inside a rear door, or a doorway to an existing bathroom can be cut through the outer wall for convenient access from the pool area.) But proximity to the house is not the only, nor even the primary, consideration. *That* is the sun.

An ideal pool location preserves the view, if any. Note the lounging area at far end. (Wall in foreground is unfinished.)

Most pools are rectangular in shape. This one is almost square. Square-cornered pools are the least expensive and simplest to install.

The topography of the lot must also be kept in mind. Here, a retaining wall was necessary, and raised the overall cost.

This pool is built far enough away from the trees to avoid falling-leaves problem. Most homeowners prefer less shade, though.

Sunlight is necessary for pool enjoyment. It keeps the water warm (although still cool enough to be refreshing), and allows the pleasure of poolside sun bathing. An obvious accompaniment to sunshine is the lack of shade, such as that provided by trees. The pool should be located away from trees, not only because they block sunlight, but also because falling leaves and seeds can be a pool nuisance. Roots, too, can be a problem, so build the pool as far as possible from large trees.

Other considerations include the location of underground piping and wiring and of such equipment as filters and pumps. If the pool is built away from the house or garage, you may want to construct outbuildings to house such equipment. You may also want to build separate dressing rooms, perhaps combined with the utility building, to keep the postbathing mess from being tracked through the house.

Human organs are often imitated by pool-builders. Here's one in the shape of a kidney.

No shape is impossible, however, as this attractive free-form pool demonstrates.

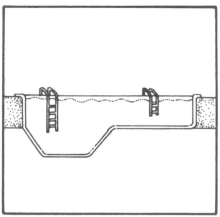

In-ground pool.

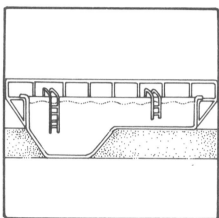

On-ground pool.

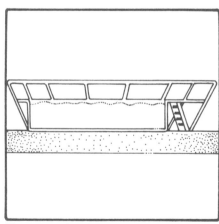

Above-ground pool.

Pool Size

The size of your pool will be determined by location, intended use, and, of course, budget. Big costs more than little, no matter what you're buying.

As a general rule, allow 36 square feet per swimmer. If there are four in your family, a 12x12-foot pool would be a minimum—but don't forget the neighbors. They won't forget you once that pool is there. For divers, 100 square feet is the recommended minumum. If a diving board is part of the plan, a minimum depth of 7½ feet should be allowed.

In-Ground Pools

There are three basic types of pools: in-ground, on-ground, and above-ground. Of these, the in-ground is by far at the head of the class—in appearance, in prestige, and in cost.

An in-ground pool generally can be built to blend in nicely with its surroundings. But it will cost considerably more to install than other types, and you will probably also have to shoulder the burden of increased property taxes once it is installed, a prospect which no homeowner views with detachment. Check this out with your local tax assessor's office; the bite may not be too bad. Or it may. Better to know in advance.

Concrete is the most commonly used material for in-ground pools. There are various methods of building concrete pools.

Poured concrete pools are structurally strong, especially when they are bolstered with steel reinforcing rods, but this is a job for a skilled contractor—no do-it-youselfers need apply. A properly poured pool should last many years. The only inherent danger is the possibility of serious cracks that are difficult to repair. These are usually caused by unstable soil conditions around the pool walls.

Gunite (pneumatically applied) concrete pools are quite strong, especially if steel reinforcing rods are used. Skilled workmen must do the job. One big advantage of a Gunite pool is that it can be just about any shape your heart desires—even heart-shaped, if that's your desire.

Dry-pack concrete construction is somewhat of a cross between poured concrete and Gunite. Stiff concrete is poured and molded over reinforcing wire placed in the excavation. No forms are used, so that almost any shape can be achieved—heart, kidney, lung, diamond, club, spade, star, moon—even your profile if you want to be immortalized in water. Dry-pack is slightly less strong than other concrete pools, and the walls are generally somewhat rough, exposing swimmers and divers to the possibility of bruises and abrasions. But the cost is usually considerably less than for other types of concrete pools. Just make sure that you deal only with a reputable and knowledgeable contractor—this, again, is no job for an amateur.

Precast pools in various materials are factory-built and lowered into place at the site. Corners, strengtheners, and sometimes the floor are constructed at the building site. Installation is rapid and economical, but structural strength is not as good as poured concrete or Gunite pools. Because of the special equipment required, this is not a job for the do-it-yourselfer.

Vinyl-lined pools are very popular because of their relatively low cost. The structural framing can be metal, wood, concrete block, or concrete. The common denominator is the vinyl liner that is placed inside. A semiskilled, patient home handyman who doesn't mind sweating a bit so that he can cool his brow a little later on can build such a pool, although it is recommended that the digging be done by an excavator with the proper heavy equipment.

Another popular style is the dog-leg.

The tear-drop is another popular shape.

On-Ground Pools

An on-ground pool is similar to the vinyl-lined above-ground pools described below, with one basic difference. A "hopper" dug into the ground at one end allows diving. That hole makes the pool virtually permanent—you can't very well take it with you if you move, as the new owner of your house would likely object to a 4-foot depression in the middle of his back yard. While building such a pool can be a do-it-yourself project, there is quite a bit of digging involved, and you may prefer to leave that part of the job, at least, to the professionals.

Above-Ground Pools

The 3-foot-diameter, 6-inch-deep plastic tub in which your tots soak their toes can be considered an above-ground pool, but here we refer to adult-sized models. These usually have a vinyl liner over an aluminum, steel, or wood frame.

In addition to lower initial cost, an above-ground pool saves the cost (or backbreak) of excavating. And, perhaps best of all, it is usually tax-free. While some municipalities consider above-ground pools as permanent additions to the property, most do not tax such installations, since they can be taken down and moved (although few homeowners would bother, except for very small versions).

Most above-ground pools have some type of skirting to hide the unsightly understructure and filtering machinery. On a large lot they can be quite attractive. But they are not well-suited to very small lots. (Perhaps no pool really is.) Most above-ground pools have decking on two or three sides that adds to the length and width of the structure, so that you will probably end up with a smaller pool than you would like, as well as sacrificing most of your back yard.

Many above-ground pools have built-in railings around the deck area. An added inherent safety feature is that it is impossible to wander mistakenly into the pool and drown—a conscious effort must be made to climb the stairs or ladder first. While that may not be enough to stop a curious and determined child, it will certainly make it more difficult for him.

Most above-ground pools now come with built-in decks, and are within the financial reach of almost any homeowner.

An in-ground pool may be your dream, but if economic or other factors make an above-ground version more feasible, don't fret. It will serve the purpose just fine, and on a hot day the water will be just as wet.

Maintenance

Once that pool is in place, it will require some regular attention if it is to provide you and your family with season-long swimming fun. One of the most important elements of pool care is maintaining a proper chemical balance of the water. From the first day you fill the pool, the water's purity should be guarded by a chemical disinfectant—chlorine, bromine, or iodine. Enough of it must remain in the water to kill disease-carrying bacteria that is brought into the water by bathers. If it all sounds somewhat distasteful, just remember the delights that your pure pool will provide—and do what you are supposed to.

Chlorine is the most widely used disinfectant. Ideally it should be used in a quantity of one part per million (ppm) of water. This means only a single drop of chlorine for every million drops of water, a very small amount indeed and scarcely enough to interfere with your pool enjoyment.

Use a leaf skimmer—a long-handled tool with a net on the end—to clean the pool's surface of leaves, bugs, debris, and other floating contaminants whenever these appear. Walls should be brushed down regularly. Special vacuum cleaners are available to allow you to clean the pool bottom.

Pumps and filters should be cleaned and serviced on a regular schedule, following the recommendations supplied by the manufacturers.

In most parts of the United States, there are at least a few months of the year when the weather is too cold for swimming, even in a heated pool. Water should be left in the pool year-round, regardless of the weather. If the pool is drained, pressures created by frozen or shifting earth could damage or collapse the pool walls. Water in the pool will counteract such pressures.

Before shutting the pool down for the winter, clean it thoroughly. Drain enough water to allow removal of underwater lighting fixtures. Insert rubber plugs in all openings, then refill the pool to within 2 inches of the skimmer opening. Turn off the main drain valve. Add an extra dose of chlorine to the water, then spread the pool cover if you are using one.

Check the pool from time to time during the winter. If there is a coating of ice on top and water has receded below it, refill with a garden hose until water level is right up to the ice; suspended ice could damage the pool walls.

Here's an ingenious above-ground pool installation. Situated on a lot which sloped away from the house, it looks like a built-in model, cost only $4600.

Outdoor Building Projects

- Decks and Patios

- Furniture

- Storage

- Kitchens

- Garden

- Strictly for Kids

- Games

- Shady Spots

- Fences and Retaining Walls

- Pet Enclosures

- Miscellaneous

- Index

- Project Index

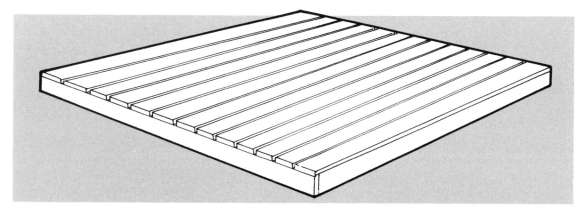

2x6 Deck

One of the simplest decks you can build is shown here. Simple, yet very solidly constructed and highly functional, it'll perform just as you would expect any good deck to perform.

First, as with any deck, mark off the area required for the deck with stakes and string. Instructions here are for a deck 10' wide (19 2x6's) and any length you wish; just repeat framing members to provide necessary support.

Sink concrete footings at 6' to 7' intervals, making their tops level with the ground. Cement an 8"x8"x4" brick on the top of each footing; when framing is installed this will raise the deck a bit higher (about 4") off the ground. If the terrain is not level you can add bricks to individual posts to achieve it.

Next, prepare nailing ledgers. Two are required. Each is made by face-nailing two straight 2x6s to each other, forming one double 2x6 or a 4"x6" assembly. As mentioned, the length of these members will determine how long the deck is.

Lay each of the ledgers across the brick-topped footings—no need to secure them in any way (their weight will hold them in place). Then simply start nailing 2x6 joists between the ledgers. The top edges of the joists should be level with ledger tops. In this situation joist hangers will greatly facilitate nailing. The joists should be secured on 2' centers.

Final step is to cut decking from 2x6 stock and nail in place across the joists (use 10d nails). Maintain ¼" space between boards as you go.

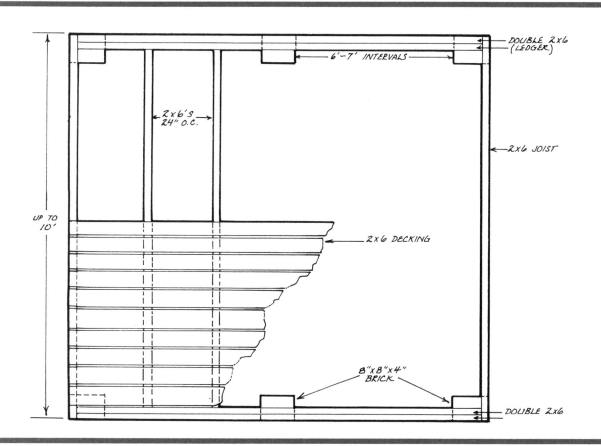

Modular Deck or Walkway

The principles of building a wood deck or walkway may be constant, but no two projects are likely to be the same. Terrain, lot size, home style, family needs and preferences, climate—all these factors will enter into planning and building the deck that you want.

One of the most simple approaches—topography permitting—is to prefabricate modular units in sizes that are relatively easy to handle, then set them individually much the same as you would a brick or block patio, but using stone or masonry units rather than a sand or gravel leveling bed as a foundation. Where the lay of the land demands, post supports can be used for the mod-

ules, or for those corners that require it. The entry "steps" in this photograph, made up of interspersed units of western pine 2x4s and 2x8s lying on their sides in alternating directions, are an attractive demonstration of this approach. The units vary in size from 4x4 feet to 4x8 feet; spacing between individual pieces of lumber is ½-inch.

Typical materials requirements for such modules are:
4x4 feet: twelve 2x(4, 6, or 8) 8 feet long; one 2x4 8 feet long; 8 feet of ½x3-inch lattice strip; 8d galvanized finishing nails; 12d galvanized annular-grooved common nails; wood preservative.
4x6 feet, with decking run in the 4-foot direction: eighteen 2x(4, 6, or 8) 8 feet; 2x4 x 12 feet; 12 feet of ½x3-inch lattice strip; 8d galvanized finishing nails; 12d galvanized annular-grooved common nails; wood preservative.

4x6 feet, with decking run in the 6-foot direction: twelve 2x(4, 6, or 8) 12 feet; 2x4 x 12 feet; 12 feet of ½x3-inch lattice strip; 8d galvanized finishing nails; 12d galvanized annular-grooved common nails; wood preservative.

From these examples, you can adapt the materials order to meet your particular needs.

First cut all pieces to length. The 2x4 base cleats are cut to fit across the width of the module (for a 4 x 6-foot unit with decking run in the 4-foot direction, they will be 6 feet long; the same size module with decking run in the 6-foot direction would have 4-foot cleats). Figure on two cleats for 4-foot-long modules, three for those 6 to 8 feet. Cut 2-inch-long spacers of lattice strip to fit over each cleat. When all wood has been cut, give it a liberal treatment of preservative, paying special attention to all cut edges and the lattice spacers.

Assemble each module on a flat surface, nailing one deck piece to the next with spacers between flush with the tops, approximately 2 inches in from each end and (for longer units) midway between. Turn the module upside down and use 12d nails to attach cleats across the bottom, nailing each cleat to each deck board below the spacers. Cleats may overhang the edges of the modular unit slightly.

The entry walkway shown is laid in several different ways. Nearest the house, it is simply set upon a concrete terrace that was already there. The module in the foreground of the picture rests directly on the ground. Most of the others in this relatively even site are leveled with flat stones, bricks, or 2-inch patio blocks at one or more corners. One module (near the middle) rests on a wood-framed planter set into the ground, fastened by 16d galvanized nails toenailed into the planter frame. The nails are countersunk and the holes filled with putty to prevent moisture from entering.

Many lots are not blessed with such flat areas. In this case, some type of post foundation, as described previously, will have to be provided. While setting posts in concrete is generally most desirable, small walkway sections may require only that the posts be dug into the ground—if the soil is compact enought to provide sturdy support. Whether this is feasible and how deep the posts should be set will depend on the soil conditions in your locality. Since these vary so greatly, it is impossible to give specific recommendations. If you are in doubt about the soil's stability, set the posts in concrete. Base cleats—not the deck boards—should rest on the posts. For modular units with boards set on edge, it is easiest to add skirt boards or a full frame for fastening to the posts, which should be set just inside the frame. Skirt boards should be of lumber 4 inches wider than the deck boards: 2x8s for a 2x4 deck, 2x12s for a 2x8 deck. The frame boards should be fastened to the deck boards with 12d nails, and to the posts with 16d nails or 3-inch lag screws. If you build a full frame around the module, the corners may be butt-joined, but mitered corners are preferred for appearance as well as moisture resistance. Miters are best cut by using a 45-degree setting on a portable power saw.

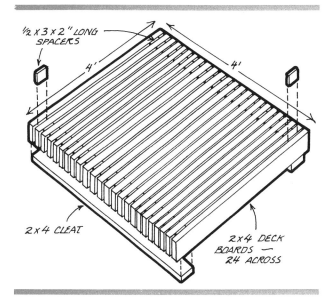

½ x 3 x 2" LONG SPACERS

2x4 CLEAT

2x4 DECK BOARDS — 24 ACROSS

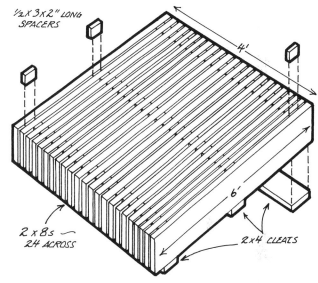

½ x 3 x 2" LONG SPACERS

2x8s — 24 ACROSS

2x4 CLEATS

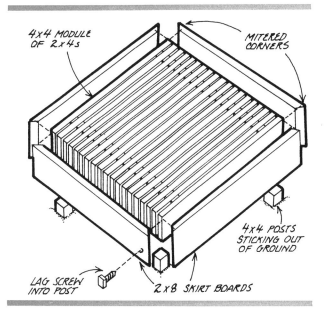

4x4 MODULE OF 2x4s

MITERED CORNERS

4x4 POSTS STICKING OUT OF GROUND

LAG SCREW INTO POST

2x8 SKIRT BOARDS

Sundeck

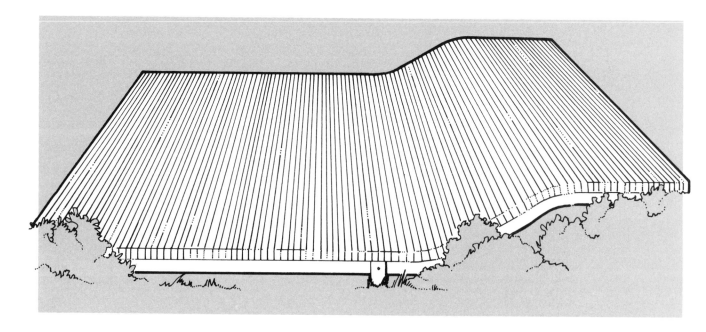

Here's a deck that's a deck and a couch in one. As you can see, it is curved to make lounging on it more comfortable than on a strictly horizontal structure.

The structure is 18' long and 8' wide. The stock you use to make it, as with most of these outdoor projects, is optional. If you don't use one of the more expensive woods, or pressure-treated lumber, you can coat the wood—even the decking members—with preservative, but give the material a couple of days to dry out thoroughly before reclining barebacked on it.

The deck has three stringers supporting it, each composed of three pieces of 2x6 joined by plywood gussets.

First, cut the stringer members: One 2x6 about 11'2" and angled 30° at one end, another piece 4' long and with square-cut ends and another piece 3'6½" long angled 60° at one end. Repeat the procedure twice.

Next, cut gussets. To facilitate this, follow this procedure, as indicated in Fig. A. Cut a piece of plywood that is 96" long and 24" wide. Divide this in half (draw a line) down the length, then proceed, from each end, to mark the panel as shown—at 6" and 12½" intervals from each end. Draw the 12½" lines straight across the board. Then, cut a piece of 1x2 that is 46" long. Measure 45" from either end of it and drive a nail, centered, through the board. Placing the strip on the plywood—the nail on the centerline—proceed to mark off curved lines at the 6" points.

When *all* the marking is done, cut along the lines you made. You'll end up with 12 gussets, six concave and six convex that are ready to link the 2x6 stringer pieces together.

Following details in Fig. B, do just that—assemble the stringers with two gussets at each joint. Only minimal trimming of the gussets will be required after they are nailed on.

Next, referring to Fig. C, dig post holes as previously described. Drive sharpened 2x4 stakes into the ground near the post holes. There should be three stakes at what is to be the low end of the deck and three at the high end. To these tack temporary 2x6's (Refer to details in Fig. B) so that the tops of the 2x4 are flush with the tops of the 2x6's, the low-end stakes protruding one foot from the ground, the high end stakes 2'.

Following Fig. D, cut posts, notching them about 5" and secure to the stringers with carriage bolts. In turn, lay each of the stringer-post assemblies on top of the temporary framework so the posts hang down inside the holes. Level the stringers, then pour the concrete in the holes and let set.

Next, remove the temporary framework and proceed to nail on the decking. Use 2x2 boards, nailing on the bottom (or low end) strips first and maintaining ⅛" spaces between boards. Countersink nails as you go.

Materials	
Quantity	Description
138'	2x2 lumber for decking
40'	4x4 lumber for posts
1 piece	of ¾" plywood (24"x96") for gussets
55'	of 2x6 lumber for stringers
	⅜"x3½" carriage bolts

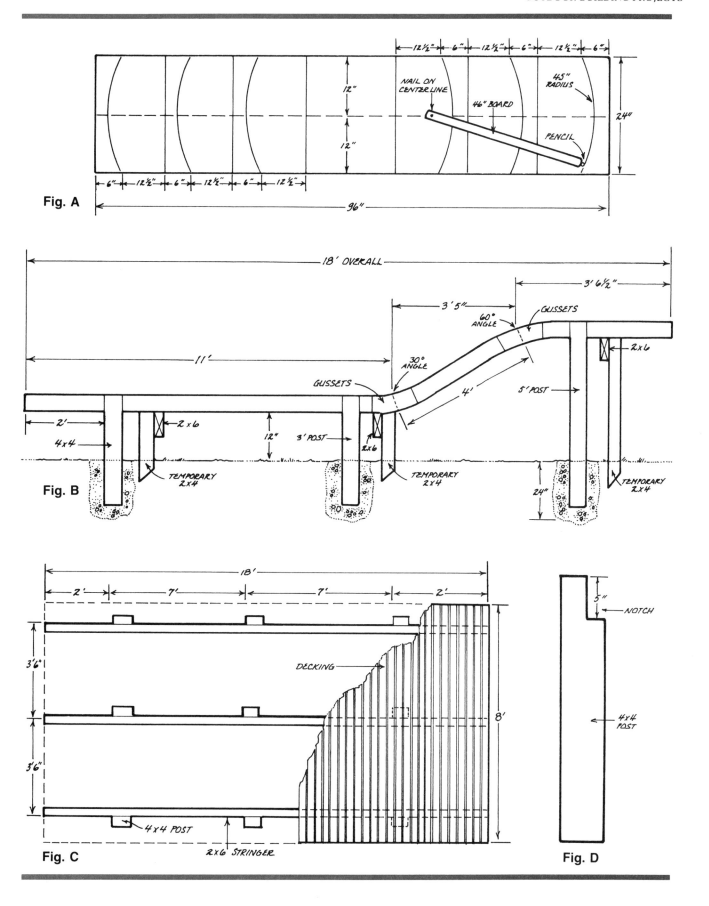

Fig. A

Fig. B

Fig. C

Fig. D

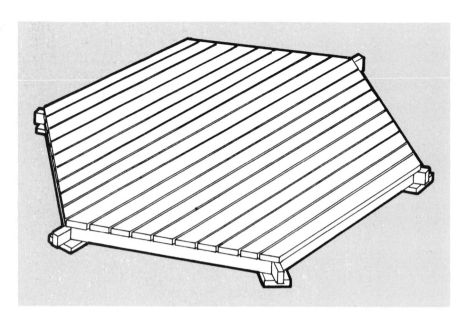

Hex Deck

In some settings a freestanding deck may be a desirable form for the outdoor living room, possibly because of the proximity of the house to the neighbors or to a busy street. While a simple square or rectangular structure can suffice, more visual interest—and thus a more inviting environment for outdoor enjoyment—can be created with a less conventional shape, such as this hexagonal deck. It is designed for building on relatively flat terrain.

The deck rests on seven concrete piers—one at each corner of the hexagon and one in the center. In addition to the foundation materials and wood preservative, materials for a 12-foot-square hexagonal deck include nine 12-foot 2x6s, thirteen 12-foot 2x4s, ten 10-foot 2x4s, ten 8-foot 2x4s, 16 feet of 1x4 (western fir, pine,

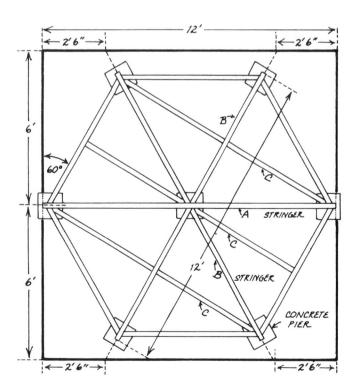

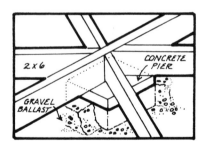

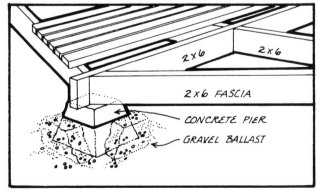

or spruce are easily worked for a deck such as this), 10d and 8d galvanized annular-grooved common nails. You will also need a 12-inch length of 2x12 or two 12-inch 2x6s, which your lumber dealer may have as scrap. Adjust materials list as necessary for larger decks.

Lay out the dimensions of the deck on the ground with chalk lines or stakes and strings. Excavate pier holes at each corner to firm soil, as previously described. Determine the exact center of the deck and excavate for the center pier. Erect forms as needed and pour the concrete piers; corner piers can be pyramidal in shape, at least 12 inches square at the base and not less than 6 inches square at the top. The center pier should be 12 inches square at the top, and 1½ inches lower than the corner piers to allow a nailer board to be placed on top. When forms are in place, use a 12-foot 2x6 (pick the straightest one) and a carpenter's level to make sure that they are all even. Then pour the concrete, strike off level with the tops of the forms, and allow to cure before removing the forms and backfilling around the piers.

Set the 12-inch length of 2x12 on top of the center pier, beneath the long stringer. Set the 12-foot-long 2x6 main stringer (A) in place on two opposite piers, and toenail it to the nailer boards on the center pier. Cut four 6-foot-long 2x6 secondary (B) stringers, squaring one end and mitering the other with a 60-degree setting on the power saw (you can also make the cut with a hand saw, marking the angle with a try square). Temporarily support the outer edges of the secondary stringers with lengths of 1x4 set on the ground, and toenail them to the center of the main stringer and to the nailers. Cut 2x6 fascia boards to fit between the six stringers, 2 inches in from each outer end—miter both ends of the fascia boards to 60-degree angles. Toenail the fascia boards in position. Measure in place, cut, and toenail six tertiary support stringers (C), four between corner piers and secondary stringers and two between the center pier and the fascia. Sharpen lengths of preservative-treated 1x4 and drive them into the ground alongside the stringers (use at least four stakes). Make a final check of the framing to make sure that it is level, then nail the stakes to the stringers to firmly anchor the structure in position.

The 2x4 decking is laid perpendicular to the tertiary stringers. Begin applying it at the center of the deck—the first deck board should be centered on the 12-foot stringer. Allow the boards to overhang the ends. Use two 10d nails to secure each board to each stringer; you can use 10d nails slightly below the surface of the wood. Check the alignment of the boards frequently, and make adjustments by increasing or decreasing the gap between deck members.

Cut a straightedged 1x4 approximately 7 feet long to serve as a trim guide. Tack it along one edge of the deck and trim the edges with a power saw, allowing a 2-inch overhang. Repeat the process along all six sides. Ease the cut edges with a wood rasp or file.

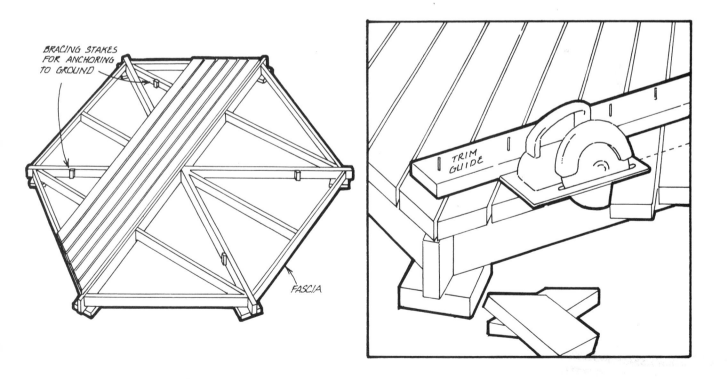

BRACING STAKES FOR ANCHORING TO GROUND

FASCIA

TRIM GUIDE

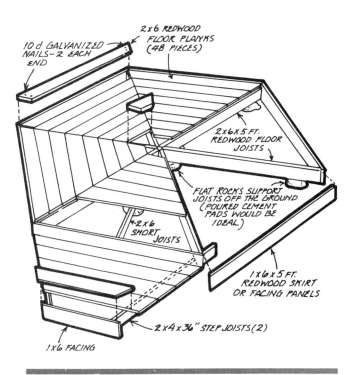

Hex Step Deck

Here is a variation on the basic polyangular deck just detailed—a slightly smaller (10-foot outside dimension) version two steps above ground level, with deck boards laid in a manner to accentuate the hexagonal shape. It may look a bit more complex, but as shown it was designed and built by a do-it-yourselfer as a weekend project. He used California redwood, spending approximately $100 for the materials. This does not include the optional umbrella stand and table.

Lumber requirements for a deck this size are twenty 10-foot 2x6s, one 4-foot 2x6, one 6-foot 2x4, three 10-foot 1x6s, and one 3-foot 1x6. 10d and 12d annular-ringed galvanized or aluminum nails are used for fastening. The joists of the deck shown were simply set on a foundation of flat rocks; concrete piers, excavated and poured as previously described, would be preferable.

Begin construction by marking off on the ground where the deck will be, using a chalk line or strings tied between stakes driven into the ground. Place stones or cement pads or piers at four of the corners, leveling them at the appropriate height (note that two of the corners of the deck are supported by the 2x4 step joists; for a more stable unit, these too should be supported by rocks or concrete, leveled 3½ inches below the rest of the foundation). Find the center of the deck area and place a rock or cement pad there also.

Cut two 3-foot-long step joists and set them on the rock or concrete foundations. Cut six 2x6 main joists, each 5 feet long. Bevel their inner ends to a 30-degree angle so that as they are fitted together a hole is formed to accomodate the umbrella pole (if your deck will not include an umbrella, cut the bevels so that the ends form a point, and fit them tightly together). Bevel the outer ends of the joists 30 degrees on each side to form a point. Set the joists in place on the foundation pads and the step joists and toenail together (the final joist may be difficult to toenail, so simply lay it in position; deck boards will hold it in place). Toenail the main joists to the step joists.

Cut six 4-foot, 11½-inches-long 1x6 skirt boards, beveling each end inward at a 30-degree angle. Nail them to the outer ends of the joists, with the top edges of the skirt boards 1½ inches above the top edges of the joists. Similarly, cut and nail on the step facing.

Cut the six short (2-foot) joists. Fasten one midway on each skirt board, at the same height as the main joists, driving 12d nails through the skirts into the ends of the joists. The short joists should be leveled, with their inner

ends simply resting on flat rocks or bricks—no need to pour concrete foundations for these.

Measure and cut each deck board individually to insure a perfect fit. The cutting diagrams show the most economical way to cut so that you can get all the needed pieces from the specified amounts of lumber. Start from the outside of the deck, fastening the six A pieces against the skirt board with 10d nails. Continue in sequence with deck boards B through H, allowing a ¼-inch gap between boards—a couple of scraps of ¼-inch lattice make the spacing easy.

With the deck completely covered, nail step piece I in place, beneath the skirt board. Nail pieces J through M to complete the step.

If you used redwood for the deck, all you need do is insert an umbrella pole assembly from your lawn and garden furniture store through the hole in the center of the deck and you are ready to enjoy the fruits of your labors—such as tomatoes in a zesty Bloody Mary or tart limes in a delicious icy daiquiri or even a cooling lemon squash, if that is to your liking. If you used some other wood species, refer to the earlier section on Finishes before you break out the cocktail shaker.

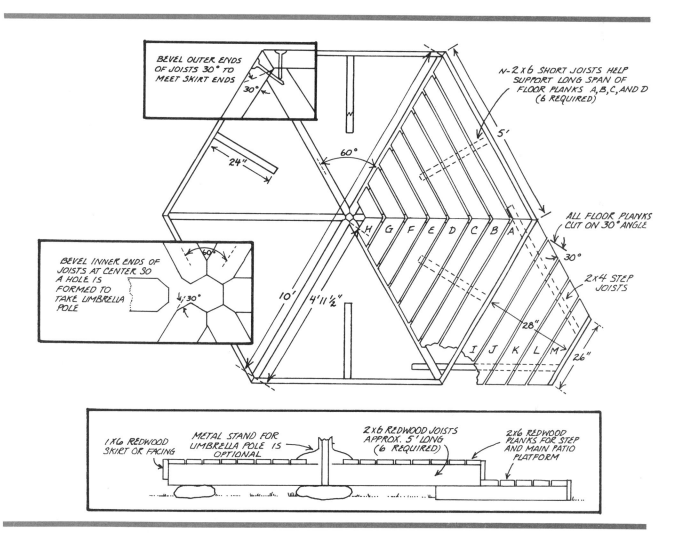

Redwood-and-Brick Patio

A rich and unusual—but not unheard of—marriage can be made between redwood and ordinary brick to create a patio that's handsome and functional. The reddish hues of the materials blend nicely and the different textures—smooth and rough—add an equally nice accent.

Following are two ways you can combine the materials: when you have a flat surface, and when the land is hilly.

For the flat surface, assuming you want to cover a 16'-long area by 8' wide, proceed as follows; you can adapt instructions for the particular dimensions you are dealing with.

First, level the entire 8'x16' area, excavating and laying a sand base as previously described for brick.

Stake two 16'-long redwood 2x4s to the ground as edge pieces; their tops should be flush with the ground surface (see Fig. A.).

Divide the area into two 8'x8' sections by staking a redwood 2x4, on edge, between the 16'-long edge pieces. If you want it there permanently, nail it in place to edge pieces.

Cut three sleepers, each long enough to fit between the edge pieces across the patio. Place each flat on the sand and a 2x4 thickness (1½"x3½") beneath the tops of the edge pieces and equal distances apart. Nail the sleepers to the edge pieces, then proceed to cut and nail the redwood 2x4 decking pieces to the sleepers; maintain spaces for drainage.

Now, lay the brick. The thickness of each is approxi-

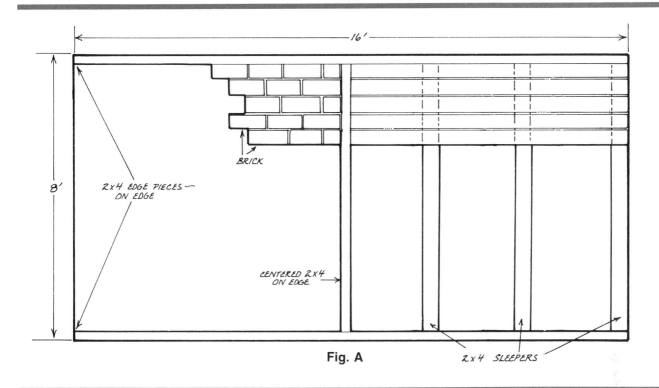

Fig. A

16'

8'

2×4 EDGE PIECES ON EDGE

BRICK

CENTERED 2×4 ON EDGE

2×4 SLEEPERS

mately 2″. Lay them in a running bond pattern; when you come to the redwood dividing piece it will be necessary to cut the bricks to fit.

If you want to butt the bricks against the ends of the redwood decking it is suggested that you make the redwood strips in uniform but staggered lengths; the dividing strip, of course, will be eliminated (see Fig. B).

If you wish to create a transition between brick and redwood decking on hilly terrain, you can follow the details in Fig. C: Just build standard decking supports and butt the bricks against the ends of the boards, either cut off evenly or staggered, as shown in Fig. B.

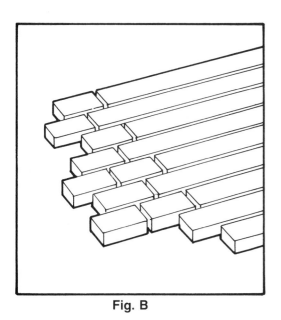

Fig. B

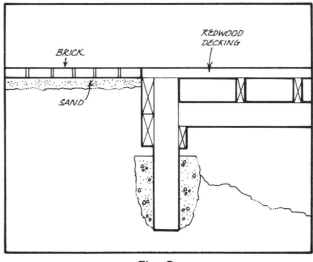

REDWOOD DECKING

BRICK

SAND

Fig. C

Deck—For a Mobile Home

While a mobile home can be a compact, economical, efficient way of serving a family's needs, the simple fact is that it can also be a mite claustrophobic. There's no way to escape except to walk around the grounds of the mobile home park.

This deck represents a nice solution to the problem. It is a deck in every way and then some, complete with seating facilities and a privacy fence, yet the structure is not permanently attached to the home. This means, in most cases, that you can build it without violating local building code laws or tacking on taxes. You should, of course, make doubly sure that you're legally in the clear before you begin.

First, mark off ground for post holes (Fig. A). Excavate for foundation blocks and install them. These can be the standard pour-your-own variety, but it is simpler to buy blocks with post-accepting hardware in them. All you do is set the post end in the U-shaped metal projection, then bolt through the holes in the metal to anchor it.

When the blocks are in, cut nine posts from 4"x4" stock. How long these will be depends on the terrain and the finished height the deck must be in relation to the front entrance; on level ground, posts can each be 1'3" long. Whatever their individual height, the middle three posts should each be ¾" longer than the others. This is so that when the plywood decking is laid on the framing it will be crowned or "peaked" in the center and drainage will be sufficient. Without good drainage plywood—even the exterior types specified here—will succumb to rot. Referring to section drawings a, b, and c, drill holes and secure posts to the block hardware with ½" carriage bolts. Then proceed to cut the perimeter framing pieces—two sides, each 2"x12"x16'5½"; two ends, each 2"x12"x15'9"; and the two boards that flank the center posts, each 15'9". Secure 2"x2" cleats to what will be the inside faces of the side (longest) pieces with the top edge of each cleat approximately 5½" (the width of a 2x6) from the top edge of the side.

Drill holes and secure all framing pieces to posts with ½" carriage bolts, then cut and install 2x6 deck joists on 16" centers, resting the ends of each on the cleats and anchoring them in place by nailing through the 2x12 perimeter pieces into the joist ends with 8d nails.

Next, install ⅝" plywood decking (Fig. B) with the following criteria in mind: 1) If you use regular square-edge plywood, support unsupported panel edges with 2x4 blocking (fig. B) nailed to joists and other framing pieces; if you use tongue-and-groove material this isn't

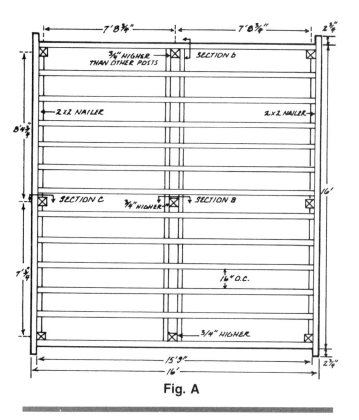

Fig. A

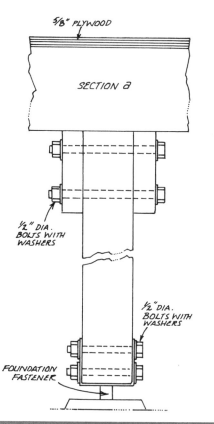

SECTION a

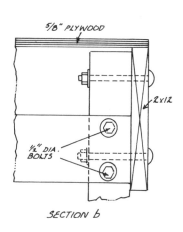

SECTION b

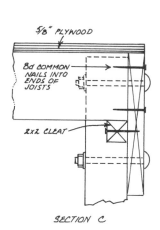

SECTION c

necessary; 2) Place plywood panels at right angles to the joists; 3) Space panel edges ⅛″ apart, panel ends ¹/₁₆″; 4) Stagger panels so ends of adjacent pieces don't rest on the same joists—too-close nailing can split joists; 5) Use 6d nails for securing panels, spacing nails 6″ apart around the edges and 10″ across the interior.

Finish the deck with a preservative, then apply a good-quality exterior paint or other type of outdoor flooring.

Steps

Simple wood steps can be constructed for this deck. First, measure the distance from the deck that the steps will occupy. (Three steps here project about 35″, but this would vary according to the deck height.) Build a concrete slab slightly longer than this and approximately 3″ wide.

Referring to Figs. C and D, cut 2x12 stringers to size, then nail steel joist hangers to stringers so the lips of the L-shaped devices are flush with the stringers' back edges. Cut and fasten 2″x2″ cleats with lag screws to stringers; top edges of cleats should be a tread thickness from tops of stringers. Set stringers on concrete pad and nail through joist hangers into deck to secure. Complete the steps by nailing 2x6 stair treads to the cleats.

Bench

The simple bench designed for use with this deck can be made as extensive as you wish—to go all the way or only part way around the deck. It's basically just 2x3 stock nailed to supports flanking posts that are, in turn, bolted to deck framing.

Start construction by cutting 4″x4″ posts. There are nine in all, each 2′3″ long. Cut eighteen 2x6 supports (see Fig. E). Bolt two supports to the top of each post, then bolt the posts to the deck at intervals indicated in Fig. F. For a finished appearance you also bolt 2x12s to the posts before you secure these to the deck.

Finally, nail on 2x3 seating boards. Use two 10d nails per support; space boards about ⅛″ apart.

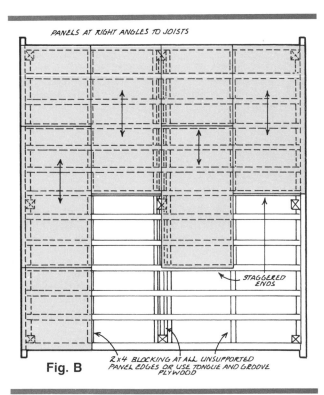

PANELS AT RIGHT ANGLES TO JOISTS

STAGGERED ENDS

2 x 4 BLOCKING AT ALL UNSUPPORTED PANEL EDGES OR USE TONGUE AND GROOVE PLYWOOD

Fig. B

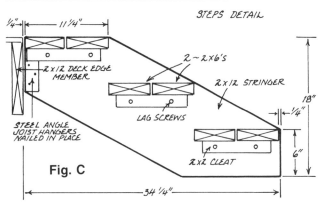

STEPS DETAIL

1/4"   11 1/4"

2 x 12 DECK EDGE MEMBER

2 ~ 2 x 6'S

2 x 12 STRINGER

LAG SCREWS

18"

1/4"

6"

STEEL ANGLE JOIST HANGERS NAILED IN PLACE

2 x 2 CLEAT

Fig. C

34 1/4"

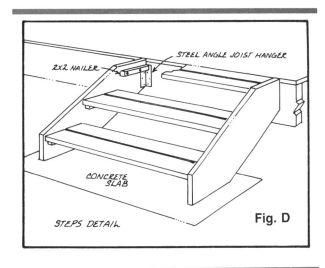

STEEL ANGLE JOIST HANGER

2 x 2 NAILER

CONCRETE SLAB

STEPS DETAIL

Fig. D

Materials, Deck

Quantity	Description
9	Post brackets cast in concrete blocks
9	4"x4"x1'3" support posts
2	2"x12"x15'9" edge support framing members
2	2"x12"x16'5½" framing members
32'	2"x2" cleats
13	2"x6"x15'9" joists (11), and (2) center support framing members
48'	2"x4" blocking (not required if plywood is tongue and groove)
8	4'x8'x⅝" plywood panels
	½" diameter x 8" galvanized hex-headed bolts (with 2 washers per bolt)
	16d galvanized box nails
	8d box nails
64'	28 ga. galvanized deck trim

Materials, Bench

Quantity	Description
1	2"x12"x17' bench trim member (cut to fit)
1	2"x12"x11' bench trim member (cut to fit)
1	2"x12"x7' bench trim member (cut to fit)
9	4"x4"x2'3" bench posts
18	2"x6"x1'3⅜" bench supports (cut as shown)
3	2"x3"x18' bench seat
3	2"x3"x16' bench seat
3	2"x3"x11' bench seat
3	2"x3"x10' bench seat
3	2"x3"x7' bench seat
3	2"x3"x6' bench seat
	½" diameter x 8" galvanized hex-headed bolts (with 2 washers per bolt)
	10d galvanized casing nails

Materials, Fence (Two 10' sections)

Quantity	Description
2	2"x8"x10' outside rails
2	2"x8"x9'5" outside rails
2	2"x6"x10' inside rails
2	2"x6"x9'5" inside rails
3	4"x4"x8' posts
18	11½"x48" pickets
	⅝" plywood
	5d galvanized box nails
	10d galvanized box nails
	16d galvanized box nails

Materials, Steps (For 3 steps)

Quantity	Description
2	2"x12"x4' stringers (cut to size)
6	2"x6"x3' stair treads
6	2"x2"x10" cleats
2	28 galvanized steel angle joist hangers
	⅜" diameter x 2½" lag screws
	10d galvanized casing nails

Fence

The fence around the mobile home is made in 10' sections with each section bolted to posts set in the ground; or, more accurately, to foundation blocks.

To make one section, start by cutting 4"x4" posts needed. Cut two posts 5½" long. Excavate and set two foundation blocks in the ground 9'8½" from center to center. Bolt the posts to the projecting hardware.

The top and bottom rails of the fence each is composed

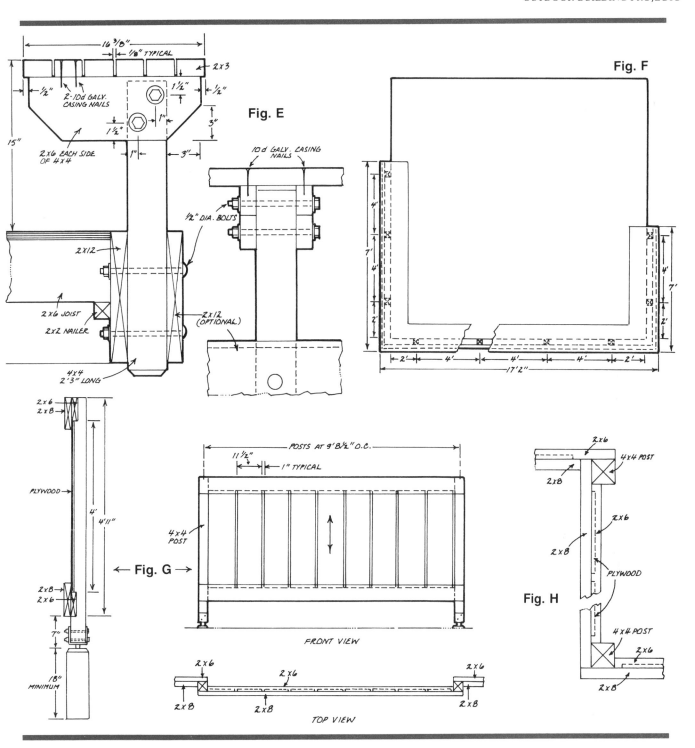

of two boards—a 2x8 and a 2x6. Cut the 2x8 10' long and the 2x6 9'5" long. Lay the 2x8 flat and nail (use 10d nails) the 2x6 to it so that the top edges of the boards are flush and the 2x6 is centered on the 2x8—this will give you an overlap (of the 2x8) of 3½" on each end, and the two-board assembly will have a recess. Set the rail on the outside faces of the posts, flush with the tops, and fasten with 16d nails, driving the nails through the overlaps.

Make the bottom rail required the same way. Secure it

to the posts about 7' from the ground level. Cut ⅝" exterior plywood (textured looks very good) into strips, each 11½" wide and 48" long. Set strips in the rail recesses and nail in place with about 1" space between each. (Fig. G)

You install the next section the same way, except the rails go on opposite sides of posts and board lengths are reversed. Here, the 2x6's are longer—10'—and the 2x8's 9'5". To turn the corner with the fence, see Fig. H.

Deck makes a cozy "conversation pit." Center table can also be used as a seat.

Convenience Deck

This 10-foot-square deck is surrounded by benches. The center table is actually a fire pit with a lift-off top. It's all built of western wood, with the fire pit of concrete blocks. As shown, the deck simply rests on a 3½-inch bed of gravel. For a more permanent installation, you may wish to pour concrete piers to support the 4"x4" lumber sleepers. If you measure carefully, you can pour the piers at the same time you pour the concrete foundations for the bench posts.

The unit pictured has deck boards laid in a "ripple" effect. The alternate patterns shown require less cutting and fewer trim ends. If you build such a deck 12 feet square, you can purchase 2x4s in 6-, 8-, or 12-foot

lengths to eliminate wasteful trimming. For a 9-foot-square deck, 6- and 12-foot lengths can be used. Plan your lumber needs carefully and you will be bucks ahead, or at least have enough left over to buy snacks and potables to serve on your new deck.

While the benches are shown surrounding the deck, they can also be freestanding anywhere in the yard. Canvas- or plastic-covered cushions will make the lounging easier.

Build the benches first, since the bench posts must be in place and their foundations poured before the deck can be laid. For the unit shown, there are two 9-foot and two 7-foot benches, the latter two flanking the deck

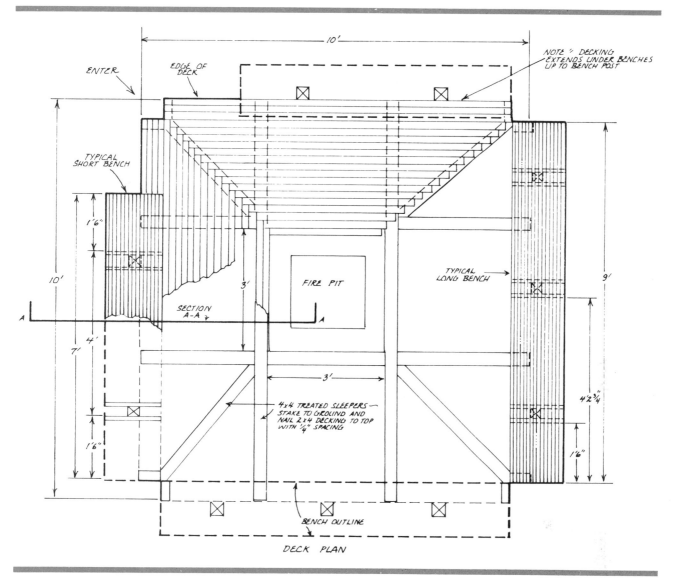

ENTER

EDGE OF DECK

NOTE " DECKING EXTENDS UNDER BENCHES UP TO BENCH POST

10'

TYPICAL SHORT BENCH

1'6"

10'

FIRE PIT

TYPICAL LONG BENCH

9'

4'2¾"

1'6"

SECTION A-A

A

3'

A

4'

7'

3'

4x4 TREATED SLEEPERS — STAKE TO GROUND AND NAIL 2x4 DECKING TO TOP WITH ¼" SPACING

1'6"

BENCH OUTLINE

DECK PLAN

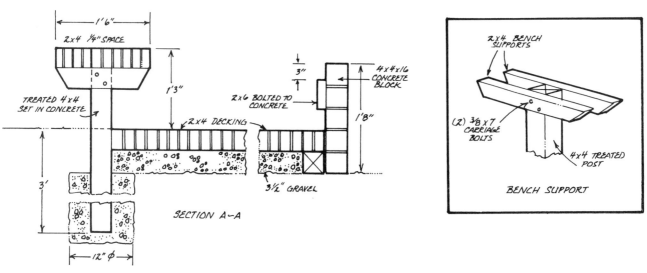

1'6"

2x4 ¼" SPACE

TREATED 4x4 SET IN CONCRETE

1'3"

3"

4x4x16 CONCRETE BLOCK

2x6 BOLTED TO CONCRETE

2x4 DECKING

1'8"

3'

3½" GRAVEL

12" Ø

SECTION A-A

2x4 BENCH SUPPORTS

(2) ⅜ x 7 CARRIAGE BOLTS

4x4 TREATED POST

BENCH SUPPORT

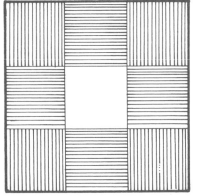
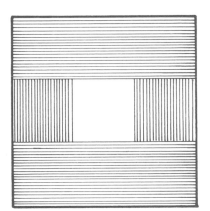
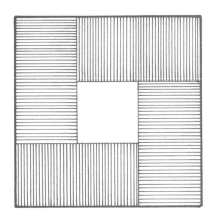

Alternate deckboard patterns.

Construct 2x4 frames for the bench seats.

Place 2x4 seat boards inside the frame, with ¼-inch spacers between.

Nail through the end caps into the seat boards.

"entryway." The longer benches have three legs or posts, the shorter ones only two.

For each bench, cut ten 2x4 seat boards 3 inches shorter than overall length (8 feet, 9 inches and 6 feet, 9 inches), and two end caps 1 foot 5½ inches long. Make a frame by nailing two of the seat boards between the end caps, flush with edges. Working on a flat surface, place the remaining 2x4s inside the frame, using scraps of ¼-inch plywood or lattice as spacers between the boards. Nail through the end caps into the seat boards, making sure all are flush. Remove the spacers.

Cut the 4x4 legs to rise 11½ inches above the deck, and to extend to the bottom of the poured foundation (see next paragraph). Make sure that they are thoroughly treated with preservative, particularly on the end grain. Cut two 2x4 seat braces for each leg, 17½ inches long, with ends angled 30 degrees. Center on each side of the leg, using a carpenter's square to make sure that they are perfectly perpendicular to the leg, and fasten with 16d nails. Drill two $7/_{16}$-inch holes through braces and leg and insert 7-inch carriage bolts. Slip on washers and nuts and tighten down. Place bench upside down and set legs in position, with the outer brace 18 inches from each end. On the longer bench, the third leg is midway between the other two. Toenail through the braces on each side and at the ends into each 2x4 seat board.

Lay out the dimensions of the deck on the ground, using stakes and strings. Use a line level or a long straightedge and level to make certain the strings are perfectly horizontal and 6 inches above the median grade. Dig the ten holes for the bench posts, 3 feet deep or below the frost line. The inner edges of the holes will be 4¼ inches inside the outer perimeter of the deck. If you are planning a permanent foundation for the deck and the fire pit, dig the holes for piers and fire pit foundation at the same time. The earth holes themselves will serve as forms for the concrete pour. Place 4 or so inches of gravel in the bottom of each hole.

Set the benches in position, with the posts in the holes, resting on the gravel. Carefully measure, align, and level the benches, using the string as a guide. Use temporary bracing to prop the benches in position, stak-

Nail braces to top ends of treated 4x4 posts.

Drill 7/16-inch holes through post and braces.

Insert 3/8-inch carriage bolts through holes.

Place washers over bolts and tighten down nuts.

Toenail leg braces to each 2x4 seat board.

Materials

For two 9-foot and two 7-foot benches

Quantity	Description
5	8' 4x4s
10	14' 2x4s
2	12' 2x4s
21	10' 2x4s
20	3/8"x7" carriage bolts, nuts, washers
Assorted	6d, 16d galvanized nails; 1/4" plywood scrap spacers; pre-mix concrete

For the 10-foot-square decks

Quantity	Description
1	14' 4x4
4	10' 4x4s
1	8' 4x4
8	16' 2x4s
8	14' 2x4s
8	12' 2x4s
17	10' 2x4s
13	8' 2x4s
Assorted	8d, 12d galvanized nails
3	cubic yards gravel

For the fire pit

Quantity	Description
40	4"x4"x16" concrete blocks
1	bag mortar mix
2	7' 2x6s
8	3/8"x6" carriage bolts, nuts, washers

For the fire pit cover/table

Quantity	Description
16	8' 2x2s
1	4' 2x2
	8d galvanized nails

ing the bracing to the ground if necessary. Pour concrete to within 7 inches of the surface, following directions for mixing and curing given in an earlier section.

While you are waiting for the concrete to harden, you can start laying the 4x4 sleepers (unless you are placing them on concrete piers also, in which case you had better let the concrete harden for a few days at least). Make sure they are thoroughly treated with preservative after cutting. The sleeper pattern will depend on the deck board pattern. For our rippled design, two 10-foot sleepers are laid across the width of the deck, 3 feet apart (3 feet 2½ inches in from each side). A cross pattern is created by laying two 3-foot and four 3-foot 2½-inch sleepers perpendicular to the first, also 3 feet apart. Sleepers are then run from the cross joints to the outside corners to support the ends of the deck boards. Finally, short sleepers are set to support the outermost deck boards. Carefully level all sleepers, building up with earth or gravel where necessary, or cutting down high spots in the earth. Spread gravel in the excavation (except for the center opening) to a depth just below the

DECKS & PATIOS

2x4 deck boards are laid on treated 4x4 sleepers; ¼-inch spacers separate boards.

Decking is toenailed to sleepers with 8d nails.

At corners, deck boards are nailed together with 12d nails.

A 2x6 frame is bolted to the concrete block fire pit.

A 2x2 frame on underside of tabletop fits around fire pit.

tops of the sleepers, being careful not to disturb the sleepers. Make a final check for level.

Build the fire pit in the center of the sleeper framing, following the directions for laying concrete block given in an earlier section. The unit is five courses high. Cut four 3-foot, 3-inch lengths of 2x6, mitered at both ends. Drill ⅜-inch-diameter holes through each 2x6 centered 7 inches from each end, then use a $^7/_{16}$-inch carbide tip bit to drill corresponding holes through the concrete block, centered 5¾ inches from the top of the fire pit. Bolt the 2x6s around the fire pit. Nail through the mitered corners with 8d galvanized finishing nails.

Cut a number of ¼-inch plywood scraps at least 4 inches long to use as spacers. Cut two 2x4s 3 feet long and two 3 feet, 3 inches long. Place them on edge around the fire pit and toenail them to the sleepers with 8d finishing nails. Nail together at the ends with 12d nails. Cut two 2x4s 3 feet, 3½ inches long and two 3 feet, 6½ inches long. Place spacers between the first and second courses and nail the second course of 2x4 deck

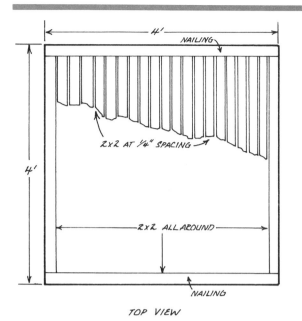

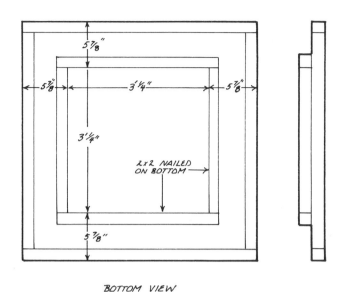

TOP VIEW BOTTOM VIEW

FIRE PIT COVER

boards in place as you did the first. Continue fastening deck boards in this manner, leaving spacers in place until several succeeding courses are securely nailed.

When all deck boards are secured, remove bench bracing.

The fire pit cover/table is made of 2x2s. Cut two 4-foot lengths and twenty-seven 3-foot, 9-inch lengths. Assemble a frame of the 4-foot pieces and two of the shorter lengths, using 8d galvanized nails, then fill in with the remaining shorter pieces, spaced just over ¼-inch apart. Cut two 3-foot, 3¼-inch lengths and two 3 foot, ¼-inch lengths and nail to the underside of the cover, centering them to form a frame that will fit outside the fire pit.

Stain or otherwise finish the deck, benches, and table/cover as you wish, following directions given in the chapter on working with wood. Then stoke up that fire and let's have a luau.

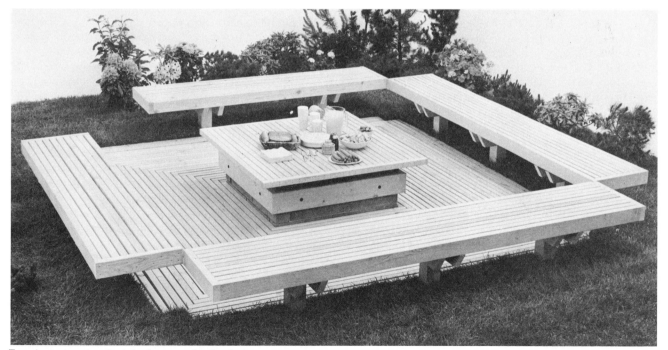

Two shorter benches flank the "entryway" to the deck.

207

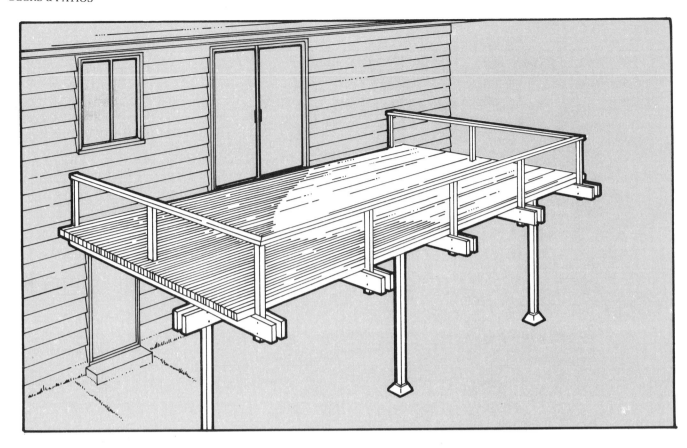

High Deck

A sun deck such as this one could be just the thing outside a master bedroom; indeed, the plans for many fine homes include just such a structure. It can be a pleasant place to have one's morning coffee, or just to pass the time of day. Access can be through a regular door, but one with sliding glass panels works especially well. Indeed, sliding glass doors tend to make any outdoor area used more frequently because it's easier to get to—and visually more apparent.

The deck shown is 14′ x 20′ but it can easily be made smaller or larger to suit your own property. Every 10′ span of structure should be supported by a pier anchored to a concrete block at each end. For example, this 14′ x 20′ deck requires three piers; a 14′ x 10′ one would require only two piers; a 14′ x 30′ deck four piers.

Start the project by drawing a horizontal line a few inches below the spot where you plan the door. The line should be straight and extend 20′. A straight 2x3 makes a good "ruler," but you can also snap a chalk line.

Temporarily nail two 2″x8 boards end to end to the house, making their top edges flush with the line. This is the face plate part of a nailer. Locate 2x4 studs beneath the siding. (They'll likely be 16″ apart, but if the house is older they may be 24″ apart.) Drill holes through the face

plate into the studs and secure it permanently with 4½″ lag screws. If the siding is beveled, use furring strips as filler to bring the face plate to true (Fig. A).

Complete the nailer (Fig. B) by fastening two 2x4s to the face plate. The bottom edges of the 2x4s should be flush with the bottom edges of the face plate. Use 16d nails, two per stud location.

Measure out 10′ from the face plate at both ends. Drive stakes into the ground and run a string that crosses both marks. Adjust the marks so they are exactly 20′ apart. Measure 10′ inward along the line from either mark and make another mark. These three marks indicate where the centers of the three concrete pier blocks required should be located.

Excavate and install pier blocks as previously described. Cut three piers from 4x4 stock, each long enough, when installed, to extend from the top of the pier to a few inches above the level of the deck. Drill centered holes in the ends of the piers; slip the boards onto the spikes projecting from the blocks (Fig. C) and brace into position with scrap lumber.

Install the beam next. Cut four 2″x8″ boards, each 11′ long. Bolt (use 8½″ carriage bolts) them end to end to the piers; board ends should be centered on the middle

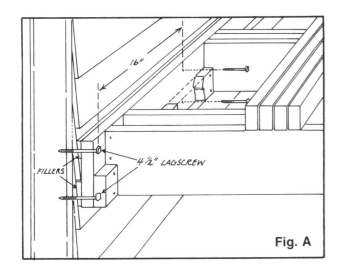

Fig. A

16"

4 1/2" LAGSCREW

FILLERS

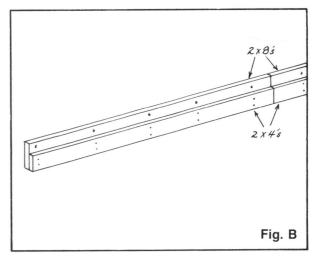

2 x 8's

2 x 4's

Fig. B

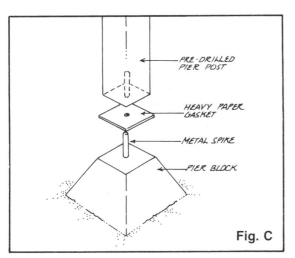

PRE-DRILLED PIER POST

HEAVY PAPER GASKET

METAL SPIKE

PIER BLOCK

Fig. C

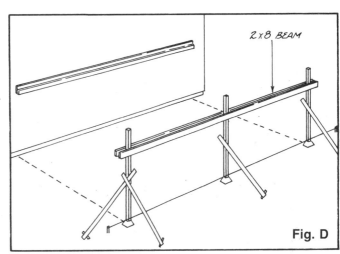

2 x 8 BEAM

Fig. D

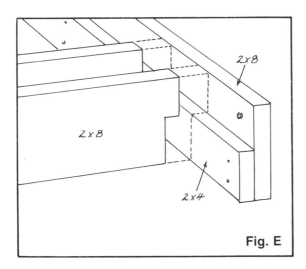

2 x 8

2 x 8

2 x 4

Fig. E

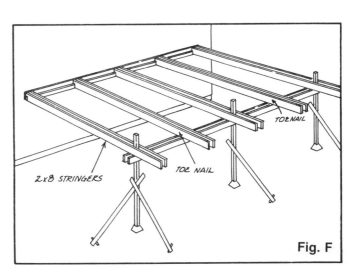

2 x 8 STRINGERS

TOE NAIL

TOE NAIL

Fig. F

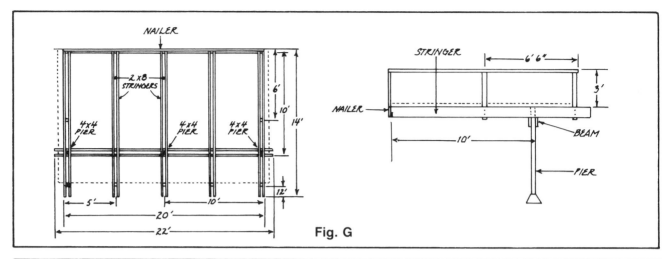

Fig. G

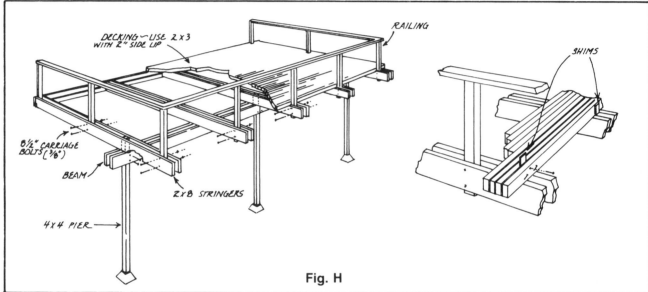

Fig. H

pier, their top edges level with the bottom edge of the nailer. Completed, the 22′-long beam should have all three piers sandwiched between it (Fig. D).

Cut ten 14′-long stringers from 2″x8″ stock. Notch them (Fig. E) at the ends to fit snugly against the nailer. Bolt three pairs of stringers to the piers and nail their ends to the nailer. Toenail two other pairs of stringers to the beam; nail as usual to the house nailer (Fig. F). When stringers are installed, cut off pier tops flush with them. Overall layout of members is shown in Fig. G.

Cut 4″x4″ post supports next. Each should be about 3′10″ long. Keeping tops level, secure them to the framing. Bolt five to the stringers along the 20′ side of the deck; bolt one each in the stringers in the 14′ side, 6′6″ from the other posts. Use 2x4s for rail supports at the house, nailing each to stringer and house stud.

Install 2x3 decking (Fig. H) with the narrow side up, spacing boards ⅛″ (use ⅛″-thick shims as a guide);

secure each board with two 10d nails wherever it crosses a stringer. As you go, cut decking to fit around the rail supports. Finally, cut and nail on 2x4 rails.

Materials

Quantity	Description
2	2″x8″x10′ boards for face plate
4	2″x8″x11′ boards for beam
10	2″x8″x14′ boards for stringers
2	2″x4″x10′ boards for attaching to face plate
3	4″x4″ piers (length: from pier block to stringer)
150	2″x3″x10′ boards for decking
7	4″x4″ boards for rail supports
2	2″x4″x4′ boards for rail supports at house
40′	2″x4″ for rails
	Carriage bolts of various sizes
3	pier blocks

Log Slices Patio

If you can handle a chain saw you can make yourself a simple, rich, natural patio rapidly and for practically nothing. Patio components are slices from logs.

Start by marking off the area that you want for the patio. Install 2x4 form boards on two opposite sides of the area. Excavate to a depth of 2½″. Then, just as you would screed sand for a patio, run a knocked-together 2x3 screed (nominal 3″, actual 2½″, side down) across the excavated area, letting the ends of your screed ride along the top edges of the forms. Tamp the earth down (a rented manual tamper is good), then check again with the screed, digging out or filling in as needed to get as level a surface—2½″ deep—as possible.

When you are satisfied, start cutting the log slices. Though this is a simple patio, the patio will be difficult to walk on if the slices are not level. This means that you should try to cut them the same thickness—2½″—so that when laid they will be level. To maintain better cutting control you may want to make a saw buck as shown.

Lay the slices on the ground, tapping them with the end of a stout board to get them as level as possible. To check whether adjacent pieces are level, hold a straight 2x4 across the slices. If there are gaps, or pieces are too high, compensate by digging out from under or building up earth under the offending ones.

To preserve the life of the pieces, it's a good idea to coat them with a preservative. A clear sealer is good, though there are other formulations you can use. One thing not to do is to use a coating that shoes can pick up and track elsewhere.

When all slices are laid (butt them together as tightly as possible), backfill around them with earth, pull up form boards and back-fill those mini-trenches.

With the method just described, weeds and other vegetation are almost sure to grow, eventually, between the slices. To avoid this you can lay 4-mil polyethylene sheeting on the excavated area before installing slices, and back-fill with washed gravel, marble chips, or the like. The stone will not only prevent (with the help of the film) vegetation from growing, but will add a touch of good looks.

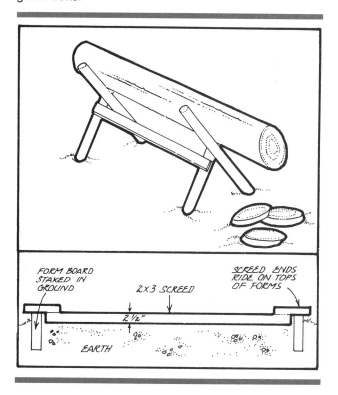

FORM BOARD STAKED IN GROUND

2X3 SCREED

SCREED ENDS RIDE ON TOPS OF FORMS

2½″

EARTH

Multileveled Deck

The basic design of this multileveled deck can be altered to meet your personal needs and the terrain of your yard. The only important thing to remember when building a multileveled deck is that each level must have sufficient strength.

Each deck level is supported by 4"x4" redwood posts placed at every corner and spaced 5' apart, as shown in Figs. A and B. Sink the posts into the ground or use post bases. 2"x6" beams span the posts on center and are attached with metal connectors. Joists are placed 2' on center across the beams and are attached with joist hangers. The bottom 2" of the exposed joist ends are beveled 45° (see Fig. A). Use U-shaped metal connectors whenever the joists run atop a beam. Note that wherever there is an "open" end, insert a diagonal joist as shown in Fig. B to insure that each deck plank end has a secure support at the corner.

Once the framing is complete, lay out the 2"x4" decking with 1⁄8" spacing between each board. Predrill the ends of the decking to prevent splitting, and use one nail per bearing, alternating sides of each deck plank to prevent cupping. When the deck is in place, nail the 2x4 fascia across the ends of the decking (see Fig. A).

Materials

4"x4" redwood stock for posts
2"x6" redwood stock for joists
4"x6" redwood stock for beams
2"x4" redwood stock for decking
16d galvanized nails
U-shaped hangers
Joist hangers

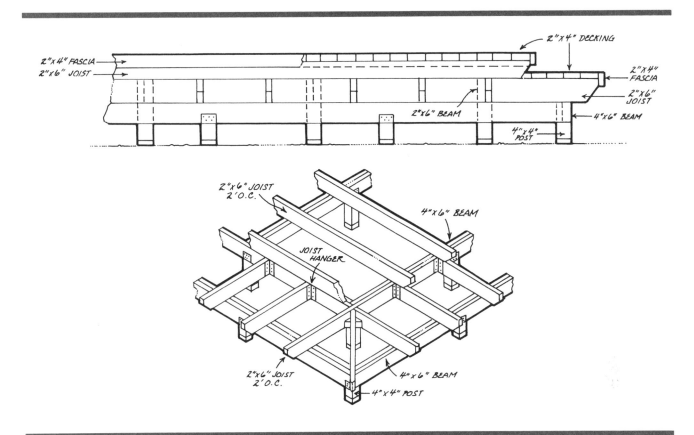

Rustic Table and Benches

The secret to this heavyweight table and benches is in the wood you use. Made of 3″ thick western cedar, this is a project that will stand where you put it and give you years of heavy-duty service. The table and benches can actually go anywhere—in the ground, into a concrete slab, or even on a finished wood deck. If you choose a deck, you will have to surface-anchor the posts with right-angle steel straps and lag bolts. Otherwise, dig holes for the table and bench posts, although if you are going through concrete, you will have to do some patchwork on the surface after the installation.

The table post is a telephone pole stub 48″ long (you could also use a railroad tie) and at least 12″ in diameter. Soak the 21″ that will be in the ground with a good wood

preservative and set the post so that the tabletop will be approximately 30″ above the ground. The four bench posts are between 6″ and 8″ in diameter and 28″ long. They are sunk deep enough so that each bench stands 18″ high. The bench posts are set 4″ from the ends of the seats. Allow 4″ of space between the inside of the benches and the perimeter of the tabletop. The table post is notched on opposite sides to accept a pair of 2″x4″x45″ supports which are bolted together with two lag bolts. The four bench posts are notched at the outside and back edges. The sides have a 2″x3″x11″ brace bolted to each post. The posts are spanned across their backs by a 2″x3″x34″ support which is screwed to the poles.

Use 3"x6"x4' or 2"x6"x4' untrimmed western cedar for the table itself. The planks are laid down with a ⁵/₁₆" space between each and are held together by screwing two 1"x4"x34" braces into each board. Put the top on the table post and screw the 2x4 supports to the bottom of the planks. Now mark out a circle 4' in diameter and cut the planks.

The benches are assembled on their supports, leaving ⁵/₁₆" of space between each plank. Mark and cut the benches, using the same 2' radius as the tabletop. Round off all corners. As a final touch, drill a hole 10" to 12" deep through the center of the table and into the post to accept an umbrella.

Materials

Quantity	Description
13	3"x6"x4' western cedar planks for table and bench tops
2	2"x4"x45" stock for table supports
2	1"x4"x34" stock for table braces
10'	2"x3" stock for bench supports
4	6"-8"-diameter peeled poles for bench posts, 28" long
1	12"-diameter peeled pole for table post, 4' long
As needed	Lag bolts, screws, and plugs

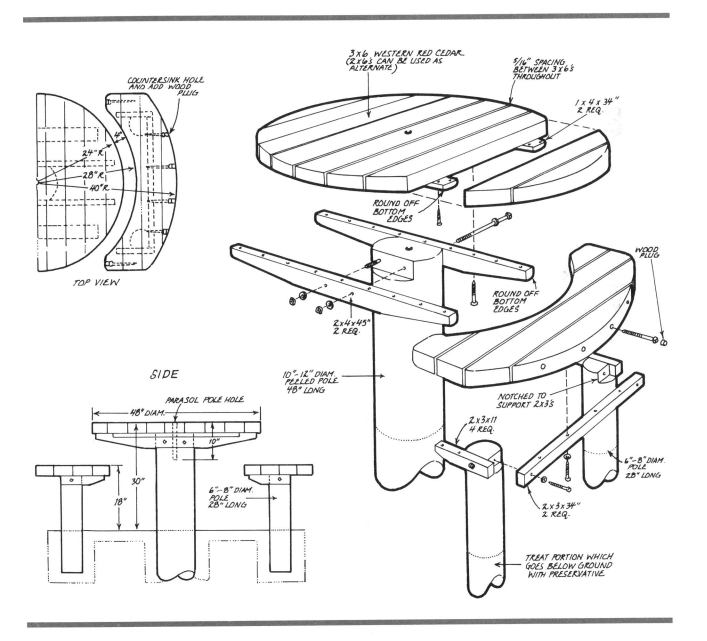

215

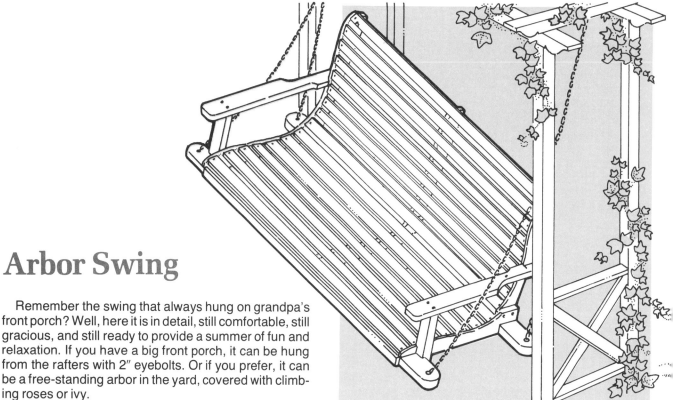

Arbor Swing

Remember the swing that always hung on grandpa's front porch? Well, here it is in detail, still comfortable, still gracious, and still ready to provide a summer of fun and relaxation. If you have a big front porch, it can be hung from the rafters with 2″ eyebolts. Or if you prefer, it can be a free-standing arbor in the yard, covered with climbing roses or ivy.

If you are making an arbor with the swing, begin by sinking four 4″x4″x9′6″ posts three feet into the ground. The post ends are treated with preservative and the foot-square post holes are filled in with concrete. The two posts at each end are placed three feet apart (see Figs. A and C) with 78″ between the outside edges of the end sets. The two 4″x4″x94″ horizontal and the two 4″x4″x48″ end pieces that tie the posts together at the top can either be scroll-cut as shown in Fig. B, or mitered 45°. ⅜″x10″ lag bolts fasten the end cross pieces and horizontals to the top of the arbor posts. Use ⅜″x8″ carriage bolts to attach the remaining five top cross pieces to the horizontal pieces. The six 1″x2″x94″ horizontal slats spaced 7″ apart over the cross pieces are nailed into place with galvanized 10d nails.

The arbor posts are stabilized by 2x4 cross braces nailed between the posts as shown in Fig. C. These are set 6″ and 30″ above the ground and are 28¾″ long. The two diagonals between each set are 2″x4″x37¾″ and mitered at each end to fit snugly against the braces. When the arbor is assembled, all corners are rounded before painting or varnishing the wood.

The swing itself can be made either with a straight or curved back. The straightback is illustrated in Figs. A and B. The details of the curved version are shown in Figs. D and E. Cut the six back and seat cleats from 1⅛″ hardwood stock, such as oak or maple. The inside of the curved edge of the two 1⅛″x2½″ outside back and seat cleats is rabbetted with a ½″ router bit. The 1⅛″x2″ center cleats are not rabbetted. All three cleat sets are joined with a half lap joint as shown in Fig. D1. The lap joint then fits into a ½″ dado cut in the back chain

support. The two chain supports are made from 1⅛″x2½″x58½″ hardwood stock and rounded at each end. The cleat sets are glue-screwed to the chain supports as in Fig. E. Now screw the nine ½″x1½″x47″ seat slats, and the eight ½″x1½″x44¾″ back slats across the cleats, using #8 (1″) brass screws. The ¾″-thick armrests and 1⅛″-thick supports are cut and notched to fit against the seat and back cleats as shown in Fig. E.

Drill holes in the #2 and #6 arbor cross pieces (see Fig. A) and insert ⅜″x4″ eyebolts. Eyebolts are also put in the ends of the chain supports (see Fig. E). The swing chain is attached between the eyebolts (Fig. B).

Materials	
Quantity	Description
63′	4″x4″ stock for arbor posts, horizontal and cross pieces
48′	1″x2″ stock for six arbor top slats
22′	2″x4″ stock for arbor side braces
16′2″	1⅛″x2½″ hardwood stock for outside seat and back cleats and chain supports
77″	1⅛″x2″ hardwood stock for center cleats
30′	½″x1½″ stock for seat and back slats
4′	¾″x3″ stock for armrests (hardwood)
18″	1⅛″x2⅛″ stock for armrest supports
14½′	porch swing chain
As needed	#8 (1¼″), #10 (1¾″), #8 (2¼″), #8 (1¾″) brass flathead wood screws
4	⅜″x2″ eyebolts for chain support
2	⅜″x4″ eyebolts for arbor cross braces
4	⅜″x10″ lag bolts with washers
10	⅜″x8″ carriage bolts with washers

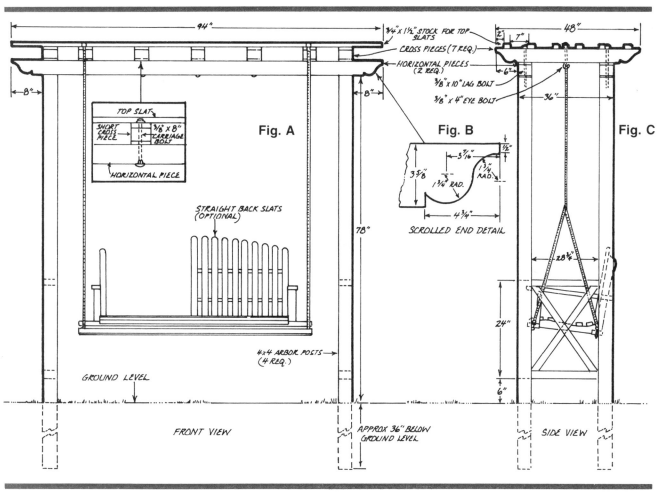

94"

¾" x 1½" STOCK FOR TOP SLATS

CROSS PIECES (7 REQ.)

HORIZONTAL PIECES (2 REQ.)

⅜" x 10" LAG BOLT

⅜" x 4" EYE BOLT

48"

Fig. A

Fig. B

Fig. C

TOP SLAT

SHORT CROSS PIECE

⅜" x 8" CARRIAGE BOLT

HORIZONTAL PIECE

STRAIGHT BACK SLATS (OPTIONAL)

SCROLLED END DETAIL

3⁵⁄₁₆

3⅝

1¾" RAD.

½"

1¾" RAD.

4¾"

28¾"

24"

6"

8"

8"

78"

36"

4x4 ARBOR POSTS (4 REQ.)

GROUND LEVEL

FRONT VIEW

APPROX 36" BELOW GROUND LEVEL

SIDE VIEW

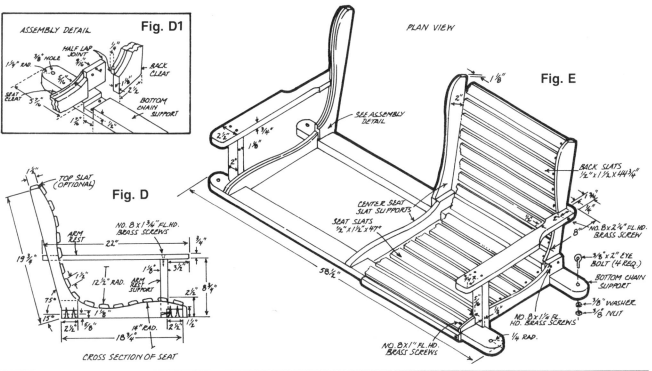

Fig. D1

ASSEMBLY DETAIL

HALF LAP JOINT

⅜" HOLE

1⅛" RAD.

BACK CLEAT

SEAT CLEAT

BOTTOM CHAIN SUPPORT

PLAN VIEW

Fig. E

SEE ASSEMBLY DETAIL

BACK SLATS ½" x 1½" x 44¾"

NO. 8 x 2¼" FL.HD. BRASS SCREW

⅜" x 2" EYE BOLT (4 REQ.)

BOTTOM CHAIN SUPPORT

⅜" WASHER

⅜" NUT

CENTER SEAT SLAT SUPPORTS

SEAT SLATS ½" x 1½" x 47"

NO. 8 x 1¼" FL. HD. BRASS SCREWS

NO. 8 x 1" FL.HD. BRASS SCREWS

¼" RAD.

58½"

Fig. D

TOP SLAT (OPTIONAL)

NO. 8 x 1¾" FL.HD. BRASS SCREWS

ARM REST

ARM REST SUPPORT

19¾"

22"

12½" RAD.

75°

15°

14" RAD.

18¾"

CROSS SECTION OF SEAT

Planter Box Benches

Here are two handsome patio benches that let you exercise your green thumb in comfort. One version is a straight bench just over 7 feet long (you can, of course, alter the lengths and other dimensions to suit your needs and space requirements) with a planter box in one end and a handy storage box for your gardening tools and whatever at the other. The second bench provides round-the-corner seating; it's 85 inches long on each side, with a planter at each end and an optional storage box in the corner.

Bench tops are made of 2x2 and 2x4 lumber; preservative-treated WWP grade-stamped Western wood was used for the units shown. The boards are spaced an inch apart to allow rain or lawn-sprinkling water to drain through readily. Planter and storage boxes are of APA grade-trademarked 303 textured siding.

Materials	
Quantity	*Description*
straight bench	
1 panel	⅜" x 4' x 8' plywood
52'	2x4 lumber
53'	2x2 lumber
6'	1x3 lumber
2'	1"-diameter dowel
corner bench	
1 panel	⅜" x 4' x 8' plywood
108'	2x4 lumber
96'	2x2 lumber
6'	1x3 lumber
2'	1"-diameter dowel
for both	

No. 8 2½" wood screws, 4d galvanized or aluminum finishing nails, wood putty, wood preservative, water-proof glue, finishing stain

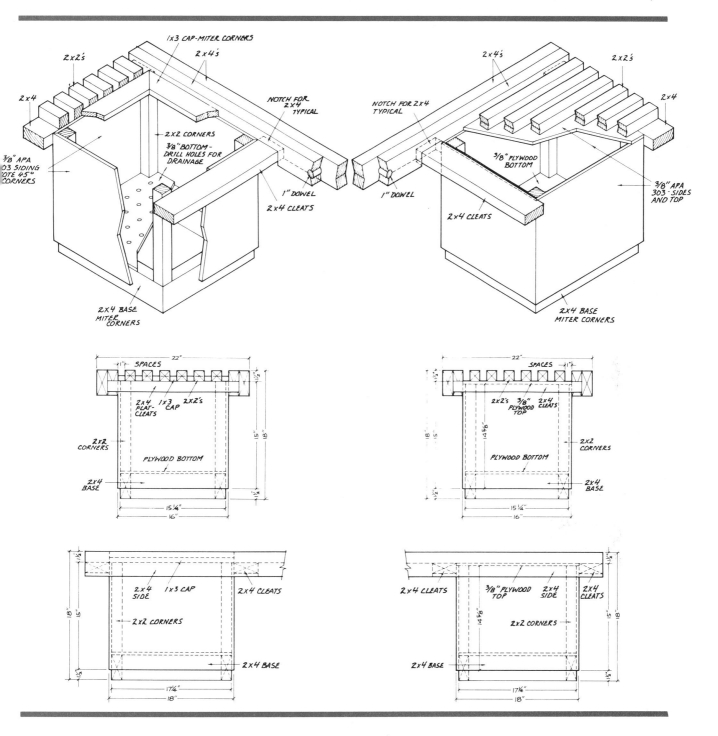

Assemble the support boxes (planter or storage) first. For the straight bench, both boxes have the same outside dimensions. Cut four 15¼- and four 17¼-inch 2x4s; miter all ends. Assemble with glue and nails to form two bases. Check with a carpenter's level to make sure the bases are square.

Cut the plywood box sides, following the cutting diagrams. Miter the mating edges. Cut four 2x2 corner frames 12⅝ inches long for the planter box,

and four 12¼ inches long for the storage box. With glue and nails spaced about every 3 inches, assemble the boxes and corner frames with the frames flush with the top edges of the sides.

Cut the two box bottoms as shown in the cutting diagram. Drill a series of ⅜-inch holes at approximately 2½-inch intervals in the planter bottom to allow for drainage. Place the two box shells upside down and slide the bottoms into place, nailing them to the 2x2 corner frames. Set the boxes onto the

2x4 bases, sliding them down so that the bottoms rest on the 2x4s. Nail through the box sides into the base pieces.

Planter boxes for the L-shaped bench are assembled the same as for the straight bench. The corner box measures 16 inches square. Mitered base 2x4s are 15¼ inches long. If the corner box is a storage unit, 2x2 corner frames are 12¼ inches long; if the box is for support only, cut them 12⅝ inches long. Assemble box shells as above, with the corner frames ⅜-inch from the top edges of the sides. In order to cut all pieces from a single sheet of plywood, the bottom of the storage box is in three sections (if you would prefer a solid bottom, you can probably find a 15¼-inch-square piece of plywood in your lumber dealer's odd-size bin). Nail the two end pieces to the bottoms of the corner frames, then place the shell over the 2x4 base. Nail the center bottom piece to the 2x4 base. If the box is not used for storage, simply slide the four-sided shell over the base, with the corner frames resting on the base 2x4s.

For the straight bench, cut five 19-inch 2x4 cleats, six 63½-inch 2x2 slats, and six 3½-inch 2x2 slats. Fasten the 3½-inch slats to one of the 2x4s, 2½ inches from each end with a 1-inch interval between slats. Use glue and wood screws driven through predrilled holes in the 2x4 into the 2x2s. Fasten the long slats to the three intermediate 2x4 cleats similarly, spacing the cleats as shown in the drawings. At the cleat that will be alongside the storage box, drive screws into each slat 1 inch from the outer edge of the 2x4. Wipe away excess glue at all slats. Glue-nail the plywood box top to the underside of the slats, against the flanking cleat, making sure to maintain slat spacing. Mark a line across the slats, centered on the flanking cleat; cut through the slats.

Notch the 2x4 inner rails to fit over the 2x4 cleats.

Fasten flush with the ends of the cleats, using glue and wood screws driven through predrilled holes in the cleats into the rails. Fasten the two end cleats (the one with short slats at the planter end) to the rail. Fasten outer rails with screws driven through the inner rails. Drill 1-inch-diameter holes through both rails, 6 inches from each end and at two equally spaced intermediate points. Coat 3-inch lengths of dowel with glue and drive into the holes, flush with the surface.

Set the bench top on the planter and storage boxes. Drive screws at 3-inch intervals through the box sides and corner frames into the rails and cleats. Cut frame pieces of 1x3 lumber to fit inside the planter opening, mitering at the corners. Assemble the frame with glue and nails. Place in the opening and nail to the corner frames. Toenail to the 2x4 cleats and rails at 3-inch intervals. Countersink the nails and fill the holes with wood putty. Apply a thorough coating of preservative inside the planter box, then stain or otherwise finish the bench and boxes as desired.

The bench assembly for the L-shaped unit is similar, except at the corner, where slats, cleats, and rails are mitered. If the box is not to be used for storage, assemble the slats and the cleats, then nail the box top to the bottoms of the mitered corner slats. Notch the inner corners of the cleats that flank the corner box, as shown in the drawing. Fasten the rails as above, with screws and dowels. You will need a helper to set the assembly on the planters and corner box. Fasten to planters as above, and nail through the box top into the box corners. You will need a nail set to drive nails between the slats.

If the corner box is for storage, assemble the two sides of the L, mitering at the corners. Place screws 1 inch from the outer edge of the cleats flanking the box. Glue-nail the box top to the underside of the slats, then cut the slats along the center line of the two cleats. Rails are then fastened as above.

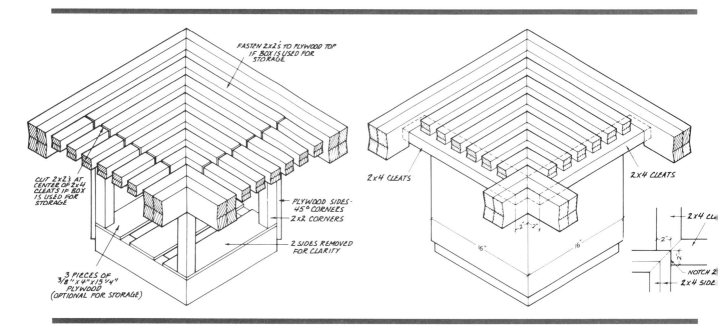

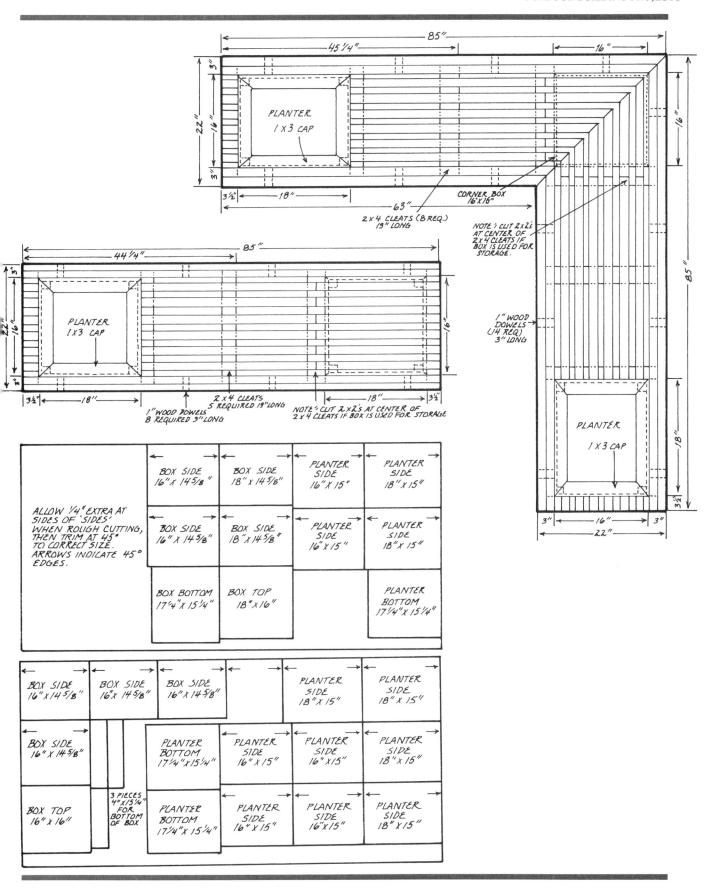

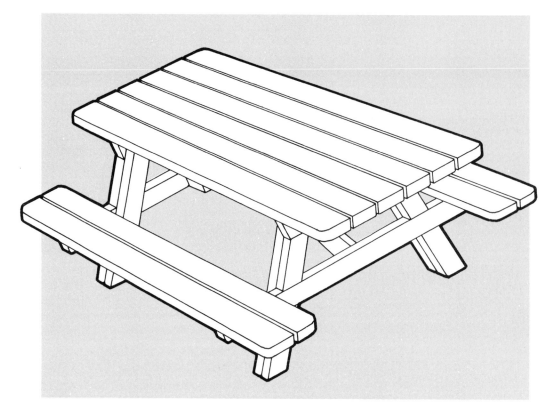

Picnic Table and Benches

Try this durable redwood or western cedar picnic table in your back yard for the next several years. Once you've built it, there is nothing you'll have to do to take care of it.

Cut all 2"x6" and 2"x4" stock according to the lengths given in the Materials List. Lay out the six 6' tabletop boards parallel to each other, leaving ½" of space between each board. Center the 2"x4"x3 center table brace at right angles across the boards. Glue and screw the brace to the top boards, using one #6 screw in each

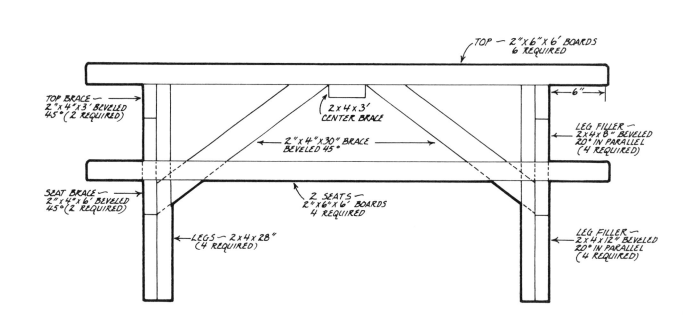

board. (All screws in this project should be countersunk and plugged.) When the center brace is in place, turn the top over and stand it on the two 2"x4"x3' table end braces. The braces should be positioned exactly 6" from the ends of the top boards. Glue the braces and use two screws in each end of every board (Figs. A, B).

The four 2"x4"x28" legs are attached directly under the second and fifth top boards and extend outward toward the sides of the top. Each leg is held against the inside of the end braces by two #6 screws. The four 2"x4"x8" leg fillers are glued against the bottom of the end braces and screwed to the tops of the legs, using two screws in each. The two 2"x4"x6' seat braces are placed across the bottom of the fillers and screwed to the main legs with a pair of screws in each leg. Finally, the 2"x4"x12" fillers are butted against the bottom of the seat braces and also screwed to the main legs (Figs. B, C).

Next, position the two 2"x4"x26¾" diagonal leg braces between the center table brace and the middle of each seat support. Two screws should be used in each end of the diagonal braces. Stand the table on its legs so that the four seat boards can be glued and screwed across the seat supports, two on each side with ½" space between boards (Fig. C).

Finish the project by rounding off the outside corners of the table and benches. If you have used cedar, no finishing is necessary, but over the years the wood will turn a pewter gray from weathering. A good soaking in wood preservative will prevent the project from discoloring, though some people like this effect. Redwood actually needs no treatment at all, although a clear preservative will prolong life. The project may also be painted, but if you do that, plan on having to repaint at least once a year.

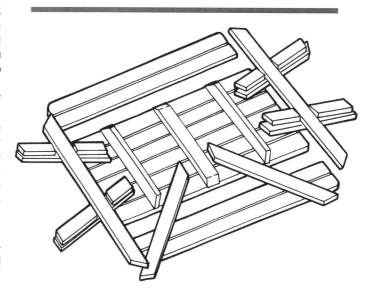

Materials	
Quantity	Description
10	2"x5"x6' table and bench top boards, square cut
1	2"x4"x3' center table brace, square cut
2	2"x4"x26¾" diagonal leg braces, beveled 45° at each end
2	2"x4"x3' table end braces, beveled 45° at each end
22"x4"x6'	bench supports, beveled 45° at each end
4	2"x4"x28" legs, beveled 20° in parallel
4	2"x4"x1' leg fillers, beveled 20° in parallel
4	2"x4"x8" leg fillers, beveled 20° in parallel
60	#6 (3") flathead screws

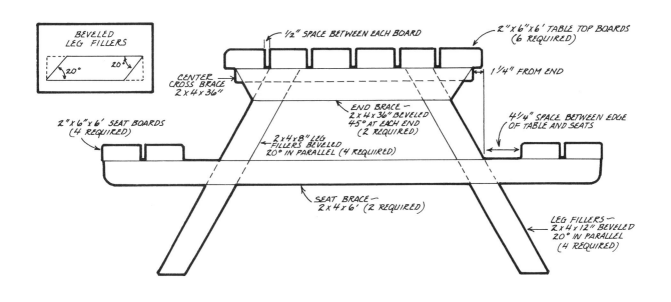

BEVELED LEG FILLERS

20° 20°

½" SPACE BETWEEN EACH BOARD

2"x6"x6' TABLE TOP BOARDS (6 REQUIRED)

1¼" FROM END

CENTER CROSS BRACE 2 x 4 x 36"

END BRACE — 2 x 4 x 36" BEVELED 45° AT EACH END (2 REQUIRED)

2 x 4 x 8" LEG FILLERS BEVELED 20° IN PARALLEL (4 REQUIRED)

4¼" SPACE BETWEEN EDGE OF TABLE AND SEATS

2"x6"x6' SEAT BOARDS (4 REQUIRED)

SEAT BRACE — 2 x 4 x 6' (2 REQUIRED)

LEG FILLERS — 2 x 4 x 12" BEVELED 20° IN PARALLEL (4 REQUIRED)

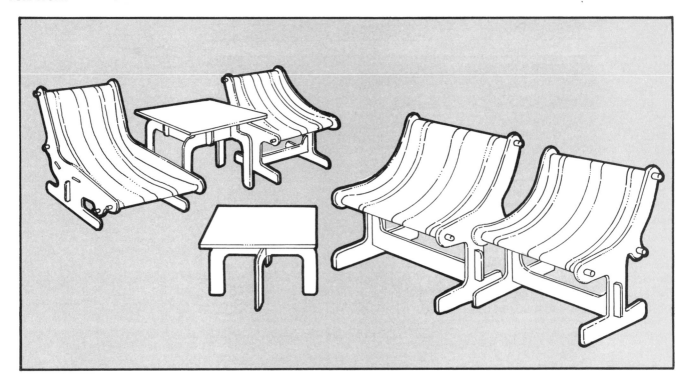

Stowaway Outdoor Furniture

You may need the use of a sewing machine to finish this project. If you can't operate one, try to enlist the help of someone who can. This set of outdoor furniture will give pleasure and comfort to everyone who uses it. Easily disassembled, the pieces can all be stored flat during the winter months and then put together for yet another summer of relaxation and fun.

Following the dimensions given in Figs. A, B, C, D, and E, draw cardboard templates which can be traced on the four panels of ¾" exterior plywood. Six of the eight chair sides (Fig. B) can be arranged on one sheet of plywood. The remaining two chair sides, plus one large table leg (Fig. C) and the large tabletop (Fig. G) fit on another panel. The tabletop is 48" square with rounded corners which have a 7" radius. Put three large table legs and the two chaise sides (Fig. A) on the third panel. The two small table legs (Fig. D), the five chair and chaise stretchers (Fig. E) and the small tabletop go on the last panel. The small table (Fig. H) is 24" square without rounded corners. When the patterns have been traced on the plywood, cut out all pieces and drill all dowel holes. Assemble the pieces to be sure everything fits properly. Then fill and sand all edges and paint the pieces. Add the glides to all legs.

The two tables are assembled by interlocking the slots in their legs. The large table legs form a crosshatch (see Fig. G) and are held to the tabletop with eight 1" angle irons. The small table legs form a cross and are placed diagonally (from corner to corner) under the top (see Fig. H). Four 1" angle irons are screwed to the legs and top to hold them together.

The chaise requires a canvas seat measuring 32"x86", plus two separate straps measuring 5"x32" and two 1"x48" tie straps. Fold the sides and ends of the canvas seat over and stitch as shown in *Fig. I*. Fold the ends of the straps over and sew them to the seat cover at the sides only. Attach the tie straps. Put the dowel at the top of the back of the chaise through the canvas end nearest the tie straps. The dowel at the foot of the chaise is inserted through the other end of the canvas. The two straps are pulled through the slots in the sides of the chaise. Insert a ⅜"x7" dowel through the loops at each end of the two straps. Tie the tie straps to the dowel at the bottom of the chaise back.

Each chair requires a piece of canvas measuring 32"x45" and two tie straps 1"x30". Overlap the ends of the canvas and stitch as shown in Fig. I. Add the tie straps. The top and bottom dowels in the chairs are inserted through the loops at the ends of the canvas. The tie straps are tied to the remaining dowel.

Assemble the chaise and chairs by interlocking the stretcher in the slots in each side and inserting the four ½"x3" dowels in the stretcher tenons. Put the top and bottom 1⅜" dowels through the sides and canvas. Drill a ⅜" hole through the dowel on each side of the furniture sides (see Fig. F) and insert the ⅜"x2½" dowels in the holes.

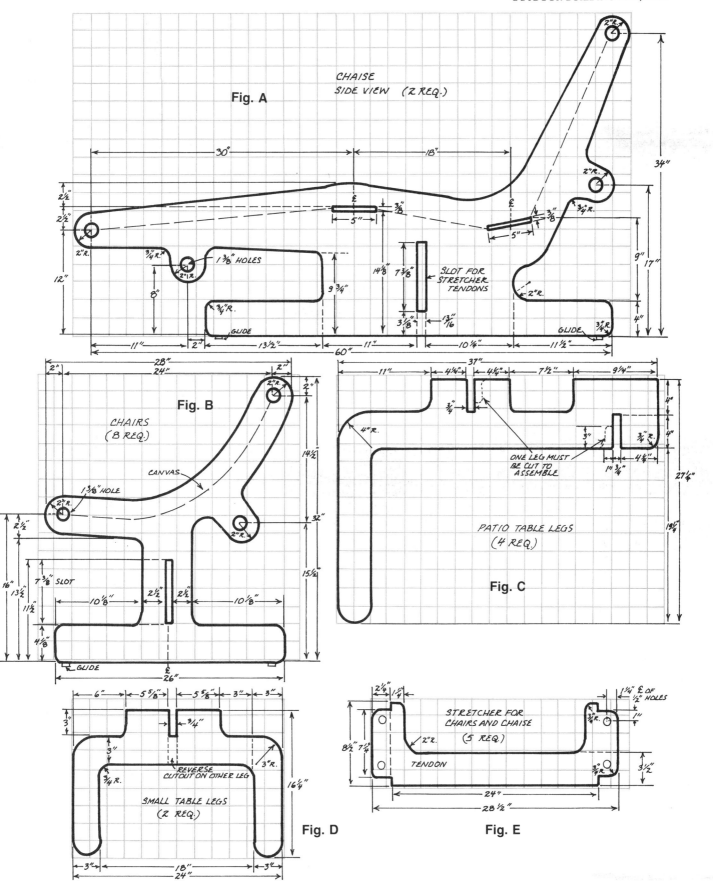

Fig. A

CHAISE
SIDE VIEW (2 REQ.)

Fig. B

CHAIRS
(8 REQ.)

CANVAS

1 3/8" HOLE

SLOT FOR
STRETCHER
TENDONS

GLIDE

Fig. C

PATIO TABLE LEGS
(4 REQ.)

ONE LEG MUST
BE CUT TO
ASSEMBLE

Fig. D

SMALL TABLE LEGS
(2 REQ.)

REVERSE
CUTOUT ON OTHER LEG

Fig. E

STRETCHER FOR
CHAIRS AND CHAISE
(5 REQ.)

TENDON

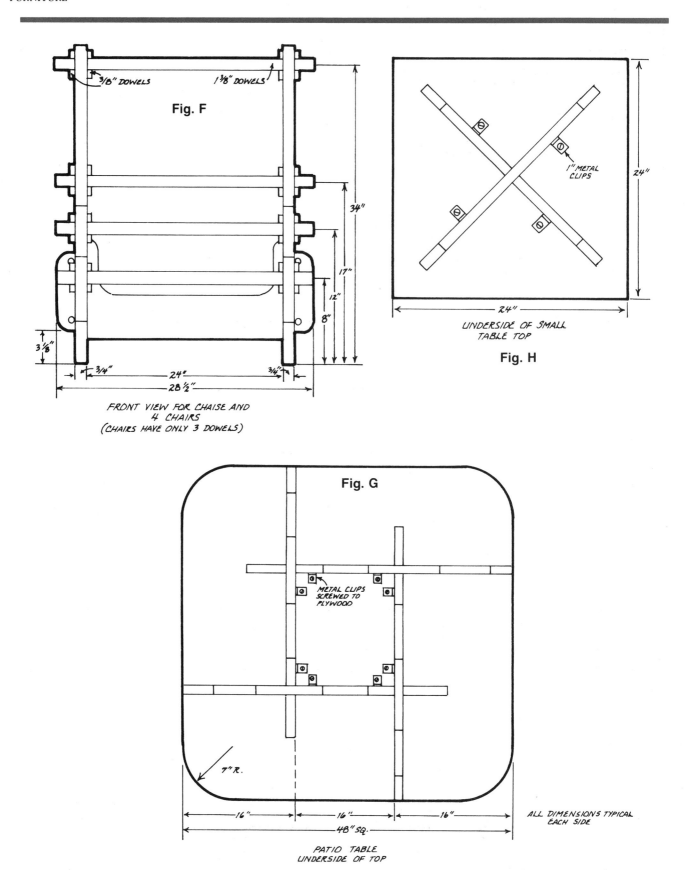

3/8" DOWELS   1 3/8" DOWELS

Fig. F

34"

17"

12"

8"

3/8"

3/4"   24"   3/4"

28 1/2"

FRONT VIEW FOR CHAISE AND
4 CHAIRS
(CHAIRS HAVE ONLY 3 DOWELS)

1" METAL
CLIPS

24"

24"

UNDERSIDE OF SMALL
TABLE TOP

Fig. H

Fig. G

METAL CLIPS
SCREWED TO
PLYWOOD

7" R.

16"   16"   16"

48" SQ.

ALL DIMENSIONS TYPICAL
EACH SIDE

PATIO TABLE
UNDERSIDE OF TOP

Materials

Quantity	*Description*
4	¾"x4'x8' exterior plywood panels, good on both sides, for all parts

Material for one chaise

2	sides cut from plywood
1	stretcher cut from plywood
4	⅜"x3" dowels for holding canvas seat straps
4	1⅜" x 28½" dowels to hold canvas seat
16	⅜"x2½" dowels for holding 1⅜" dowels in place
4	½"x3" dowels for holding stretcher tenons in place
4	glides
1	32"x96" piece of canvas for seat and straps
2	1"x48" strip of canvas for seat tie straps

Material for four chairs

8	sides cut from plywood
4	stretchers cut from plywood
16	½"x3" dowels for stretcher tenons
12	1⅜"x28½" dowels for holding canvas seats
48	⅜"x2½" dowels for holding the 1⅜" dowels in place
16	glides
4	32"x45" pieces of canvas for seats
4	1"x30" canvas strips for tie straps

Material for tables (one 2'x2', one 4'x4')

2	tops, cut from plywood
6	legs, cut from plywood
12	1" angle irons and screws
8	glides

As needed
Paint, varnish, wood filler

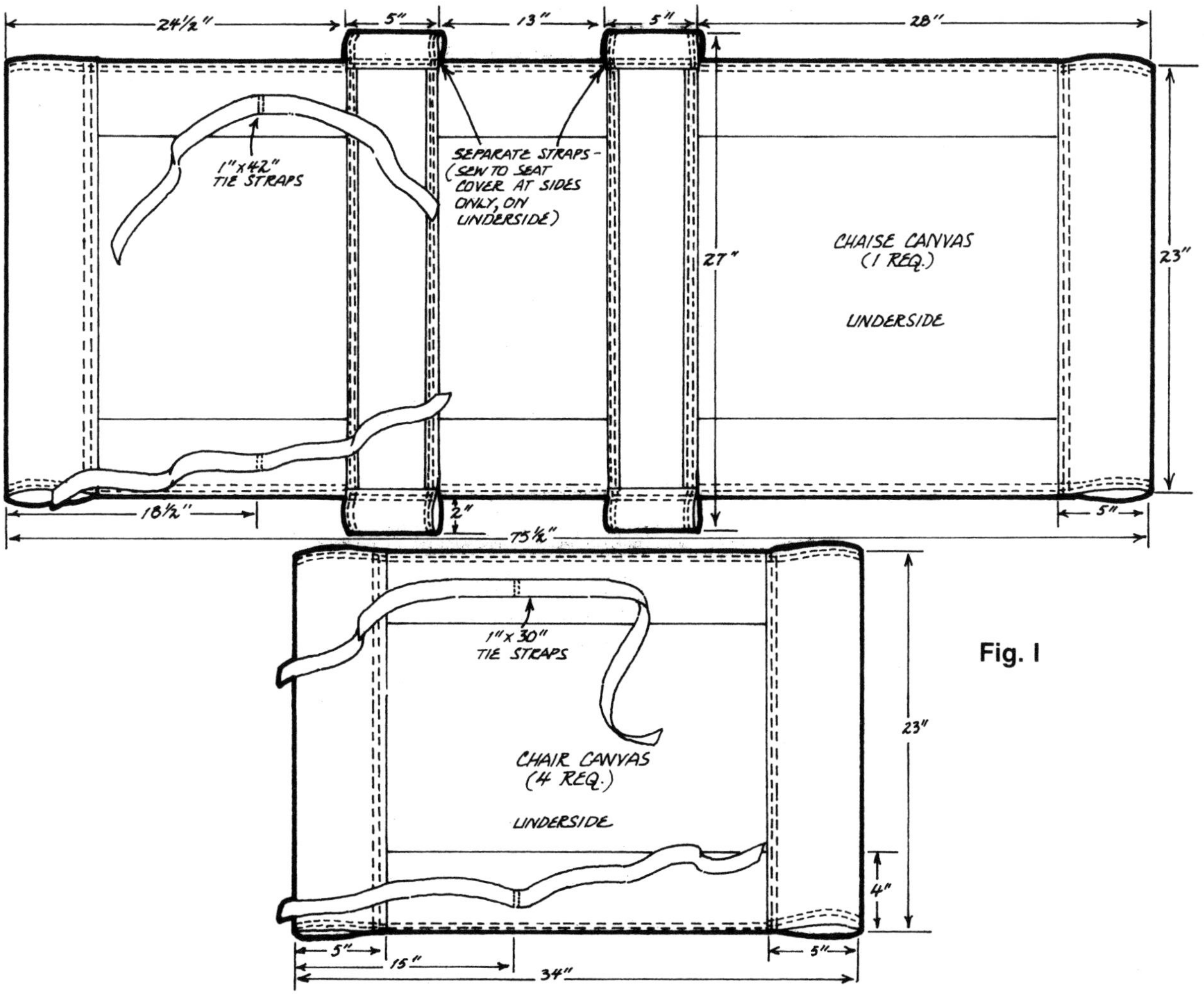
24½"
5"
13"
5"
28"
1"x42" TIE STRAPS
SEPARATE STRAPS - (SEW TO SEAT COVER AT SIDES ONLY, ON UNDERSIDE)
27"
CHAISE CANVAS (1 REQ.)
UNDERSIDE
23"
18½"
2"
75½"
5"
1"x30" TIE STRAPS
CHAIR CANVAS (4 REQ.)
UNDERSIDE
23"
4"
5"
15"
34"
5"

Fig. I

Built-On Deck Bench

If you have a deck that needs some seating, this idea may be for you. It's a bench you build onto the existing railing. You can do it if the existing railing, in its new capacity as bench back, is strong enough to take the strain of people leaning against it.

The idea is simple. Bolt a pair of 2x4s to each railing post and to the top of a 2x4 bench leg; in other words, sandwich the post and leg between the 2x4s. Then, simply lock-anchor the leg(s) to the floor with metal angle(s).

For strength, these 2x4 supports should be installed every five feet. They should be long enough so that when bolted in place the seat area is between 20″ and 21″ wide; the legs should be long enough so that when the seating material is added to them the bench is around 16″ off the deck.

When all the supports and legs have been secured, add the seating material. In the case shown, this is 1x2, spaced ½″ apart. For an easier job, follow this procedure. Every five feet nail on spacer blocks. Drill through the 1x2s before hammering them to the supports with 10d finishing nails.

For an easier job of nailing, use 2x6 seating, or some other wide stock. Make sure, in the interest of harmonious design, that the new components you add are the same type of stock originally used to construct the deck.

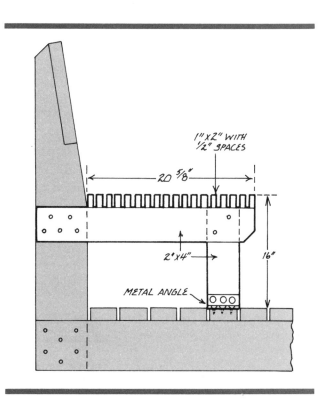

Simple Bench

All you need to make this bench (other than fasteners) is two boards—a 2x12 plank and a piece of 2x4 which is used as a brace. And you can build the bench—which though simple is very sturdy—in less than an hour.

Cut two 14″ pieces off the ends of the plank—these will be the legs. Cut a 4′ length of 2x4—this will be the brace between the legs. The remaining plank section is the seat and it is almost 6′ (68″) long.

Center the brace between the legs so its bottom edge is 4½″ from the leg bottoms. Secure brace with either 20d nails and glue or 5″ lag screws. If you use screws, remember to use pilot holes.

There are a couple of ways to attach the seat to the leg-brace assembly. You can screw or nail it on, going through the top of the seat into the assembly, or toenail (and glue) it on from below.

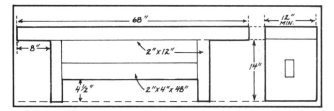

Children's Table and Seats

Here is a table and matching seats that are exactly the right size for small children. The design produces a sturdy yet easy-to-make project that will serve your children for years to come.

Mark the plywood panel for cutting as indicated in Fig. A. Be careful to leave a ⅛″ space between lines to allow for the kerf of your saw. Since the table and seats are all assembled in exactly the same way, repeat the following procedure for each:

Cut out all pieces and glue-assemble the legs by interlocking them at the notches. Place them on the underside of the table or seat top, and drill holes for the #8 (4″) screws (Fig. B.) Countersink each screw at least 1″ but not more than 1¼″. Glue and screw the legs into place. Glue the four triangular braces between the legs and countersink the #3 (1″) screws ¼″.

Sand all edges, rounding them slightly, and fill with wood dough or filler. Finish with a primer and enamel, varnish, or polyurethane. Three or four coats of polyurethane will help to weatherproof the entire project if you are planning on leaving it outdoors.

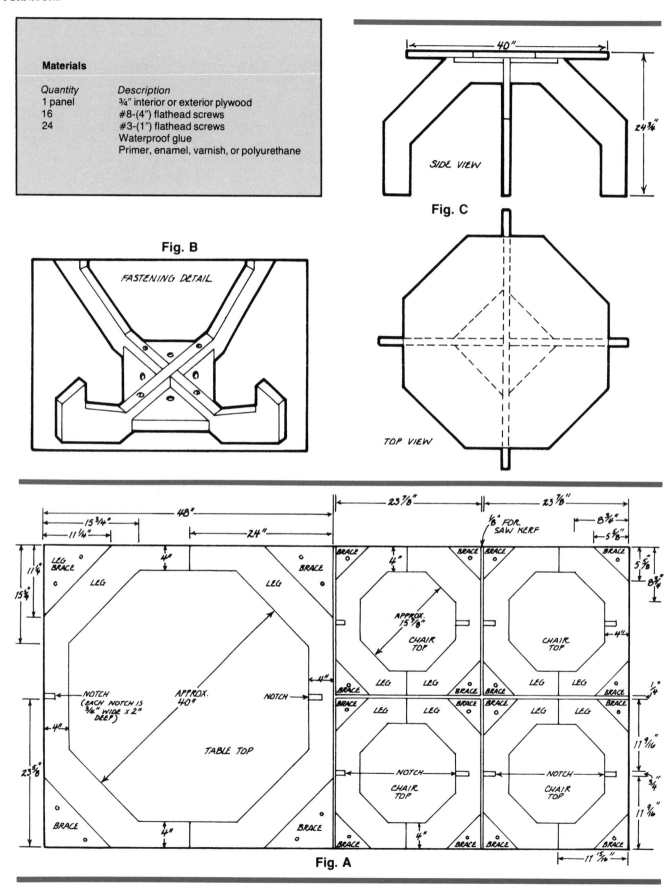

Materials

Quantity	Description
1 panel	¾" interior or exterior plywood
16	#8-(4") flathead screws
24	#3-(1") flathead screws
	Waterproof glue
	Primer, enamel, varnish, or polyurethane

Fig. C

SIDE VIEW

40"

24¾"

TOP VIEW

Fig. B

FASTENING DETAIL

Fig. A

48"

15 ¾"

11 ¼"

24"

23 ⅞"

23 ⅞"

⅛" FOR SAW KERF

8 ¾"

5 ⅝"

LEG BRACE

LEG

BRACE

LEG

4"

BRACE

BRACE

BRACE

5 ⅝"

8 ¾"

11 ¼"

15 ¾"

APPROX. 15 ⅛"

CHAIR TOP

CHAIR TOP

4"

NOTCH (EACH NOTCH IS ¾" WIDE × 2" DEEP)

APPROX. 40"

NOTCH

4"

LEG

LEG

BRACE

BRACE

LEG

LEG

BRACE

¼"

TABLE TOP

BRACE

LEG

LEG

BRACE

BRACE

LEG

LEG

BRACE

11 9/16"

23 ⅝"

4"

NOTCH

CHAIR TOP

NOTCH

CHAIR TOP

¾"

BRACE

BRACE

4"

BRACE

BRACE

BRACE

11 9/16"

11 15/16"

Folding Outdoor Furniture

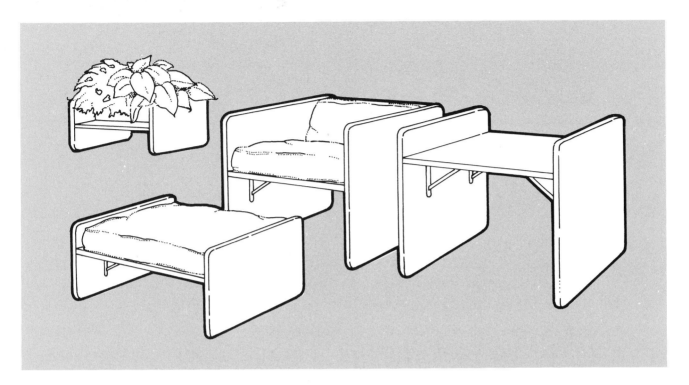

The beauty of this project is that the design can be applied to a whole variety of furniture—lounge chairs, high or low tables, ottomans, or planters. Aside from being quick to build, each piece is easy to set up, or fold flat for storage. Yet they are all strong and stable.

Mark out as many sides, backs, seats, or tops as you need on ¾″ plywood panels. Use a 1½″ radius to plot the curve for all corners (Fig. A). Cut out the pieces and true all plywood edges with coarse sandpaper. Fill the edges with wood putty or filler and sand smooth when dry. All of the furniture is assembled in the same way. Check the schematics for positioning of seats and tabletops.

When assembling the chair, screw the folding shelf brackets 8″ from the edges of the sides. The rear brackets should be 1½″ lower than the front ones. Screw the seat to the brackets and hinge the seat back 3¾″ from the rear edge of the seat. Screw a 1½″ angle iron to each side approximately 3″ from the back edges. Attach the metal furniture guides, prime and enamel or varnish the chair, and you are finished. Cushions for all furniture can either be purchased or made.(See Fig. B.)

The high and low tables and stool have no seat back. Otherwise, they are assembled in the same way as the chair, except that the folding brackets are all placed at the same height on the sides. To make the planter, simply construct a low table and screw two 3″x28½″ end pieces across the open edges of the top. A metal liner can be made to fit inside the box if you wish.

To make matching trays that fit on the tables, cut all parts from ¾″ plywood. The tray bottoms should measure 10½″x26¾″. Tray ends are 3″x10½″ and the sides are 3″x28¼″. Predrill, countersink, and glue-screw tray parts together. Your tables are all large enough to hold two trays at a time, with just enough room to spare.

Materials (for one piece)

Quantity	Description
¾″x4′x8′	exterior-grade plywood panels as needed
2 pair	8″ folding shelf brackets with screws for folding parts
4	furniture glides (approx. ¹⁵/₁₆″ diameter)
1 pair	3″x3″ lightweight hinges (for chair back only)
1 pair	1½″ angle irons (for chair only)
Wood filler, primer, enamel or varnish	

Parts (for one furniture project)

Part	No.	Description
A	1	28½″x30″ for all seats and tops
B	2	22″x30″ for sides of chairs and high tables
C	2	15″x30″ for sides of low tables and planter
D	1	11½″x28½″ for seat back
E	2	3″x28½″ ends for planter box
Tray		
F	2	3″x10½″ for tray ends
G	2	3″x28¼″ for tray sides
H	1	10½″x26¾″ for tray bottom

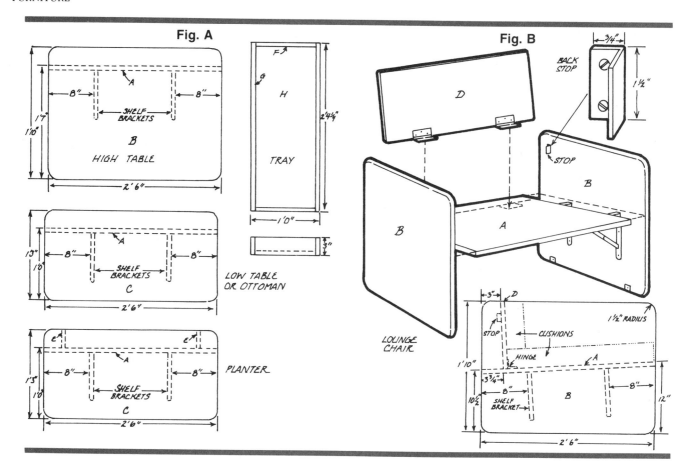

Fig. A

A

8"   SHELF
BRACKETS   8"

1'7"
1'10"

B

HIGH TABLE

2'6"

A

8"   SHELF
BRACKETS   8"

13"
10"

C

LOW TABLE
OR OTTOMAN

2'6"

E   A   E

A

8"   SHELF   8"
BRACKETS

1'3"
1'0"

C

PLANTER

2'6"

F
G
H

TRAY

2'4½"

1'0"

3"

Fig. B

BACK
STOP

¾"

1½"

D

STOP

B

B   A

LOUNGE
CHAIR

3"   D

STOP

HINGE

1½" RADIUS

CUSHIONS

A

1'10"

3¾"

8"   B   8"

10½"

SHELF
BRACKET

12"

2'6"

Lean-To Shed

1 4x8 (no cutting needed)
1 2'x8'—this pairs up with the 4x8 to sheath the roof
1 4'x7'—lower part of the outside wall
1 2'x7'—pairs with the 4x7 to form outside wall
1 4'x8'—cut at an angle as shown in Fig. C. The large pieces form the back wall, the small pieces go over the door opening.

Finish the shed according to the material that's on the building—beveled siding or whatever. You can match the roof with the house shingles also, or simply use roll roofing. To do this, lay it on the shed, lapping it a couple of inches up the wall. Nail roofing on every 3″, then seal the joint between the roofing edge and house with roof cement. (If you live in a concrete house, a couple of variations on the above instructions will pertain.) Fasten 2x4 posts to the house with masonry nails (a stud driver is excellent in this situation). When you install the roofing, lap it on as for a wood house, but adhere it with a generous bead of roof cement on the inside edge, then cover the lap with a joint of cement.

No outdoor projects book would be complete without the classic storage unit—a lean-to shed. It makes a great place to store all kinds of things. Made of hefty stock and sheathing, it can be finished with the same material as used on the house. Handy, yet unobtrusive.

The shed is supported against the building and at two corners. First, measure out 3'10″ from where the wall that you're building against is. Run a line at this point parallel to the building and make two marks 7' apart. Dig two footing holes there. Fill the holes with concrete, then set a 6″½″ bolt in each, letting each bolt protrude about 2″. Bolts should be exactly 3'10″ from the house wall.

Now, proceed to build the shed framing. Cut two 2″x4″ posts, each 7'8½″ long; secure them to the wall, then spike a 7' 2x4 across the tops of the posts.

Start construction of the outer wall by cutting two 4x4s, each 6' long. Working on any convenient flat surface, spike a 7' 2x4 across the tops of the 4x4s. Cut another 2x4 to fit between the 4x4s and toenail it in place 6″ from the lower ends. Then cut two 2x4s and nail in place equal distances (from end posts) apart. (See Fig. A.)

Cut four rafters, each 6' long, following Fig. B for angling ends to fit against the roof and notches to fit pieces on the outside of the structure (where outer and side walls meet). Nail the rafters in place. Make certain the rafters are evenly spaced and parallel to make the roof material easy to install.

Just like a house, sheathing is used to cover the framework. To save strain on your part, you can have your dealer cut it to the size needed: In all four sheets of ½″ sheathing are required and should be cut as follows:

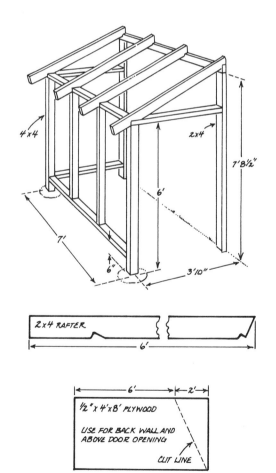

2x4 RAFTER

6'

½″ x 4'x8' PLYWOOD

USE FOR BACK WALL AND ABOVE DOOR OPENING

CUT LINE

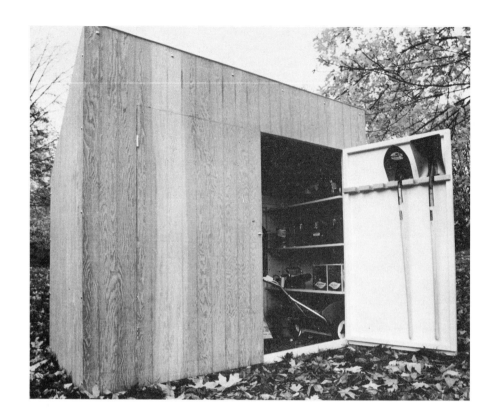

Garden Storage Shed

Here is a low-cost way to organize your outdoor equipment under one roof at a minimum of cost and space, providing a place for everything (it's up to you to make sure that everything is kept in its place). As designed by Jeff Milstein, AIA, the shed rests on a bed of gravel. A more permanent foundation would be needed only in harsher climates; a concrete slab could be built as described in an earlier section of the book.

Occupying 4x8 feet of ground space, the spacious shed has wide double doors to admit the largest pieces of outdoor equipment. Hooks, brackets, and shelving can be attached inside to suit your requirements—(enough plywood will be left over after cutting the shed side panels for a number of shelves). The roof slopes from a height of 6 feet 8 inches in front to 4 feet 6 inches in the rear and will withstand normal snow loads. The redwood or preservative-treated sills resist deterioration. As shown, the shed is fixed to the ground with steel pipe stakes bolted to the frame; this allows easy relocating if desired. If built on a concrete foundation, anchor bolts should be provided around the slab perimeter, and the sills drilled to fit over the bolts.

The roof and siding are of ⅜-inch rough-sawn plywood. It can be stained or left to weather naturally, and blends well with any outdoor setting.

Cut all the plywood panels as shown in the cutting diagrams. Cut lumber framing to the lengths given in the Materials List. Treat the lumber with a wood preservative (unless redwood or another decay-resistant wood is used), taking special care to thoroughly treat end grain.

Glue-nail framing to the inside of the front, back, and side panels, and the doors, as shown in the elevations.

Sills should extend 1 inch below the plywood. After they are in place, cut the top side framing pieces at angles at both front and back. Glue roofing paper to the underside of the roof panels. Fasten the roof framing to the panels, ripping the front and back framing pieces to follow the roof's contour (see detail drawings 3 and 4).

Excavate the area where the shed is to be located to a depth of 2 inches. Spread medium to fine gravel in the excavation and level it, using a straightedge and a carpenter's level. Set the back panel in position and have a helper hold it steady. Run a bead of caulking compound down the end frame pieces, then lift one side into position and drill holes through both corner frames. Insert bolts and tighten on wing nuts (see detail 1). Repeat with the other side, then fasten the front. Drive steel pipes into the ground inside the shed along each side near the corners, flush with the tops of the sills. Make sure that the sills are even and level and that the corners are square, propping the frame up with gravel where necessary. Drill ⅜-inch holes through siding, sills, and pipes, and bolt the structure to the pipes.

If you are building the shed on a concrete slab, lay the sides, back, and front in place on the ground around the slab. Drill through the sills at the locations of the anchor bolts. Lift the back into position over the bolts, then place washers and nuts on the bolts and tighten down. Proceed with sides as above, placing them over the bolts. The front should have anchor bolts at the ends only, so that they do not interfere with the opening.

With the shell in place, lift the roof into position (you will definitely need help for this operation). Fasten as shown in detail drawings 3, 4, and 5.

Cut 1¼-inch-wide (or whatever width suits your needs) slots in the 2x4 tool hangers, spacing them to fit your garden shovels, rakes, hoes, etc. Notch them at the ends and screw onto the door framing. Cut the ends at an angle where the doors meet so as not to interfere with closing. Hang the doors with flush-mounted or mortised hinges (see alternate details in front elevation drawing). Install magnetic catches above the doors. Attach door knobs. Install hooks, shelves, perforated hardboard, etc., as needed to accommodate tools and equipment in the shed.

Materials

Quantity	Description
Plywood	
6 panels	⅜"x4'x8' rough-sawn 303® APA grade-trademarked plywood
Lumber*	
2	2x3, 7'9" long, for front and back sills
2	2x3, 4' long, for side sills
4	2x2, 5'1½" long, for door framing
2	2x3, 3' long, for door framing
2	2x2, 2'9" long, for door framing
2	2x4, 3' long, for door-mounted tool hangers
2	2x2, 4' long, for rear side framing
2	2x2, 5'3" long, for center side framing
2	2x2, 6'4" long, for front side framing
2	2x2, 4' long, for bottom side framing
2	2x2, 4'9" long, for top side framing
1	2x2, 7'9" long, for upper back framing
3	2x2, 3'11½" long, for vertical back framing
2	2x2, 3'1¾" long, for vertical back framing
2	2x2, 3'9¾" long, for back horizontal framing
2	2x4, 7'9" long, for longitudinal roof framing, ripped to fit (see details 3 and 4)
3	2x4, 4'3" long, for roof joists, cut at angles to fit (see details 3 and 4)
2	2x2, 6'3" long, for front framing
1	2x4, 7'6" long, for header over door
2	2x2, 5'2" long, for hinge strips
1	2x2, 8" long, for joint above door
1	2x2, 7'9" long, for top front framing

Other Materials

Quantity	Description
4	¾" x 12" steel pipe for anchor posts
4	#8 wood screws for door-mounted tool hangers, 2½" long
2	Magnetic door catches
4	Door hinges
14	⁵⁄₁₆" carriage bolts with wing nuts, 4" long for sides
4	³⁄₁₆" carriage bolts with wing nuts, 3" long
20	⁵⁄₁₆" carriage bolts with wing nuts, 2½" long
As required	6d aluminum or galvanized box nails
As required	16d aluminum or galvanized common nails
As required	Drain gravel to layer 2" deep
As required	Silicone caulk to seal all joints
As required	Glue for glue-nailing (resorcinol type recommended)
As required	Paint or stain for finishing 4'x8"x8' roofing paper.

*NOTE: All lumber lengths are approximate. You may need to trim some of the framing to fit.

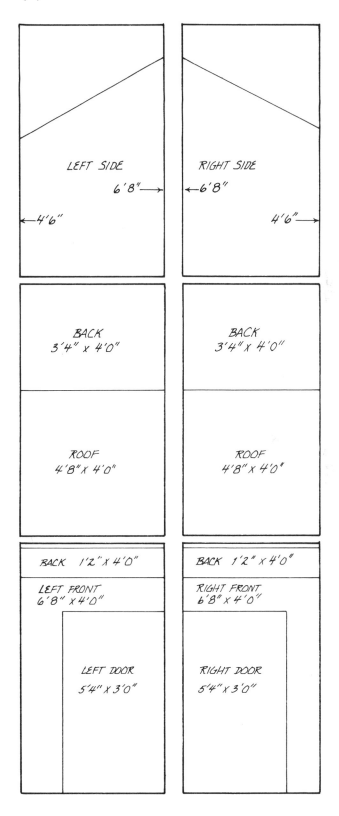

LEFT SIDE 6'8" → ←4'6"

RIGHT SIDE ←6'8" 4'6" →

BACK 3'4" x 4'0"

BACK 3'4" x 4'0"

ROOF 4'8" x 4'0"

ROOF 4'8" x 4'0"

BACK 1'2" x 4'0"

LEFT FRONT 6'8" x 4'0"

LEFT DOOR 5'4" x 3'0"

BACK 1'2" x 4'0"

RIGHT FRONT 6'8" x 4'0"

RIGHT DOOR 5'4" x 3'0"

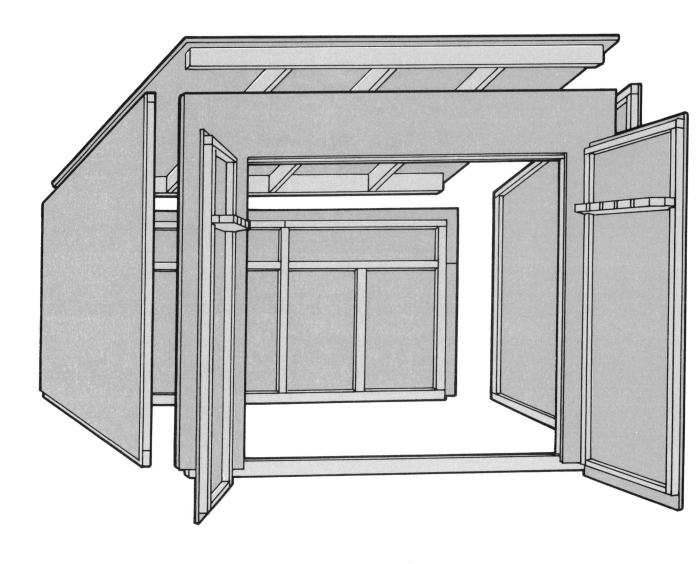

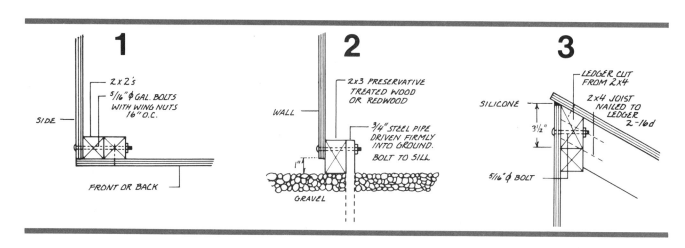

1

SIDE —

2x2's

5/16"∅ GAL. BOLTS
WITH WING NUTS
16" O.C.

FRONT OR BACK

2

WALL —

2x3 PRESERVATIVE
TREATED WOOD
OR REDWOOD

3/4" STEEL PIPE
DRIVEN FIRMLY
INTO GROUND.
BOLT TO SILL

1"

GRAVEL

3

SILICONE —

LEDGER CUT
FROM 2x4

2x4 JOIST
NAILED TO
LEDGER
2-16d

3½"

5/16"∅ BOLT

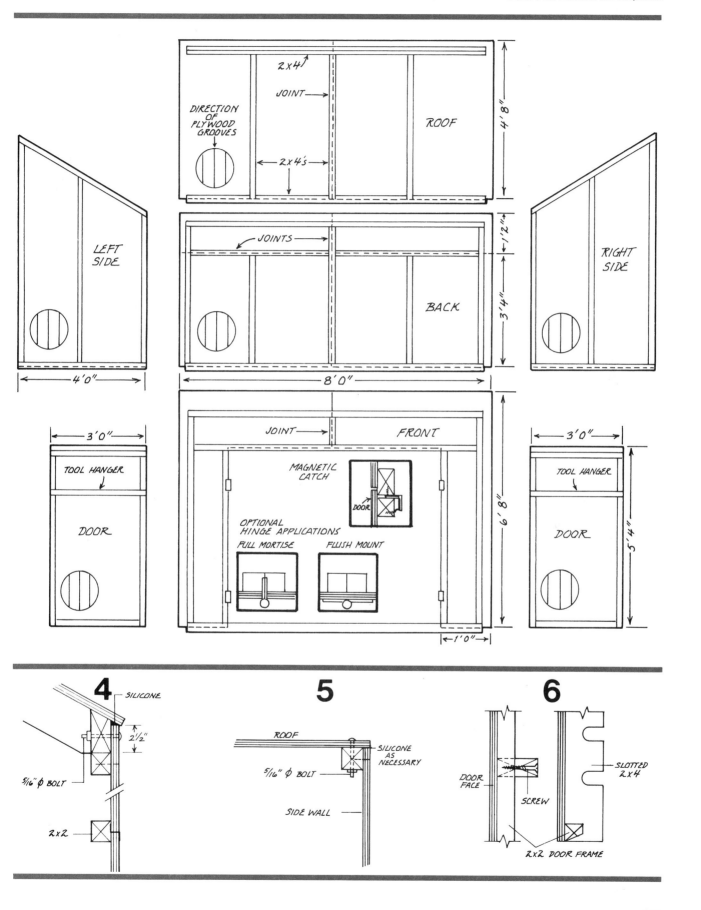

A Good Hangup for Garden Tools

It's nice to have garden tools—everything from rakes to power mowers—handy, rather than having to lug them out of the garage every time you want to use them. This hanging storage cabinet puts them close by. Here it is shown mounted between carport framing members, but it could be mounted anywhere space is available. If it is installed in an area where the unit's back faces an open area, a portion of the back can be cut away making the unit accessible from both sides.

The unit is basically a 14"-deep cabinet crosshatched inside with shelves and dividers.

Following Fig. A for dimensions, cut bottom, top, sides, back, and long divider from ¾" plywood. Lay the back on a flat surface and assemble as follows: Nail (use 8d nails) and glue the bottom to the back, nail sides in place, then the top, then the long divider, driving nails for this through the back as well as through the top and bottom into divider edges. Then, fill in with shelves and dividers according to your storage needs. (Note: box depth can be varied—enlarged—to accommodate larger power mowers.) Here there are four shelves but you might choose to have only a couple or none; see Fig. B for locations of shelves in this plan. Also, if you wish to have the unit accessible from the back, cut out

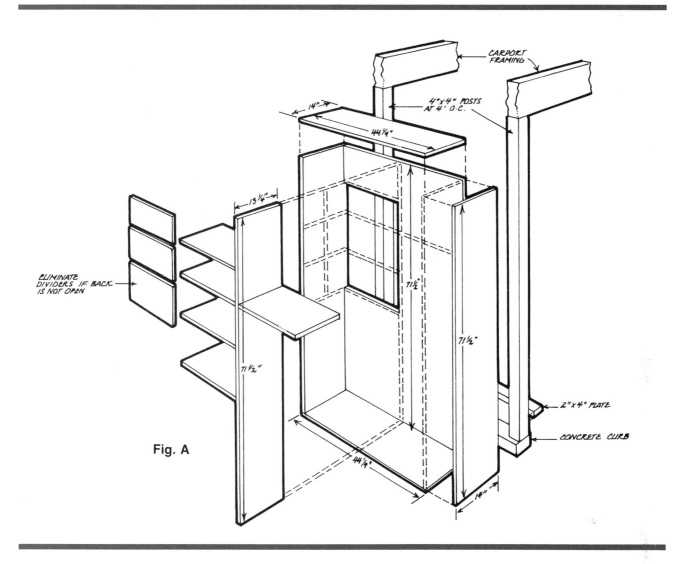

Fig. A

the plywood piece indicated (approximately 29″ deep by 21⅜″ wide) and eliminate the shelf dividers.

Finish to suit, then mount the cabinet (minus the doors) on posts or house studs using lag screws or bolts as needed. Finally, hang the doors with three pairs of hinges each and install door hardware.

Materials

Quantity	Description
3	¾″x4′x8′ sheets of exterior plywood
4′	of 2x4 stock for plate (if required)
3 pairs	of door hinges
2	door pulls
	Door catches
	6d and 8d finishing nails

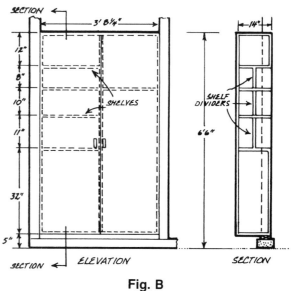

Fig. B

Hanging Storage Boxes

A unit such as the one shown can be a handy and handsome addition to a patio area, and it's simple to make—four boxes nailed to vertical 4"x4" posts.

The unit may be constructed wherever you have a structural arrangement where support posts can be anchored at the top—such as to a porch or patio roof.

Here four boxes are shown, but you can build as many as suits your purposes. Each box is 24" wide by 16" high and is made of ¾" exterior plywood. Cut the parts as indicated in Fig. A, then assemble them with nails and glue, and attach the door with a pair of butt hinges. Repeat procedure for other boxes.

Next mount the 4x4 posts. There are three, and they should be cut to fit and anchored depending on your particular patio situation. In the unit shown, for example, the posts butt against the patio slab and are nailed at the top to a 2x4 nailed to the rafters; in this case the 4x4s actually support the overhang. If you were going to mount the posts in the earth, they would have to be handled as you would handle any posts placed directly in the earth.

The boxes may be nailed through the sides into the posts with no further support necessary. In the photo 2x4s are used, but these are more decorative than supportive.

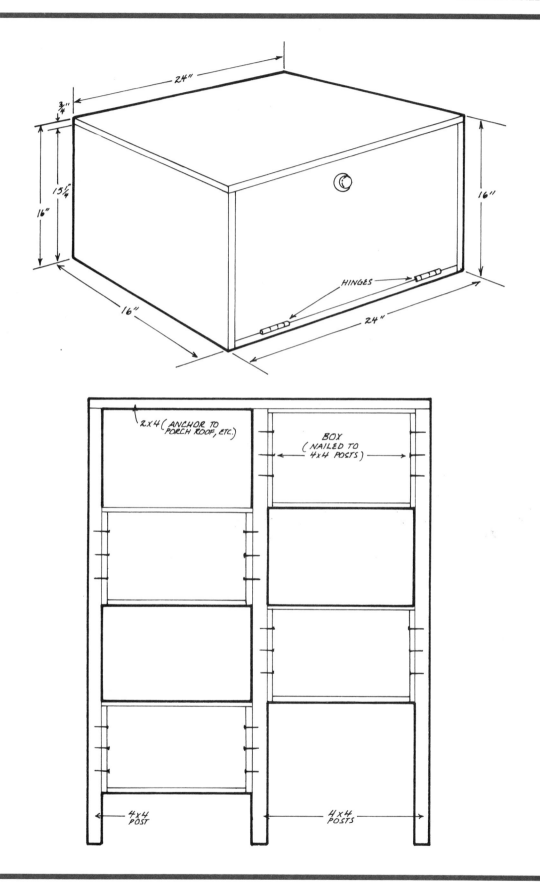

Modular Storage—Plus

Here's an interesting and unusual idea. Modular storage units that not only can provide space galore, but are designed so that they can support things between them—table, bench, play equipment for the kids—the accessories are many. And, colorfully painted, their modern design is sure to dress up a back-yard area.

The basic module is essentially a plywood box—4'x4' square and 8' high. It is bolted to a 4'-square foundation of heavy stock (4"x4" material is used). Parts are bolted together with carriage bolts and wing nuts. Should you move it will be an easy matter to disassemble the unit(s) to take with you.

Start construction by building the foundation (Fig. A), hammering it tightly together with 16d galvanized nails. Cut out all plywood components needed—floor, back, walls, short front panel, and base. Dimensions are shown in the cluster of drawings designated Fig. B. Note that the walls have slots cut in them. These are to support accessories.

Cut all 2x2 framing pieces needed (also Fig. B) and nail them to panels as called for. Cut five cleats for shelves and attach at points shown; 4" pegs for hanging things may also be attached at this time.

Sand and fill the parts as needed, then paint them. As mentioned, modern design is the keynote here, so you can paint different panels different colors without worrying about a garish effect.

Start assembling the pieces by setting the two walls on edge, back or slotted sides up, and lightly clamp the roof and base to them. Drill through the roof and base into the wall framing for bolts (see Fig. B for hole locations); holes should be ¼".

Fasten the roof to the sides with bolts and wing nuts (each bolt is ¼"x2¾"), but leave the base as is—clamped on.

Lay the back panel in place. It will be recessed and rest against the side framing members. Drill holes and bolt it on, then drill holes through the roof into the back's framing and bolt there. Also drill holes through base into back but don't bolt it on (keep it clamped on).

Turn the assembly over onto its back. Lay the front panel in place and secure it by drilling through the roof into the framing on the front, then bolt these components together. Follow by drilling holes into the side framing on the front; bolt on.

Remove the base from the assembly. Square the piece on the foundation and secure with nails and glue. Using the holes in the base as guides, drill through the foundation. Set assembly—walls, roof, back—on the base and bolt it on with ¼" carriage bolts 6" long and wing nuts. These should be countersunk at the bottom.

Nail shelves for cleats, first notching the boards to fit around projecting framing members in the corners.

Check all wing nuts for tightness. Tighten as needed. It would also be a good idea, as you assemble the various components, to apply mastic to the joints. Overall assembly is shown in Fig. C.

Install a catch and door lock (optional) on the door panel. Hang the door with a piano hinge. The door handle (Fig. D) may be made of plywood as shown, but ordinary hardware is okay.

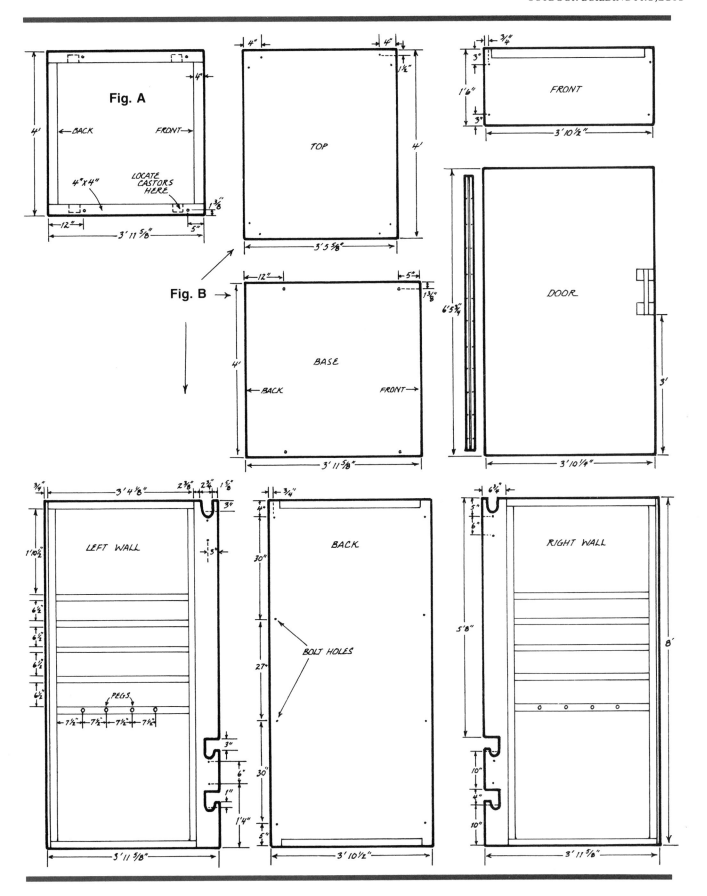

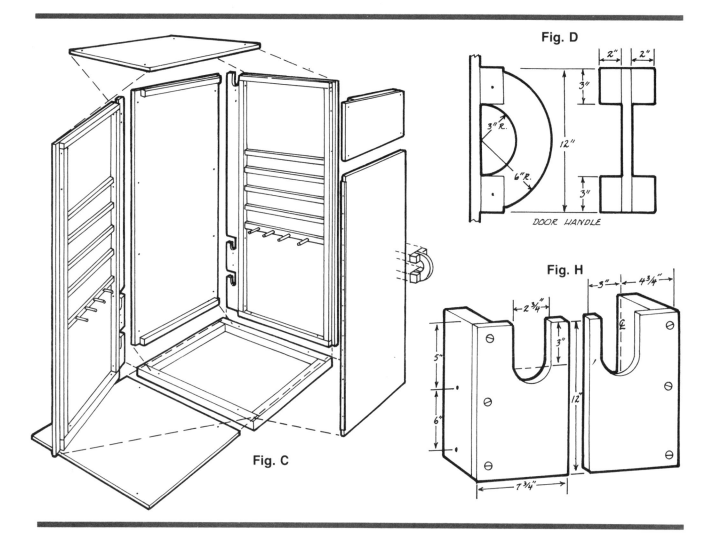

Fig. D

DOOR HANDLE

Fig. H

Fig. C

As mentioned, a variety of accessory structures can be made and mounted on the storage units—however, you need at least two storage units to hang accessories. The accessories are easy to build. A few are shown in Figs. E, F, and G. To hang one, situate two modules back to back, a few feet apart (this distance depends on accessory size). Then simply slip the dowel frame members in the slots made in the backs of the modules. That's all the support you need.

If you want the doors to be side by side or facing the same way you can build connectors (Fig. H) and secure them to the sides of the units near the front edges (Fig. I.)

A few arrangements of modules and accessories are shown (Figs. J, K, and L). Experimentation and your own imagination will likely produce additional accessories. Only one caution: If you make any play equipment—such as the monkey bar shown—the modules should have their foundations anchored to spikes or bolts set in concrete. Free-standing modules (or ones on casters) will not be a solid enough base to take the stress of active children.

Materials

Quantity	Description
16'	4"x4" stock for foundation
60'	2"x2" stock for framing and door-handle blocks
40'	1"x2" for shelf cleats
4"	½" dowel for shelf pegs
	6d nails for framing
8	16d common nails for foundation
20	¼"x2¾" carriage bolts with wing nuts for assembly
6	¼"x6" carriage bolts with wing nuts for securing assembly to foundation
	2³/₁₆"x4" carriage bolts, washers and nuts for door handle
8	#10 1½" flathead screws for door handles
1	6' piano hinge for door
	#4 ¾" brass screws for piano hinge
1	door catch
1 sheet	exterior plywood for roof and base
2 sheets	exterior plywood with paintable surface for front and back
2 sheets	exterior plywood, rough-sawn finish, for walls

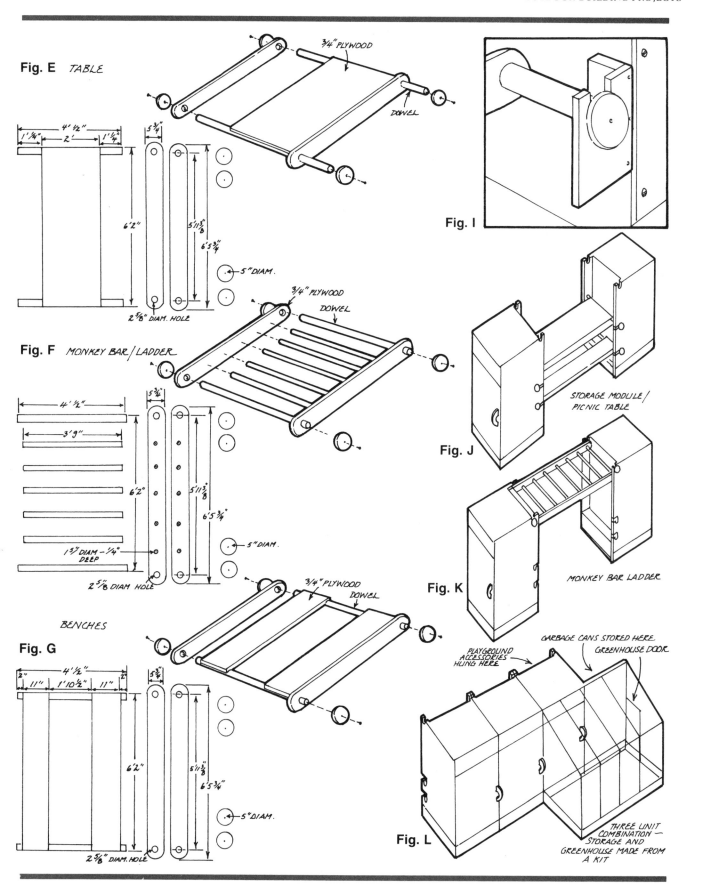

Fig. E *TABLE*

4' 4½"
1' 3¼"
2'
1' 3¼"
5 ¾"
6'2"
5'11⅜"
6'5¾"
5" DIAM.
2 ⅝" DIAM. HOLE

¾" PLYWOOD
DOWEL

Fig. F *MONKEY BAR / LADDER*

4' 4½"
3' 9"
5 ¾"
6'2"
5'11⅜"
6'5¾"
1 ⁵/₁₆" DIAM – ¼" DEEP
2 ⁵/₈" DIAM HOLE
5" DIAM.

¾" PLYWOOD
DOWEL

BENCHES

Fig. G

4' 4½"
2"
11"
1' 10½"
11"
2"
5 ¾"
6'2"
5'11⅜"
6'5¾"
5" DIAM.
2 ⅝" DIAM. HOLE

¾" PLYWOOD
DOWEL

Fig. I

Fig. J

STORAGE MODULE / PICNIC TABLE

Fig. K

MONKEY BAR LADDER

Fig. L

PLAYGROUND ACCESSORIES HUNG HERE
GARBAGE CANS STORED HERE
GREENHOUSE DOOR

THREE UNIT COMBINATION – STORAGE AND GREENHOUSE MADE FROM A KIT

Basic Storage Barn

Need more storage space for your garden tools, lawn mower, even the kids' bikes? The mini storage barn needs only an 8'x8' corner of your back yard, yet it is large enough to hold all your outdoor equipment and then some.

Cut and frame out all ten sides of the barn before you start any assembly. (See Basic Framing Sketches) The two roof sections, F and G, are ½" panels left 8' long but trimmed to a width of 3'3". Each panel has three 2"x4"x2'10¾" braces mitered to a 60° angle at each end. The braces are nailed across the width of the panel with the outside ones placed 4½" from the ends. The middle brace divides the panel exactly in half. All three braces are ¾" from the top edge of the panel and will be nailed to the ridge beam. Panels E and H are also made from ½" plywood, trimmed to 3'3¾" wide. Both sections have three cross braces 2"x4"x2'9¼" long with a 60° miter at one end. The square ends of the cross braces are nailed to a 2"x4"x7'3" beam which is anchored along the top edge of the panel. One cross beam divides the panel in half. The two end braces are nailed 3½" from the ends of the panel.

The two side panels, D and J, are trimmed from ⅝" exterior plywood siding to a width of 3'9". Since the decorative grooves in the panel must run vertical, the panel must be cut in half and reassembled. Cut each half so that it measures 3'9"x3'9½" and butt them together so that the grooves run across the width of the panel. The panel now measures 3'9" wide by 7'7" long. Nail a 2"x4"x7'3" along the top edge, leaving 2" at each end of the panel. Then nail the two 2"x4"x10½" end braces at right angles to the long brace. These will extend 1½" beyond the width of the panel. Nail a second 2"x4"x7'3" brace between the ends of the side braces.

The brace will overlap the panel approximately 2" so that they can be nailed together. Now place the 2"x4"x3'7" center brace along the butt line with its 4" side against the panel. Nail both halves of the panel to the center brace.

Cut the front and back panels according to the accompanying diagram. Two side Ks and two side Bs are required. Cut doors A and C from the B sides. Cut 2x4 frames and nail them along outside edges with the 4" side against the panels. The two halves of both the front and back walls are butted together and held by a center brace as shown in the diagram. Note that the frames along the sides where panels D and J will join are set ⅜" in from the edges of the plywood. The 2x4 header across the top of the door frame is allowed to extend 1" below the panel. The frame across the bottom of both walls extends 1½" below the panels.

The doors are framed with 1x4 stock on both sides. The inside frame ends 1" from the top of the door. The outside framing is nailed to the outer edges of the panel on all four sides and includes a diagonal brace which divides each half of the doors.

Materials	
Quantity	**Description**
4 panels	½" medium-grade exterior plywood
6 panels	⅝" exterior plywood siding
283'	2"x4" framing (based on 8' lengths)
8'	2"x6" stock for ridge beam
176'	1"x4" trim stock (based on 8' lengths)
12	¼"x3½"-long lag bolts
5½'	¾" steel pipe (cut in 16" lengths)
2 pairs	3" strap hinges for doors
As needed	Roofing material to cover 96 sq. ft.
As needed	10d common and 8d finishing nails

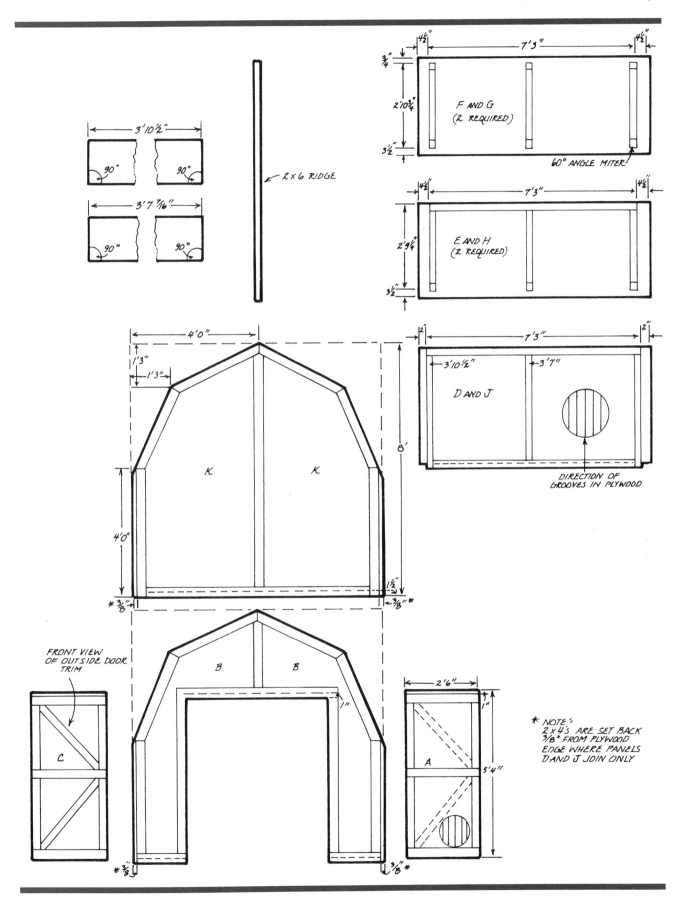

2 x 6 RIDGE

3'10½"
90°   90°

3'7 7/16"
90°   90°

4½"   7'3"   4½"
¾"
2'10¾"
F AND G
(2 REQUIRED)
3½"
60° ANGLE MITER

4½"   7'3"   4½"
2'9½"
E AND H
(2 REQUIRED)
3½"

2"   7'3"   2"
3'10½"   3'7"
D AND J
DIRECTION OF
GROOVES IN PLYWOOD

4'0"
1'3"
1'3"
8'
K   K
4'0"
1½"
* ⅜"   ⅜" *

FRONT VIEW
OF OUTSIDE DOOR
TRIM
B   B
1"
C   A
2'6"
1"
5'4"
* ⅜"   ⅜" *

* NOTE:
2 x 4's ARE SET BACK
⅜" FROM PLYWOOD
EDGE WHERE PANELS
D AND J JOIN ONLY

When all pieces are cut and framed, assemble the barn by nailing the back and front walls between the sides wherever the 2x4 frames butt together. Next, attach roof sections E and H, and finally sections E and G are nailed to the 2"x6" ridge beam. Nail roof flashing over the peak of the roof, using mastic to insure a watertight seal. Overlap and nail 1x4 trim stock to both sides of all corners and around the doorway. When hanging the doors, bolt the hinges through the trim, panel, and 2x4 frame.

To stabilize the entire structure, drive a 16"-long ¾" pipe into the ground at the back corners and on both sides of the door. Drill a ¼" hole through the pipes and base of the walls to accept lag bolts. The roof may be finished with any of several materials including shakes, shingles, or roll roofing.

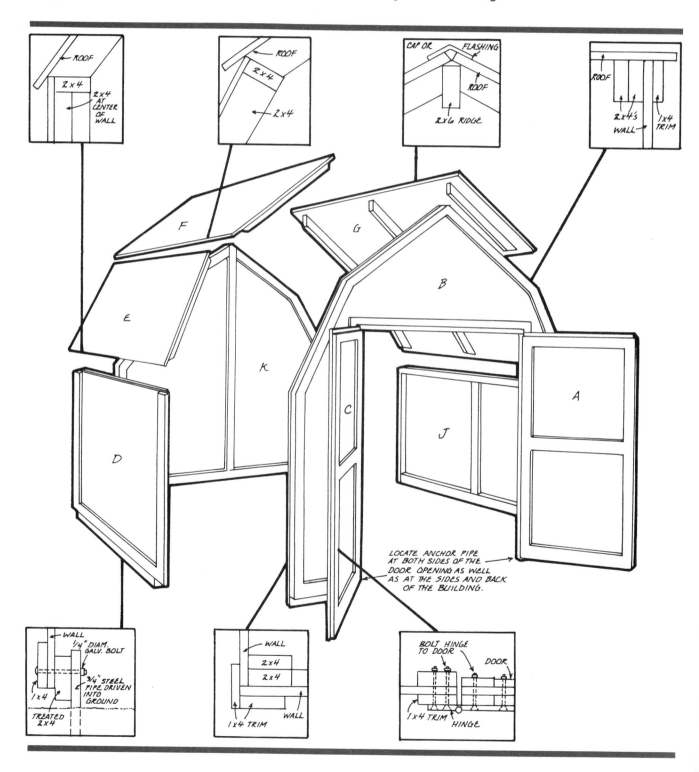

Outdoor Garden Storage

This easy-to-build, yet invaluable outdoor storage house provides a flexible place to keep all your outdoor tools and patio items. There is a wide choice of textured plywood siding for the outside. Inside, shelves, counters, and hangers can be placed anywhere they suit your needs.

Cut the 2"x4" stock and assemble the floor frame, nailing the supports 2' on center. The outside dimensions of the completed frame measure 6'x8'. Place the 4"x4" skids on the ground and make sure they are level. The skids are soaked in preservative and placed 8' apart. Toenail the frame to the skids, as shown in Fig. A, and nail ⅝" plywood flooring over the frame (Fig. B).

Cut and assemble the front, back, and end wall

Materials	
Quantity	Description
4	⅜" exterior plywood panels for roof
9	4'x8' plywood siding panels for walls, door and ramp
2	⅝" exterior-grade plywood panels for floor and counter
23	2"x2"x8' stock for wall studs, top and bottom plates, and counter framing
7	2"x2"x10' stock for rafters
3	2"x2"x12' stock for roof framing
4	2"x4"x8' stock for floor framing
3	2"x4"x6' stock for floor framing
2	4"x4"x6' stock, treated, for skids
4	1"x2"x12' stock for fascia
13	1"x2"x8' stock for corners and trim around door
5	1"x6"x6' stock for door shelves and framing
1	1"x4"x8' for shelf fronts
3	3½"x3½" fast pin zinc-coated hinges
1	key-lock and latch
Assorted galvanized nails	

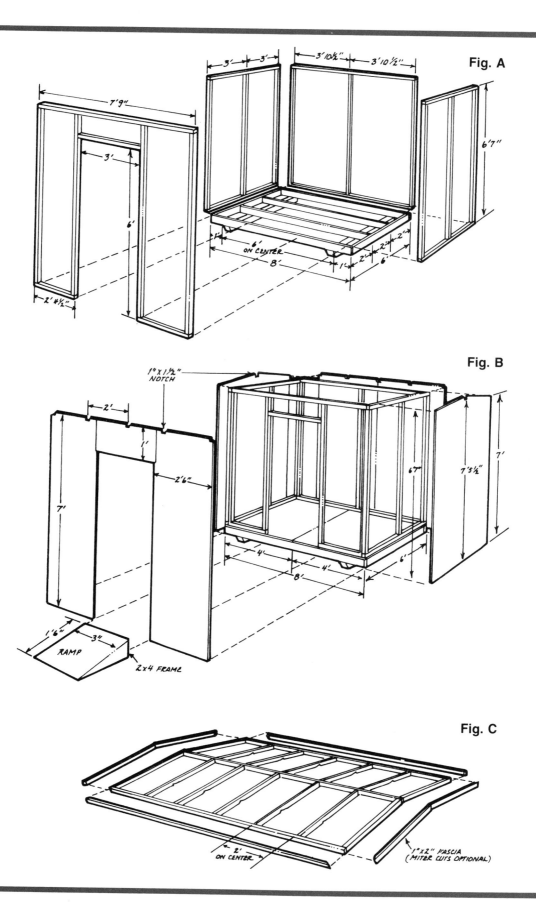

Fig. A

Fig. B

Fig. C

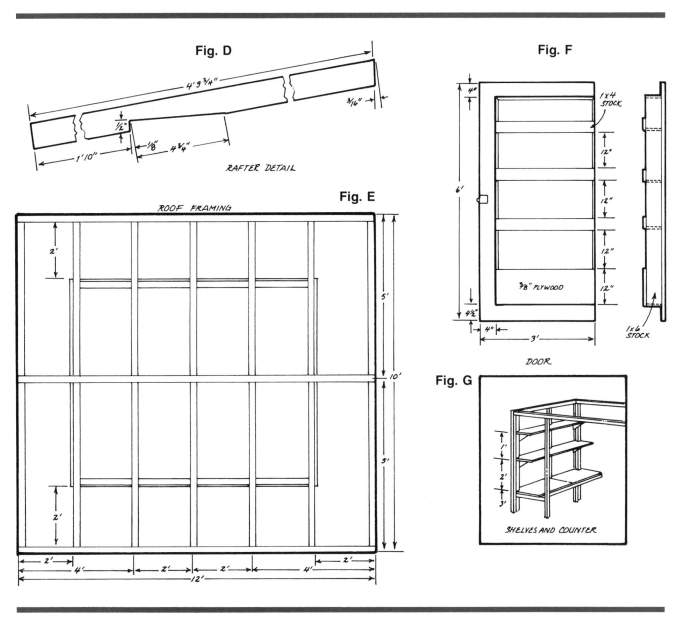

Fig. D

RAFTER DETAIL

Fig. E

ROOF FRAMING

Fig. F

DOOR

Fig. G

SHELVES AND COUNTER

frames from 2"x2" stock (see Fig. A). The side frames measure 6'x6'7". The front and back are 6'7"x7'9". The door frame in the front wall has an inside measurement of 3'x6'. Stand the walls into place on the floor and nail them together at the corners and bottom plates, making sure they are plumb, as shown in Fig. B. Now nail the ³⁄₈" plywood siding to the outside of the wall frames. Note that the top edges of the front and back walls have 1"x1½" notches cut every 2' on center. The peak of the roof in the end panels is 5½" higher than the 7' sides and is also notched (see Fig. B). The ends are made from two 3'-wide panels that butt at the center of the notch in the peak. When the siding is in place, overlap 1"x2" stock around each corner. 1x2 stock is also nailed flush with the door frame.

Cut and notch the ten rafters from 2x2 stock as shown in Fig. D and assemble them to the ridge beam and fascia boards (see Figs. C and E). Cut the ³⁄₈" plywood roof sheathing and nail it over the frame. Add the 1x2 fascia and nail the roof into place on top of the walls. Each of the rafters fits into the notches in the top wall edges. The roof is finished with built-up or 90-lb. roll roofing over the plywood.

Construct the door by nailing 1"x6" stock to the back of a 3'x6' piece of plywood siding, as shown in Fig. F. Glue-nail 1x6 stock and ³⁄₈" plywood to the 1"x6" frame to make the shelves and their fronts. Nail a 1"x2" strip to the latch side of the 2"x2" door frame to act as a door stop, and hang the door. Cut plywood shelves and the counter as shown in Fig. G and set them between the studs, using plywood brackets and 2"x4" supports. The plywood ramp is made from two pieces of plywood cut 3'x1½' and nailed together over a 2x4 frame.

A-Frame Garden Shed

Here is an unusual and attractive potting and garden tool storage shed which is easy to build and even easier to use. When the basic structure is finished, you can add hooks, shelves, workbenches, and whatever else will serve your particular gardening needs.

The 8'2"-long by 9'-wide base is made from patio bricks, or you can pour a concrete slab. Anchor the 2"x6" base plate around the perimeter of the base, as shown in Fig. A. Now stand two of the 2"x4"x10' rafters on the front corners of the base and bring them together at the top. Mark the angles to be beveled at both ends of the rafters (approximately 120° at the peak and 45° at the base). Cut all ten rafters to the same angles and assemble the two side frames as shown in Fig. A. The rafters are spaced 2' on center with 2"x4" pieces of blocking placed at the 4-foot and 8-foot heights, as well as at the base. Stand the frames on their sides and nail the tops of the rafters to the 1"x8"x8' ridge beam. The rafters are braced by five 2"x4"x2' cross beams mitered 45° at each end, which are centered across the rafters under the ridge beam (see Fig. B).

Now stand the A-frame on its base and nail it to the base plate. Nail the door studs in place at each end of the shed, leaving 36½" between them for the doors. The header is placed 6'8" above the base plates.

Nail the 26"x10' corrugated fiberglass panels to the side frames, with their ridges running up and down; mastic is put between each of the 2" overlaps between the panels to insure a watertight seal. Predrill all nail holes and use aluminum nails with neoprene washers,

nailing the fiberglass to the studs every 12". Nail four 26"x2' sections of fiberglass to both sides of the roof peak and the mitered cross braces under the ridge beam. Attach the ridge roll as shown in Fig. B. Corrugated panels are nailed to the ends, around the door frames. Leave ½" of the door frames exposed to act as door stops and trim the fiberglass to conform with the angle of the sides.

The doors are framed with 2"x4" stock (see Fig. C). Notch the side frames for the cross brace in the center and add glue blocks to the corners. Nail flat fiberglass paneling to the outside of the doors, allowing it to extend ½" beyond latch side and top of the frame. Fiberglass is also nailed to the inside of the top, angled portion of each door. Hang the doors.

Materials

Quantity	Description
34'	2"x6" stock for base plate
25	2"x4"x10' stock for framing
1	1"x8"x8' stock for ridge beam
8'	ridge roll
10	26"x10" corrugated fiberglass panels for walls
2	3'x8' flat fiberglass panels for doors
2 prs.	3" door butts
2	latches
As needed	16d common nails, aluminum nails with neoprene washers, mastic, patio blocks or cement

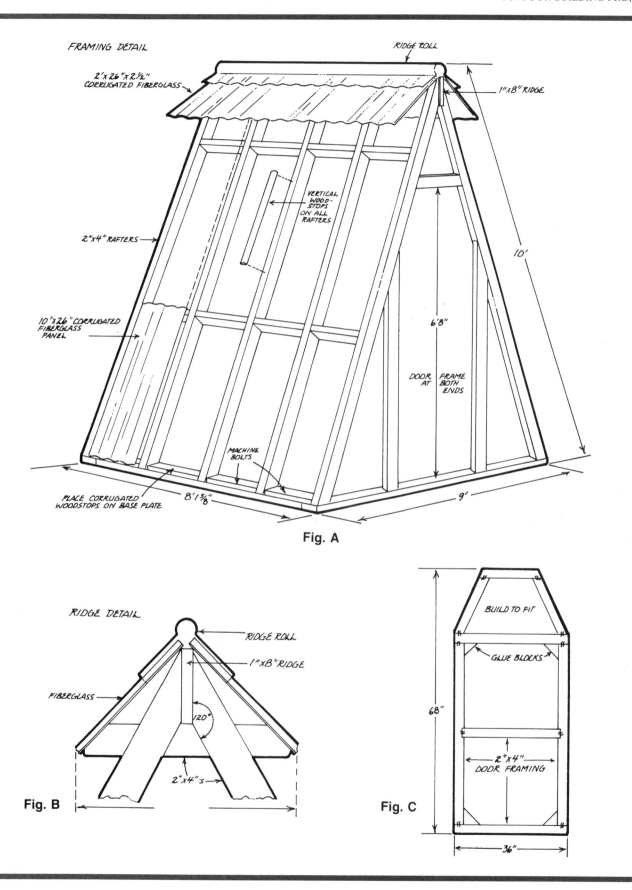

FRAMING DETAIL

RIDGE ROLL

2"x 26"x 2½"
CORRUGATED FIBERGLASS

1"x 8" RIDGE

10'

VERTICAL
WOOD-
STOPS
ON ALL
RAFTERS

2"x4" RAFTERS

6'8"

10'x26" CORRUGATED
FIBERGLASS
PANEL

DOOR AT FRAME
BOTH ENDS

MACHINE
BOLTS

PLACE CORRUGATED
WOODSTOPS ON BASE PLATE

8'1⅝"

9'

Fig. A

RIDGE DETAIL

RIDGE ROLL

1"x 8" RIDGE

FIBERGLASS

120°

2"x4"'s

Fig. B

BUILD TO FIT

GLUE BLOCKS

68"

2"x4"
DOOR FRAMING

Fig. C

36"

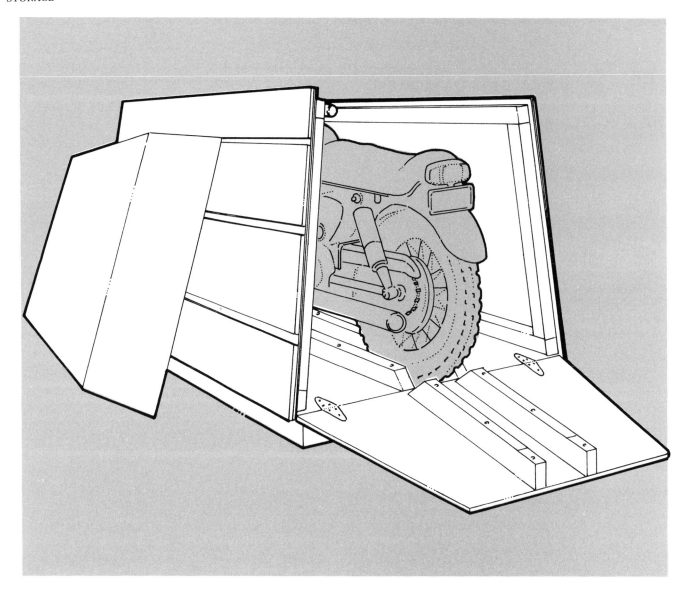

Garage for a Motorcycle

This mini-garage will keep a motorcycle protected from weather and from those who would wish to relieve you of it without your knowledge. Basic material used is ⅝" rough-sawn plywood. You can vary this as you wish. Perhaps you will want to paint the structure the same color as your house.

Start the construction by building the base, shown in Fig. A. Cut two side pieces from 2"x4" stock, each 83¼" long, and two end pieces, each 40¾"; cut a brace that is also 40¾". Nail (use 4d nails) the pieces together into a rectangular frame with the brace centered as shown in the drawing.

Cut a 46½"x84¾" piece from ½" plywood; set the piece so it overlaps 1¼" on the sides and slightly (½") overlaps in the back but is flush with the front edge. Secure it with 8d nails.

You can make all the walls (sides, door, back) of the garage next, but they will not be installed until after the wheel guides are in. Cut side panels from ⅝" rough-sawn plywood, each 85¼"x40⅜". To each attach a framework of 2x3s around the inside face, observing the locations in Fig. B.

Cut the back (Fig. C) from a piece of rough-sawn plywood, making the section 34⅜" at the top, 46½" across the bottom, and 39½" high. Cut the same size door (Fig. D). Next, install a pair of spaced 2x3s. Cut the

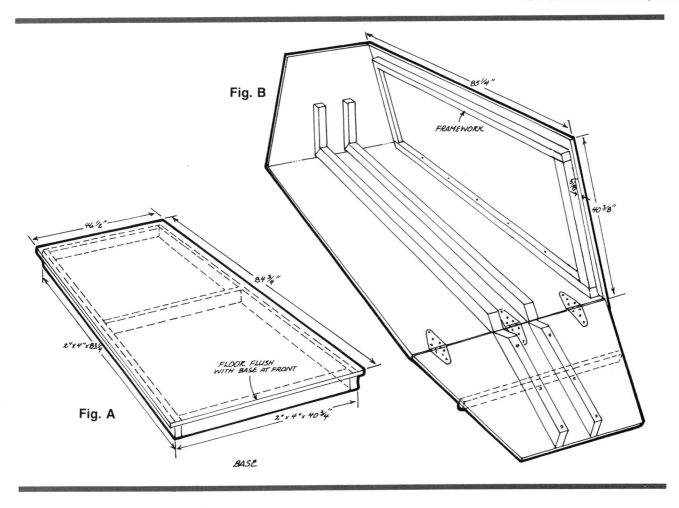

Fig. B

85¼"

FRAMEWORK

5⅛"

40⅜"

46½"

84¾"

2"x4"x83¾"

FLOOR FLUSH
WITH BASE AT FRONT

Fig. A

2"x4"x40¾"

BASE

2x3s as long as the base, sawing the front end at 45° angles; this is so that when the door is closed, it can fit into proper positions against the corresponding 2x3 guides of the door which when down serves as a ramp.

Referring to Fig. B, tack the 2x3s in, along the center of the base, forming a slot that will accept the particular size tires your motorcycle has. Then drill holes and anchor the boards permanently, with ¼"x5" carriage

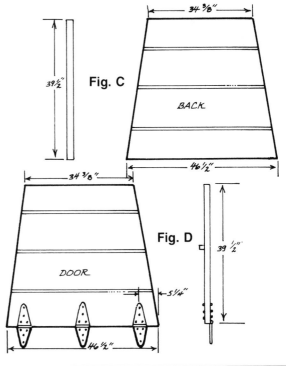

34⅜"

39½"

Fig. C

BACK

46½"

34⅜"

Fig. D

DOOR

39½"

5¼"

46½"

Materials

Quantity	Description
1	4'x8' sheet of ⅝" rough-sawn plywood
1	4'x8' sheet of ½" exterior plywood
1	4'x8' sheet of ¼" exterior plywood
22'	of 2x4 stock
24'	of 2x3 stock
10'	of ¾"x6" stock
3½'	of 2x2 stock
3	heavy-duty butt hinges
2	4½" hasps
	¼"x6" carriage bolts for door hinges
	¼"x5" carriage bolts for wheel guides
	⅛"x1½" screws for door hinges anchored to base

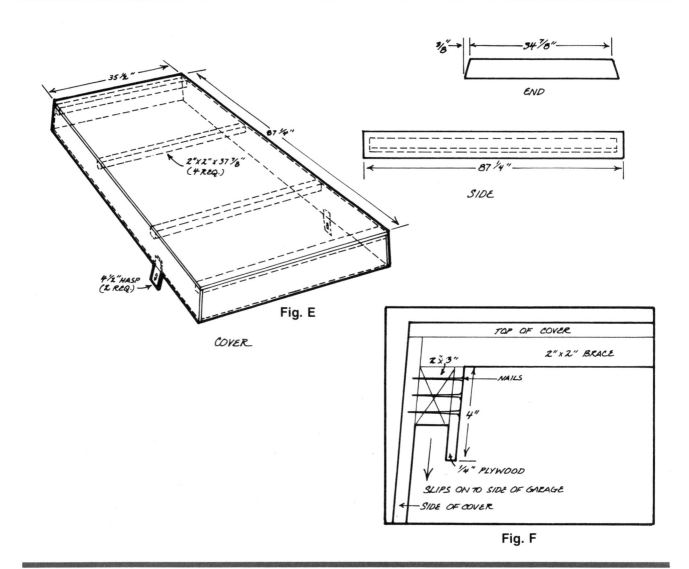

35½"

2"x2"x37⅞"
(4 REQ.)

87¼"

4½"HASP
(2 REQ.)

Fig. E

COVER

⅜"   34⅞"

END

87¼"

SIDE

TOP OF COVER

2"x3"   2"x2" BRACE

NAILS

4"

¼" PLYWOOD

SLIPS ON TO SIDE OF GARAGE

SIDE OF COVER

Fig. F

bolts. One bolt 3" from each end and one centered are recommended for each 2x3. Cut and attach guides the same way on the back (Fig. B).

Set door panel into position next to base and mark both for hinges—3 pairs of 6" heavy-duty butt hinges. Drill holes for bolts and screws; hinges may be screwed to the base but should be bolted to the door.

Cut and attach (with carriage bolts) 2x3 guides to back side of the door, following method used for the base and back. Here, the 2x3s are angled at 45° at the ends closest to the base—those corresponding 2x3s mentioned earlier.

Begin assembly of the garage by lightly nailing the sides to the base. Slip the back in place, then bend in the sides and nail the parts together with 6d nails. Attach hinge leaves to the door, then screw the other leaves to the base.

Next make the cover, or roof. Following Fig. E, cut the two sides and the two ends needed; note angled ends. Nail the pieces together with 6d nails.

Cut the top for the cover—a piece of 35½"x87¼" plywood. Nail in place. Cut four 2x2s, each 37⅜" long, and nail to the assembly in postions shown in Fig. E to brace it.

The cover has a lip on each side (inside) which rests on the garage sides. To make these lips, cut a piece of ¼" plywood 4" wide and 87" long. Nail these pieces to a 2x3 also 87" long with one long edge flush with a long edge of the plywood strip. In turn nail this assembly inside the cover flush against the braces. The lip thus formed is about 1" deep. (see Fig. F). Repeat the procedure for other side of the cover.

Finally, install hasps (one on each side) and finish to suit.

Hanging Bike Rack

Here is a neat way of saving space in your garage. The rack is not difficult to build, but you will have to supply some of the dimensions yourself, since the width of the rack depends on the space between the joists in the area where you plan to put it. In any case, you will need approximately two-thirds of a ¾″ plywood panel to complete the project.

Before starting, measure the spacing between joists to determine the exact width of the compartment. Mark out the sides, back, top, gussets, bottom, shelf, and doors on a plywood panel and cut them out. Glue and nail a 1x2 brace to the compartment sides and back to support the middle shelf. Use 6d nails to glue and nail the top, bottom, and back to the sides. The shelf may or may not be installed permanently, depending on your needs. Hang the doors.

Cut the two 2″x4″x57″ hangers and nail the plywood gussets to one end of them. At the other end of the hangers, sandwich triangular gussets (cut from ¼″ plywood scrap) between the 2x4 hanger and the 1″x3″x21″ bicycle supports, using nails. Lock the supports to the hangers with two carriage bolts. With just one bolt, the support will tend to rotate anytime only one bicycle is on the rack. The supports have a 1″-diameter notch placed 3″ from each end. A suggestion for drilling these half holes is to clamp a piece of scrap lumber to the edge of the 1x3 piece and drill through it, using the hole in the scrap as a guide to hold the bit in place.

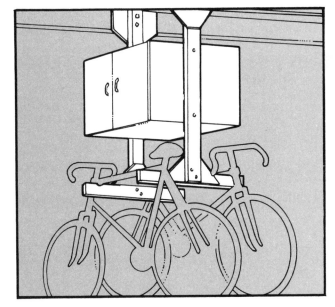

Now bolt the compartment between the hangers, using two carriage bolts on each side. Lift the rack up against the joists and pin it in place by nailing the gussets to the rafters. Then drill holes through the hangers, gussets, and joists for carriage bolts, allowing for two bolts in each hanger.

Drill a hole through the bottom of the hangers so that a locking chain can be put around the bicycle frame. You might also consider drilling the notches half an inch larger and lining them with scraps of carpeting to protect the finish on your bikes.

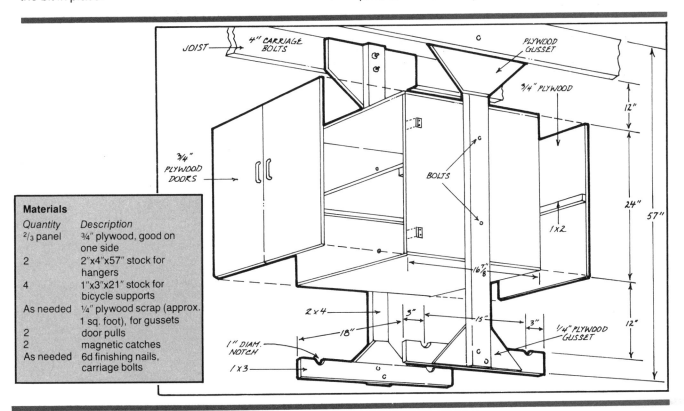

Materials	
Quantity	Description
⅔ panel	¾″ plywood, good on one side
2	2″x4″x57″ stock for hangers
4	1″x3″x21″ stock for bicycle supports
As needed	¼″ plywood scrap (approx. 1 sq. foot), for gussets
2	door pulls
2	magnetic catches
As needed	6d finishing nails, carriage bolts

Patio Cart

To make patio dining more flexible, here is a cart that not only rolls, but its tray lifts off to make serving easier. The cart is designed to hold everything from extra charcoal to plates, cups, and food. You can even put hooks on the sides to hang cooking utensils.

Mark and cut out the pieces (as shown in exploded view) on a ¾″ plywood panel. All curved ends in pieces J, K, and the two F parts are made with a 3″ diameter. Drill all holes in the four L pieces as well as pieces K and J. The positioning of the three 4½″ holes in side J is shown in Fig. B.

Assemble the cart by glue-nailing both ends A to the outside of bottom part I. Center wall B stands between ends A. Attach shelf C on the right side of B, 12″ below the top edges of the cart. Partition D is inserted against B and C, 7″ from front end A. The two H pieces are glue-nailed to the front of the 11½″x12″ cabinet, as shown in exploded view. Glue-nail side K flush with the top edges of the two As and part D, and locate the two L pieces in the top outside corners formed by K and ends A. Part F is glue-nailed flush with the bottom of the cart with the 12″ leg at the back of the cart.

The left side of the cart is assembled by attaching leg-wheel support F against the bottom edges of twin parts A and part I. Part G is glue-nailed to the edges of parts A 9″ from the bottom of the cart. Shelf C is attached between ends A 18″ from the bottom of the cart. Side J is glue-nailed to the outside of C and the two A ends. Partitions E are positioned between the holes in J as shown in side detail. The two L tray supports are nailed inside the corners mady by J and the two As.

Insert the 1½″x22″ dowel handle in the 1½″ holes in sides K and J and glue-nail in place. Drill a hole for the axle in the center of the wheel supports 6″ from the top edge of part F. Assemble the axle and wheels.

Cut out the 28″-diameter tray and place it on top of the cart. Mark the holes in the L pieces on the bottom of the tray. Now drill ¾″ holes ⅛″ deep in the bottom of the tray and glue the four ¾″x1″ wood dowel legs in the holes. Next, glue a 2″x7′8″ strip of wood tape around the edge of the tray allowing the excess width of the tape to extend above the top of the tray. When the tape is dry, wrap a second strip of tape around the first, staggering the butt joints of the two layers. Apply a third layer of tape. The dowels in the tray will fit into the holes in parts L, or will act as legs for the tray when it is being used as a server, so do not permanently attach the tray to the top of the cart.

Materials	
Quantity	*Description*
1	¾″x4′x8′ plywood panel, exterior or interior, good both sides
22″	1½″ wood dowel for handle
2	10″ spoked wheels with axle and caps
23′	2″ wood tape, for tray rim
As needed	8d finishing wheels, wood putty, white glue, paint or varnish

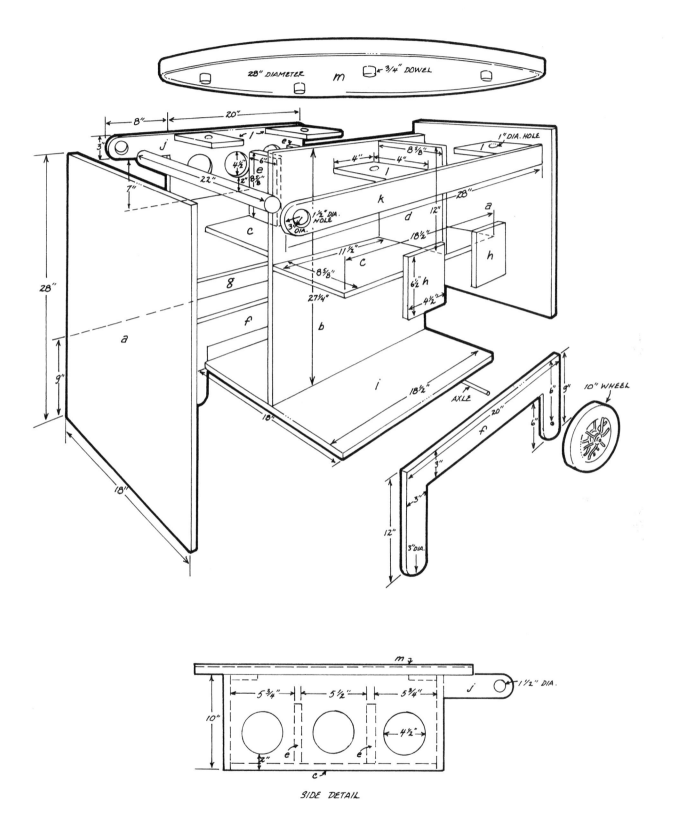

SIDE DETAIL

Buffet Table

Designed for convenience, this buffet table is a serving bar, a dining table, and a storage center all in one. It consists of three units—a drop-leaf table and two rolling carts—that nest together to take up only 2'x6'x30¼' of space.

Start by framing the table and leaf tops, using 2"x2" stock. Cut four pieces 72" long and miter them 45° at each end. Now cut and miter two 24" and two 12" pieces. Nail the two frames together so that the tabletop is 24"x72" and the leaf is 12"x72" (see Fig. A). Nail strips of 1"x1" around the inside of the frames, attaching them ¹⁄₁₆" from the bottom edges of the 2"x2" stock. Rip the 1"x4" stock to a 3" width and install the cross braces as shown in Figs. A, B, and C. The end braces are 51" between their outer edges, and the middle brace is placed on center between them. Use the remainder of the trimmed 1"x4" stock to make the 16"x48" leg support frame and center it on the cross braces. Cut the 21"x69" tabletop and the 9"x69" leaf top from ⅝" plywood and glue-screw them into the tops of the frames. Glue the laminate to the plywood tops. Laminate is also nailed to the underside of the leaf.

The two legs and their attending leaf supports are all made in the same way. Assemble two 17½"x28"x⅝" leg frames from 1"x2" stock. The two leaf frames are 12½"x28"x⅝". Nail 1"x1" stock on center around the inside of the frames. Cut the four 16"x27"x⅛" legs from ⅜" plywood. The leaf supports are ⅜"x11"x27". Glue-

nail the plywood pieces inside their frames (Fig. D). Note that the leaf supports are ⅛" shorter than the legs. Line the bottoms of the legs and the leaf supports together and attach each set with a piano hinge. Now bolt the legs to the leg support frame (Fig. C). The leaf is attached to the tabletop with four 3" butts.

The shelf and drawer carts are identical in size and

Materials	
Quantity	**Description**
1¼	⅜" interior plywood panels
2	⅝" interior plywood panels
32'	2"x2" stock for tabletop framing
77'	1"x1" stock for tabletop frames, cleats, leg and leaf framing
30'	1"x2" stock for leg and leaf support framing
8'	1"x3" stock for interior framing
7'	1"x4" stock ripped to 3" wide for interior framing
5'	2"x4" ripped to 2½" width for interior framing
1 piece	21"x69" laminate for tabletop
2 pieces	9"x69" laminate for leaf top and bottom
2	28" piano hinges for leaf supports
4	3" butts for leaf top
6 prs.	22" drawer slides, for drawer cart
8	2" casters for shelf and drawer carts
6	2½" carriage bolts to attach legs
As needed	4d and 8d finishing nails, flathead wood screws, glue

are assembled in the same way. The shelf cart is made by cutting a tall side (23¾"x28") and a short side (23¾"x25½") from ⅝" plywood. The back measures 16¾"x25½" and the three shelves are 16¾"x23"x⅛". Assemble the shelf cart as shown in Fig. E, using 1"x1" stock for the shelf cleats. Attach the four casters and add a 1⅜"x16¾" plywood strip across the back of the top shelf. The drawer cart is identical to the shelf cart

except that the drawer slides are positioned as shown in Fig. F.

The three drawers are identical, too. The sides are 2⁵/₁₆"x23⅜"; the backs are 2⁵/₁₆"x14⅝"; the faces are 3½"x16⅝" all cut from ⅝" plywood. Use ⅜" plywood for the 2⁵/₁₆"x14⅝" drawer inner faces and the bottoms, which are 16½"x22⅜". When all drawer pieces are cut, assemble the drawers as shown in Fig. G.

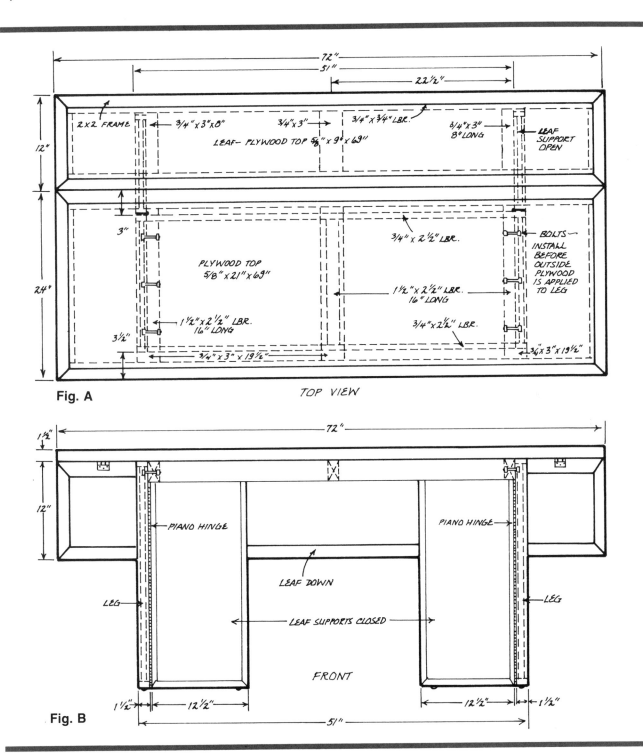

Fig. A TOP VIEW

Fig. B FRONT

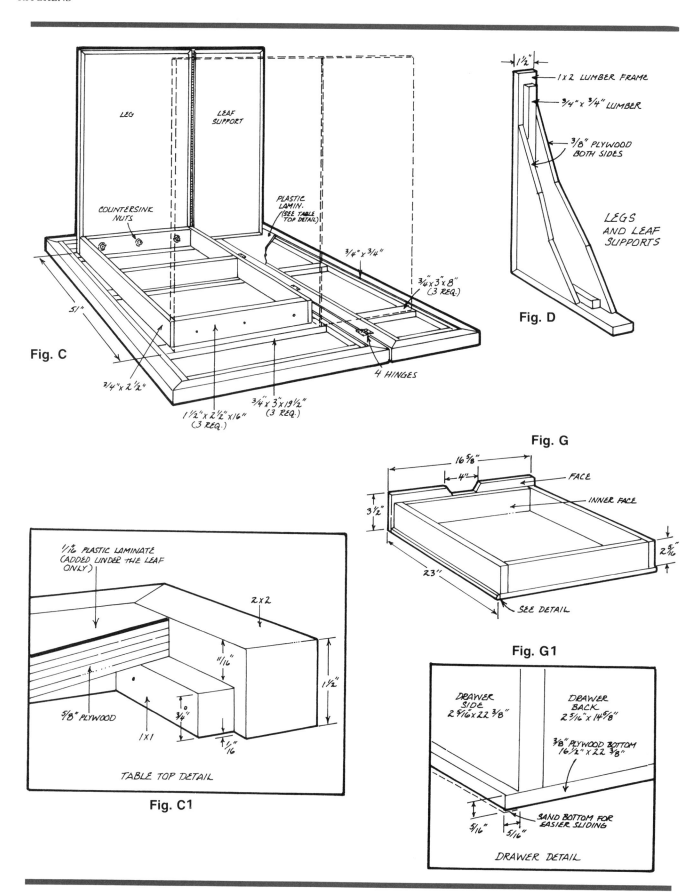

LEG

LEAF SUPPORT

COUNTERSINK NUTS

PLASTIC LAMIN. (SEE TABLE TOP DETAIL)

3/4" x 3/4"

3/4" x 3" x 8" (3 REQ.)

51"

3/4" x 2 1/2"

4 HINGES

1 1/2" x 2 1/2" x 16" (3 REQ.)

3/4" x 3" x 19 1/2" (3 REQ.)

Fig. C

1 1/2"

1 x 2 LUMBER FRAME

3/4" x 3/4" LUMBER

3/8" PLYWOOD BOTH SIDES

LEGS AND LEAF SUPPORTS

Fig. D

16 5/8"

4"

FACE

INNER FACE

3 1/2"

23"

SEE DETAIL

2 5/16"

Fig. G

1/16 PLASTIC LAMINATE (ADDED UNDER THE LEAF ONLY)

2 x 2

11/16"

1 1/2"

5/8" PLYWOOD

1 X 1

3/4"

1/16"

TABLE TOP DETAIL

Fig. C1

DRAWER SIDE 2 5/16 x 22 3/8"

DRAWER BACK 2 5/16" x 14 5/8"

3/8" PLYWOOD BOTTOM 16 1/2" x 22 3/8"

5/16"

5/16"

SAND BOTTOM FOR EASIER SLIDING

DRAWER DETAIL

Fig. G1

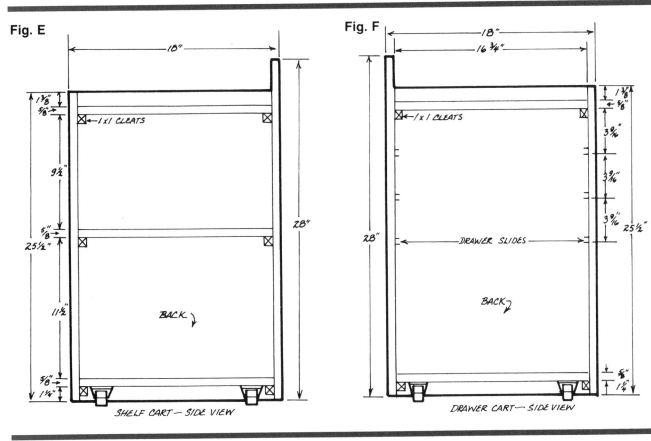

Fig. E SHELF CART — SIDE VIEW

Fig. F DRAWER CART — SIDE VIEW

Basic Brick Barbecue

There are many different kinds of barbecue units, but if there is a classic unit this brick design is probably it. Simple, straightforward, solid, it will give years of service if built properly.

How you build it depends to some degree on your patio situation. If you have a concrete slab, this barbecue can go directly on it without further ado. You can also build on earth, but the earth must be well drained; compact it thoroughly before you start building.

If the earth is not well drained, then a slab is called for. It should be constructed like any other concrete slab—to last. Make it 4″ to 6″ thick, suitably reinforced with rods and sloped for water runoff, and mount the slab on an excavation that is 6″ to 8″ deep filled with gravel.

Follow the sketch to build the barbecue, also referring to basic brick techniques spelled out earlier in the book. Note that the first course is crucial to the squareness of the entire structure, and this should be laid out dry first, as noted in the drawing. Note, too, that the sixth course of bricks protrude slightly to form a ledge for a charcoal pan.

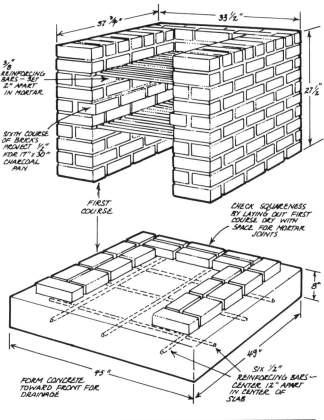

263

Grill Garage

This grill garage is a time-saver and space-organizer all in one. It can hold everything you need to do all your outdoor cooking, and it gives you a place to prepare and serve any meal, be it for two or two hundred.

The unit can be free-standing or built against a fence or wall. Choose a well-drained area and be sure that the 6'x3' base is level. The base is made from patio bricks, concrete, or the garage can stand on a wooden deck. When the base is completed, frame the three walls, using 2x4 stock (see Fig. A). The middle and right wall frames are identical, while the left wall has one less cross brace. When the vertical frames are finished stand them on the base and nail the top and back cross beams in place. Note that the front studs are ¾" higher than the back wall to provide a ¼" slope per foot in the roof for drainage. Four of the rafters are 3'1" long. The center rafter is 3'5" long and extends beyond the back wall to support the roof drain.

Consult Figs. B and C for shelf dimensions and assembly. 2"x2"x2'9¾" supports are nailed along the bottom edges of the 2x4 braces marked "B" in Fig. A. The supports have two 2x2 cross supports positioned between the front 2x4 studs, and the center of the frame (see Fig. C). The sliding shelf is ¾" plywood cut 2'9¾" square and covered either with Formica or the sheeting used for the grill garage roof. Nail 1"x1"x2'9¾" runners

under two opposite edges of the plywood board. A 1"x2"x2'8¼" shelf stop is nailed between the back edge of the runners so that it extends ¾" below the 1x1 stock. Complete the shelf by nailing a 1"x2"x2'9¾" strip of western cedar across the front edge of the shelf and attaching a pull. Put the shelf on its 2x2 supports and nail pieces of 1x1 stock to the 2x4 braces ⅛" above the shelf top. The shelf can now be pulled out until the stop strikes the center brace.

Cut a 3'x3' square of ¾" plywood and notch the corners to fit around the front and back studs. Nail the shelf to the top of the cross braces (marked C in Fig. A) below the sliding shelf. The top shelf is 1'x6' and cut from ¾" plywood. The back corners and center are notched to fit around the studs, and the shelf is nailed to the top braces (marked A in Fig. A). Two 1"x4"x2' boards are also notched and nailed to the "A" braces so that they extend from the top shelf to the front edge of the studs, as shown in Fig. B.

Nail a 1x2 piece along the underside of the front roof support (marked D in Fig. A) to act as a door stop. The 2x2 cross support under the sliding shelf will stop the cabinet door under the shelf, so neither of these should be covered by cedar siding. Notch the ½"x4'6"x2'10" plywood wall to go around the top shelf and nail it to the center studs as shown in Fig. B.

Cut the metal or plastic sheeting used for the roof to a

Fig. A

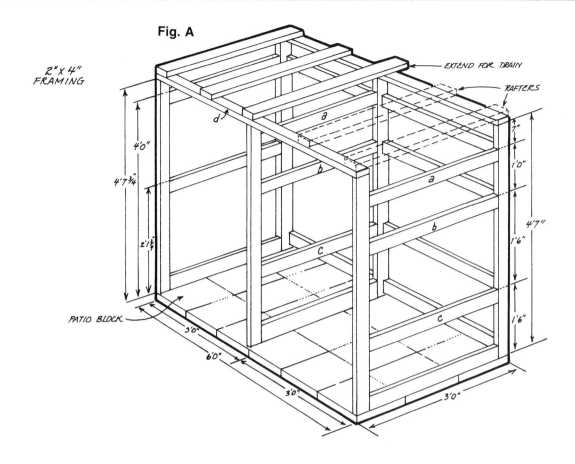

2"x 4" FRAMING

EXTEND FOR DRAIN

RAFTERS

7"

1'0"

4'7"

1'6"

1'6"

a

b

c

d

a

b

c

4'0"

4'7¾"

2'1½"

PATIO BLOCK

3'0"

6'0"

3'0"

3'0"

Fig. B

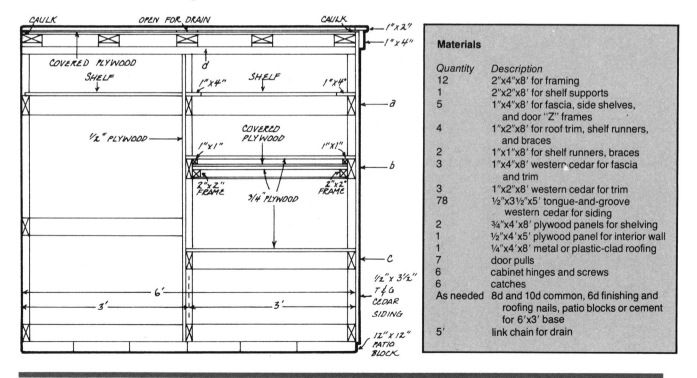

CAULK

OPEN FOR DRAIN

CAULK

1"x 2"

1"x 4"

COVERED PLYWOOD SHELF

d

1"x 4"

SHELF

1"x 4"

a

½" PLYWOOD

COVERED PLYWOOD

1"x 1"

1"x 1"

b

2"x 2" FRAME

¾" PLYWOOD

2"x 2" FRAME

c

½" x 3½" T&G CEDAR SIDING

6'

3'

3'

12" x 12" PATIO BLOCK

Materials

Quantity	Description
12	2"x4"x8' for framing
1	2"x2"x8' for shelf supports
5	1"x4"x8' for fascia, side shelves, and door "Z" frames
4	1"x2"x8' for roof trim, shelf runners, and braces
2	1"x1"x8' for shelf runners, braces
3	1"x4"x8' western cedar for fascia and trim
3	1"x2"x8' western cedar for trim
78	½"x3½"x5' tongue-and-groove western cedar for siding
2	¾"x4'x8' plywood panels for shelving
1	½"x4'x5' plywood panel for interior wall
1	¼"x4'x8' metal or plastic-clad roofing
7	door pulls
6	cabinet hinges and screws
6	catches
As needed	8d and 10d common, 6d finishing and roofing nails, patio blocks or cement for 6'x3' base
5'	link chain for drain

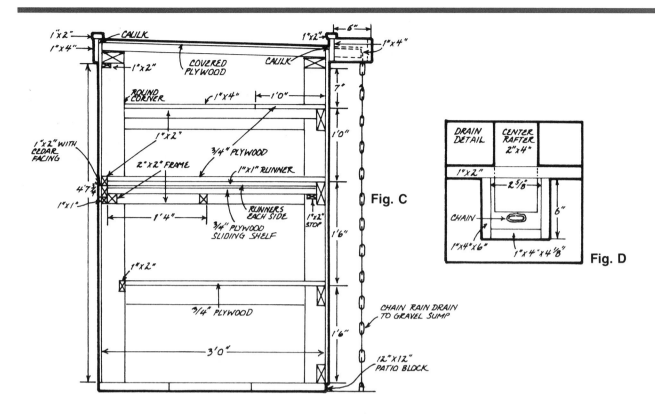

Fig. C

Fig. D

width of 3'5" wide by 6'1" long. Attach the roof to the rafters with neoprene washer nails and caulk the edges of the sheeting. Now nail the cedar T&G siding to the sides and back of the garage. Corners may be either mitered or overlapped. Strips of siding 1⅝" wide are nailed to the exposed edges of the studs in the front wall. When the siding is in place, add the 1"x4" fascia with its 1"x2" top to the roof (see Figs. B and C). The 1x2 piece

along the rear wall is nailed around the extending center rafter to form a drain box 6"x⅝" (see Fig. D). Attach the 5' length of chain to the rafter and stake it in the ground, as shown in Fig. C.

Cut and assemble the doors from T&G cedar. Blind-nail the braces as shown in Fig. E, using 1x4 stock to make the "Z" frames. Hang the six cabinet doors, adding their pulls and catches.

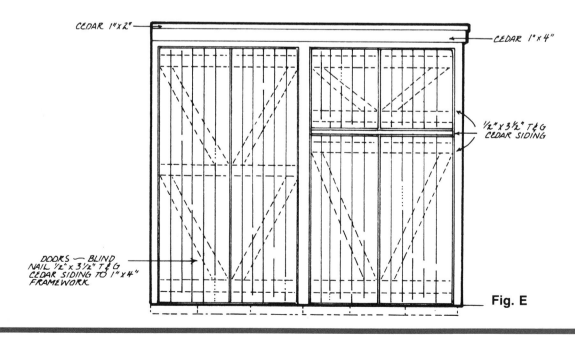

Fig. E

Brick-on-Sand Patio

Many people feel that a patio area should be articulated in some way—set off from the rest of the back yard. This can be done with well-placed storage units, or furniture placement, or various kinds of screens. A durable and pretty way also to do it is shown here, with brick. The patio itself—i.e., the flooring—is brick on sand, but around it is a solid wall of concrete incorporating a useful barbecue center. While the wall is low—only six courses high—it does effectively define the area as a patio—a place to rest, take in the sun, enjoy each other's company.

Dimensions on this project can be varied to suit your particular patio situation. The one shown is approximately 18′ long x 11′ wide.

As with any brick-on-sand patio floor, an edging is required. In this case the edging is the wall that goes around the patio; wherever there are walkways—or perhaps you'll just want one walkway—the perimeter bricks should be mortared in place or otherwise anchored to prevent interior bricks from moving.

Wall

The wall is built like any brick wall. After the foundation is in, carefully set your string guidelines. Start laying the bricks at the corners. Finish one corner, then lay up the next adjacent one, using a straightedge with a level to keep the bricks true. Then lay the intermediate bricks. Make frequent use of the level.

Note that in this installation the bricks are laid in standard fashion for five courses but that the top course is laid at right angles to the others (Fig. A).

When mortar on the wall has cured properly, you can proceed to lay the floor. Prepare it with a sand base, then simply lay the brick in the pattern shown in Fig. B. Finish by filling cracks and joints between bricks as previously described.

Barbecue

It's a good idea to start building the barbecue more or less from the middle out; that is, the barbecue door. You can build one side of the barbecue, set the door in place, then build around it. This is far easier than trying to build the barbecue and leave a perfect opening for the door. A detail of this is shown.

The barbecue itself is of simple, straightforward design. As the sketches indicate, it is one course thickness. The gate (a cast-iron type is good) can be supported by bricks as shown and should be set loosely on the brick supports. The grill may be supported in a variety of ways. One possibility is shown.

Note, also, the slanting floor of the barbecue. This is to make clean-out easier.

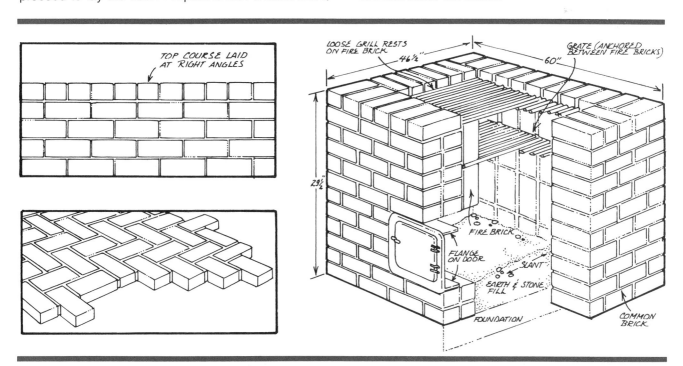

Simple Flower Boxes

There are three different designs here. You can make one of them or all three. Use ¾″ exterior-grade plywood. They will serve you well, and the basic instructions can apply to a box of your own design and size.

Choose the design(s) you want to make and mark out the pieces on a panel of ¾″ textured plywood. See Figs. A-F for dimensions of the sides, bottom, and ends of the boxes. The ends and sides are mitered at the corners and are glue-nailed to each other, as well as around the bottom. Be certain that all joints are tight and flush, to prevent any leaks when the boxes are in use.

Cut the 2″x4″ and 2″x2″ bottom framing pieces and glue-nail them under the sides and ends of the boxes. If you are building design 1 or 3, the frames must be beveled to fit the angle of the sides and ends. Reinforce the box corners with angle irons. Drill three holes in the bottom of the box so that water can drain into the base. Miter the 1″x2″ top frames and nail them into place as shown in Fig. I.

Cut and drill the sides and ends for the base box and assemble them around the base with waterproof glue and nails. Nail the base in place under the box. Both the base and the flower box are coated with a suitable repellent to protect the wood from water. Round all corners before finishing the project.

Materials

Quantity   *Description*
Use a textured ¾″ plywood exterior grade

PLANT BOX # 1		PLANT BOX # 2		PLANT BOX # 3	
2	12″x46″ for sides	2	12″x40″ for sides	2	12″x46″ for sides
2	12″x22″ for ends	2	12″x16¾″ for ends	2	12″x22″ for ends
1	16″x39¼″ for bottom	1	15¼″x38½″ for bottom	1	16″x39½″ for bottom
2	4½″x32″ for sides of base	2	4½″x32″ for sides of base	2	4½″x32″ for sides of base
2	4½″x10½″ for ends of base	2	4½″x10½″ for ends of base	2	4½″x10½″ for ends of base
12′	1″x2″ for top framing	10′	1″x20″ for top framing	8′	1″x2″ for top framing
2′	2″x4″ for bottom framing	2′	2″x4″ for bottom framing	5′	2″x2″ for bottom framing
7′	2″x2″ for bottom framing	7′	2″x2″ for bottom framing	2′	2″x4″ for bottom framing
4	1″x3″ angle braces with screws	4	1″x3″ angle braces with screws	4	1″x3″ angle braces with screws
1	10½″x30½″ for bottom of base	1	10½″x30½″ for bottom of base	1	10½″x30½″ for bottom of base

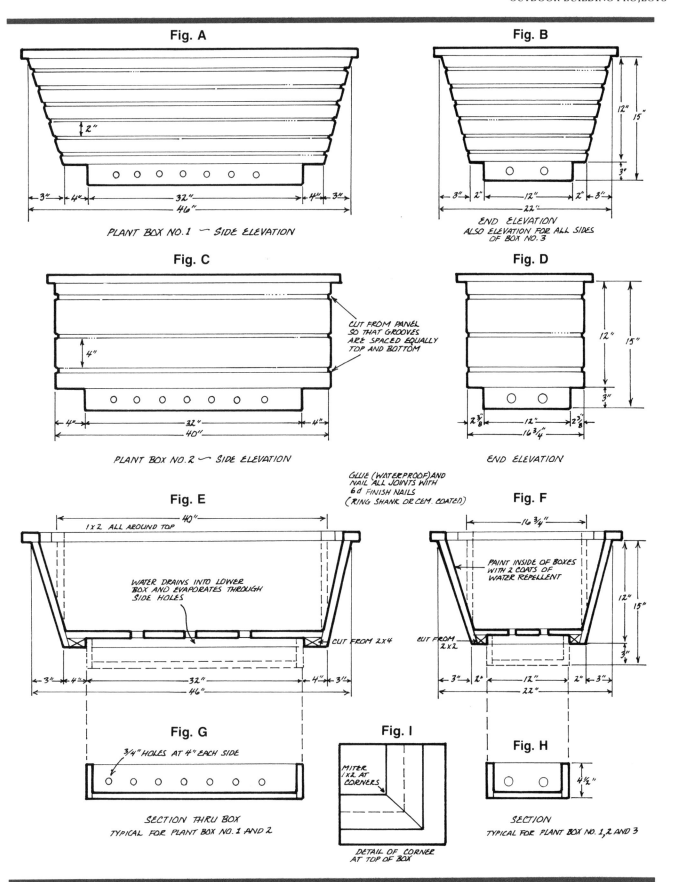

Fig. A

PLANT BOX NO. 1 ~ SIDE ELEVATION

2"

3" 4" 32" 4" 3"
46"

Fig. B

12" 15"

3"

END ELEVATION
ALSO ELEVATION FOR ALL SIDES
OF BOX NO. 3

3" 2" 12" 2" 3"
22"

Fig. C

PLANT BOX NO. 2 ~ SIDE ELEVATION

CUT FROM PANEL
SO THAT GROOVES
ARE SPACED EQUALLY
TOP AND BOTTOM

4"

4" 32" 4"
40"

Fig. D

12" 15"

3"

END ELEVATION

2 3/8" 12" 2 3/8"
16 3/4"

GLUE (WATERPROOF) AND
NAIL ALL JOINTS WITH
6d FINISH NAILS
(RING SHANK OR CEM. COATED)

Fig. E

40"
1 x 2 ALL AROUND TOP

WATER DRAINS INTO LOWER
BOX AND EVAPORATES THROUGH
SIDE HOLES

CUT FROM 2x4

3" 4" 32" 4" 3"
46"

Fig. F

16 3/4"

PAINT INSIDE OF BOXES
WITH 2 COATS OF
WATER REPELLENT

CUT FROM
2x2

12" 15"

3"

3" 2" 12" 2" 3"
22"

Fig. G

3/4" HOLES AT 4" EACH SIDE

SECTION THRU BOX
TYPICAL FOR PLANT BOX NO. 1 AND 2

Fig. I

MITER
1x2 AT
CORNERS

DETAIL OF CORNER
AT TOP OF BOX

Fig. H

4 1/2"

SECTION
TYPICAL FOR PLANT BOX NO. 1, 2 AND 3

Fiberglass Greenhouse

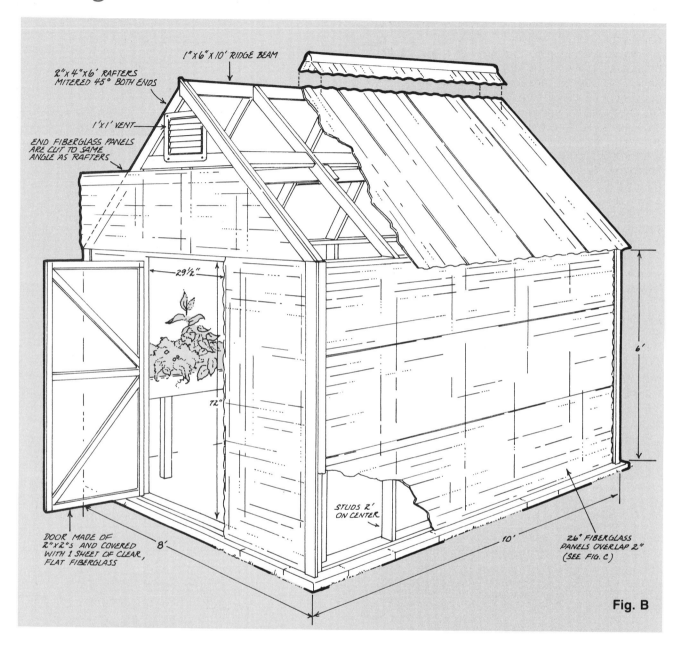

Fig. B

Virtually indestructible, this fiberglass greenhouse, made with clear, fluted panels rather than glass, offers years of service with little or no upkeep.

When selecting a place to build the greenhouse, bear in mind that you may want it to be accessible to water, gas, and electricity, depending on your needs. If you plan to use it all year around, you should also consider putting in heaters and vent fans. Also check your local building department for any pertinent information about building codes and permits in your area before you start work.

Once you have selected a location for your greenhouse, lay out the twenty-nine patio blocks in an 8′

x 10′ rectangle, (see Fig. A) making sure they are level. For a more permanent installation, use concrete footings. Next, cut and assemble the 2x4 lumber into two 10′ x 6′ frames for the side walls. The back and front wall frames are 8′ wide and 6′ high. All studs should be nailed on 24″ centers. When assembling the walls on the patio block base, be sure they are plumbed and squared before nailing them together (see Fig. B). The doorway in the front wall is framed out to accept a 29½″x72″ door.

Next, precut all twelve 2x4 rafters to the desired pitch (approx. 45°), and brace them against the 1″x6″ ridge board. The rafters are nailed into place, 24″ on center

270

and stabilized by collar beams at their midpoint (3').

The clear, 26"-wide corrugated fiberglass panels can be cut with any circular saw using an abrasive disc blade. All nail holes must be predrilled. Use aluminum nails with neoprene washers to prevent leakage. The panels should be nailed lengthwise to the walls. Start at the bottom of each wall and work up to the roof. Each panel overlaps the panel beneath it with mastic applied at every overlap to insure a watertight seal (as per Fig. C). The two aluminum vents are installed in the front and back walls, as close to the peak of the roof as possible before the panels go on. The top front and back panels are trimmed to fit the pitch of the roof. When nailing fiberglass to the roof, begin at one end of the greenhouse. After each section is paneled on both sides, fasten the aluminum ridge roll flashing over the fiberglass, using plenty of mastic to make a waterproof seal.

The door is made by assembling a rectangle from the 2"x2" stock measuring 29½"x72". The frame has a divider in the center and diagonal braces bisecting both halves of the frame. Cover the frame with a panel of flat, clear fiberglass. Hang the door and finish the greenhouse by nailing trim lumber around all corners and to the front and back walls where the panels meet the roof. Complete the project by painting the trim.

Materials

Quantity	Description
29	4" x 8" x 16" patio blocks (one to be cut in half)
23	2" x 4" x 6' lumber for studs
13	2" x 4" x 10' lumber for framing side walls and rafters
4	2" x 4" x 8' lumber for framing front and back walls
1	1" x 6" x 10' lumber for ridge board
2	2" x 2" x 8' lumber for door
2	2" x 2" x 6' lumber for door
12	1" x 3" x 8' lumber for trim
2	12" x 12" aluminum vents
5	26" x 12' corrugated clear fiberglass panels (cut in half for roof)
6	26" x 10' corrugated clear fiberglass panels for sides
9	26" x 8' corrugated clear fiberglass panels for front and back
1	29½" x 72" flat clear fiberglass panels for door
1	hardware kit for door
5	2' aluminum ridge rolls
6	boxes of aluminum nails w/washers
	10d common nails
	Tube of mastic

Fig. A

LAYOUT OF 29 PATIO BLOCKS

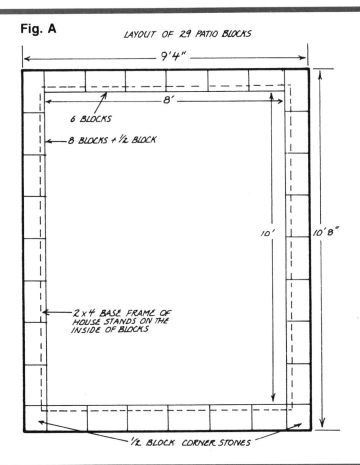

9'4"

8'

6 BLOCKS

8 BLOCKS + ½ BLOCK

10'

10'8"

2 x 4 BASE FRAME OF HOUSE STANDS ON THE INSIDE OF BLOCKS

½ BLOCK CORNER STONES

Fig. C

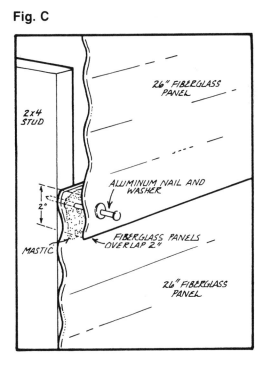

26" FIBERGLASS PANEL

2x4 STUD

ALUMINUM NAIL AND WASHER

2"

FIBERGLASS PANELS OVERLAP 2"

MASTIC

26" FIBERGLASS PANEL

Compost Tank

Compost is a necessary enriching ingredient in most gardens, but a pile of it in a corner of the yard does not make a very pretty sight. This circular tank, painted a bright color, will not distract from the yard's appearance and it is designed so that fresh cuttings, compost maker, and leaves can be shoveled in at the top and shoveled out—as compost—at the bottom.

The basic material for the job is a 4'x8' sheet of exterior plywood ¼" thick—or thin. Cut four pieces from the panel, each 24"x48". Cut four 2x2 legs, each 32" long and sawed at a 45° angle at the tops. Referring to Fig. A, overlap the four plywood pieces 3" each, laying each leg in the position shown, and join the sections with four equally spaced 1¼" No. 4 galvanized screws and glue. It's best to predrill pilot holes for the screws.

Stand the assembly up and bend it into a circle (Fig. B). Apply glue to free ends and overlap them 3" as before and drive screws home.

Treat the legs and inside surfaces with a preservative; paint the exterior with a couple of coats of primer and finish paint.

Set the structure in final position and dig out five or six inches of soil under each leg. Sink the legs into the soil, packing it in tightly around them. If you wish, a concrete floor could be poured with 1¼" galvanized pipe substituted for the wood legs. If this is done, paint legs with a metal primer and finish paint before bolting them to the assembly.

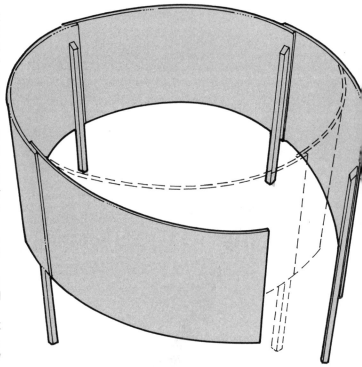

Fig. B

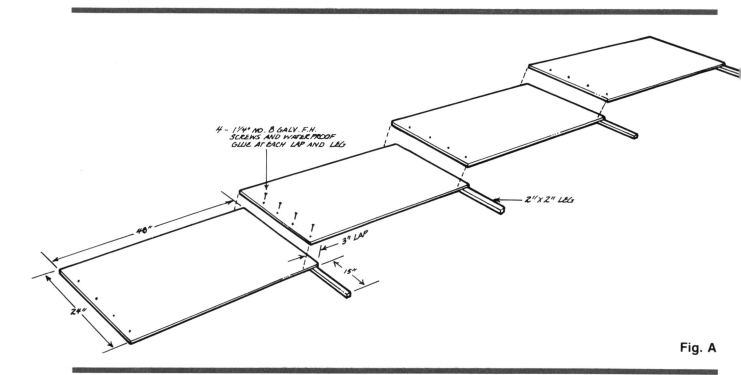

4 - 1¼" NO. 8 GALV. F.H. SCREWS AND WATER PROOF GLUE AT EACH LAP AND LEG

2" X 2" LEG

48"

3" LAP

15"

24"

Fig. A

Sturdy Back-yard Swing

This heavy timber swing might just as well be made of steel—it's that strong. Unlike steel, however, the wood members won't rust.

You can make the swing with any kind of good-grade 4"x4" stock you wish. Redwood and cedar are good choices, though expensive. You might want to opt for one of the cheaper kinds (fir, pine, spruce, etc.) that is pressure-treated with preservative.

The structure basically consists of two A frames with vertical center posts running up through the peaks with the frames joined by a cross member across the post tops.

Build one A-frame first. Lay out with chalk an 8' equilateral triangle (all sides 8') on a flat surface. Also make a mark that bisects the triangle from the peak down, and another that runs horizontally 2' from the base line. The A can be laid out using this triangle as a guide.

Cut an 8'-long center post. Lay this post down the center of the triangle so its bottom end butts against the 2' line.

Cut two legs, each 8' long. Bottom ends should be cut square, but the tops at 30° angles. Lay the legs down so their outside edges are flush with the legs of the triangle and their beveled ends rest against the center post. Tack ends to the post.

Lay an 8' length of 4"x4" across the legs so that its top edge is aligned with the horizontal chalk mark; in other words, if laid in position the center post would butt against its top edge. Mark where this horizontal crosses the legs. Cut excess off, thereby creating 60° angles at each end. Tack horizontal to legs.

Next, proceed to join the members permanently. Use plated, rustproof ⅜"x8" lag screws and washers, first drilling a ⅜" hole in one member, then a ¼" pilot hole in the other—the one the screw goes into.

When the A-frame assembly is completed, build another just like it—use the first as a template for cutting pieces for the second.

Using the A-frames as guides, measure and cut the remaining components—the 10' cross member that joins the As and their diagonal supports. Drill holes for lag screws as before—⅜" and then ¼" holes.

Carry all the parts to the site. Stand up the A-frames (a helper is needed unless you want to brace them) and attach the cross member and supports, running lag screws into the prepared holes.

Large screw eyes are used to hang the swing; these also should be rustproof. Drill through the angled portion of each support and run lag screws into the cross member. Tie the ropes onto the screw eyes. Knot the ropes' ends to notched seat boards, or fasten a screw eye to each end of the seat and tie cord ends to these.

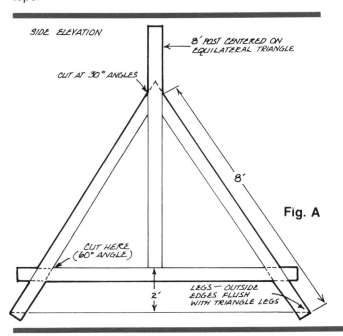

SIDE ELEVATION

8' POST CENTERED ON EQUILATERAL TRIANGLE

CUT AT 30° ANGLES

8'

Fig. A

CUT HERE (60° ANGLE)

2'

LEGS — OUTSIDE EDGES FLUSH WITH TRIANGLE LEGS

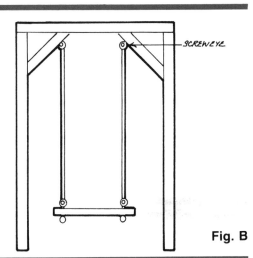

SCREW EYE

Fig. B

Super Sandbox

This sandbox has a number of excellent features. There is a canopy that can be raised or lowered or angled toward the sun to provide shade; the same canopy forms a cover at night to keep small animals from contaminating the sand. There are two storage chests—one at each end of the unit. They have hardware cloth bottoms: Excess sand sifts through instead of piling up.

Build the sandbox proper first. Assemble base framing: a single 2x4 set on edge and notched to accept perimeter 2x2s, nailed in place. Build the box itself—plywood bottom and four plywood sides—separately, nailing the pieces together at overlapping corners. Set the box on the base so that its edges are flush with the framing edges. Nail through the box bottom into the base. (See Fig. A.)

Now put in the framing members that flank the box on the storage chest sides. Nail the pieces—the 2x4 and 2x2 legs and the 2x2 strips that sit on top of the legs—directly to the box sides, piece by piece. Note that these framing assemblies extend a bit (1½") beyond the box edges. This creates a recess on each side which the remaining two framing assemblies fit into. (Fig. B.)

When framing is complete on the storage chest sides, add 2x2 framing assemblies to the other sides, again nailing directly to the box (and through to the other framing). Note here that the completed assemblies create a slot on each side which accepts posts on which the canopy can be moved up and down.

Build the storage chests separately. Each consists of a 2x2 base with two sides (no end pieces yet) nailed to it and a divider/stiffener in the middle. It's a good idea to nail the hardware cloth to the base (s) before you secure

the sides and stiffener. Attach precut lids with bent strap hinges. (Fig. A.)

Nail on the structure-length 6'-long sides. These cover the framing and form ends for the storage boxes.

Construct the canopy. Cut angled ends out following sketch (Fig. C); note hand holes and centered holes for carriage bolts. Assemble canopy ends to two 1x2s (each 3'5½") to form an open rectangle. Stretch a piece of canvas cut to fit across the 1x2's and between the ends; the edges of the canvas should be flush with the bottom edges of the 1x2's. Nail other 1x2's (each 3'5½") to overlapping canvas edges to secure it.

Support posts for the canopy should each be cut about 5½'. If you can't get 2x3 stock you can make up the posts from ¾" plywood.

Drill $^7/_{16}$" holes along the length of each post, spacing the holes about 4" apart. Holes needn't be drilled more than about one-third of the way down, starting from the top.

Slip bolts with wing nuts through the holes in canopy and posts to hang the canopy. To move the canopy up or down, or angle it, you remove the bolts, locate the canopy at the holes at the level you wish, slip bolts in, and tighten wing nuts. If you wish to angle the canopy, tip it to the pitch you wish and tighten wing nuts—that'll be enough to hold it in position.

Finish the structure with a good-quality paint as detailed in the wood chapter. Since this box will be the province of tots, make sure that the paint is safe—lead-free—for their use. They may decide to make a meal of the structure and though unsafe paints have been largely outlawed, one shouldn't take a chance.

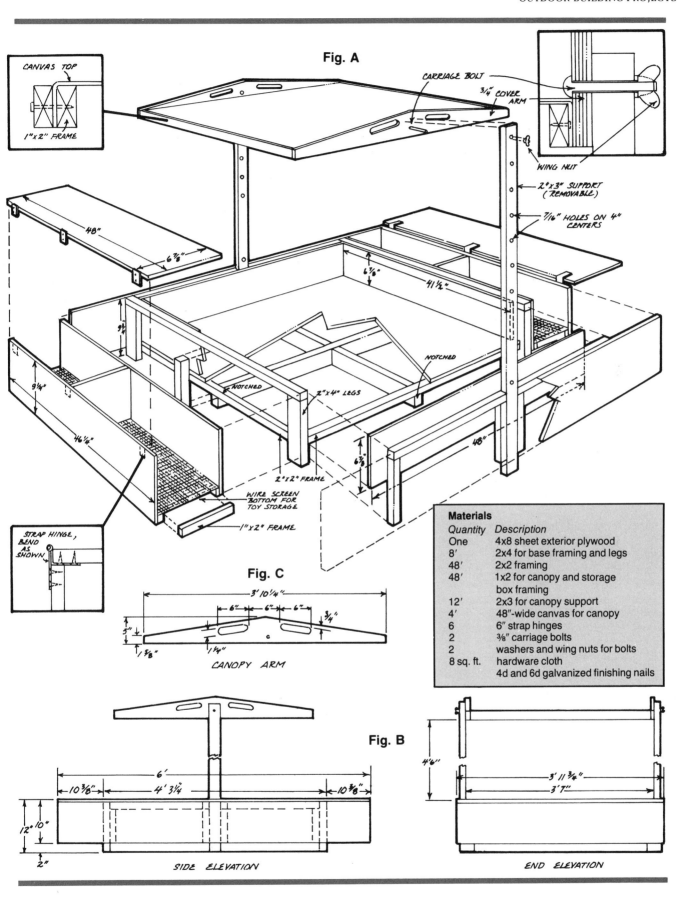

Fig. A

CANVAS TOP

1"x 2" FRAME

CARRIAGE BOLT

3/4" COVER ARM

WING NUT

2"x 3" SUPPORT (REMOVABLE)

7/16" HOLES ON 4" CENTERS

48"

6 7/8"

6 1/8"

41 1/2"

NOTCHED

9 1/4"

NOTCHED

2"x 4" LEGS

9 1/4"

6 7/8"

48"

46 1/4"

2"x 2" FRAME

WIRE SCREEN BOTTOM FOR TOY STORAGE

1"x 2" FRAME

STRAP HINGE, BEND AS SHOWN

Fig. C

3' 10 1/4"

6"   6"   6"

5"

3/4"

1 3/8"

1 1/4"

CANOPY ARM

Materials

Quantity	Description
One	4x8 sheet exterior plywood
8'	2x4 for base framing and legs
48'	2x2 framing
48'	1x2 for canopy and storage box framing
12'	2x3 for canopy support
4'	48"-wide canvas for canopy
6	6" strap hinges
2	3/8" carriage bolts
2	washers and wing nuts for bolts
8 sq. ft.	hardware cloth
	4d and 6d galvanized finishing nails

Fig. B

6'

10 3/8"   4' 3 1/4"   10 3/8"

12' 10"

2"

SIDE ELEVATION

4' 6"

3' 11 3/4"

3' 7"

END ELEVATION

Shingled Playhouse

The kids can help shingle their own homelike playhouse. And if you are really courageous, you could let them paint it themselves, too. The design produces a sturdy, "climb-overable" structure that will still be around to give the grandchildren some fun of their own.

Mark out and cut the plywood pieces according to the layouts shown in Fig. A, using five panels of exterior-grade ⅝" plywood. Now assemble the floor support frame and legs (shown in Fig. B). The legs are nailed into the ends of the 2x4 supports and braced on each side with gussets #16. Make certain that the center support beam lines up under the ⅝"x2' slot cut out of the floor (#1). Nail the floor to the support frame, setting it back ⅝" from the two long sides of the frame. Nail the front (#3) and back (#2) walls between the two sides (#4). Note that in cutting the two #4 sides, the top 4'-long edge is mitered 45° to accept the roof. Sides #2 and #3 stand outside the edges of the floor, on the ⅝" extensions of the floor support frame. The two sides (#4) are placed on the floor itself with the mitered edge even with the angle of the front and back walls.

Insert interior wall #5 in the floor slot and install wall #7 and floor #8. The 1'5⅜" sides of wall #7 must be mitered 45° so that the panel fits snugly between back wall #2 and interior wall #5. Nail the two roof panels

(#6) in place. The 4' sides of each panel are mitered 45° in parallel.

Now assemble the two window towers from parts #9, #10, and #11. Parts #10 must be mitered 45° along both 2'9¾" sides to conform with the angle made by sides #11. Nail the towers to the top of the house, as shown in Fig. B. Assemble the stairway as shown in Fig. B by nailing the two #13 parts, #14 and #15 between the two sides, #12, and nail the entire structure to the front of the archway of the house. The finished house may be either shingled or simply painted inside and out.

Materials	
Quantity	**Description**
5	⅝" plywood panels, exterior. Use two good sides if the project is to be painted. Use one good side if the exterior is to be shingled.
4	2"x2"11⅜" stock for legs
3	2"x4"x5'8¾" stock for floor frame sides and center brace
2	2"x4"x3'10" stock for floor frame ends
2 lbs.	6d finishing nails
As needed	Shingles, paint

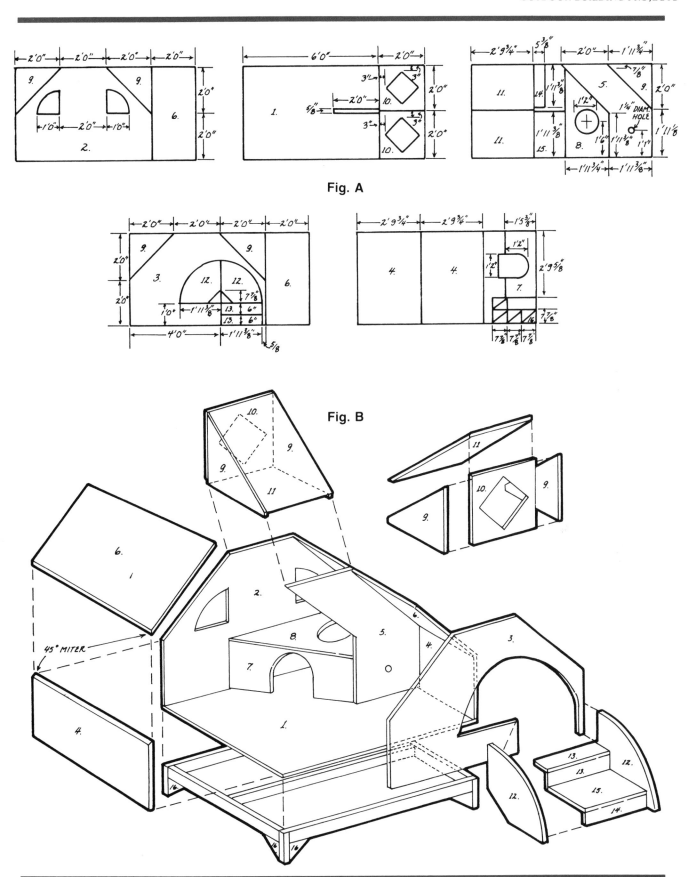

Fig. A

Fig. B

45° MITER

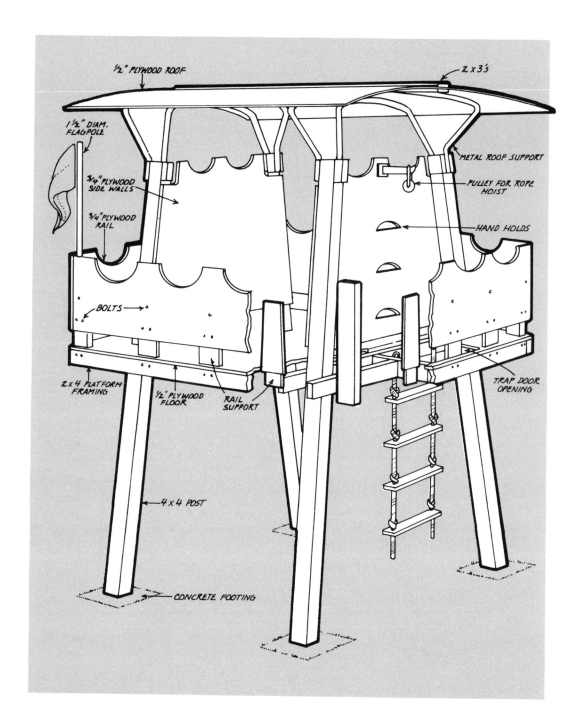

½" PLYWOOD ROOF

2 x 3's

1½" DIAM. FLAGPOLE

METAL ROOF SUPPORT

¾" PLYWOOD SIDE WALLS

PULLEY FOR ROPE HOIST

¾" PLYWOOD RAIL

HAND HOLDS

BOLTS

2 x 4 PLATFORM FRAMING

½" PLYWOOD FLOOR

RAIL SUPPORT

TRAP DOOR OPENING

4 x 4 POST

CONCRETE FOOTING

Tower Fort

The scalloped edges on this fort give it a slight medieval flavor. While there isn't a moat, it does have a rope ladder that can be pulled up and give some measure of protection against invasion.

The structure basically consists of an 8'-square platform mounted on pairs of 4'x4'x10' posts. You can do the basic layout work on the ground, but make sure it's flat.

First, lay out a line that is absolutely straight—at a 90-degree angle. Follow the same procedure to get each pair of posts symmetrical: Lay the posts roughly parallel to this line, then position them so the top ends are each 2'3" from the line. Measure down the line 3'8" and position posts so they are each 3" from the line at that 3'8" point. Tack the posts together in position with temporary strips—one across the top ends, another a few feet from the bottom ends.

Follow the cutting diagram and cut out a side wall; you'll note it has handholds—cut them now. Lay the wall in proper position on the posts, then fasten it on securely with #8 1½" flathead wood screws. Remove the temporary strips.

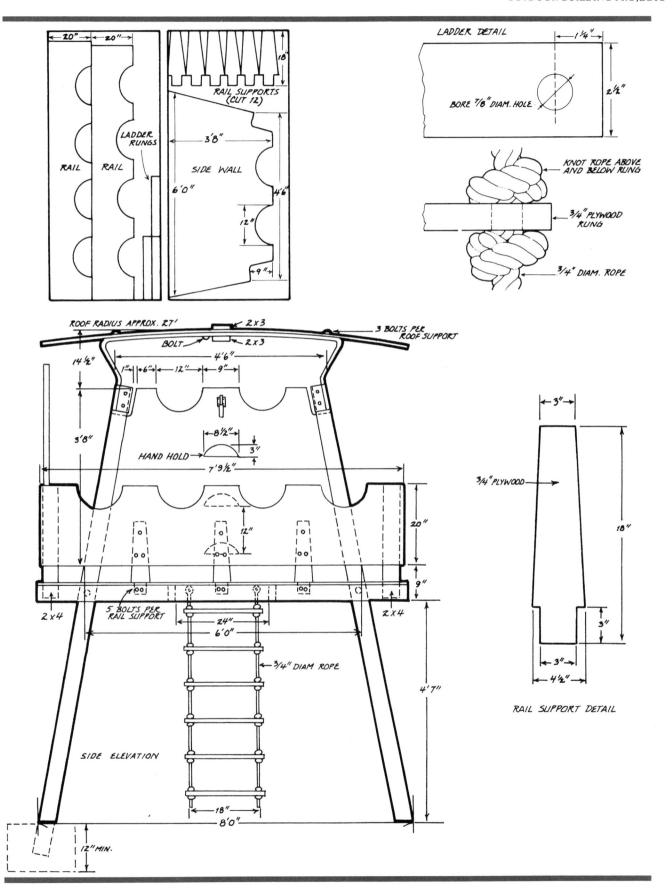

20" 20"

RAIL RAIL

LADDER RUNGS

RAIL SUPPORTS (CUT 12)

18"

3'8"

SIDE WALL

6'0"

4'6"

12"

9"

LADDER DETAIL

1¼"

BORE ⅞" DIAM. HOLE

2½"

KNOT ROPE ABOVE AND BELOW RUNG

¾" PLYWOOD RUNG

¾" DIAM. ROPE

ROOF RADIUS APPROX. 27'   2x3

3 BOLTS PER ROOF SUPPORT

BOLT   2x3

14½"   1" 6" 12" 9"   4'6"

3'8"

HAND HOLD   8½"   3"

7'9½"

12"

20"

9"

5 BOLTS PER RAIL SUPPORT   24"

6'0"

¾" DIAM ROPE

4'7"

2x4   2x4

SIDE ELEVATION

18"   8'0"

12" MIN.

3"

¾" PLYWOOD

18"

3"

3"   3"

4½"

RAIL SUPPORT DETAIL

279

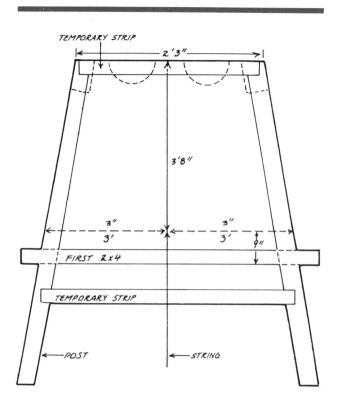

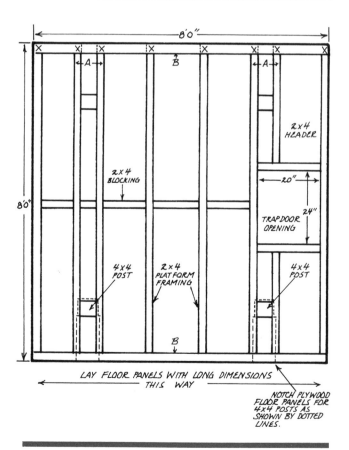

Next, mark the posts (use same procedure for both pairs) for the first floor framing member (A). Measure down 9″ from the bottom of the side wall and draw lines across the posts. The first member—a 7′3″ 2x4—should be laid with its bottom edge even with these lines. When it is, tack it on temporarily.

Turn the assembly over and tack on another 2x4 the same size as the first and parallel with it, then bolt the 2x4s to the posts with 8″ carriage bolts.

The ends of the posts should be embedded in concrete. Mark off the hole locations and then excavate—the holes should be at least a foot deep. Set the two post assemblies in the holes; hold them in position with scrap lumber bracing.

Cut two 8′-long 2x4s (B). Nail these to the ends of the 2x4s bolted on the posts. To make this and subsequent floor framing easier, first mark the posts off as indicated in the framing detail sketch. The X's represent where the end of the main flooring members should fall. Cutting and marking the members on the ground beats doing while you're on a ladder.

When 8′ boards are nailed home, fill in the rest of the floor framing. As you work, make sure the pieces are level to one another. To do this, raise (prop up) or lower (dig soil out from underneath) the post ends.

Flooring panels come next. Two 4′x8′ sheets of ½″ plywood are used. In order to install them they must be notched to fit around the posts. Do this carefully, saving the cutouts. When the panels are in, replace the cutouts, trimming then as needed. Complete floor installation by cutting out the material over the trap door opening. One final step: Check for level.

Pour the concrete. Let cure and proceed to put in the rest of the components. Cut twelve rail supports. Measure off five equal parts on each side of the platform. Using auger, keyhole saw and square rasp, make slots for the supports at your middle three marks on each side (the corners get treated differently). Slip the supports into the slots and bolt them to the framing. Cut the rails and bolt these to the supports.

The corners require 2x4s. Follow this procedure to install each. Cut a 2x4 long enough to span from the bottom edge of the framing to top of rail. Cut a notch in the flooring, slip the 2x4 through and bolt it to framing and rail.

Supports for the roof are made with steel rod, bent over and welded to special metal brackets on the post ends. If you are familiar with metalworking, the sketch details will enable you to make the supports and brackets needed. If not, bring this plan down to a welder and have him make up the components for you.

To make the roof, butt two 4′x8′ panels lengthwise. Screw an 8′-long 2x3 to cover the joint on each side. The roof is bolted in three places to the metal roof support rods. When you bolt the roof in place it should be located so that as you tighten up on the bolts the panels bend crosswise rather than lengthwise—they'll bend easier this way.

Now add those details that will give extra delight to the

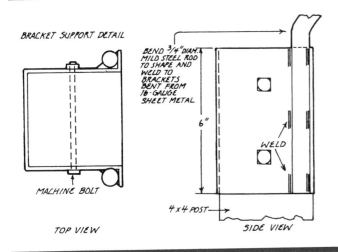

BRACKET SUPPORT DETAIL

MACHINE BOLT

TOP VIEW

BEND ¾" DIAM. MILD STEEL ROD TO SHAPE AND WELD TO BRACKETS BENT FROM 16-GAUGE SHEET METAL

6"

WELD

4 x 4 POST

SIDE VIEW

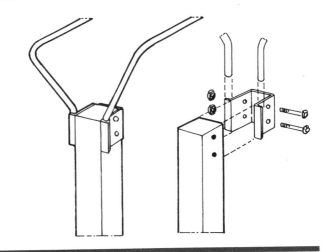

kids. Cut ladder rungs from ¾" plywood, each 2½" wide and about 20" long. Drill ⅞"-diameter holes near the ends for the ropes, then thread ropes through, knotting as shown. Hang the ladder from the trapdoor framing with two large screw eyes. You can also mount a pully that hangs down through the trapdoor (it's perfect for fort supplies). A 3" length of 1½" dowel mounted in a corner makes a good flag post.

Paint the structure inside and out with a good-quality exterior paint—two prime coats and a finish coat.

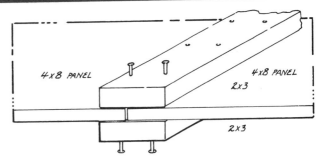

4x8 PANEL   4x8 PANEL
                   2x3
                   2x3

ROOF BATTEN

Materials

Quantity	Description
2	sheets ¾" exterior plywood for side walls and rails
2	sheets ½" exterior plywood for roof and floor
17'	of 2x3 lumber for roof battens
40'	of 4x4 lumber for posts
88'	of 2x4 for platform framing
1	piece 1½" dowel 3' long for flag post
	4½"x8" carriage bolts for framing
	¼"x3" carriage bolts for rail supports
	¼"x2" carriage bolts for rail and roof brackets
	⅜"x4½" machine bolts for roof-to-rod fastening
	⅜"x2" eye bolts for rope ladder
	¾" manila rope for ladder
	6d galvanized box nails, #8 wood screws

4'   4'

8'   8'

2x3

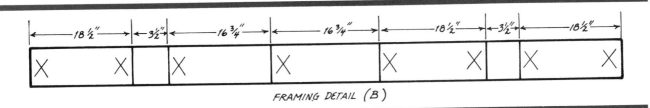

18½"   3½"   16¾"   16¾"   18½"   3½"   18½"

FRAMING DETAIL (B)

Final assembly of the teepee—fastening of the final two sides together—is done with hinges instead of staples. Lay a strip of canvas (5" wide, 8' long) along the edge of one of the remaining pieces so that half the width of the strip is on the wood. Screw the strip in place equally spacing five hinges along its length. Lift the assembly up (you'll need a helper) and maneuver the sides so the structure is in a teepee shape, then secure the flap of canvas to the remaining side by screwing through the free hinge leafs.

Bright paints work well in finishing the teepee. You might paint the sides different colors, or you might decide on designs. If you use designs, it's best to outline each design with masking tape before you paint, stripping the tape off after each section is dry. This will insure clean lines between various colors. Before you do any finish painting you should prime the outside and seal all edges.

Materials

Quantity	Description
3	sheets exterior grade ½" plywood
3	yards of light canvas
4	boxes No. 5 staples
9	pairs of 1½" galvanized cabinet hinges
2½	quarts exterior primer and high-quality exterior house paint

Plywood Teepee

This structure should be a hit with small Indians of all tribes. It should be a winner with the chief who constructs it, too—it's quite easy to make. It consists of six triangular-shaped pieces of plywood held together at the edges by strips of stapled-on canvas. It stands eight feet high and its radius will allow it to accommodate quite a few young warriors.

Materials for the job include three 4'x8' sheets of exterior-grade plywood, 3 yards of light canvas, four boxes of No. 5 cloth staples or the equivalent amount of upholsterers' tacks, and nine 1½" galvanized hinges.

Start by cutting out the triangular-shaped sides. Each panel yields two sides. First, divide the panel by drawing a line between diagonally opposite corners. Measure eight feet down the line from each of these corners and make marks; join these marks with other lines going to the respective adjacent corners. Cut the pieces out.

Arrange the pieces on the ground in a semicircle, like pieces of pie. Pick any two of the sides near the middle of the semicircle and cut the doors out of them; each door should be about 3' high and 2' wide at the base. Attach the doors to the sides you cut them from with hinges—two for each door. The hinges should go on from the outside.

Next, join the sides. You'll be able to do all except those pieces on the outside of the semicircle. The method is the same. Butt sides together, lay a strip of canvas 8' long and 5" wide along the joint, then staple or tack the canvas on. The strip above the doors is only 5' long.

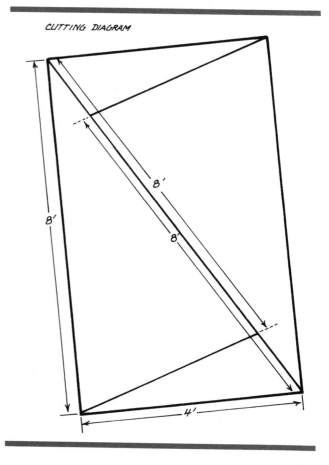

CUTTING DIAGRAM

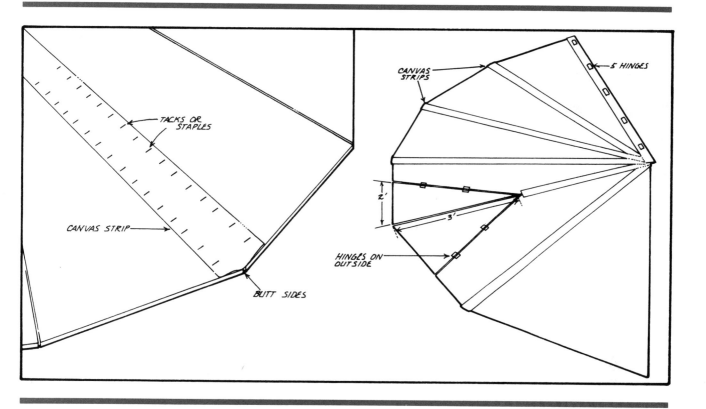

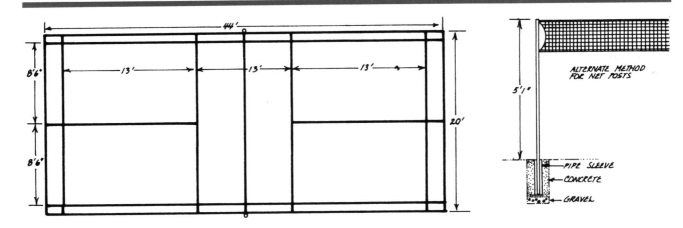

Badminton

Contrary to popular belief, the name of badminton does not refer to a minton who was bad but, rather, to the place where the game became popular—Badminton, Gloucestershire, England.

The court may be set up on a temporary or permanent basis. In either case, it's a good idea to pick an area which has hardy grass—or where you can plant some. A meadow fescue or rough-stock meadowgrass works quite well.

To set the court up on a temporary basis, simply drive the net posts into the ground at the appropriate points and hold them that way with guy wires tied to stakes in the ground.

For a permanent installation, you can install sockets for the posts in the ground. Using a post-hole digger, excavate the holes necessary to a depth of 16″. Pour a couple of inches of gravel into the holes, then slip in pieces of galvanized pipe that are slightly larger than the ends of the posts; the pipe should be at least 14″ in the ground. Then backfill around the sockets with earth or pour concrete.

If you wish, you can also mark the boundary lines of the court by installing driven-in pieces of wood or concrete markers set 2″ below grade as described in the croquet instructions.

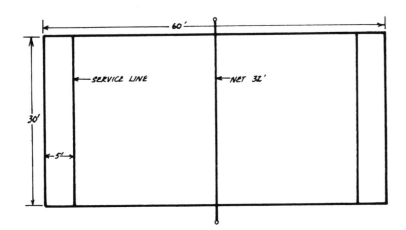

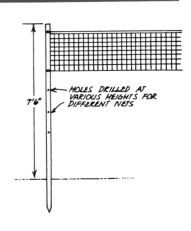

Volleyball

This is another game that can be played on grass so long as it is level and free of hazardous bumps and depressions.

You can follow the same method for setting up the court as for badminton—pipe sockets in the ground,

markers etc. However, if you don't mind stretching the rules and the court a bit, you could use the badminton court for volleyball. Use the same posts for both games, simply drilling holes at various heights to accommodate both the volleyball and the badminton nets.

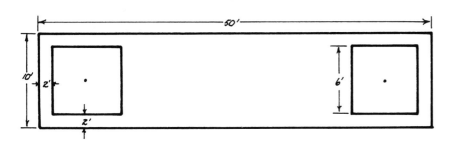

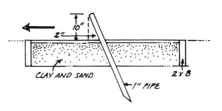

As a game, horseshoes goes back a long way—probably as long as horses have been shod. Indeed, there are records of Roman soldiers introducing the game to Britain when Rome conquered that country way back around 100 A.D. At any rate, it's still quite a popular game.

If you want to play on an official horseshoe court—and it really takes away from the fun if you don't—you should have space in your back yard for a court that's 10' wide by 50' long. A couple of feet in from each end of this area there should be a pit that is 6' square.

Start construction by excavating the 6'-square areas to a depth of 7" or so. Frame each area with an assembly (four boards) of 2x8's, hammering the pieces together with 10d nails. Also screw ¼" strap iron to the top edges of the 2x8s—this will protect it from splintering if an errant horseshoe collides with it. The framework edge should protrude from the ground an inch or so.

Level the area within the square pits, and fill them to frame-edge level with potter's clay or clay and sand.

Next drive a stake into each area. The stakes should be 1" in diameter and 36" long—use either hardwood dowel or galvanized pipe, driving the stake into the exact center of the pit so that it rises 10" above the framework and slants about 2" forward.

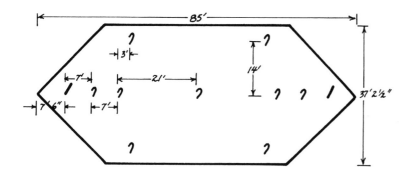

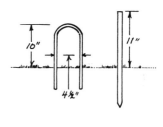

Croquet

If golf and tennis can be called the IN games of today, then croquet was the game in mid-Victorian times. It is not too difficult to imagine the men of the time, with their waxed handlebar moustaches, and the ladies, in their white dresses and bustles, playing the game under a bright sky—at a time when you could see the sky.

Today, there seems to be a resurgence of interest in croquet. To make the field needed for it is super simple.

Following the sketch, mark the field off—you'll note that you need a quite a large area. There is a variety of ways to mark. You can simply draw boundaries with a stout cotton cord, or use lime or flour. Or, if you will play croquet fairly frequently, make the markers permanent by driving wood stakes into the ground at all six corners of the field, or setting lengths of galvanized pipe flush with the ground, or small sections of concrete.

The wickets—the curved pieces the balls are driven through—can simply be driven into the earth at the points noted in the layout. Or, if croquet is about as popular around the house as eating, the wickets and two stakes required can be set permanently: Simply embed wire wickets (galvanized) and galvanized pipe in concrete whose surface is 2" below ground level, then fill around wickets and stakes with sod.

It should be noted that a permanent installation such as above can be hazardous at some future date if you move away. And mowing around galvanized wickets and stakes will take a bit of extra time.

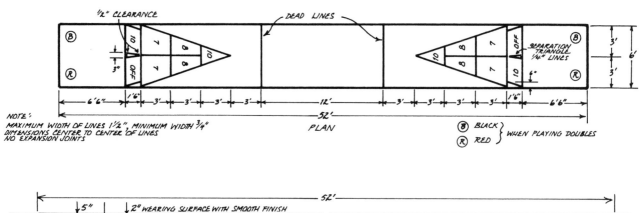

Shuffleboard

If you have an unused part of your yard that measures 6'x52', why not install a shuffleboard? Shuffleboard, once known as Shove-Groat, Slide-Groat and Shove-Penny, was first introduced in England in the 15th century. Since then, the game has enjoyed world-wide popularity, particularly on board ships. It not only requires a surprising amount of playing skill, but is considered an excellent form of exercise. Moreover, building a concrete shuffleboard is not much different from laying a good cement sidewalk, except that a little more attention must be paid to securing a smooth and level surface.

Construct a 12" high wooden frame that has an inside measurement of 6'x52'. The ground inside the frame is tamped and rolled to a uniform depth and made as level as possible. If the soil is well drained, the cement can be placed directly on it; if not, lay a sub-base of well-compacted coarse gravel or cinders 6" deep, and make it as level as possible.

The concrete is put down in two layers: the base layer is 3" thick and composed of one part cement, two and a quarter parts clean, coarse sand, and three parts crushed stone or gravel, mixed with no more than 6 gallons of water per bag of cement. The cement is leveled, and then a reinforcement of wire mesh weighing between 60 and 100 pounds per square foot is laid down.

The playing layer is put on within 45 minutes after the base layer is struck off. This layer is 2" thick and consists of one part cement, one part clean sand, and one and three quarters parts fine, crushed gravel. Troweling is begun as soon as the concrete is hard enough, in order to prevent excess material from working to the surface. The concrete should be carefully hand troweled until the smoothest possible finish is achieved. This project is not meant for one totally unskilled at cement work. You might want to hire a mason just for these finishing touches.

The finished surface is kept continuously wet for seven days, so that the cement will cure properly. Apply water directly on the concrete as soon as it is hard enough not to be marred. Or, an excellent way of keeping the surface wet is to cover the concrete with 2" of sand, or a layer of burlap, and keep the covering constantly wet by sprinkling it during the one week curing period. Remember that the more attention paid to the curing process, the more durable the concrete will be.

When the concrete is completely cured, allow the court to dry for another four or five days. Then paint the lines shown in Fig. A on the concrete, using a high-quality paint. If a waxed finish is desired, treat the cement with paraffin wax dissolved in turpentine, followed by a coating of powdered wax rubbed in. You can also achieve a smooth surface by scrubbing the concrete with a strong soap solution. Polishing the surface is best done with powdered boric acid.

Materials

126' lumber for framing.
As needed: Stakes to hold frame in place.
As needed: Cement, gravel, sand, cinders.
1 qt: A high quality oil or varnish based paint.
312 sq. ft. wire mesh (60-100 lb. per sq. ft.) for reinforcement.

Back-yard Basketball Court

Ideally, basketball should be played on an asphalt or concrete surface. If you want to do this—and have the room—you can simply follow directions given earlier in this book for making a concrete patio slab and make a court following dimensions in figure A.

Another court possibility—and one that is widely used—is a driveway. Usually this is so located that a minimum number of house windows are in danger of being broken.

The backboard and basket may be mounted in a variety of ways. Wherever it is mounted, there should be some room under it (at least 18″ from its face to the nearest obstruction), so a hard-driving player has just that—room to drive.

A particularly sturdy way to mount backboard and basket is to a pipe. Just sink a 3″ diameter galvanized pipe 14′ long) into a concrete base, making sure the

pipe is plumb, then mount backboard and basket to it. (Fig. A.) You can rig your own hardware for hanging the backboard and basket but sporting goods stores commonly sell kits, complete with all hardware, for the purpose.

Another place to mount the backboard and basket is to a tree. This setup is shown in Fig. B. Two holes are drilled through the tree and two pieces of plywood, each 2′ square, are attached to ¾″ threaded rod run through the holes and locked to the tree and plywood pieces; 12 nuts and washers per rod are required.

The backboard is then attached to the ends of the plywood pieces with 2″x2″ angle irons and the basket is attached so that its rim is the required 10′ above the ground. This method will not damage the tree in the slightest.

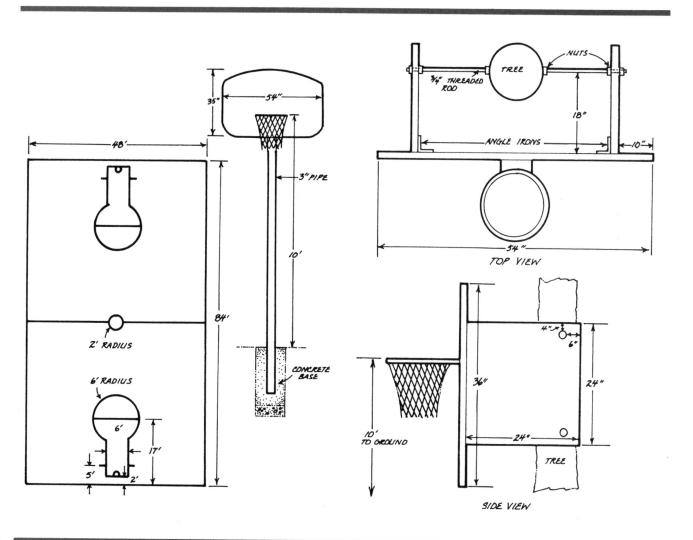

TOP VIEW

SIDE VIEW

Garden Gazebo

The dictionary defines "gazebo" as "a balcony with windows." This modern design of an ancient worldwide structure is an octagon with eight windows. It is made with redwood stock, which guarantees it will stand for years, but you are in for a lot of heavy sawing, so be sure your power saw blade is good and sharp.

Sixteen of the 4"x4"x8' posts are plowed their full length on center. The groove is ¾" deep and ¾" wide. While you have your dado blade(s) on, also plow 25' of 2"x2" stock, and the 32' of 2"x4" top plate on center to the same depth and width. Put four of the plowed 4"x4" posts aside. All of the remaining sixteen 4"x4" posts are now beveled at a 70° angle. In each case, the beveled side is opposite the routed edge, as shown in Fig. A. Nail the beveled edges together to form eight angled posts, as shown in Figs. A and B.

Mark out the octagonal gazebo on the patio where you plan to build it. The posts can be erected in holes, with angle irons, or on bases. Cut the four 1"x12"x2'8" and two 1"x12"x4'8" baseboards (see Fig. A) and insert them in their slots as the posts are lifted in place. When the posts and bases are assembled, cut the 2"x4" plowed top plates. There are four 3'x2' lengths, two 5'2" lengths and two 4' lengths, mitered 70° at each end. Nail the top plates between the posts.

The eight curved trusses are marked and cut from 1"x12" and 1"x6" stock as shown in Fig. D and glue-screwed together with half lap joints. When the trusses are assembled, they are raised in position (see Fig. E) and toenailed to the top plates. Three-eighths-inch lattice strips are nailed between the trusses (Fig. E) approximately 18" apart.

The ⅜" lattice strips are measured and cut to fit diagonally into the plows in the posts and are nailed to the sides and top plate. The windows are framed from 2"x2" stock which is plowed on center along the outside edges to receive the lattice strips. The curve in the window tops is a 12" radius. Cut and splice the 2"x2" stock to form the curve and sand the frame smooth before putting the frames in place (see Fig. E). When the lattice is finished, cut the fascia as shown in Fig. F, from ⅜"x8" stock. Cut the stock into four 3'2" pieces, two 4' pieces, and two lengths of 5'2", and nail them flush with the top of the top plates. The decorative ball on top of the gazebo can either be turned on a lathe or purchased already made from a cabinet shop.

Materials	
Quantity	Description
20	4"x4"x8' redwood stock for posts
4	1"x12"x2'8" stock for baseboards
2	1"x12"x4'8" stock for baseboards
4	4"x4"x3'2" grooved for top plates
2	4"x4"x4' grooved for top plates over doorways
2	4"x4"x5'2" grooved for top plates over windowed sides
25'	2"x2" stock for window frames
4	⅜"x8"x3'2" for fascia over sides
2	⅜"x8"x4' for fascia over doorways
2	⅜"x8"x5'2" for fascia over windowed sides
32'	1"x6" stock for trusses
32'	1"x12" stock for trusses
500' (approx.)	⅜" lattice stock

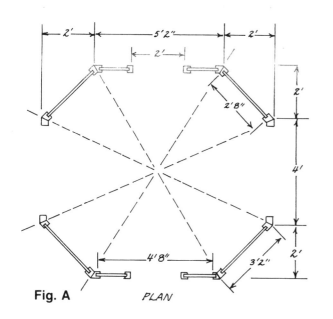

Fig. A PLAN

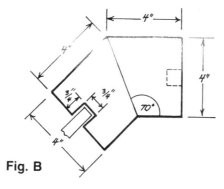

Fig. B

CORNER POSTS

TWO 4"x4" JOINED
REQUIRED PER GAZEBO: 8' LENGTH
FOUR DOUBLE PLOWED
FOUR PLOWED ONE SIDE ONLY

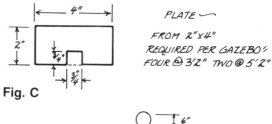

PLATE

FROM 2"x4"
REQUIRED PER GAZEBO:
FOUR @ 3'2" TWO @ 5'2"

Fig. C

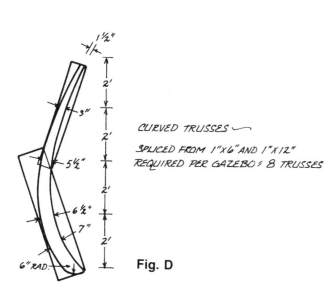

Fig. D

CURVED TRUSSES

SPLICED FROM 1"x6" AND 1"x12"
REQUIRED PER GAZEBO: 8 TRUSSES

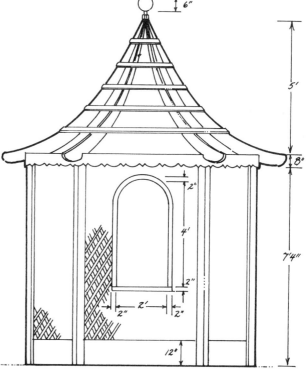

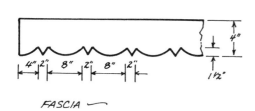

FASCIA

FROM 3/8" x 8"
REQUIRED PER GAZEBO:
FOUR @ 3'2" TWO @ 4' TWO @ 5'2"

Fig. F

Fig. E SIDE ELEVATION

Gabled Patio Cover

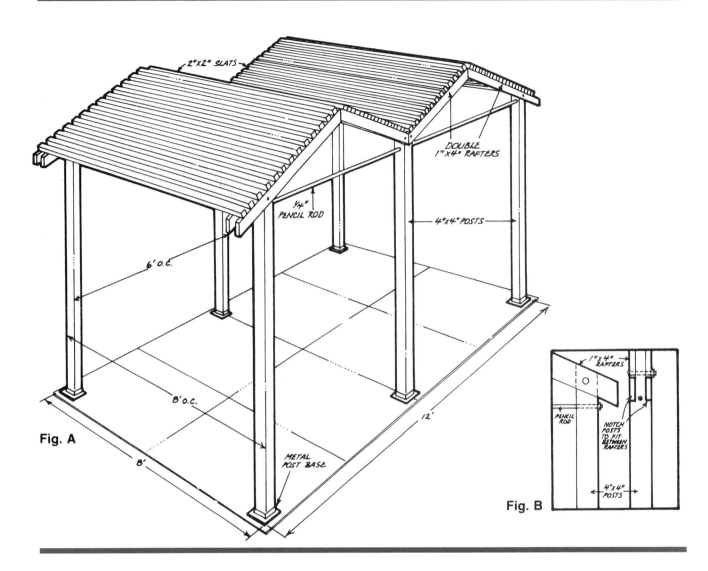

Fig. A

Fig. B

The roof may look like the back of a camel, but this timeless double-gabled patio cover design will add beauty, as well as comfort, to your patio living.

The gabled roofs are bolted to six redwood posts, or one end of them can be attached to the eave of your house. To build a "floating" cover, set six 4"x4" post bases 8' apart and space them every 6' as shown in Fig. A. Miter the tops of the four 4"x4"x8' corner posts 20° (see Fig. B) and cut notches on both sides of the miter. The notches are 3½" long and ¾" deep so that the 1"x4" rafters can fit flush against the sides of the posts. The two middle posts are notched with a V that conforms to the joint made by the two gables. Now bolt the posts to their bases and tie their tops together with the two ¼" pencil rods, as shown in Figs. A and B. Keep the posts plumb by tying them together with temporary support boards.

Cut the 1"x4"x4' redwood rafters, mitering them 20° in parallel at each end. Assemble the rafters in pairs, butting them at the peaks by nailing a piece of scrap wood between them at the joint. Now bolt the rafters to the posts, as shown in Fig. B. Nail the 2"x2"x8' roof slats across the rafters, leaving 1½" between each slat.

Materials	
Quantity	Description
6	4"x4"x8' redwood posts
6	4"x4" metal post bases
2	¼"x24'1" pencil rods to tie posts together
16	1"x4"x4' redwood rafters, mitered 20° at each end in parallel
52	2"x2"x8' redwood roof slats
8	¼"x4" bolts for attaching roof rafters

Redwood Screen Divider

If nothing else, this attractive screen divider is both massive and solid. The details given below are for building one section of it, but you can assemble as many sections as you need. Sections can be smaller than the 6'x6' dimensions suggested here, of course.

Posts for a 6'x6' section are 4"x6"x8' redwood stock set at least two feet in the ground and aligned 6' apart on center. When the posts are in place, attach the 4"x6"x6' bottom rail with 6" L straps as shown in Fig. A. Toenail the rails to the posts with 16d galvanized nails.

Now construct the two identical frames that form stops for the diagonal boards from 2"x4" stock. Cut the horizontals to fit tightly between the posts (approximately 5'7"). The 2"x4" verticals are 4'8" long. Lay one of the frames flat and position the 1"4" boards diagonally across it, leaving ¾" spaces between boards (see Fig. A). Nail the boards using two 8d galvanized nails at each board end, and trim the the boards flush with the outside of the frame. Nail the second frame to the boards, sandwiching them as shown in Fig. B.

Nail the frame on center between the posts, centering it on the bottom rail. Cut the top rail and nail it in place (see Fig. B), as well as attaching it to the posts with 6" L straps on both sides of each end.

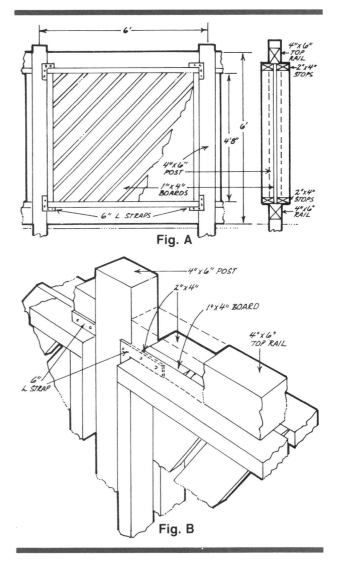

Fig. A

Fig. B

Materials

For one 6'x6' section

Quantity	Description
2	4"x6"x8' redwood posts
2	4"x6"x6' redwood horizontal rails
44'	2"x4" redwood stock for frames
96' (approx.)	1"x4" redwood boards for slats
8	6" L straps to attach top and bottom rails

291

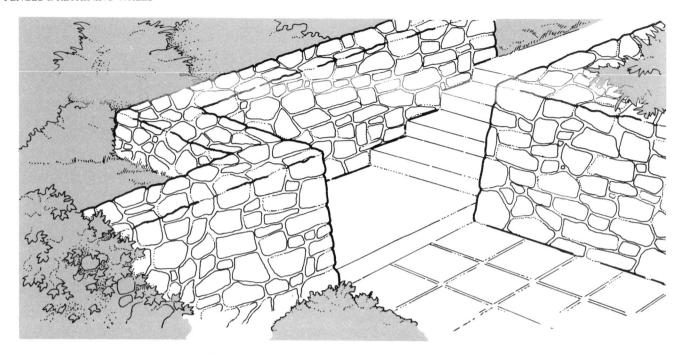

Retaining Walls

Retaining walls retain earth and have a wide variety of uses around the home, both decoratve and functional: as walls for plant beds, to hold hillside earth, to shore up walkways and so on. There are a variety of materials that can be used, including brick and decay-resistant wood (redwood, notably), but stone is a popular do-it-yourself item. In limited amounts it's easy to use and available in a wide variety of types and colors to complement outdoor decor: slate, sandstone, granite, limestone, and quartzite are all available in different textures and colors for the job.

There are two ways to lay up a stone retaining wall—dry (without mortar) and wet (with mortar).

A dry retaining wall is relatively easy to make. It depends upon the weight and friction of one stone on another for stability. Therefore, walls over 2' high require a "batter" or slanting of the stones 2" back for every 1' in height.

When starting a dry wall, lay the first stones about 6" below grade. (No footing is required for a dry wall since the stones are not bonded together and will not raise and lower with the frost.) The first stone layer, of course, should be larger stones. String a line along the wall as a guide to keep it straight.

Batter boards are wedge-shaped—flat on one side, sloping on the other. When driven into the ground at the edge of the wall, they afford a quick check on inward sloping. Be certain the batter boards are at right angles with the ground by checking with a level.

For best results, lay stones as flat as they would lie naturally on the ground. As you go, pack the back of the stones with earth, jamming large stones into the hillside. Try to break up joint lines. A continuous joint is not as attractive or as structurally sound as a broken one.

If the wall is to be less than 2' high you don't need a batter—not much earth is being retained. A stone coping can be placed on this type of wall—as well as a taller wall to finish off.

A wet retaining wall is very much like a dry one, except that mortar holds the wall up rather than the friction of stones together. For this type wall, a footing of stone or concrete, as indicated in Fig. C, is required, and there should be drainage weep holes—pieces of rustproof pipe run through the wall at intervals to allow water out (intervals depend on moisture in soil). The big advantage of a wet wall is its solidity—stones can't be jarred out of place and dirt won't flow through it.

After the footing is installed, the wall is erected like a dry wall. The batter on this should be 1" for every foot in height. For mortar, use one part cement to every two parts sand and mix with water to a workable consistency. Make sure you pack all voids and take care not to get mortar on the faces of the stones.

Another wet wall variation is shown in Fig. D. Pour a concrete footing 8" thick, 24" wide (for a 12"-thick wall) at the frost line. Lay up concrete or cinder block to just below grade. Lay a 4" block, leaving a 4" shelf to receive veneer. Place wall ties between the block as the veneer is laid. This type construction should also have a coping of some sort to cover the veneer and exposed block wall.

One big advantage of this kind of wall is the almost unlimited choice of 4" veneer stones. In both cases (veneer and nonveneer) you will probably have to use a drain tile bedded in coarse gravel unless the soil is especially well drained.

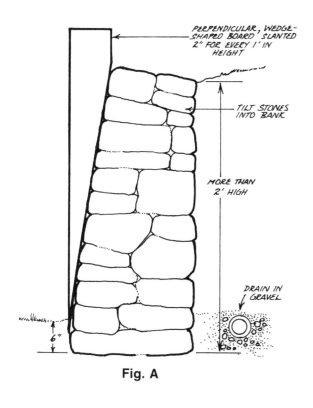

PERPENDICULAR, WEDGE-SHAPED BOARD SLANTED 2" FOR EVERY 1' IN HEIGHT

TILT STONES INTO BANK

MORE THAN 2' HIGH

DRAIN IN GRAVEL

6"

Fig. A

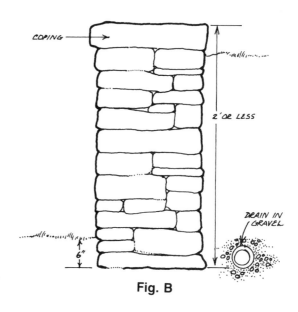

COPING

2' OR LESS

DRAIN IN GRAVEL

6"

Fig. B

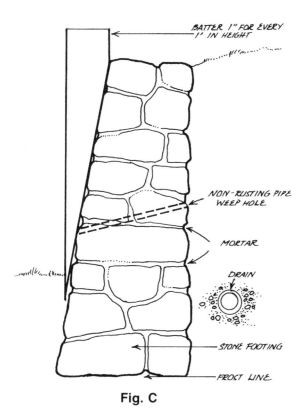

BATTER 1" FOR EVERY 1' IN HEIGHT

NON-RUSTING PIPE WEEP HOLE

MORTAR

DRAIN

STONE FOOTING

FROST LINE

Fig. C

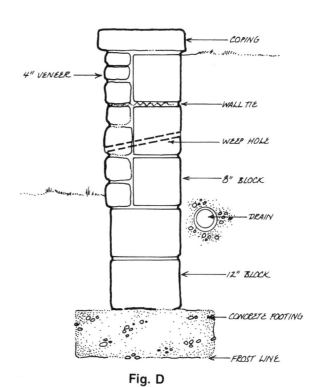

COPING

4" VENEER

WALL TIE

WEEP HOLE

8" BLOCK

DRAIN

12" BLOCK

CONCRETE FOOTING

FROST LINE

Fig. D

Fence— With A View

The windows in this handsome divider can be left open, or filled with hanging plants, vines, or decorative inserts. The dimensions of the divider you build depend on your personal needs, so purely for the sake of clarity, the plans given here are for a divider 6' high and 13' long.

Posts are 4"x4"x8' redwood stock set 4' apart, and at least two feet in the ground. Posts also flank the windows and are set 19½" on center, so that the width of each window will be 15½", as shown in Fig. A. When the posts are aligned, nail the top 2"x6" rail to one side of them, flush with their tops. The bottom rail is nailed to the same side of the posts, approximately 3" above the ground.

Now cut the 2"x12" stock to fit tightly between the window posts and the rails and assemble the windows as shown in Fig. B. Nail the frames between the posts and the rails. Cut and nail 2"x4" stringers between each of the posts, on center between the top and bottom rails (see Fig. A). Nail the 2"x2"x6' slats to the frame, leaving a ½" of space between each. Six-inch lengths of 2"x2" stock are nailed to the top and bottom rails above and below each window.

Materials

Quantity	Description
6	4"x4"x8' redwood stock for posts
3	2"x6"x13' redwood stock for stringer and rails
78	2"x2"x6' redwood stock for slats
28'	1"x12" redwood stock for window frames

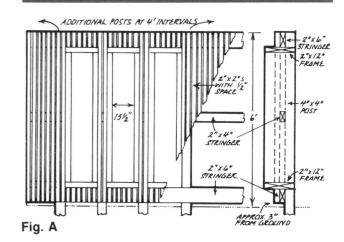

Fig. A

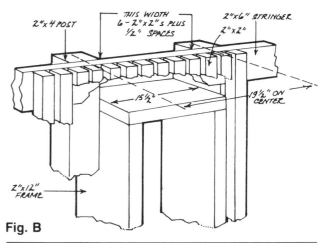

Fig. B

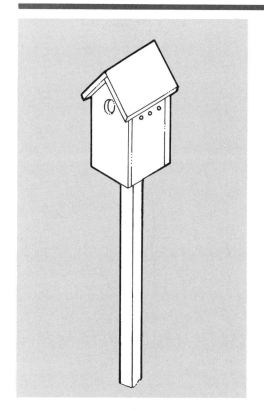

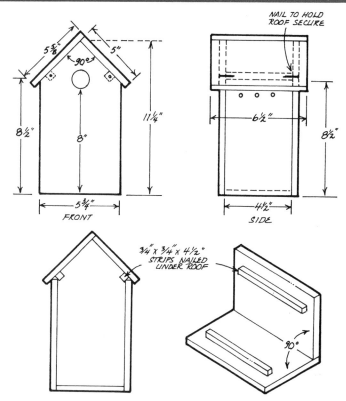

A Pair of Birdhouses

While we cannot picture a bird shopping around for a home the same way we humans do, experts say that smaller birds who ordinarily live in tree hollows and on branches prefer a home with a rustic look. Hence, the pair of birdhouses here have been designed with this in mind. The basic material is 5/8″ rough-sawn redwood plywood. The material is inexpensive in the amounts you need it and will withstand weather without any problems whatsoever.

Dimensions you use to build these birdhouses will be good for a number of species: wren, white-breasted nuthatch, tufted titmouse, tree swallow, and eastern bluebird. But you should size the entrance hole to suit the bird that will frequent the house; different birds also like their domiciles to be certain distances above the ground, as follows:

Name of Bird	Entrance Width (Diameter)	Height Range
Wren	1″	8′-18′
White-breasted nuthatch, Tufted titmouse	1½″ ″	12′-25′ ″
Tree swallow	1⅜″	8′-30′
Eastern bluebird	1⅝″	8′-20′

You can build either or both of the birdhouses following the sketches (Figs. A and B) and using 4d nails. To make the houses easy to clean, the roofs lift off. You can

hold them in position (Note: they should not be removed while the birds are in the house) by first drilling through the sides to penetrate roofing members, then slipping nails loosely in the holes. For ventilation, note also holes (⅜″) drilled in the sides of the structures.

The homes may be mounted on posts sunk into the ground. To keep squirrels and other small creatures away from the houses these posts should be some type of tubular metal.

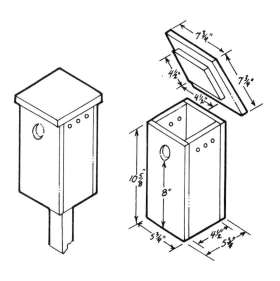

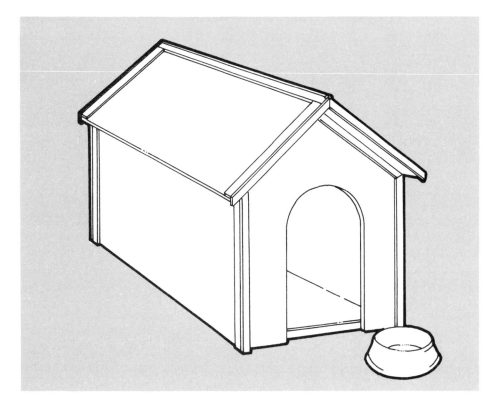

For the Larger Dog

Here's a snug house for the larger dog. It's built with handsome textured plywood and rests on a base of 2x4s, which keeps it off the ground and dry. You can build it in prefab sections, which makes assembly fast and easy. Another feature is the wide doorway, which makes housekeeping easier.

You can start construction by building the floor/base. Cut a piece of ½" plain plywood flooring 46"x33¼". Cut out the five 2x4s required for the base, then glue and nail the flooring to the base pieces laid flat. It's best to nail to the long (or side) base pieces first, then fill in with cross members.

Sides are the same size (46"x25") and each has nailers running around the edge on the inside. Cut all the pieces out; then, as with the base, nail the sides to the nailers. Note that the nailers that run vertically do not go all the way down to the bottom edge—they're 2" from the edge.

The front and back are also the same size. Cut them out, also cutting the entry in the front. Cut four nailers, each about a foot long. Center each of the nailers on the sloping (or top) edges of the front and back, and nail in place.

The house is now ready for assembly. Start with either side. Nail it to the base, then nail the front to the base, then the other side and the back. Lock the structure together by nailing through the front and back into the sides.

Install the ridgepole next. Measure between the front and back, cut a 2x2, then end nail it in place.

Cut two pieces of plywood for the roof (each 4' 7¾"x23"). Supporting the ridgepole from underneath,

nail the roof sections on—to sides, front, back, and ridgepole.

Between roof sections there will be a small gap which must be sealed. One good way is with bullnose aluminum flashing, normally used on house corners. Cut a strip long enough to span the roof lengthwise. Bend back the flashing slightly, lay it over the gap, then nail the metal lips onto the roof.

Trim the house with spruce furring strips, tacking the pieces in place. For an extra measure of good looks, corners on the front and back sides of the house should be mitered.

The house can be finished any way you see fit, but to preserve the beauty of the textured plywood we suggest a stain. To protect the wood, also seal all edges with a water repellent, and apply a coat of the repellent to the floor of the structure.

Materials

Quantity	Description
2 sheets	⅜" textured plywood (for walls and roof)
½ sheet (4'x4')	exterior-grade plywood for floor
16'	2x4 lumber
24'	2x2 lumber
52'	⅜"x1¼" spruce furring strips
½ lb.	4d galvanized nails
5'	aluminum bullnose flashing
	Finish
	Water repellent

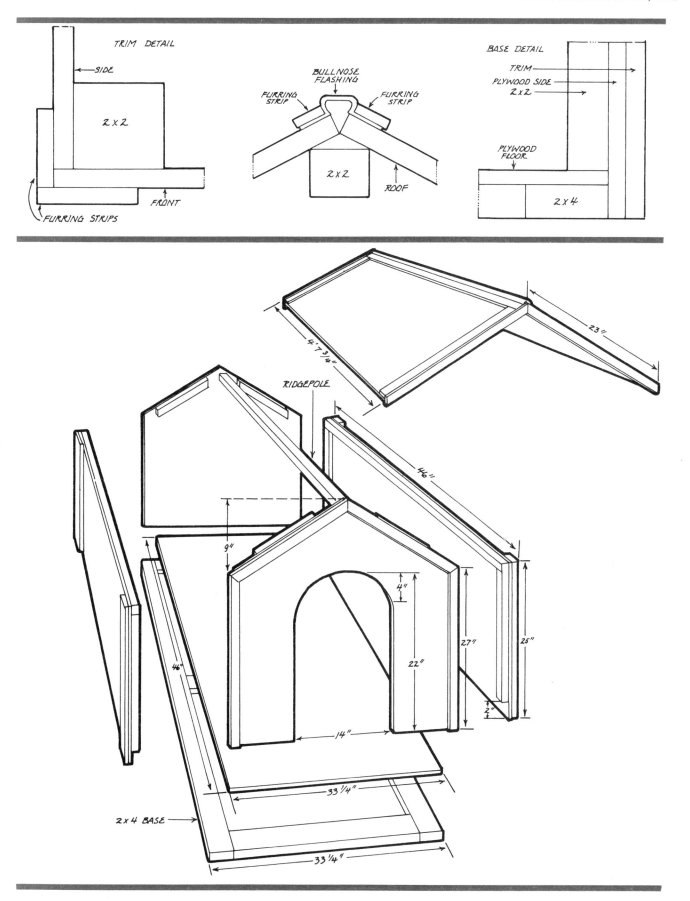

TRIM DETAIL

SIDE

2 x 2

FRONT

FURRING STRIPS

BULLNOSE FLASHING

FURRING STRIP

FURRING STRIP

2 x 2

ROOF

BASE DETAIL

TRIM

PLYWOOD SIDE

2 x 2

PLYWOOD FLOOR

2 x 4

4' 7 3/4"

23"

RIDGEPOLE

46"

9"

4"

27"

25"

22"

2"

14"

46"

33 1/4"

2 x 4 BASE

33 1/4"

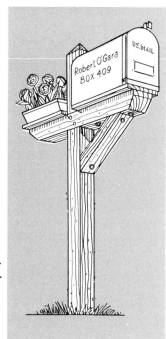

A Mailbox That Will Endure

The problem with most mailboxes, aside from the fact that they won't win any beauty contests, is that they're skimpily made. The beefy unit shown here can't be accused of that. It's made of 4"x4" lumber and, while it probably wouldn't fare well under direct mortar fire, it will resist assaults from weather and pranksters. Adding a nice touch to its construction is a spot on it where you can set a box of fresh flowers every day.

Start by cutting the main 4x4 post required; cut top at angle shown (in main drawing) for a decorative touch. The post should be as long as necessary to let it project 54" above ground, and sunk to the proper depth—here that depth is 30". Sinking it in concrete will make it as sturdy as possible.

Measure 38½" up the main post from where the ground line will be. Saw out a notch there that is 3½" wide and 1¾" deep (see main drawing and joint detail). Cut the horizontal arm required (where the mailbox and flower box rest); this should be 37" long, angled at the ends as indicated. Mark the arm for the same size notch as made in the post (see main drawing for notch location). Saw the notch.

Join the arm to the post at the notches, then fasten the members together at the joint with a pair of machine bolts. Cut a 19"-long brace, angled 45° at each end. Hold the brace in position under the mailbox side of the arm and secure with lag screws through the angled ends—one screw into the post, another into the arm.

Sink the main post into the ground, or anchor in concrete. When firmly in place, cut wood pads or bases for mailbox and plant box from 1"x6" stock. Nail the plant box pad to the arm with 8d nails. Nail the mailbox piece into place, then lay the mailbox on top of it and bolt it onto the arm with carriage bolts. Finish to suit.

Materials	
Quantity	Description
12'	of 4"x4" stock
3'	of 1"x6" stock
2	5/16"x4" carriage bolts
2	5/16"x4" lag screws
2	5/16"x5" machine bolts
10	5/16" washers
8d	common nails

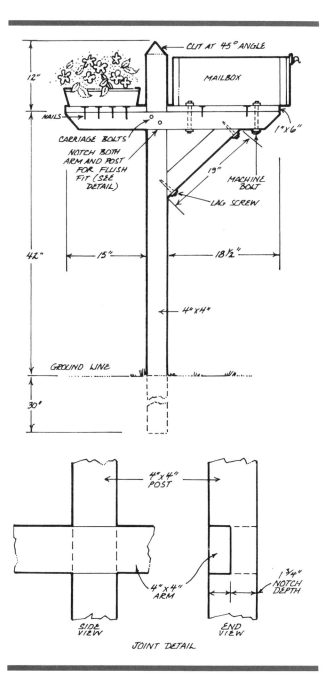

job—based on their size and toughness—is a chainsaw. Spikes must be driven with a sledgehammer.

Ties do, of course, have advantages. They come treated with preservative and will last virtually forever. Their strength is formidable, and they have their own natural beauty.

Artwork shows some situations where ties can be used. Keep the following points in mind:

• Use galvanized spikes for fastening them together.

• If you are making a walkway or patio from them, use edge members, just as with other free-floating materials. Drive 2x4 stakes into the ground to hold the ties in place.

• When using ties for retaining walls, keep the wall low. If you build a high retaining wall of railroad ties, they have to be anchored into the ground with engineering precision, and it is likely a job for an engineer.

Railroad Ties

No extensive step-by-step instructions are furnished here on using railroad ties for two reasons: they're not easy to get, and they're very difficult to work with. In the interest of those who will want to do some work with them, however, following is some information on them. Three ideas are also presented.

Probably your best bet to get the ties is at a railroad yard; if you live in a large city, you may be able to get them from the subway system. Another possible source is a lumber yard, but here you must usually get them on special order—and they're expensive. They weigh, figuratively speaking, a ton, and freight won't be cheap.

As mentioned, ties are difficult to work with. In addition to being heavy, they're very hard to cut, and experts say that the only really practical tool for doing the

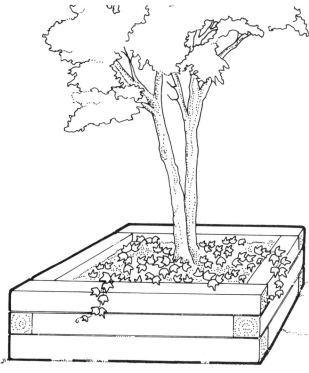

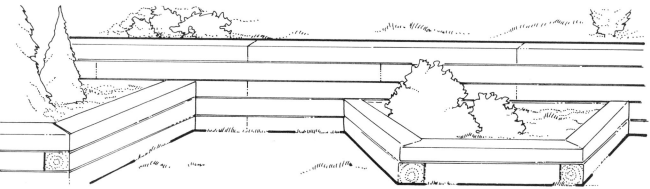

Sliding Glass Door

The big idea in getting the most out of an outdoor area is to make it easily accessible—and visible—to persons who live in the house. If one doesn't do that, no matter how inviting it has been made with accessories, barbecues, what-have-you, it simply won't be used as much as it could be.

The pre-eminent way to make it such is the installation of a sliding glass door. The unit not only "advertises" the outdoor living area all the time and makes it easy to get to, but makes the room it's in look bigger—a big part of one wall is the great outdoors.

Patio doors are available in a variety of styles. There is the classic kind—two all-glass panels in a plain frame—but there are also Colonial, French Provincial, Italian Provincial, and other modes to meld with interior—and exterior—decor. To make the glass easy to clean, some doors come with a snap-off mullion—you take it off and wipe an expanse of glass rather than little segments.

It should be remembered that sliding glass doors have perennially rated high (in the top ten) on government most-dangerous-household-products lists. Kids are especially prone to bang into them; a hard-charging youngster can't distinguish between that clear glass and the great outdoors. Hence, some sort of grillwork or decorative design should be installed on the door to clearly define it.

Doors usually come with one fixed and one movable panel; the sliding one can be gotten on the left or right side. Doors with three panels—one fixed in the middle, two sliding ones flanking it—are also available. Sizes here range up to 12′.

Doors are either wood or metal (usually aluminum). Metal ones come in various painted and brushed (bronze) finishes. Wood cousins (or distant relatives) come either primed, ready to be finished, or clad with a hard plastic (the best kind of door) that never requires finishing—washing is all.

Door glass may be tempered or tempered and insulated—a dead air space is trapped between glass panels. This is a good feature that will ultimately more than pay for itself in fuel savings.

The doors may also be obtained with screen inserts—a nice feature on warm days that lets you look out and feel the breeze without insects flying in. The frames come either knocked down or assembled but the glass panels and their frames always come assembled.

A patio door may be installed anywhere you wish, even if plumbing or heating units are in the way. These can be readily moved. Most people install doors, granted easy accessibility to the patio, where windows exist. This makes the job easier because a big part of the wall opening that must be made is already there.

Following is the installation procedure for installing a standard-size patio door, in this case a wood one (ponderosa pine) clad with vinyl. Installation for other doors may vary a bit but the basics will pertain.

First, remove the siding and wall material (siding and sheathing) within the area where the door will go, exposing studs. A keyhole saw works well for plasterboard removal. Remove siding carefully—you may be able to reuse some pieces when refinishing around the door.

Next, build a temporary wall inside the house—about 30″ from the studs, following this procedure. Cut two 2x4s 1″ longer than the width of the opening you'll make. Nail together to make a plate. Cut a 2x4 shoe the same length. Cut two 2x4s ¾″ longer than the distance between the floor and the ceiling, less 4½″. This will make the studs ¾″ longer than the distance between the plate

Fig. A

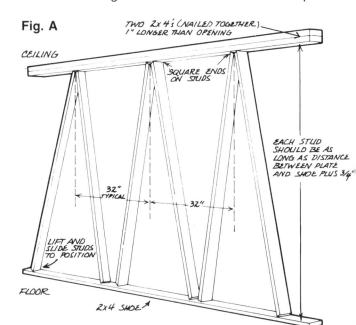

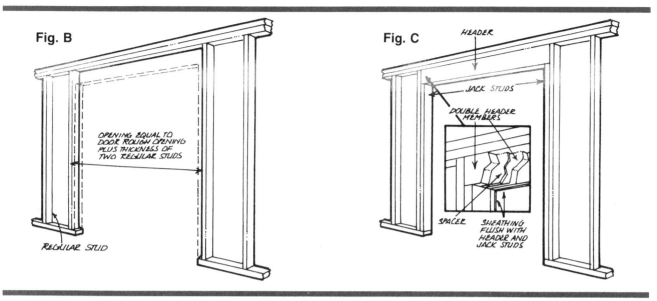

Fig. B

REGULAR STUD

OPENING EQUAL TO DOOR ROUGH OPENING PLUS THICKNESS OF TWO REGULAR STUDS

Fig. C

HEADER

JACK STUDS

DOUBLE HEADER MEMBERS

SPACER

SHEATHING FLUSH WITH HEADER AND JACK STUDS

(3″) and shoe (1½″) when they're installed. Have a helper hold the plate against the ceiling (30″, you'll recall, from existing studs) and lay the shoe on the floor, aligned with the plate. Wedge the two studs between plate and shoe, hammering and prying them together into an A shape as shown in Fig. A. Repeat the procedure with other pairs of studs, wedging them between plate and shoe and observing the distances between pairs as specified in the drawing (Fig. A).

When the temporary wall is in you can cut out studs to create the opening and frame it for the door. Exactly what you do will depend on the construction of your house—brick, block, or frame—and the dimensions of the door to be installed. Frame construction—the most common type—is shown here.

First, cut out studs to create a rough opening for the door that is equal to the door width plus studs (3″). See Fig. B. Frame out the door with two jack studs—studs cut off at the top so the header, the main beam that supports the wall, can rest. Normally, this header can be a sandwich of two 2x8 boards with filler between (Fig. C). This arrangement can handle spans of up to 12′, which is quite strong, but to be on the safe side you should check it out with your local building code. Nail the

framing pieces in place making sure that they are true and level. If the framework isn't, your door won't be, and that can cause operating problems. Remove the temporary wall.

If required, assemble the door frame. Then, run a bead of sealant all around the opening where the frame will sit. Set the frame in place from the outside and tip it in place. Check it for level at the sill. Use pieces of shingles (or other slim, wedge-shaped pieces) and level it. Clamp in place with C clamps, then permanently fasten with color-coated 8d nails (use color-coated nails or screws wherever they show), carefully hammering them along the inside frame lip every 12″ or so.

Next, check sides for true. Wedge cedar shingles to make it so if required (Fig. D), clamp in proper position, then drive #10 2½″ screws through predrilled holes. To ease the job, predrill holes in jack studs.

Repeat the leveling procedure for the top of the frame, anchoring it in place by driving #10 screws through the predrilled holes. Finish the frame by securing metal sill facing with 8d nails spaced 12″ or so.

Install the stationary glass panel. Place it in the outer track and force it into the jamb track with wood wedge. Check for trueness and tightness. Brace and wedge (Fig. E) in position, permanently secure with brackets provided using #8 1″ screws. Complete installation of the fixed door by screwing the parting stop to the framework with #8 1½″ screws.

Rest the movable door on the inside track at bottom. Tip it up so the rollers slip onto the track. Screw the head stop piece in place with #7 1⁹/₁₆″ screws.

Check how the door slides. It should slide easily. If it doesn't, look on the outside of the door at the bottom rail. There will be two adjusting sockets. Remove the caps from them, then insert a screwdriver and raise or lower the door as required until the door rides smoothly. Refinish the areas, inside and outside, around the door.

And make provision with grillwork, decorative tapes, etc. to make sure people know the glass is there.

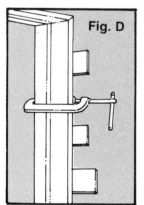

Fig. D

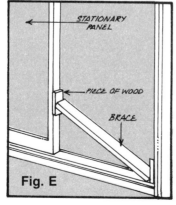

STATIONARY PANEL

PIECE OF WOOD

BRACE

Fig. E

Garden Pool

The good thing about this garden pool is that it is free-formed—no precise formwork is required.

The depth of the finished pool will depend on what you're going to stock it with—fish or plants. For fish, a good finished depth is 14″; 16″ to 18″ is better for plant growth. A saucer-shaped pool is easiest to dig.

For a pool that is 14″ deep, dig the saucer-shaped hole to a depth of 20″; the edges of the "saucer" should be about 6″ deep all around, i.e., 6″ from the surface. Later, when you put in a 3″ sand base and 3″ of concrete on top of this, the resulting rim will be above the water-line.

Following detail in the drawing, set up pool drain with 2″ pipe, coupled together and run (note elbow) to either another drain or a dry well. To drain, the top piece of pipe is unscrewed.

With piping completed and disturbed earth replaced, drive 9″ stakes, marked at 3″ intervals, 3″ into the ground as a guide for laying the sand base and pouring the 3″ of concrete. Make the stakes 18″ apart.

Lay the base of sand, smoothing it out using the 3″ mark as a guide to depth; gravel may also be used.

Next, lay ¼″ reinforcing bars, crisscrossing on the sand and bending as necessary to the shape of the hole.

Mix concrete to a very stiff mixture. The idea is to make it thick enough so that when placed on the sand it does not sag.

Start your pour in the bottom of the pool and work your way up the sides. Level the mix with the tops of the stakes, pulling them as you go. When all the concrete is poured and the stakes removed, smooth the concrete with a trowel or float.

The rim of the pool may be left as is or you can mortar rocks to it for a decorative look.

It's a good idea to fill and empty the pool with clean water a few times before placing the fish in it. Subsequent cleanings will depend on the type of fish you have, and you should get advice from a pet store on this.

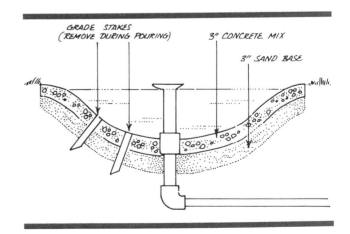

INDEX

Building Installation & Techniques

PROJECT INDEX

Outdoor Building Projects